F
IT'S A
F

It's a Long Way from Penny Apples is a book about a journey ˱.˲ poverty to wealth, from deprivation to fulfilment. And Bill tells us about that journey with all the mesmeric charm of a born storyteller. The evocation of Dublin life at that period is fascinating in a way that equals the autobiography of Sean O'Casey and much of the work of Brendan Behan. But it's not only the life of the city that is brilliantly evoked: the life of the Cullen family is portrayed with a simplicity, honesty and accuracy that will haunt readers for a long time to come. And Bill brings out the comedy of that deprived life in a manner that establishes the wit and wisdom of his people, particularly the sharp, patient wisdom of his mother. The world Bill creates is natural, irrefutable, authentic. It will bring joy and sadness, tears and laughter into the hearts of all those privileged to read it.

Professor Brendan Kennelly, Trinity College Dublin

This book is very different from the literature of whinge which specialises in demonising parents and which has become a feature of contemporary Irish writing. It is about people who want to make life glow instead of huddling around snuffed-out candles. The dialogue reflects what Joyce called the 'sacred eloquence' of his city. A light-fingered garage employee going out the door draws the comment: 'Jaysus, look at yer man, he's got so many car parts under his coat that if you pushed him he'd start.' Someone says about Bill's mother, Mary Cullen: 'Sure the Ma could talk Christ down off the Cross.' Lucky for us that Bill Cullen had the ear to catch this sort of talk and with an accomplished pen has set it down for us to read today.

Ulick O'Connor, poet, author and playwright

Too many imaginative fictions are unashamedly presented as actual memoirs of an Irish childhood. This book rings with truth. Bill Cullen tells of his life with unflinching honesty and unvarnished language so the reader hears an authentic voice. Although Cullen's story begins in the tenements, it is not sad: far from it. *It's a Long Way from Penny Apples* provides an exhilarating example of what one can achieve with determination and good humour. Yet in spite of his success he remains irrevocably Irish, keeping his roots deep in Irish soil. Cúchulainn and Brian Ború would be proud of this latter-day hero.

Morgan Llywelyn, author of *Lion of Ireland, 1916* and *1921*

MERCIER PRESS

Cork

www.mercierpress.ie

Trade enquiries to CMD BookSource,
55a Spruce Avenue, Stillorgan Industrial Park,
Blackrock, County Dublin

First published in 2001 by Mercier Press

This paperback edition, 2003

© Bill Cullen, 2001

ISBN: 978 1 85635 400 4

15 14 13 12

A CIP record for this title is available from the British Library

This book is sold subject to the condition that it shall not, by way of trade or
otherwise, be lent, resold, hired out or otherwise circulated without the publisher's
prior consent in any form of binding or cover other than that in which it is
published and without a similar condition including this condition being imposed
on the subsequent purchaser.

No part of this publication may be reproduced or transmitted in any form or by
any means, electronic or mechanical, including photocopying, recording or any
information or retrieval system, without the prior permission of the publisher in
writing.

Printed and bound in the EU.

IT'S A LONG WAY FROM
PENNY APPLES

BILL CULLEN

WITH A FOREWORD BY
FORMER TAOISEACH BERTIE AHERN TD

MERCIER PRESS
IRISH PUBLISHER – IRISH STORY

Liam's parents, Billy Cullen and Mary Darcy,
on their wedding day, 8 September 1935

'You've borrowed eighteen million pounds. God bless you, son. That's a long, long way from penny apples.'

MARY DARCY TO HER SON LIAM, SHORTLY BEFORE HER DEATH

This book
is dedicated to
my greatest supporter
JACKIE LAVIN
and all the women of the world
who make so many sacrifices
and give so much of themselves,
their strength, their fortitude,
to support their families.

THE MA, MOLLY DARCY, THE DA

We all owe a huge debt of gratitude to our parents. But for me and my brothers and sisters, my parents were extra-special.

The Da, Bill Cullen, diligently tried to teach us his army habits of doing things right. The Ma, Mary Darcy, taught us to do the right things and do them right now, as she worked around the clock to support the needs of her ever-growing family.

They made so many sacrifices to create a better life for their children. Always giving, giving, giving.

All the time, our grandmother, Molly Darcy, was there to give a sense of peace and wisdom to the frantic pace of life in Dublin's inner city of the forties and fifties. She gave me the self-confidence, the values and the beliefs of the Celtic warriors.

Rare Ould Times

Raised on songs and stories,
Heroes of renown,
The passing tales and glories
That once was Dublin town.

The hallowed halls and houses,
The haunting children's rhymes,
I remember Dublin city
In the rare ould times.

Pete St John

CONTENTS

Author's Note
and Acknowledgements

This book, of necessity, combines memory with imagination. Where I was present, I painted the picture as I remember it. Otherwise, it's as the story was told to me, or as I imagined it from my experience of the people involved. Some names have been changed to protect the innocent.

*

The film of *Angela's Ashes* was depressing. I had a childhood of similar poverty and deprivation but my memories of it are happy. The people I knew in Dublin's inner city in the forties and fifties were good Christian neighbours, rich in humour and compassion. They supported and helped one another and shared a world of few expectations. I felt obliged to tell the story of those communities, particularly the street-trading women who worked their stalls in hail, rain and snow. Women who sacrificed their whole existence to give their children a better life.

Kevin Kearns motivated me from the backwoods of Vermont in the USA. Pushed me to get up at four o'clock in the mornings to write a few pages every day before heading to the office. Jackie put up with me taking two weeks on Mangerton Mountain writing twelve hours a day, ignoring the beauty of Killarney. Ivor Kenny encouraged me to tell the story to a wider audience and advised on the draft manuscript.

I wrote six hundred longhand foolscap pages, and I would like to offer sincere thanks to my friends who read the manuscript: Tighe O'Donoghue in Lough Guitane; Derry O'Donovan in Sandymount; Rosemary Evans in Howth; Dolores Daly on Robin's Hill; my sister Vera in Finglas; Father Paul Murphy in Waterford; and Páidí Ó Sé in Ventry in the Kingdom of Kerry. A special thanks to Gay Byrne for his encouraging support, and also to Ulick O'Connor for his unique literary perspicacity and knowledge of Dublin, its people and its history.

My daughter Hilary acted as researcher and critic, and Jackie encouraged me and put up with my nocturnal vanishing acts. My assistant Christine Fitzpatrick did all the typing, checking and collating. A big hug for them.

A special thanks to our northside Taoiseach, Bertie Ahern, who took time out to read the book. Molly Darcy would have added a new incantation to her Rosary: 'May God help our pal Bertie with all his endeavours for peace on this little island. Lord, hear our prayers.'

Special thanks to Jo O'Donoghue and all the team at Mercier Press: Seán, Claire, Caitríona and Jane. Jo believed in the book from day one and got it into the shops for the Christmas market.

I hope the readers enjoy, as much as I have, walking down the memory lanes of a vanished Irish era.

FOREWORD

This is an incredible story of life in Dublin through the twentieth century. Bill's recollection of events spans generations of Irish history. The book, though auto-biographical in tone, combines fact and fiction, memory and imagination. It is full of colourful anecdotes and characters that leap off the page. For me, its greatest strength is its marvellous description of Dublin's places and people, which are both familiar and intriguing at the same time.

Penny Apples is essentially a story of one ordinary Dublin family and their extraordinary journey through life in an ever-changing city. It is a social and personal history that combines blunt realism with the everyday humour of northside Dublin life. From the grubby poverty of the Summerhill tenements to the life of a millionare in a country mansion, this is a bracing story.

Cullen's memoir, however, does much more than follow the standard rags-to-riches trajectory. Across three generations, the author, with real dramatic flair, brings to life the people, the passion, the politics and the repercussions of historic events on a Dublin family, their circle of friends and the wider community.

The story is told in a voice that is quintessentially Dublin, yet Bill's powerful memoir is not just a beautifully written portrait of a Dublin family. History and fiction are interwoven, and the novel is loaded with both comic and poignant moments.

It is clearly the author's intention to give us a close-up view of some of the seismic events in our capital, such as the bombing of the North Strand and the 1916 Rising, and to allow us to view them from the inside. Famous names such as the irrepressible Lord Mayor Alfie Byrne, the charismatic genius Brendan Behan, the master tailor Louis Copeland, war leader and statesman Michael Collins and that giant of Gaelic football, Mick · O'Connell, are just some of the renowned figures from Dublin life that dot the pages of this book. But the striking panorama of characters never overshadows the rich and complex tale of the Cullen family. The real story is that of Molly Darcy, Bill's grandmother, who carried messages for Collins; it is the story of Bill's father, 'the Da', the dockland ganger whom Alfie Byrne helped get a job; and it is the story of 100,000 supporters crammed into Croke Park to marvel at the skills of the players.

In his memoir of poverty-stricken youth, Limerick author Frank McCourt wrote: 'Worse than the ordinary miserable childhood is the miserable Irish childhood.' Bill Cullen's novel *Penny Apples* contains similar wrenching accounts of poverty in the 1950s Dublin of his childhood. But the great strength of Bill's book is its humour, not its pathos. It is this factor which carries the plot through hard times with disarming wit and the optimism for which Dubliners are renowned. It is the story of a city that has good times and bad and of a people who have prospered both in spite of and because of their past.

I want to congratulate Bill Cullen for this deeply

moving and personal account of Dublin life in turbulent times. This is a family story, a history of Dublin, a social commentary and a love story all rolled into one. Most of all, it is an incredible book. It is a work worthy of much acclaim.

An Taoiseach Bertie Ahern TD, October 2001

1

THE GERMANS BOMB DUBLIN

Billy Cullen was heading back to bed when he heard it. A faint drone, but slowly getting louder. A bloody aeroplane. He took the clock from the shelf to the window and saw that it was twenty-five past one in the morning. Listening carefully, he guessed the plane was down in the south-docks area, around Ringsend. Heading up the River Liffey. As the drone faded to the west, he sat on the chair and realised that it must have been the plane's second time to go over, as he had wakened about ten minutes before. Pulling on his trousers, he went over to the bed and shook his wife's shoulder.

'Wake up, Mary,' he said, and she was awake like a shot. 'I'm going out the back because there's a plane mooching around up there. Remember they accidentally dropped a bomb in Terenure a few months back.'

He lit the oil lamp and moved to the door while Mary hopped out of bed and put her shawl around her.

'Mind yourself, Billy,' she whispered as he let himself out.

'I'll be okay,' he said. 'Just bolt this door behind me and open it on my five taps when I get back.'

Billy stepped down the stairs in his bare feet and out

the back door, to the scrubland behind the Summerhill tenements. On the way, he heard scuffles and murmurs from the spunkers in the basement and thought they'd have no chance down there if any bombs fell. When he got out to the yard, he saw the dockland searchlights weaving patterns in the sky. That would happen only if they had no information from Collinstown Airport on the passing plane. It could be a lost British bomber trying to get home, but he should be heading east to the British coast, not west into the Irish midlands. If it was a German, he too could be lost, and might mistake Dublin for Belfast, or even a British city, if his instruments were faulty.

In the moonlight, he could clearly see the old stable buildings at the end of the yard stretching over to the Twenty-seven Steps, where his wife's brother, Bob Darcy, had his horse and cart stabled. Just when he was thinking he could go back to bed, he heard the aeroplane again. The noise was louder now, definitely down by the docks but on the northside this time, and suddenly he saw the plane picked out by the searchlights: there was a German swastika on the side. He turned and dashed up the back stairs. He gave his 'shave and a haircut' taps and Mary opened the door.

'Get dressed, get the kids up,' he said. 'We'd better get out of here; it's a bloody German bomber up there.'

The words were hardly out of his mouth when he heard the 'crump, crump, crump' of bombs landing. He pulled Mary to the floor. There was another 'crump, crump', and then the noise of the aeroplane filled the room as it passed overhead. As the noise faded, Billy thought he heard another 'crump' before everything went quiet. But the silence was broken now by the

Summerhill tenements in 1913.
Molly Darcy is on the extreme right.

sound of shouts and screams. Mary picked up the two girls: Rita, who was four, and two-year-old Betty. The baby, Vera, was still asleep.

'Don't touch any gas taps, Mary. Only use this oil lamp. And get the girls down to Molly's,' he said, as he pulled on his boots and gansey. 'That's bombs the bloody so-and-so dropped, and it's not far away either. I'll have to report to the Local Defence Force in Rutland Street School.'

Mary had herself ready and was dressing the girls. 'It's okay, Billy,' she said, 'I'll take care of things here and check out Mother Darcy. You make sure you get Big Bob with you down there, so give him a shout first.'

As Billy turned to leave, the door burst open, and Missus Carey from upstairs came in, crying, 'Jesus, Mary and Holy Saint Joseph, Mister Cullen, they're going to murder us in our beds! Himself is after dropping on the floor with the fright.'

Mary put her arm around the old dear and said, 'Off

you go, Billy, I'll look after all this. Take care of yourself.'

Billy moved out the door with his usual 'You too', and he threw a dabble of holy water on himself from the small font nailed to the wall under the picture of the Sacred Heart of Jesus. Down the stairs he went, moving a few people aside on the way, and when he got out onto the street he saw his neighbour Tommy Farrell on the footpath.

'It's down towards the Five Lamps, Billy. We'd better get moving to the school. Here's Bob,' said Tommy, pointing down the street, where Big Bob Darcy was coming up the middle of the road. He was fully dressed.

'Bejaysus, a fella can't even have a bit of a hooley with his pals but either the guards hoosh us out of the pub or some bloody German in his aeroplane tries to blow us all up. This is some state of affairs,' said Bob, and it was obvious from the white froth on his upper lip that he'd still been scooping Guinness when the bombs fell.

Billy looked over at Bob Darcy, his brother-in-law. A big tough man he was, a full six feet four inches and over eighteen stone: he wasn't called Big Bob for nothing. While he was a gentle sort of fella, he was known to be fond of the Guinness and with the drink on him would take on any man in a fight. Billy Cullen didn't touch the drink – in fact would never go into a pub – and from that point of view he had little time for Bob Darcy.

Billy knew that no matter how much booze Bob had in him, he would never show it. He had seen him outside the pub after a night's drinking, still able to outfight a younger, sober opponent, keen to be able to

Big Bob Darcy (centre) on his wedding day.
Uncle Ned is on the extreme right.

say he'd floored Big Bob Darcy. For tonight's work his size and strength would be needed. Billy felt a shiver down to his boots as he saw the smoke and flames in the distance.

Up Summerhill they went, with people calling nervously from the hallways. Men with only their trousers on and the women in shawls.

'What's up, Mister Cullen, are we in for a hiding?' someone shouted.

'No, it's okay,' said Billy. 'It was only one aeroplane, and it's off home by now. Go back to bed, the LDF boys will take care of things.'

As he was saying this, they could hear the clanging of fire-brigade bells not far away. They came to the door of Rutland Street School – called the Red Brick College on the Hill by the locals. Jimmy Corbally was at the door. In they went, to find Captain Bolger and about twenty other men in the large hall.

'Well done, lads,' Bolger said to the new arrivals.

'We're just ready to head off. The word on the phone is that the houses up at Newcomen Bridge on the North Strand Road have been severely hit. We're to get up there fast and help the fire-brigade lads, so grab your kit and double up outside and we'll move into Killarney Street and up to the Five Lamps. Let's go.'

As they came up to the Five Lamps, they could see that there was chaos. People were running in all directions, some in their nightclothes, many others arriving half-dressed. Fire-brigade units were already in action. Billy couldn't believe his eyes: the houses on both sides of the North Strand Road up to Newcomen Bridge were in ruins.

'We'll have to set up rope cordons to hold back the crowds,' said Captain Bolger, 'and then we'll need every man we can get to help remove that rubble.'

Billy looked at Bob, who was now grim-faced and quietly sober. 'We've some night ahead of us here, Billy Cullen, and that's a fact,' Bob said, looking at two battered bodies lying in the rubble just a few yards ahead.

It was Sunday evening at six o'clock. The whole of Summerhill Parade and the North Strand Road had been blocked off since Friday night. Only emergency-crew members were let through. The ambulances had been ferrying people to hospital for two days. Mary Darcy was listening to the six o'clock news on the wireless. It was hard to believe that thirty-four people were dead and hundreds were injured in hospital. The rescue work was coming to an end and wives could expect the crews from the emergency forces to get home soon. Mary had left her children down in Number 17 with Mother

Darcy and had the coddle simmering away on the hearth.

Outside on the street, she heard a shout of 'Here they come', and she stuck her head out the window. Sure enough, a bunch of lads was trudging down from Rutland Street, looking like coal miners. They were filthy and unrecognisable, except Big Bob, who stood out a mile in any group because of his size. And her Billy, who still walked like a soldier on parade, with his chest out and his head high. She rushed down the stairs to the hall just as the group was passing, and Billy and his pal Tommy Farrell turned in to the footpath.

'See ya later, Billy,' said Bob. 'Mind him, now, Mary me girl, he's knackered.'

The North Strand bombing, which took place on 31 May 1941. Thirty-eight people were killed and 141 were injured in the attack.

Billy said, 'So long, lads', and walked quickly into the hall. The smell of decay hit him and he shook his head sadly.

Mary put her shawl around his shoulders. 'Come on, Billy,' she said, 'let's get you cleaned up. I've some hot water on the boil upstairs.'

She stripped off his gansey and shirt, his boots, socks and trousers. They were filthy and she saw cuts and bruises all over his arms and legs. His hands were in a terrible state, bleeding and gashed, with some of his nails broken. With a clean cloth and the Sunlight soap, she washed the grime from his body, then sat him down and let him steep his hands in a fresh basin of hot water. He was quiet as she gently cleaned his hands finger by finger.

'We'll need something for these. Just as well I've got some Germolene.' She rubbed the pink antiseptic cream into the cuts and scrapes.

'Where are the girls?' he asked.

She smiled at him. 'They're down with Mother Darcy. She's minding them tonight. You know poor Martin was to make his Confirmation yesterday but it was cancelled by the Archbishop? So they've been playing together all day and I'll pick them up in the morning.' Martin was Mary's youngest brother. He and his sister Angela, who was fourteen, together with Big Bob, lived in Number 17 with Mary's widowed mother, Molly Darcy.

He looked up at her and gave a wry smile. 'Well, at least young Martin will have his day later,' he said, and she felt the desolation in his voice.

'Come on now, Billy, and have a plate of this coddle,' she said, and busied herself serving the stew. He got stuck into the coddle with his big spoon and ate three platefuls without a word from him.

At last he sat back. 'That's the finest meal I've ever tasted, Mary,' he said.

'Hunger is the best sauce,' she said. 'Put on this clean vest and get yourself into bed before you pass out.'

She went out through the curtain, and as he pulled the vest on over his head he heard her bolting the door. He was sitting on the edge of the bed when she came back and she sat beside him and put her hand on his. There wasn't a sound as they sat together for a while and then she felt him shudder.

'It was horrible, Mary,' he said. 'Poor women, old men and children all blown to bits. I pulled out Tommy Carroll and he'd no legs. Doris Fagan had her head blown off. Not a scratch on it, but the rest of her missing. And Harry Browne is dead, and so is his mother, his wife and their four lovely children.'

The tears were streaming down his face, his chest was heaving and he just couldn't get any more words out. Mary pulled back the bedcover and moved him into the bed, pushing his legs under the sheet. She undressed and quickly slid in beside him and held him tight as the tears flowed down her shoulder.

'It's all right, Billy,' she kept repeating, 'it's all right', and slowly the spasms subsided as she held him fiercely to her. She pulled him down to her breast as she slowly lifted the end of his vest.

Almost nine months later, on a cold day in February, Mary Darcy gave birth in the Rotunda Hospital to a wee boy she named after his proud father: William Patrick Cullen.

2

THE LUCKY BABY
BORN IN A CAUL

Mary came out of the Rotunda Hospital with her new baby in her arms, and Billy beside her, to see Mother Darcy standing across the road with the three girls and Big Bob behind them. When they'd crossed the street, Bob said, with a big smile, 'Well now, Billy, the lad is the image of ya. But he has his mother's smile,' he added quickly, to be sure he didn't cause offence. Mammies can get snappy after a new baby, you know. Mary held the baby so the girls could see and coo at it, while Mother Darcy slipped a half-crown into the baby's hand.

'That's so you'll never have a need for money as long as you live, son,' she said quietly, and turned to head for Summerhill.

But Big Bob said, 'Well, I'll just finish me pint here in Conway's Pub with the lads and I'll see you later.'

'Good luck, Bob,' said Mary. 'I suppose you're marking the spot where Padraig Pearse surrendered in 1916. It was right here that himself and Nurse Farrell were taken away, you know, only there was no pint of Guinness waiting for him – just a lonely death from a British firing squad.'

They passed the Parnell Monument, where Charles Stewart Parnell's effigy stood pointing straight across at the maternity hospital, and went up to Summerhill, where Mary was stopped by many a woman who pressed a coin into the baby's hand. All the coins were quickly passed over to Rita to mind because she was carrying her mother's handbag.

'What's his name?' Mary was asked. She replied, 'Well, he's another Bill, but we'll have to call him Liam or we'll have too many Bills in the house. Yes, he's Liam under our roof, but he'll be his own Bill when he moves on.'

A few weeks later, they had the christening in Lourdes Chapel in Seán MacDermott Street with Mary's brother and sister, Bob and Angela, as the godparents. Then it was back to Number 28 for tea and scones. The women hunched over the fire, whispering low, while the men sat around the table playing cards in the glow of the gas globe. Missus Farrell was inquisitive.

'So it's a lucky baby, Mary,' she said. 'There's no doubt about it, but the Lord gives and he takes away. You lost little Tony to the fever and you've got a lovely wee boy from the death and desolation of the bombing. It's all your prayers down there in the chapel to Our Lady of Lourdes, and sure, the good Lord, he does move things in ways we don't understand. But tell us now, Mary, is it true? About the birth, I mean, and him born in a caul?'

Mary was smiling quietly. The women leaned forward to hear her words. Only Molly Darcy remained upright, a mug of tea in her hand and a proud, knowing look on her face. Molly wasn't very tall but her stocky build, together with her dark eyes and black hair, gave her a strong presence.

'Yes, it's true,' said Mary. 'I didn't know what was happening, with all the nurses rushing around and them laughing and giggling and congratulating me. "Here's your lovely baby boy," said Doctor Mulligan to me, "and here, Missus Cullen, is the caul he was born in. Keep it safe because he's a privileged child – only once a year or so do we have such an occasion." The nurses opened a bottle of Taylor Keith Lemonade and the baby and mother were toasted.'

The four neighbours were straining to hear every word, and Mary looked from face to face. Her friends were all bursting to ask the question.

'It's all right,' she said, 'you can see the caul tomorrow. Molly has it down in Number 17 in a safe place.'

'Oh, the wonder of it all,' said Missus Farrell. 'Are you going to keep it?'

It was Molly Darcy who answered that question. 'Well now, Missus Farrell, you know how a baby survives in his mother's waters for nine months. That's why a sailor believes he can never drown if he has a caul in his possession. There's more ships being sunk out there in this war than you and I have seen hot dinners. Sure we've already had Missus Redmond's husband up offering ten pounds for the caul before he heads out of port next week. Do you think Mary can turn her back on that sort of money?'

The women nodded knowingly to each other. 'You're right,' said Missus Farrell. 'There's no doubt about it at all. Ten pounds, begob! We can call him Lucky Liam all right,' she said, touching the child's head gently.

'What's all that whispering you girls are at over there?' asked Bob from the table.

'Sure, it's woman-and-baby talk we're at, Bob,' Molly

replied. 'Things you men know nothing about!'

'And that's a fact,' said Bob. 'But there's one thing I do know something about, and that's porter. This is a dry house, with the pair of you teetotallers. Billy, is it okay if I pop across the road to Lynch's for a few bottles of Guinness for the lads? We can call it invalid stout for the women. What do ya say?'

But Billy shook his head and Mary said, 'Off you go to the pub, Bob Darcy, if it's drinking you want to do. You know myself and Billy are Pioneers and no drink comes under our roof.'

Bob stood up. 'Well, that's fair enough with me, but I'm out of here to Killane's. I'll see you through the week.' The gathering quickly broke up, all the visitors heading down the stairs and Billy seeing them to the hall door with the oil lamp. When he returned, Mary was standing by the fire.

'I didn't mean to break up the party, Mary,' he said. She looked at him, knowing that he thought she was upset at her mother and brother moving out because of his stand on the drink.

'It's all right, Billy,' she said, 'I agree with you completely, and so does the Mother. She's a nondrinker too, but she won't stop Bob bringing in his bottles.'

The following week, Bob Darcy did the dealing on the caul in Thomas Delaney's pub down on the North Wall docks. He was in great fettle altogether as he stood at the bar with a pint of Guinness looking like a tiny whiskey glass in his giant hand. He sank the black with a few slugs on one short visit to his mouth and then faced the crowded bar.

'Okay!' he roared. 'Give us a bit of quiet around here

because the young McGregor from the Scottish herring ship is in the saddle. He's put a bid of twelve pounds on the lucky caul and I'm selling. I like the Scotsmen – sure aren't we Celtic brothers under the skin – but this lad is not as brave as his ancestor, Rob Roy McGregor. He's willing to pay for some heavenly assistance to get through the war safely. And that's what this is, me lads!' shouted Bob, as he held aloft the folded caul. 'It's signed here clearly by the good Doctor Mulligan in the Rotunda Hospital. The genuine article, and that's a fact. So do I hear more? Who wants to die in a dry bed with their children around them?'

The bidding moved up by ten-shilling bids until it was still young McGregor at sixteen pounds ten shillings.

'Okay,' said Bob, 'it's going once, if you're all done.' There was silence in the room.

'It's going twice to my friend the Scotsman, who'll be buying me a few pints as well for my trouble,' said Bob, and there was silence again.

Bob raised his hand above the counter, but just then a voice from the door shouted, 'I'll make it twenty pounds!' in a twangy accent. A tall, slightly built young man dressed in the uniform of the American navy walked over to Bob, pulling four big white English five-pound notes from a wallet.

'Here you are, sir, twenty pounds for the caul,' he said. Bob looked at McGregor, who shook his head sadly.

'Going for the last time,' said Bob, 'to my American friend here, who'll be buying a few Irish whiskies for the seller', and he gave the counter an almighty slap that rattled pints up and down the whole bar.

The American took a fifth fiver out. 'That, sir, is for your trouble,' he said. Bob handed him the caul and took the five fivers.

'Will you join me for a drink to seal the bargain?' asked Bob.

'The bargain is well sealed,' said the American. 'I've got the caul and you've got the dough, and my ship gets under way in twenty minutes. So thank you for your hospitality and I'll say goodbye.' They shook hands and Bob watched him walk briskly out the door into the grey, wintry evening.

'They're something else, them Yanks are,' he said to Tommy Farrell, who was standing beside him. 'They have money to burn, you know. If I ever get to America, I could sell them Galway Bay a million times over, and that's a fact.'

Tommy nodded. 'Sure, you're out on your own, Bob; you could sell sand to the Arabs. So are we going to have a few scoops now?'

Bob gave him a big wink. 'We are, Tommy me boy,' he said, 'but not here where everyone in the bar knows I've a fortune of money in me pocket. We'll grab Denis and Joe Boy there and we're off home to Killane's. Even the sailors will think twice about tackling four of us.'

Tommy cackled with glee. 'There's no doubt about it,' he said, as the four pals headed out the door, 'you know what I'm going to tell you, Bob Darcy – you only look stupid.' Big Bob Darcy tucked his hands in his pockets, the five fivers clutched tightly in his right fist.

'This money is going to my little sister, Mary, and those four wee kids of hers,' he thought to himself, while out loud he said, 'And that's a fact, Tommy Farrell.'

FOOD RATIONS: THE MIRACLE
OF THE LOAVES AND FISHES

Mary Darcy was deep in sleep, enjoying the happy dream of herself with her young child running through the grass. It wasn't just grass, though – it was the well-cared-for lawn of the park in St Stephen's Green. Young Tony was an exuberant one-year-old and she had slipped away with him for an hour to feed a bag of crumbs to the ducks in the pond. The young fella was still a bit wobbly and moved deliberately, feet and arms in tandem, going faster all the time to keep his balance. Mary grabbed him at the last minute, just as he was about to fall on his face. She bent and plucked him into her arms and then rolled with him in the grass. Over and over she went, with Tony clutched tight to her breast. The boy squealed with delight as they came to rest and lay catching their breath. On the ground, the smell of freshly cut grass was exhilarating, and through the summer haze she could see the top floors of the St Stephen's Green mansions above the treetops. The massive façade of the Shelbourne Hotel was right opposite her, and she wished that she was one of the ladies alighting from the carriage she had seen at the door as she entered the gates of the park. Mary felt the boy's intense gaze and looked at him. His arms were around her neck and his dark-green eyes were sparkling. She felt a surge of love for the young lad. She brushed the blond curls from his forehead and lay back on the grass, closed her eyes and experienced a feeling of pure joy as the heat of the sun touched her.

She awoke slowly, with the sun on her right arm. Not opening her eyes, but gradually realising that it was a dream of yesterday. This was today, and the sun on her arm was the first ray of the summer morning. She guessed it was after five o'clock, but the alarm, which was set for half past five, hadn't gone off yet. She reached out for the clock and opened her eyes to see that it was twenty past five. She clicked the alarm off, put the clock back on the shelf and slowly looked around the room that was home: the first-floor front room of a five-storeyed dilapidated tenement house only a stone's throw from O'Connell Street in the middle of Dublin.

The small cot was right beside the bed, and baby Liam was fast asleep. Across the room from the bed was a table and four chairs, and beside the big open fireplace was a long workbench with shelves above it: that was her kitchen. On the other side of the fireplace was a dresser that her husband Billy had made. Here the enamel cups and mugs and plates were stacked on top and the bottom cupboards stored their food supplies. This was really only half of the big room, which was cut in two by a curtain of sheets held up by a wire cable that stretched from wall to wall. The sheets were home-made from old white flour sacks collected over many months and sewn together by herself and her mother,

Molly Darcy. The rear half of the room was split in half again with a similar curtain of flour sacks. One of these quarters was the children's bedroom, where her three girls – Rita, Betty and Vera – were asleep in a single iron bed. She could hear them sleeping quietly in the still of the morning. The other quarter was the entrance area, with the door from the landing, which was used for storage – for the Da's bike, turf overflowing from a wooden tea chest, the baby's pram and other household odds and sods.

The walls were bare brick, covered with mould from the leaks around the windows. Even in summer it was damp and depressing, but Mary had learned that it was no use getting depressed. You just had to ignore the things you could do nothing about and get on with life. It was time to get up and get the porridge on for breakfast. Billy was asleep beside her and he had to be up and away to catch the army lorry at six o'clock down in Gloucester Diamond at the back of the tenements.

She got out of the bed in her ankle-length nightdress and quickly dressed in the corner. She put her freshly ironed white wraparound apron on over her skirt and cardigan, tied it around her waist with the attached strings and set to work, making breakfast. The oatmeal flakes went into the pot; then she added water from the bucket of fresh water on the worktop, which Billy brought up from the tap in the backyard last thing every night. She filled the big teapot with water and lit the gas stove. The only other thing to eat was a stale half-loaf of bread, which she cut into slices. She stuck a slice on the end of a big fork and pushed it into the gas flames under the teapot.

Billy hadn't budged while all this was going on.

The Ma with Rita and Betty, in matching frocks at front, baby Vera, and neighbours' children, at the rear of the Summerhill tenements in 1940

Unlike Mary, who spent as little time as possible asleep, Billy was as still as a sack of spuds in the bed. So she started pushing his shoulder and whispering to him to get up. It took a few minutes for him to open his eyes.

'Okay,' he said. 'I hear you. Time to get up and at them, is it? Well, it's great to see the sun shining.'

'It's a pure beautiful morning, Billy,' said Mary. 'Get yourself ready now, because that truck will leave on the dot of six.'

Billy came out of bed in his long vest – down to his knees nearly it came. Over to the corner, where he pulled on his underpants and trousers, while Mary poured some hot water from the teapot into his enamel shaving mug. Billy got the bar of Sunlight soap, dipped his shaving brush into the water and set about shaving.

'Janey Mac,' he said, 'we'll have to get a decent mirror. This yoke is cracked and speckled so much I might as well be looking at the wall.'

When he'd finished shaving, he poured some cold

water from the bucket into the basin. He washed his face, neck, hair and armpits with the sunlight suds and dried off vigorously with the towel. On went his shirt, his army socks and his well-polished boots. Then he combed his hair and sat down to the steaming bowl of porridge that Mary had put out for him.

'No milk, I'm afraid,' she said. 'I gave the last drop to Betty last night, but there's a slice of nice hot toast with your tea.'

Mary filled an enamel mug with hot water. She kept her back to Billy as she squeezed the old tea leaves from yesterday's meal by pressing the leaves against the side of the mug with a knife.

'I see it's weak tea again,' said Billy, guessing what she was up to. 'Didn't you get any tea on the ration vouchers I gave you?'

'They had no tea in Findlater's yesterday,' she said. 'With a bit of luck I'll get some today.'

She wasn't telling him that she had got tea the day before but had given it to her mother, Molly, who hadn't seen tea for a week.

'I've wrapped some bread slices for you,' she said. 'Missus Farrell next door tells me she's got some bacon lard she'll give Tommy, so you can make sandwiches between you. And now you'd better get a move on — it's ten to six. Go on, off you go.'

Billy picked up his woollen gansey and the lunch wrap, gave Mary a hug, put a massive hand on baby Liam's head and slipped through the curtain. He paused and looked at his three daughters: Rita and Betty, still fast asleep in their bed, cuddled together like spoons in a box, and Vera looking at him as she sucked quietly on her soother. He blew them a kiss, stuck a finger in the holy water font and paused under the picture of the Sacred Heart.

He said a quiet Hail Mary, and then out loud, 'God bless this house and everyone in it.' He pulled back the bolt and opened the door, and turned to Mary, who had followed him to the door.

'Mind yourself today,' she said. 'You too,' said he, and off he went down the stairs, taking them two at a time.

Mary slipped back over to the window. She saw Billy come running out the main hall door, where Tommy Farrell was waiting. Billy slapped Tommy on the back and then both of them set off down Summerhill. She knew they'd pass by her mother's place at Number 17 and down the Twenty-seven Steps to Gloucester Diamond, where the army trucks picked up the workers to head for the Dublin Mountains to gather turf for the day. She glanced across the road and saw a couple of lads slip up the side-entrance to the Lee Dairy yard beside Hutton's Lane. She'd be able to get some milk there in an hour or so. The door opened and her mother, Molly, came in.

'God save all here,' said Molly, taking off her black shawl and putting it on the end of the girls' bed. 'I saw himself headin' off,' she said, 'so you get a move on now and you'll just make the first Mass. Father O'Brien only went into the chapel a minute ago.'

Mary nodded, picked up her own shawl and slipped out the door, following in her husband's path down the Twenty-seven Steps. She saw the last of the army trucks vanishing around the corner into O'Connell Street as she turned the other way into Seán MacDermott Street. As always, she was struck by the different names. Seán MacDermott Street was named after a hero of the 1916 Rising, replacing the English name of Gloucester Street.

The area known as Gloucester Diamond was still called that twenty years later, however, because no one could be bothered to get their mouth around 'Seán Mac-Dermott Diamond'. So the old name stuck.

Mary slipped into the little tin church known as Lourdes Chapel just as Father O'Brien came out onto the altar to start the six o'clock Mass. He was followed by four altar boys carrying the brass candleholders in one hand and their Latin Mass cards in the other, held solemnly against their chests. The priest ascended the altar steps as the altar boys put the candleholders on the side altar and returned to kneel in twos on each side of the altar. The priest placed the chalice in front of the tabernacle, went to the right-hand side, where he opened the missal at the prayers for the day, and swept back to the tabernacle with a flourish of his flowing vestments. Down the steps he came, and knelt on the bottom step between his quartet of altar boys to begin the Mass with the introduction line of *'Introibo ad altare Dei'* ('I will go to the altar of God'), to which the altar boys replied, *'Ad Deum, qui laetificat juventutem meum'* ('To God, who brings joy to my youth').

As the service continued, Mary, with the memory of Stephen's Green still fresh in her mind, could only think of her young son. How much she had wanted him to be on that altar. 'Tony, Tony,' she whispered, 'may Jesus and his Holy Mother take care of you now.'

*

Billy and Tommy came dashing into the turf yard in Gloucester Diamond just as the trucks began to rev up. 'Come on, lads!' shouted Bob Darcy. 'You're on this

Ma and Da passing the Gresham Hotel in 1939

truck with me today.' Bob and another neighbour held out their hands from the back of the truck and pulled the two men up onto the floor as the truck lurched forward and out into Gardiner Street. They turned towards Cathal Brugha Street (named after another Irish hero), and within minutes were heading down O'Connell Street, named after the great liberator, Daniel O'Connell. The journey took them through the south side of Dublin city, through Rathmines, Terenure and Rathfarnham and on up the Ballyboden Road to the turf bogs of the Dublin Mountains. As it was a sunny morning, the tarpaulin cover of the truck had been rolled up. The six men in each truck were sitting down on the truck floor looking at the streets and houses going by. Dublin was still asleep, with only a few early risers out walking and biking – some to work and others hurrying to early-morning Mass.

'How's Mary?' asked Bob. 'Has she got over young Tony yet?'

'She's fairly good, I suppose,' Billy responded, 'but you know Mary. Even when her heart's breakin', she'd never admit it. She gets on with things, and sure the three girls are a handful. But you can see when the wistful look comes on her that she's thinking of the wee lad.'

'Yes, I've seen that look,' said Bob. 'I suppose the best cure for that was your new baby, Liam.' Bob chuckled. 'And sure if it's another baby boy she wants, there's no better man for that job than yourself, Billy.'

The lads in the truck joined in the laughter and Billy smiled at them. But inside, he was fuming at Bob's coarse remarks. 'Big and all as he is,' he thought to himself, 'I can see myself breaking his head one of these days.'

The trucks were travelling along the mountain road with a cooling breeze blowing in off the Irish Sea. The bogs stretched out for miles around them. The turf had been cut into sods and left to dry in mounds out to the side of the road. This work was done by expert bog workers using a *sleán* to cut the turf. The *sleán* was like a bladed spade, and a special type was used on the Dublin Mountains because the bogland there was much thinner than in the wet lowlands. It was really tough work and these men had arms like tree trunks. A wooden bog barrow was used to load the sods on and it would then be dragged across the slippery bog surface to the drying ground beside the road. The turf took a long time to dry, but up on the mountains the wind did a good job in quickly forming a tough, waterproof skin on the sods.

On this sunny morning, the six army trucks pulled in beside the long lines of turf that had been cut the previous year. The turf had been covered through the winter, but the covers had been removed in the fine April weather. Now after a sunny month of May, it was to be loaded into the trucks to take into the city. Sometimes the trucks went directly to the turf depots for immediate distribution, and sometimes to the storage area in Dublin's Phoenix Park for further drying. This turf was a great source of energy for Ireland during the war, when imported coal became too expensive. The minister, Seán Lemass, was able to kill two birds with one stone when he introduced his turf scheme. He curtailed coal imports – to the benefit of the Exchequer – and got unemployed men out on the bogs all over Ireland to save the turf. The turf was given out free on ration vouchers to the needy and sold to those who could afford it. From these humble origins was born Bord na Móna, which turned into a multi-million-pound state agency supplying alternative energy. Horticultural turf mould (peat moss) was also exported all over the world.

The men jumped down from the trucks and were called to order by the army corporal, who sat beside the driver in the truck cab. Each group of six men lined up beside their truck and the corporal did a roll-call from his roster sheet – 'Cullen?' 'Yes, sir.' 'Darcy?' 'Yes, sir.' – until all six of his men had replied in the affirmative.

At each truck, this was repeated, and all the men were given their turf forks and were reloaded onto their trucks. Then the trucks moved out, to pull up at varying distances along the turf lines. The men hopped to it and the hard work started, the work of forking the turf sods into the truck, with three of the lads on top of the mounds and the other three on the ground. Every half-hour they alternated from ground to top, which was the easier job. The big strong men, like Bob Darcy and Billy

Cullen, could load twice as much turf as Tommy Farrell
or some of the smaller lads. But everyone got the same
pay: ten shillings a day, plus a free bag of turf, so they
all did their best and there was no slacking accepted.
Only when a man was obviously under the weather or
off-colour was he let slip under the wheels of the truck
for a rest. The army lads set up a huge water urn on a
turf-burning range, so tea was available from about nine
o'clock, and the men took turns getting tea breaks.
Lunch hour was from one to two o'clock, when each
crew examined their lunch bags.

'The same old prairie sandwiches again,' said Mickser.
'Two lumps of bread, with wide open spaces between
them.'

'That's okay,' said Tommy Farrell. 'I've got a couple
of pounds of bacon lard. We'll give it a heat-up and
spread it on the bread for a lard sambo. Just the job.'

Sometimes some of the men would have a delicacy
like a few rashers or some black pudding. And the army
lads would always share out some of their rations.
Friday was pay day – and the truck convoy had a few
visitors, who came from surrounding mountain farms
on their carts. Usually it was the farmer's wife or son
and they would have eggs, fruit, cabbages, potatoes and
other vegetables to sell. Bob Darcy was the dealing man
for Billy's truck. He'd take five shillings from each man
and haggle and negotiate the thirty bob into as much
produce as he could get. He'd a great gift of the gab
about him, never getting down to business until he'd
paid the necessary compliments to the seller.

'There's no doubt about it,' he'd say, 'but sure the
mountain air up here must do magical things to a girl.
Your lovely skin and sparkling eyes are like a film star's.

Sure, they'll be wanting you for the next Clark Gable picture.'

And when he got to the buying, it would be: 'Now don't forget these eggs are for Tommy's sick little girl who needs nourishing. These carrots and parsnips have to feed ten kids for a month, so just throw in a few more.'

He could go to the Olympics and talk for Ireland, could Bob.

It was six o'clock before the work was finished and the trucks loaded. The men were exhausted and burnt from the sun. They had their last mug of tea, climbed up on top of the turf and headed for home. Back to the Gloucester Diamond depot. The army sergeant in charge had decided this load was ready to burn, and there were plenty of customers. Billy looked back over the mountain bog with the turf lines along the road and the mounds drying all over the place. Local people were to be seen gathering turf from their own 'pre-let' spots. Some of them had creels, which were open top wicker baskets, with a rope strap going over the neck, as the basket of turf fitted on their back. He saw an old man bent under the load of the creel, which could have held his own weight of turf.

'There's no doubt about it,' he thought, 'the good Lord will provide if you're ready and able to go out and work.'

Coming down the mountains, the trucks took it slowly, to make sure the loads of turf didn't shift on the bumpy roads. They came down a different route through Dundrum and over the road by Mount Anville Convent, from where the view out over Dublin Bay was spectacular. From the top of the truck, Billy could see from Dún Laoghaire harbour across the bay to the sand dunes of Dollymount Strand and on to the majestic Hill of Howth.

'Mary was right,' he said to Bob, 'it's a pure beautiful day, and isn't Dublin a lovely city. We'll get the kids out to Dollymount Strand this Sunday.'

*

The army trucks pulled in to the turf depot, where the men jumped down to let the trucks pull in to the unloading bays. Here a huge grab bucket mounted to a ceiling gantry was used, and it unloaded in fifteen minutes what had taken six men all day to load up.

'You know, Billy,' said Bob, 'it won't be long before they'll have machines like this up on the mountain doing the loading and we won't be getting our few shillings for the job, and that's a fact.'

Each man had received a fuel voucher with his pay packet and they handed this voucher over for a sack of turf. Bob and the rest of the lads were retiring to Killane's pub for a few jars but Billy was heading straight home. As he watched them heading for the pub, Billy knew that wives and mothers would be waiting anxiously at home for the men to return with the wages and the goodies. Most of the lads would be okay, and Bob was a single man anyway. But he knew that one or two would get drunk and spend or gamble or give away the hard-earned cash.

Billy swung the turf over his shoulder as if it were a bag of feathers and picked up the other sack of goodies. He was in great spirits as he bounded up the Twenty-seven Steps to Summerhill. From the steps, he could see the backs of the tenements, with the poles sticking out from the windows and all the family clothes out to dry. At the top, he saw Bill O'Brien in his bicycle shop next door to the gateway into Hendron's Engineering Works.

'Howaya, Bill,' he called across the street. O'Brien's greasy face smiled back at him from under the bikes hanging by hooks from the iron storage racks. Billy went over to see how his own bike was coming on, after the rear hub had seized up.

'Don't worry, Billy,' O'Brien said to him. 'I've found a matching hub on an old post office scrap bike. I'll fix it up by tomorrow evening for you.'

Billy was always ready to stop and chat with the bicycle-shop owner. He loved fixing bikes up himself but repairing punctures and fitting new spokes was as far as he got. O'Brien mainly worked on the messenger-boy bikes with the small front wheel and a mounted frame for a wicker basket. This was the standard one-manpower delivery format for the post office, the grocery shops, the butchers and all sorts of businesses. With business slack during the Emergency, the bikes were left in with O'Brien for repair and the owners were taking their time collecting and paying for them. O'Brien was hoping the war would end and business would pick up. Out of the corner of his eye, Billy saw his mother-in-law, Molly Darcy, come out of the hall door at Number 17 with her shawl around her shoulders and her big pair of rosary beads wrapped around her right hand.

'Evening, Billy,' she called to him. 'Just rushing to make the Rosary at seven in Lourdes Chapel.'

Billy nodded to her retreating back as she headed down the steps. 'That's a black mark for you, Billy,' said O'Brien, ''cause you aren't home in time to let Mary go with her. She loves going to the evening Rosary with

Mary, the way they did before you got married.' Billy knew O'Brien was right and that he'd better get on home, because Molly would quote the exact time she tagged him gossiping in the bike shop. So he bade O'Brien goodnight and stepped on up the street with his head high and his shoulders back in the military bearing that he was known for. Some young children were playing 'piggy-beds' on the footpaths and he gave them a cheery word as he marched by with his two sacks. The kids would have to be off the streets by eight o'clock, as the guards from Fitzgibbon Street would be on their rounds soon to shoo them home. There was one golden rule in Summerhill: you didn't argue with those giant Kerrymen in their blue uniforms. It was simply 'Yes, sir' or 'No, sir', and off you went about your business.

Billy went through the doorway of the tenement Number 28 and, as always, the smell of poverty and urine hit him. It was worse than usual this summer evening after he had spent the day in the mountain air, even though he knew that Mary would have spent some time washing out the hall. The two families on the hall floor had about six children apiece. Downstairs, the basement rooms were uninhabitable – but at night they were home to a handful of vagrants. These wouldn't bother to make it out to the lavatory in the backyard, and used the hall as a toilet. So Billy held his breath as he went up the stairs and vowed that he'd get out of there as soon as the war ended and he got his job back with Brooks Thomas timber merchants on the North Wall docks. He'd get his family away from the dirt, the smell and the throngs of humanity that threatened to smother his hopes for a better life for his children.

These houses had been built two hundred years before and were ready to fall down. Dublin Corporation was slowly buying out the profiteering landlords, with the intention of redeveloping. But money was scarce and it took the disaster of a building collapsing and people dying to get a building listed as being in a 'dangerous condition'. It was okay to be living in an 'uninhabitable dwelling', but you had to be in a 'dangerous building' to be moved. Number 28 wasn't too bad, as it officially housed only forty-nine residents. There were a hundred and twenty-eight people living in Number 24. So, as Mary said, we should always count our blessings – things could be a lot worse.

As he crossed the landing to the door of the Cullens' room, he could hear Mary's voice shushing the girls: 'Keep quiet now, your daddy is coming with the food.' He knew Mary had been watching for him at the window. He dropped the sack, opened the door and picked up the sack again as he stepped over the threshold, to see Mary there with baby Liam in her arms and Betty and Rita clinging to her apron, and little Vera asleep in the pram.

Mary welcomed him with sparkling eyes. 'You're burnt black,' she said, as he dropped the sack of turf inside the door.

'So I am,' he replied. 'But come on in here, me girls, and see what I've brought you home from the mountains.' He swung the sack of produce onto the kitchen chair. 'Now close your eyes,' he said, 'and count to ten, and then you'll see what I've got here.' Betty and Rita put their hands over their eyes and started to count in time with Mary, who took it slowly. Billy lined up the goodies on the table: he pulled out two heads of cabbage, filled the basin with spuds, six eggs went onto a plate, then four carrots, four parsnips, a skinned rabbit, six rosy red apples – cookers, yes, but they looked great.

'Ten! Ten! Ten!' shouted the girls, and then peeped through their fingers just as he put the last piece on the table – a freshly made loaf of bread as big as a house. 'And that's what the lads in the mountains call a turnover of bread.'

The girls squealed with delight as Billy gave each of them a handful of home-made toffees, which quickly had them sucking and gurgling on the edge of Mary's bed. Mary herself went into action, scrubbing the spuds and chopping them into pieces, which she dropped into the big black iron pot that she had had simmering all afternoon on a bed of turf in the fireplace.

'And look what I've got,' she said to Billy, showing him three ripe red tomatoes, six rashers and six sausages. 'You don't think I've been wasting my day sitting around here. The mother and meself bartered all our sugar-ration vouchers down in Moore Street for these, so we'll all be going without sugar for a long time.' She knew Billy liked his tea sweet, but even more than that he liked a Dublin coddle. 'Off you go,' she said, 'and clean yourself up while I get the food ready. Here's a towel and soap, and don't leave it behind you.'

Billy stripped off his shirt and gansey and picked up the towel and soap, and off he went out the door and down the stairs to the backyard. It was Friday night and there were a few lads having a wash under the tap. He'd already used the toilet in the turf depot rather than inflict the stench of the backyard lavatory on himself. So he quickly stripped off his vest and scrubbed his entire upper body under the tap. It took only a few minutes, then he towelled himself dry.

'You'd want to watch it, Mister Cullen,' said one of the lads, 'or you'll have the girls jumping on ya going up the stairs, showing off that big hairy chest.'

Billy blushed and quickly put his vest on, saying, 'Sure it's only young fellas like you that the girls are after.' He scooted in the back door with the words 'No, no, it's experience they're after' ringing in his ears. 'Young tykes,' he thought, 'saying things like that.'

The girls were in bed when he got back to the room. 'I gave them some mashed spuds,' said Mary. 'After those toffees, they're too full for any more. The coddle will take a while, but I got you an *Evening Herald*. You could read me the news.'

Billy knew Mary hated the fact that she couldn't read the newspaper. She was smart as a fox, could add up numbers like a flash, could understand the bullet points of an advertisement, but stumbled and faltered when trying to read a newspaper or a letter.

'Right,' said Billy, 'I'd better light the gas globe, it's getting dark in here.'

Over he went to the single-filament globe, turned on the gas tap and put a lighted match to the globe, which was illuminated with a soft glow. The room was bathed in a dim light. He picked up the paper and went through the front-page stories as Mary listened and asked questions. Within an hour the coddle was ready to serve, and she filled two deep plates with the thick stew. Billy shovelled it into his mouth with a big spoon and she watched with contentment as he wolfed the food down: a hungry man after a long day's work. She was still out of tea, but had prepared two big enamel mugs of shell cocoa and two chunks of the mountain bread, with some margarine spread on it.

Before they started, there was a light knock on the door. It was Missus Carey, looking for 'a bit of bread to make a sambo for tomorrow's lunch for himself. He's got a day's work in the turf depot.' Billy just nodded to Missus Carey and ignored the passing over of the bread. Sure it could be Mary's turn tomorrow, and in Summerhill sharing was part of surviving for everyone. When they had washed up, it was eleven – time to empty the slop bucket in the lavatory and refill the fresh-water bucket for the morning. Mary went with Billy down the stairs to the backyard, holding an oil lamp to light the way. They returned, bolted the door, and Billy quickly undressed to his vest and hopped into bed with the paper.

'Better check the hatch-match-and-dispatch columns in case someone we know has croaked it,' he said.

Mary picked up the basket of clothes which she had pulled in off the line earlier and went to work with the hot iron off the hearth. When the ironing was done, she settled into her favourite chair with a bundle of ganseys and socks and frocks for darning and mending. By this time Billy was asleep, and it was after midnight when she finished up. She checked the baby, who had finished his bottle and was fast asleep. The three girls were asleep too, but Betty was coughing a little. A bit rough, thought Mary. She'll be getting her cod-liver oil in the morning, whether she likes it or not. She undressed quickly and put on her nightdress. As she reached out to quench the gas globe, she spotted his unopened pay packet on the mantelpiece, where he always left his wages. Not a penny had he taken for himself. As she lowered the gaslight, she looked at his strong, handsome profile in the bed until the light popped out. Then she climbed into the bed and was asleep in an instant, thinking that, despite all her troubles, she was very lucky to have a good man beside her.

4
'MAY SHE REST IN PEACE'

The winter of 1942 was a tough one. There was no work
on the bogs and Mary had gone through the last of the
lucky windfall from the sale of Liam's caul. Billy went
down to the docks with Big Bob every day but there
were ten times more men than there was work. The
little money earned was often spent in Thomas Delaney's pub. It was soul-destroying seeing so many
grown men loitering around, so Billy took to carving
toys out of the wood scraps from the timber yards. Toy
guns and toy carts with solid round wheels were the
favourites, and he got some paint from the factory to
decorate the toys in bright colours. He even turned his
hand to making small stools and benches that he was
able to sell for a few shillings.

Mary was good at bartering the food-ration vouchers,
turning sugar vouchers into spuds and tea vouchers into
carrots down in the Dublin vegetable markets. Molly
had been selling fish in Henry Street for years, and when
Mary found a farmer with surplus vegetables she sold
them from Liam's pram, using Molly's street-trading
licence to keep the police at bay. There was no photograph on the licence and it said Mary Darcy, which was

Molly's christened, legal name. So more and more, Mary, her daughter, was using the licence.

This meant, of course, that Mary was heading off in the morning, leaving Billy to mind the kids. The seeds of frustration were planted. Billy loved the children, but seeing his wife publicly becoming the breadwinner was a huge blow to a proud man. He knew she was keeping the family alive as he filled his day with carving wood, cleaning the house and playing with the kids. He grew quiet and withdrawn and their evenings were spent in silence, Mary heading down to the Rosary at seven in Lourdes Chapel with her mother and getting home later and later, Billy sitting at home reading the *Evening Herald*.

To thwart her, he joined the sodality in the Pro-Cathedral in Marlborough Street, spending from half past six till ten o'clock in the church on Wednesdays and Fridays. He helped the curate with all the church duties. The tension at home culminated in accusatory rows and arguments, which started over little or nothing.

It was after one such row that they were lying in bed together – but miles apart – when they heard Betty crying. Billy got up and went through the curtain to her, as Liam woke and started bawling: he was a crier of a baby. 'She's been off-colour all day,' Billy said to Mary, 'and she hardly touched her food.'

'Why didn't you tell me?' said Mary, and saw his angry reaction.

'Don't give me that,' he said. 'Sure I didn't get a chance to get a word in edgeways. You've been giving out lackery since you came in the door tonight.'

Mary knew he was right: she was irritable and tired from running around the street all day. 'This child has a fever. Sure you just have to feel her forehead to know she's burning up,' said Mary. 'I'll take her down to the mother.'

'Oh no you won't,' said Billy. 'The last child of mine you took down to your mother came out in a box, so Betty stays right here. I'll go and get a doctor,' he said, grabbing his clothes and dressing quickly.

Vera and Rita had joined Liam in the crying as Billy grabbed his bike and slung it over his shoulder. He unbolted the door, pausing to bless himself with the holy water, and headed down the stairs.

Mary rocked Liam's cot as the girls calmed down after the angry words, and finally they fell asleep. It was an hour later when Billy returned, with a young man in tow. 'This is Dr Molloy from Temple Street Hospital to have a look at her,' he said.

The doctor laid the child on the bed and did a quick examination of her eyes, throat and pulse, then felt her knee and elbow joints. 'I'm afraid that I'll have to get this child to the hospital immediately. Wrap her tight in a blanket. Will you be able to carry her on the bike, Mister Cullen?'

Billy nodded and looked at Mary, expecting to see her wrapping up Betty. But no, she had stepped back away from the bed, with her hands to her mouth and a glazed look on her face. Billy grabbed the blanket and wrapped it snugly around the child. He stood up with the child on one arm.

'Let's go, Doctor,' he said. Billy turned to Mary as she stood staring at him, a desolate look on her face. 'Take care of yourself,' he said to her.

'You too,' she answered softly. He dabbed some holy water on the child's head as he went out the door.

Young Betty died in the hospital the next day, with Billy still there dozing in the waiting room.

Dr Molloy woke him with the bad news. 'It was viral pneumonia,' he said. 'She didn't have a chance, Mister Cullen. And you'd better move your wife and children out of that damp tenement, because they're at risk too.'

Billy clamped his teeth and glared at the young doctor with fury. 'And where do you think I'll take them to, doctor?' he asked angrily. 'To stay in the Shelbourne Hotel for the winter? Sure we're lucky to have a roof over our heads.'

The hospital was run by the Sisters of Charity, and a nun quickly came over. 'Now Mister Cullen, the doctor is only trying to be helpful,' she said. Billy looked at her calm, serene face. With the flying coif, she looked like an angel.

He calmed down and said, 'I'm sorry, Doctor. I know you did your best, and thanks for coming out in the middle of the night.'

The nun took his arm, saying, 'Come on down to the chapel and we'll say a few prayers. Sure isn't this your second young one that Christ has chosen to take, Mister Cullen? You know the procedure.'

While they were in the chapel praying, Mister Stafford, the undertaker, opened the door and wheeled in a trolley with three cardboard boxes on it. A priest was behind him and as they walked up the middle of the small church a number of nuns also appeared.

With the trolley in front of the altar, the priest turned and said, 'My brethren, we're here to ask the good Lord to accept these innocent children into the Kingdom of Heaven. May He give them the happiness in heaven that they didn't receive in this valley of tears. May the Virgin Mary bless and comfort the parents and relatives and may their souls and all the souls of the faithful departed rest in peace. Amen.' He paused, and slowly sprinkled holy water on the three boxes as he murmured his Latin blessing.

Then he smiled to the small gathering and said, 'And now will you please join me in the Holy Rosary, to pray for these unfortunate children. We'll say the Five Sorrowful Mysteries of the Blessed Virgin.' Then he started with, 'The first sorrowful mystery: the Agony in the Garden. Our Father, who art in heaven . . . '

Billy didn't join in the prayers. He was thinking of the last time he and Mary had been in Stephen's Green with the kids. Betty had spent the hour chasing butterflies in the grass and between the trees, and falling among the flowers. He remembered Mary wiping the green grass-stains from her knees and brushing the yellow dust of the buttercups from her white frock. The child's eyes sparkling with joy, her tiny hand resting on his own massive fist. So trusting, so vulnerable, so innocent.

When the Rosary was finished, Stafford wheeled the trolley out the side door of the church to an open yard, where his small, horse-drawn cart awaited. As he placed the boxes in the cart, Billy walked out.

'Can I go with you, Tom?' he said.

'Now, Billy,' said Stafford, 'we've been through all this before and you know you can't come with me. It's standard procedure with the Church to protect parents from the grief of burying a young child. It's all taken care of in private. The mothers are never let see their dead children. You go on home and look after Mary and your other kids. That's where you're needed now. I'll make sure Betty will be with your other wee lad and it's a nice sunny spot they've got too.'

He climbed up on the cart. One chuck on the reins and off the horse went over the cobblestoned yard. The three small boxes shivered as the steel-rimmed wheels hopped on the cobbles.

Billy stood there for a long time, thinking it was better for Mary not to go through this grief but wishing he knew where the children were buried. It would be nice to visit them when time had healed the pain. He didn't go back into the church but headed out the backyard of the hospital to go home to Summerhill. He walked down Hill Street into Grenville Street, across Mountjoy Square and down Gardiner Street. As he turned up Summerhill, he saw Mary leaning out the window of Number 28 watching for him. She saw that his shoulders were slumped and his head bent. She knew Betty wouldn't be coming home. She slid slowly back into the room and fainted on the floor.

*

It was the summer of 1944 in Dublin. A lovely mid-June Sunday, and Billy and Mary had the kids out on Dolly-mount Strand. The Number 30 bus from the Five Lamps took the six of them and the pram all the way out to the wooden bridge. And it didn't cost them a sausage because the conductor was Jimmy Corbally, a Local Defence Force man who had stood shoulder to shoulder with Billy on the bombsite in '41. Billy was embarrassed and wanted to pay, in case an inspector came on board. 'Don't be silly, man,' said Jimmy. 'Sure you'll have to pay up if he does get on. But we'll wait and see first.'

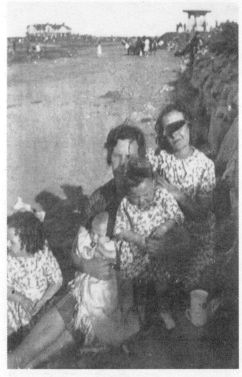

The Ma on Dollymount Strand with, from left, Vera, baby Liam, Betty and Rita. The famous Royal Dublin Golf Club is in the background. All frocks courtesy of Molly Darcy's sewing machine.

Anyway, they got all the way out for zilcho, so that meant extra sweets and ice cream for the kids. They made sandcastles, rode on the donkey and rolled down the sand dunes. They collected winkles from the rocks for cooking later when they got home. For food, Mary produced a parcel of sandwiches with tomatoes and some cold rashers, which they washed down with a couple of bottles of milk. Little baby Noel was five months old now and as good as gold. Not a bother out of him as he played with his rattler in the pram. Young Liam was big as a house for a two-year-old and was over kicking a ball with some older lads. Vera and Rita were playing house and Billy caught Mary's eye as she looked over the kids.

'Are you all right, Mary?' he asked.

'I am, Billy,' she replied. 'You know, the sun just warms the bones and makes me feel like a young one again.'

'Come off it,' he said. 'Sure you're only a colleen.'

'Oh, I'm a quare colleen at twenty-nine years old and after six babies,' she said. 'I'm looking at Liam and he's the spitting image of poor Tony. And Vera is like a twin of our Betty, may they both rest in peace.'

Billy looked carefully at her but she was all right now: her eyes were happy, and she was smiling. Doctor Mulligan had said she just needed a bit of time – and, of course, another baby to love. He was right, it was a long time since she had looked so calm and happy. He put his arm around her and held her close.

'Billy, will you promise me one thing?' she said. 'Will you promise me to keep the kids in the sunshine as often as we can? It's good for them.'

He thought of the dull, dark tenement and swore again to himself to get them out of it as soon as the bloody war was over. The American troops were kicking Hitler's arse in Europe now, so it might be soon.

'Mary,' he said, 'we'll get them out to play in Mountjoy Square every bright evening that God gives us.'

'That's the job,' she said. 'And we'll get to Stephen's Green on Sunday too.'

'There's the sparkle,' he said to himself. 'That's my Mary.'

They walked over the wooden bridge that evening hand in hand, Liam asleep in the pram with Noel, Vera in Billy's arms and Rita skipping along.

'What do you think of that for a bit of luck, Mary,' Billy said as the bus pulled in. 'It's Jimmy Corbally again. You must get dizzy going around in circles, me ould pal,' he said, as Jimmy gave him the wink and pulled the child's pram in under the stairs of the bus.

'You know, Billy,' said Jimmy cheerfully, 'it's better to be born lucky than rich.' Mary smiled from her seat and her eyes sparkled as she cradled her sleeping son Liam in her arms. Mother Darcy was right when she said life was for living. She could see now there were so many things to thank God for when she looked at her four lovely children.

'Put the past behind you, girl,' Molly had said. 'Yesterday is history, tomorrow is a mystery, so make the most of today.'

She could feel the strength coming back into her body: her lifeblood was pumping, she was switched on and ready to go. She'd get her six o'clock Mass tomorrow and go down to the market to tangle with the vegetable farmers from Rush and Skerries. Sure, she might even start the ball rolling tonight if she got under Billy's night vest. Billy was sitting across from her, delighted to see her eyes sparkling and to notice her almost laughing to herself. 'She's back in action again,' he thought, 'and it's about time too!'

5

A Boy with the Girls
in the Nuns' School

September was back-to-school time for Rita, and the first time out for Vera, who, as a four-year-old, was heading up to the Sisters of Charity Convent at the rear of Gardiner Street Church with her older sister. Sunday evening had been busy with getting all the school clothes ready. Mary had produced two new school satchels with new writing pads and rulers, all picked up at a bargain price from her old pal Mister Scott – or Hector Grey, as he called himself now.

'It's a trade name, Mary,' he said to her. 'This war will be over in months and the country will come alive again. So I'm expanding and I'm calling meself Hector Grey from now on.'

Mary looked at him and said, 'It sounds queer to me. I thought you only changed your name if you were a spy, or the police were after you. But anyway, it's your business, once I still get me wholesale discount.'

'And of course you will,' said Hector. 'I've told all me lads that whenever Mary Darcy comes into this shop, she gets the family discount.'

But as the girls were getting their school gear organised, young Liam was becoming agitated. 'Where you going, Vera?' he asked.

'To school I'm going tomorrow. Don't worry, Mother Darcy'll mind you.'

This didn't please him one bit. 'Don't want Mother Darcy. Want to go with Vera.'

He was put to bed, but as soon as Mary got up on Monday for her early-morning Mass she found the little fella sitting at the door.

'Want to go to school with Vera,' he said.

She planted him back in bed with the girls and Vera woke up and comforted him.

'Don't want Mother Darcy, want to go with Vera,' were the words in Mary's ears as she went out the door. After Mass, she got Billy off to the docks and then tackled the children.

'Now, son,' she said to Liam, 'you'll have to stay here with me, because Vera has to go to school. You're too little, and it's a girls' school – not for boys.'

The lad just looked at her with his bottom lip sticking out, repeating, 'Want to go with Vera.' When the girls were finally ready to move out, he threw himself on the floor, kicking his feet on the wooden boards and crying loudly.

'Off you go, girls,' Mary said. 'Don't mind his tantrums – he'll get the wooden spoon if he keeps that up.'

Rita and Vera skipped out the door, still looking anxiously at Liam.

'Mind yourself crossing the road,' Mary shouted down the stairs after them, and she stepped back into the room, to find the little fella dashing past her and down the stairs as fast as his legs would go.

The Ma with, from left, Rita, baby Noel, Liam and Vera in 1944. It was obviously Liam's curls that got him into the girls' school.

'Get back here, you little villain,' she shouted as she took off after him. When she got out the hall door, there he was on the footpath, with Vera holding his hand.

'Mammy, Mammy, let him come with us. I'll mind him,' said Vera.

Rita also added her piece: 'Sister Bernadette won't mind, Mammy, she's very nice. We'll tell her you have to go to work.'

The girls looked pleadingly at her. The young fella had tears streaked across his face, still with his bottom lip sticking out.

'Okay,' she said, 'back you come till I tidy him up. Take him up to the nuns and we'll see what they make of him.'

Back up the stairs they all trooped, and Mary pulled out a small white shirt and pants for Liam, washed his face and hands and then spent a few minutes styling the ringlets of his shoulder-length curly blond hair. As she put on the pants, Mary remembered the nights she'd spent with Mother Darcy, cutting up Billy's pre-war work dungarees. They had made five pairs of smaller trousers, which they shared out with neighbours' children. This pair was the one she'd finished off with double-edged stitching and matching shoulder braces. The only decent shoes in the place were an old pair of Rita's. She gave them a quick rub of Nuggets boot polish, then stuffed some newspaper up in the toes of the shoes and strapped them on.

'Now,' said Mary, 'off you go, the lot of ya, and don't you make a show of us up there with the nuns. Be on your best behaviour,' she cautioned, waving her finger under the boy's nose. Before they went out the door, she lined them up under the picture of the Sacred Heart and sprinkled the three of them with holy water from the little font.

'May God bless us and bring us home safely,' they all repeated together, then out the door and down the stairs they went.

Mary watched from the window with Baby Noel in her arms as the three children went across the road, with the girls on each side of Liam, all holding hands. They went up Hutton's Lane, skipping and swinging each other. Mary looked after them for a long while, thinking that Liam could pass for a girl with his long ringlets – until he opened his mouth, that is. She turned from the window to have a cup of tea and make the baby a bottle, feeling a quiet contentment. It was great to think that the kids were getting an education. Learning to read and write, they were – what a wonderful gift.

Up Hutton's Lane, across Mountjoy Square into Belvedere Place and left under the arch into Belvedere Row the three children went. The laneway was packed with young boys and girls, all running around, playing and shouting. The school only catered for children up to seven years of age, and Rita pulled Liam and Vera over to meet some of her pals from her last class. Before she could get talking, the side gate opened and out came Sister Bernadette, with a large bell ringing in her hand.

'Line up, children,' she called out. 'Boys to the right and girls to the left.'

Liam felt Vera squeeze his hand and his sisters dragged him to the left queue as the nun opened the main gate and the children filed in.

'Girls left, boys right,' the nun repeated, as the children marched in and went right and left respectively. No one had paid any attention to Liam, and it struck Rita that his long hair was a great disguise. When they got inside the girls' school, Rita knew she had to head off to Classroom 2, while Vera would be in Classroom 1. But they waited together in the corridor until all the children had gone into the classrooms and Sister Bernadette arrived from outside.

'Into your classrooms now, girls,' she said, and Rita started explaining that this was her brother Liam, who had come to school with her sister Vera, who was here on her first day, and they had to bring Liam, because their Mammy had to go to Moore Street to sell apples, and would it be all right, Sister, if Liam went to class with Vera, because he was a good boy and very quiet.

The words came tumbling out of her, with Vera nodding vigorously in support.

Then there was silence, with all three children looking up anxiously at the stern face of the nun towering over them. She was a formidable figure, in her long black cassock with a huge white coif that looked like a Chinese sailboat on top of her head. A white rope was tied around her waist, from which hung an over-sized set of ornate red rosary beads, with a huge crucifix on the end hanging to about the nun's knee. A ring on the rope held a bunch of jailer's keys that rattled threateningly when she moved. Liam was looking down at her feet, which were in a pair of strap sandals, and her bare toes were twitching up at him. Then the tension broke when the nun spoke in a calm voice with a country lilt.

'Well sure now,' she said, 'and isn't he a lovely child, and Sister Patricia will take care of him because she has a wee brother too called Liam. Off you go, Rita, to Sister Philomena in Class 2, and you two follow me.'

They went into Class 1, where the nun motioned Vera into a double desk beside another girl and took Liam's hand and brought him right up to the front of the classroom, lifting him up onto the seat of the teacher's desk. She had a whispered conversation with Sister Patricia, who was smiling broadly at the young-ster, and then left the room. Sister Patricia went to her desk and, spreading a white sheet of paper on it, she handed a red crayon to the boy.

'Well now, Liam, you're very welcome, and let's see what you can draw on this,' she said.

So for young Liam Cullen, it was a lucky day. He started school at two and a half years old, because he had the same name as a lonely nun's brother. Sister Patricia made a fuss of him, giving him little titbits of fudge and hard-boiled sweets. But he joined fully in the class activities of drawing and colouring animals, learn-ing to spell his 'cat' and his 'rat' and his 'hat'. By

Christmas he had his alphabet off by heart and he knew his arithmetic tables up to 'Ten by ten is a hundred.' There had been some jeering remarks from the boys at the lunchtime break in the schoolyard and it was little Vera who went on the attack, lashing out with her feet and chasing the bullies who didn't know how to handle a fighting girl. All boys were strictly taught that you never struck a girl. Only cowards and bowsies did that, so the jeers died away.

Before the Christmas break the Ma was sent for, and Sister Bernadette explained that the young fella had come along so much she was recommending he go into the boys' school – not into first babies, but straight into second class with the five-year-olds. Mary was delighted. On his last day in the girls' school, Liam arrived with his ringlets cut off and with two lace handkerchiefs made by Mother Darcy as a thank-you present for Sister Patricia and Sister Bernadette. At lunchtime they stood together, the two nuns with his two sisters, and watched him march over to the boys' playground with his bottom lip sticking out. 'Howaya,' he said to one of the boys looking at him. 'I'm Liamo. Where's Sister Frances of Class 2?'

Even as a three-year-old, you could see he had the cut of his father's jib. Chest out and chin up – ready to take on the world.

So Liam got off to a flying start in school and had an intense desire to learn everything. In the next three years in Gardiner Street, he become the number one for the three Rs: reading, 'riting and 'rithmetic. Sums were a doddle and he had the answers as quick as the questions were written on the blackboard. He was reading Rita's school books as well as his own, and he practised

The Da (marked, in dark suit and trilby) gets his 'Emergency' medal from Frank Aiken, Minister for Defence, in 1948

his writing with pen and ink during the play-breaks. He stayed in Gardiner Street until he was six, when he made his Holy Communion and moved on to the Christian Brothers in St Canice's School on the North Circular Road. St Canice's was only a stone's throw from Summerhill. Even after he had left Gardiner Street, Vera would tell him that 'Sister Patricia was asking for you today', and Mary knew the nuns were proud of Liam. There's no doubt that the nuns of Gardiner Street Convent were a first-class example of caring, loving teachers who worked very hard to set the children on the right road.

*

In May 1945, the war in Europe ended. The Cullen family were all gathered around the wireless after school, hearing how Hitler had committed suicide in his bunker before the Americans and Russians captured Berlin. The celebrations began with the people of Dublin pouring onto the streets, dancing and singing. Mary's brother, Big Bob Darcy, stood on a chair outside Killane's pub with a pint of Guinness in his hand, leading the crowd with his powerful voice. The favourites were 'It's a Long Way to Tipperary' and 'Pack Up Your Troubles in Your Old Kitbag'. The crowds sang in unison, while the children perched on the steps and railings, laughing in wonder at the adults, who were crying with joy.

In the second week in August, the news came through that the Japanese had surrendered and the war was finally over. It was a triumph for the Western World over Hitler's Nazis and the devious Japanese, of good over evil.

Mary Darcy had forgiven the Germans for the North Strand bombs. They were dropped by 'some frightened pilot who had lost his way and thought Dublin was Belfast', was her belief. But she had never forgiven the Japanese.

'You know,' she said, 'those little brown fellas sneaked up like thieves in the night and blew up the American sailors sleeping in their bunks. They never declared war. I heard their ambassador fella in the States was signing a peace treaty with the Yanks on the day the Jap planes blew up the American navy fleet in Pearl Harbour. No warning. Thousands killed. Just out of the black night they came and blew hundreds of ships into smithereens.' That had been her stance. 'Sneaky little so-and-sos,' she called them.

But now the news on the wireless was telling of the bombing of Hiroshima and Nagasaki. Atomic bombs, they were called. Two whole cities wiped out with just two bombs. Flattened buildings up to ten miles away.

Houses and people evaporated like a leaf in a flame. Half a million people killed or maimed.

That night Mary was sitting at the table having a mug of shell cocoa with Mother Darcy. 'It's hard to believe it,' said Mary. 'All them innocent people killed. What has the world come to? How can Jesus, Mary and Holy Saint Joseph let these things happen?'

'Now now, Mary,' said Molly. 'Don't be getting upset. It just reminds you how you lost your own pair. Sure we don't even know if your brother Ned is dead or alive. Doesn't the good Lord do things in mysterious ways? This war has seen millions of people killed everywhere, and at least it's over now. The dead are dead and the living have to get on with living. So let's go down to Our Lady of Lourdes and say the Rosary.'

And off they went down the Twenty-seven Steps to let the peace of the little tin chapel wash over them.

Years later, when an Asian came to buy apples at the stall, Mary's face lost its smile as she served him politely, torn between condemnation and sorrow. She shook her head when he left.

'I know they bombed Pearl Harbour, but they didn't deserve an atomic bomb,' she said to her pal Nanny Kelly, who sold beside her.

'Janey Mac, Mary, that's a Chinese fella from the takeaway down the street. He's not Japanese!'

Mary shook her head again and said, 'I don't care what he is. As far as I'm concerned, I wouldn't trust any of those little brown fellas as far as I'd throw a piano.'

Mother Darcy chastised her. 'That's wrong, Mary, that's a terrible thing to say. None of us know what we'll do when we're afraid. And you certainly can't visit the sins of the fathers on the sons. You yourself should know better.'

Mary looked at Molly for a long few minutes, then nodded slowly and said, 'You're right as usual, Mother. Sure every man is some mother's son, and the good Lord forgives every sinner. I'll talk to the priest in Confession on Saturday.'

6

SO THAT'S WHY
THE GERMANS BOMBED DUBLIN

Big Bob Darcy was in full flow, with his pint of Guinness in his hand. The usual gang were in Killane's and the talk had started about Bob's brother Ned, who was due to return from serving with the British army. They hadn't heard from him since he'd signed up, but a telegram had arrived saying he'd be home in a few days.

'Sure isn't there plenty of fellas who took the king's shilling,' said Bob. 'That's not a crime any more, when the Brits had to face them Germans. Would you like to have them Nazis in here now dragging you out of your own pub and off to a slave camp in Siberia? Pull your teeth out and starve ya to death? Say what you like about the Brits, but you have to give that old bastard Churchill full marks. He didn't back down to Hitler like the rest of them. Churchill has balls of steel. Lee-a-Roady he's got, and big ones too. I'm delighted the brother went over to back him up and if anyone here has anything to say against that,' – he paused and threw his cap on the sawdust floor – 'well, let him pick that cap up and we'll sort this out with our mitts.' There was silence in the pub as Big Bob looked slowly from face to face.

'Well,' he said, 'is there a man in this house who wants to say anything about my brother?' Not a move out of anyone.

'Right,' said Bob, sweeping his cap off the floor, 'and now I'll tell yiz all about why the Germans bombed the North Strand.'

Mister Killane behind the bar was relieved that a fight hadn't broken out. Up like a flash he was to Bob with a fresh pint. 'There you are, Mister Darcy, that's on the house', and as Tommy Farrell looked at him expectantly, he added, 'in honour of the bravery of your brother Ned.'

'May the Blessed Virgin always keep you safe, Mister Killane,' said Bob, as he picked up the pint.

'You remember, Tommy,' he began, waving his free pint to all and sundry, 'where them bombs fell that night. Go on now, just tell me exactly the spots they hit.'

He waited for a response, but sure Tommy was always slow off the mark, and Pat Cluxton, the furniture man, piped up. 'The biggest bang,' he said, 'was at Newcomen Bridge, on the North Strand Road, where you can see a couple of acres of houses were wiped out.'

'Yes,' said Bob. 'Good man, Pat, and that's a fact. Now where else would you add?'

'The next one was at Summerhill Parade at the top of William Street and another across the road beside O'Connell's School in North Richmond Street,' said Pat.

'And that's a fact as well,' said Bob. 'And where else?'

'I didn't think there was any more,' said Pat, looking at Tommy and then around the room.

There was silence for a few moments as Bob stood his full height, towering over little Tommy, and looked around with a knowing smile on his face. 'Where, me boyos, did the last bomb fall, 'cause that's the clue,' he said.

'It fell in the Dog Pond up in the Phoenix Park,' said a voice from the door.

'Be the bejaysus and that it did, and there we have the culchie Garda Byrne from Fitzgibbon Street, who does know about these things,' said Bob, pointing to the huge man in the doorway who was smiling at Bob.

'I hope Big Bob is behavin' himself, Mister Killane,' said the garda.

The publican touched his cap and said, 'Not a bother, guard. Sure he's peaceful as a lamb, our Bob is.'

The guard touched his helmet, nodded to Bob and eased his huge frame out the door, saying, 'Let's keep it nice and peaceful so.'

Bob responding softly as he left, 'Just as peaceful as it is down on the Bog of Allen.'

There was silence for a moment as the guard's shadow hesitated before moving away, and Bob with a broad grin said, 'Ya see? Them culchies only *look* stupid. That fella knows all about it. Ya have to remember a few weeks before the North Strand bombs, the first week of May 1941 it was. The Germans sent their whole bloody air force to blow Belfast off the map. Gave them an awful hammering for two solid days. Terrible it was. And do you remember what we did down here? We sent our fire-brigade units up from Dundalk and Drogheda and from Dublin to help with the fires up there.'

He paused and, looking slowly around, took a slug from his pint. 'So do you get it?' he said softly. 'We were supposed to be a neutral country but we openly went and gave the boys in Belfast a hand. Belfast is part of

Britain as far as them Germans are concerned.'

'Remember the Wexford creamery that was bombed?' Bob asked. 'That was supposed to be an accident too. But we know now what really happened. The Germans found the abandoned British supplies on the Dunkirk beaches after the retreat, and the big wooden butter boxes had Campile Creamery, County Wexford stencilled all over them. That's why the creamery was bombed – Hitler was telling de Valera to stop helping the Brits.'

There was silence in the pub. Not a sound. Mister Killane's eyes were popping out of his head as he strained to hear Bob's words from behind the bar. Bob looked at Tommy Farrell.

'Tommy, me ould flower, don't you remember your pal Jack Conroy who went to school with you in Marlborough Street? Didn't he go up to Belfast on the fire brigade from Buckingham Street? Didn't he tell us that? When we were pulling them people out of the rubble on the North Strand?'

Tommy looked at Pat Cluxton and said, 'He's right. You remember Jack Conroy, Pat. Sound as a bell. Lived up beside the cattle market on the North Circular Road. And Bob is right, the lads from the station did go to Belfast.'

'So what?' said Pat, with a wave of his hand. 'What about it?'

'So what?' echoed Bob. 'Have you any brains? Don't you see what happened? The big bombs fell about two hundred yards from Buckingham Street Fire Brigade Station. The next ones at Richmond Road, just a couple of hundred yards further on. If that aeroplane had been a few degrees to the west, he would have destroyed the fire station – and a lot of us along with it. So the bloody

Germans were paying us back, telling us to keep quiet and mind our own business.'

He paused and looked at Cluxton over the lips of his pint. 'And the last bomb?' he continued. 'Do you know where the Dog Pond is? Just across the road from the Áras an Uachtaráin, our president's palace, where our Ulster-Protestant president Douglas Hyde lives. So Hitler was giving him a kick in the arse and warning him to keep out of this war, or else.' He stopped and looked at the in—credulous faces all around him. He turned to the bar as a babble of voices and arguments broke out.

'You know, Mister Killane,' Bob said, 'that deserves another pint. They'll be coming in here for weeks discussing all that controversy.' And like any good businessman, Mister Killane had a pint up like a flash, saying, 'You're dead right, Mister Darcy.' As Bob picked up his pint, he murmured, 'And that's a fact' into the white froth, before slugging half the glass in one go.

*

As autumn turned to winter, the number of soldiers returning from the war grew bigger. There was a happy family reunion for Corporal Ned Darcy, a tall, lean, good-looking man with sad eyes. He refused to talk about his army career, where he was or what he'd done and seen. 'That's a closed book as far as I'm concerned,' he'd say, 'and I'm just glad to be home alive and in one piece.'

The saddest sight was the growing number of men sleeping rough on the Dublin streets. Men with limbs missing, moving around on home-made wooden crutches.

There were no wheelchairs. Legless men had wooden box-carts with steel ball-bearings for wheels. They pushed themselves along with blocks of wood tied to their hands and steered the single front wheel with a wooden rudder guided by two strings wrapped around their forearms. They could really hammer along and guide the box-cart at high speeds, using the wooden blocks to jam the wheels for braking.

A number of lads from rural Ireland stayed on in Dublin. They didn't relish going home to republican areas, where they might be regarded as outcasts for having taken the king's shilling. Even worse, they feared physical threats to themselves and their families, so they stayed to live a homeless, penniless, miserable life on the Dublin streets. At home, their poor mothers and families often went through the pretence that 'Poor Sean died in France, so he did.'

One shell-shocked man in a bedraggled army uniform marched up and down O'Connell Street, military-style. He was called 'Sergeant' and he spent his days taking commands as if he was on barrack drill. He was always on 'Quick march!' so the young fellas would shout 'About turn!' and he'd spin smartly on his heel and back he'd go up the street. When they'd shout 'Left turn!' he'd do a ninety-degree turn and off he'd go again. Whenever he'd be marched out into the traffic on O'Connell Street, sure the trams, the buses, the horses and carts, they would all stop to let him pass. When he did hit an immovable object like Clery's window or the wall of the GPO, he'd just mark time until someone's command moved him on. Sometimes, of course, he'd be wearing himself out marking time and looking at a wall for half an hour, so he'd be sensible enough to shout himself 'About turn!' then 'At ease' and he'd relax and then 'Dis-*miss!*' and he'd lie down in the middle of the footpath and go to sleep . . . until someone spotted him, and the shout of 'Atten-*shun!*' would see Sergeant jump up and stand straight as a flagpole, and then he'd be off, to follow the orders of all and sundry again. Sergeant was looked after on the streets by many's the people.

On a really wet day, Sergeant would cutely shout his own orders and march himself right into the picture houses, right up to the ticket usher, and they would all find a seat for him in the corner where he wouldn't bother anyone. This tactic he would use for food as well, by marching into Cafolla's or the Palm Grove. Right up to the counter with him to announce loudly, 'Sergeant here to collect the colonel's food order, ma'am!' which usually got him a bundle of fish and chips from the staff, who knew the eccentric oul' fella. If it was the case that they refused him, he'd shout out, 'Permission to return to base, ma'am!' and without waiting for a response he'd turn on his heel and march away. Sergeant marched around Dublin for years, like a clockwork toy, but always with an excited smile on his face, as if he was a child enjoying a great adventure. Mother Darcy said that when he returned to the hostel he lived in he became a normal, gentle fella and went to bed quietly. But when he was up and out the door the next morning, his shouts of 'Atten-*shun!*' and 'Company, by the left, quick march!' would start him off on another day of marching on the streets of Dublin, to everyone else's orders or to his own, as the case might be.

Eventually, in the 1950s, he vanished. No one noticed until Mother Darcy mentioned she hadn't seen Sergeant for a few days. After a couple of weeks, it was clear he wasn't on parade any more, and that was that. Molly Darcy said he just emptied his locker in the hostel, packed a haversack and walked away. Who knows where oul' Sergeant finished up?

Everyone knew 'Bang Bang'. He went around Dublin shooting people with a big old manor key which he used as an imaginary gun, shouting 'Bang! Bang!' The young fellas would fall down on the path in agony and die a death as good as any picture-house villain, and Bang Bang would blow the smoke from the barrel of his key-gun and look around menacingly with the key held high to see if anyone else wanted trouble. If anyone moved they'd get a few imaginary bullets, until Bang Bang holstered his key and strode off to another shoot-out somewhere else. He'd jump on the open platform of passing buses, and from this mobile gun wagon he'd 'Bang! Bang!' everyone in sight up and down the street. The bus conductors were well used to him and often hooshed him inside: 'In you go now, Bang Bang, and sit down where you can shoot them in comfort.' The bus inspectors humoured him because when he was asked for his bus ticket or anything else, his response was always the same: 'Bang! Bang!'

There were many characters like Sergeant and Bang Bang on the streets. This pair were the well-known ones; most of the others were ordinary homeless men scraping a meagre existence. The shopkeepers and street traders helped with handouts like an overripe apple or a handful of broken biscuits. Mary Darcy was selective in her handouts. She was a soft touch when she saw a genuine case: she'd be known to give a sick person a few shillings. But she was tough with those she considered chancers or wasters: she'd run such people off with caustic comments like 'Get out of that with yourself! Sure a strong young fella like you should be down in the markets working for your dinner' or 'Sure you're as well able to earn a few bob as we are' or 'You're not codding me with your dark glasses and white stick. Didn't I see you picking out the sweets in Woolworth's yesterday. Get yourself out of here or I'll break that "Help the Blind" sign on your head.'

And while none of the dealers had any time for spunkers (who were the real down-and-out drunks), Mary Darcy had a soft spot for them. This was a strange attitude from a woman who neither drank nor allowed drink into her own house. She'd still slip a thrupenny bit to the old spunkers, saying, 'Now you're to get yourself a cup of tea with that.'

When Nanny Kelly would chastise her for giving the spunkers money to buy their methylated spirits, she'd just say, 'Sure, he can't help it, it's his only bit of comfort and isn't he a harmless oul' fella and may the Holy Mother of God look after him.'

This attitude was the very opposite to that of her husband Billy, who detested the spunkers with a passion. 'Them spunkers are steeped in the drink and sure you can smell them a mile away,' he'd say. He'd run them off when they approached him begging and would throw them out of the tenement hall if he found them there.

*

The papers were full of stories about the war crimes. 'Wiped out millions of Jews in the gas chambers of the concentration camps, Hitler did,' people would say.

'Ya know,' said Tommy Farrell one night in Killane's pub, 'this little country of ours has had tough times. But gas chambers for the poor Jews is the worst I've ever heard. Did ya see the pictures in the *Herald*? The ones they found alive in the camps. Only skin and bone. Walking skeletons. And it said six million went for a burton.'

'That Hitler has a lot to answer for,' Big Bob Darcy said, shaking his head. 'And that's a fact. I don't think Saint Peter will be opening the pearly gates for him. Ould Nick he's with right now. Having a barbecue.' They all laughed.

'And ya know his brother was okay. Dacent man to have a few pints with,' Bob said casually. This silenced the table.

'Are you saying ya were drinking with Hitler's brother?' asked Mister Killane.

'Well, ya could hear me story if there was a pint of Guinness in me hand,' said Bob, looking at his empty glass on the table. 'Sure a man can't talk if his whistle is dried up.'

Knowing the pulling power of Big Bob's stories, Mister Killane had a pint in front of him in jig time. Bob took a swallow and smacked his lips. The others leaned forward as he began to speak, in a quiet voice.

'Mother Darcy knew him. Hitler's brother. Used to help out in Madame Barrington's house when she was up on Mountjoy Square. A butler he was, who used to give a hand with the parties. Molly said he worked as a waiter in the Shelbourne Hotel.' And he took a long, slow swallow of Guinness and licked the foam lovingly off his lips.

'Ah Jaysus, Bob, that's a hard one to credit,' said

Tommy Farrell. 'How do you know he was Hitler's brother?'

Bob leaned forward onto the table and looked around as they stretched in. ''Cause Mother Darcy met him. Went over with Tommy McDonagh to the Horse Show in Ballsbridge to work in the kitchens there, so she did. McDonagh introduced her to this fella. Knew him well. Had some great days at the showjumping in Ballsbridge, they did. Ya know what his name was,' he said as he paused for another swallow, emptying the glass, which was replaced like magic by Killane.

'His name, me good friends, was Aloysius Hitler from Austria. Told all about the soldier maniac of a brother he had. But Mother Darcy said Aloysius was a great bit of fun after a few pints. And I'll tell ya more. She also says he married Bridget Dowling from Athy in the county of Kildare.' Another swallow of Guinness.

'The brother of the bould Hitler, and he lived here in Dublin and married an Irish girl. Put that in yar pipe and smoke it,' he concluded, and with one last swallow he finished his pint as the others looked at him in amazement. 'And we all know that Mother Darcy doesn't tell lies, so that's a fact,' he said, and out he walked.

End of story. This gave a topic of conversation in Killane's pub for many's the week. And Mother Darcy confirmed it was true.

THE LORD MAYOR
GETS THE DA A JOB

With the war over, the Dublin docks were very quiet.
Billy Cullen still hadn't got his job back in Brooks
Thomas. There was no timber coming in from Norway.
It was all going to England and Europe for rebuilding
after the devastation of the bombings. He still went
down to the quaysides every morning looking for work,
but the ganger bosses picked their cronies. It was
humiliating to be constantly rejected, but you still
battled to survive the wet, cold winters in the dismal
tenements.

It was coming up to Christmas and Billy knew he had
to get out of Summerhill or he would explode from the
pounding fury in his head. After a few fruitless visits to
the Dublin Corporation Housing Department in Lord
Edward Street, he decided to try a long shot and call to
see the best-known man in Dublin – Alfie Byrne. Alfie had
been Lord Mayor of Dublin for eight years in the thirties.
He was a small, dapper man with a three-piece suit and a
fob watch and chain straddling his waistcoat. His grey,
pointed moustache and shining patent-leather shoes gave
him an air of impeccable elegance.

Alfie worked tirelessly for the city of Dublin and its citizens and was well known for helping the poor. It was Alfie who had pushed for the new housing estates in Cabra and Donnycarney, where tenement dwellers were being rehoused in single-unit family homes. While Alfie used to canvass the tenements at voting time, he hadn't been seen around Summerhill for years. So Billy set off to find him, with a letter marked 'Personal' and addressed to Alderman Byrne in his pocket; the letter was in Billy's best copperplate handwriting. Billy had been on personal terms with Alfie ever since the Eucharistic Congress in Dublin in 1932.

Back then, Billy had been a twenty-four-year-old corporal in the Free State army. He was in charge of one of the many platoons of soldiers delegated to prepare the Phoenix Park for the visit to Ireland of the Papal Nuncio, Pascal Robinson. Mass was to be celebrated by the Archbishop and the Nuncio in the open air. The army had the job of building the altar, setting up rows of seating for the thousands of dignitaries and erecting the cordons for the various areas of visitors. Even then, Billy was a member of the sodality in the Pro-Cathedral and was well known to the priests who were involved in the logistics of the event.

Alfie Byrne came to the Park every day during the preparations to make sure 'that this Congress puts Dublin on the global map for the whole world to read about', as he put it. Alfie soon found out that Billy Cullen was a lad with a foot in two camps: the clergy and the army. So when Alfie wanted some changes made, it was Billy who acted as facilitator. Whether it was an extra cleaning team for the Wellington Monument, or the sodality banners to be moved from the centre aisle to the sidelines, Billy Cullen could make it happen smoothly. Over a million people were there that September day in 1932 to witness the historic event and confirm to the world the staunch Catholicism of the Irish nation. The ceremony was broadcast on the wireless and there's no doubt but that the whole country came to a halt.

'There wasn't a soul to be seen moving on any street in any town in Ireland that day. All on their knees glued to the wireless,' was how Bob Darcy described it. 'And for the whole four hours not a man in Ireland had a drop to drink. If the priests pulled that stroke every day, sure Guinness would have to move out of the country.'

After the event ended, Billy and the soldiers spent another few weeks in the Phoenix Park. The altar and seating had to be dismantled and removed. Army lorries hauled away hundreds of tons of litter and restored the park to its former green glory. On the last day of the work, Lord Mayor Alfie Byrne addressed the gathering of soldiers, police and other helpers with a loud hailer, thanking them for their service to Dublin city. As the last convoy was moving out, Alfie came over to give a personal thank-you to Corporal Billy Cullen. 'I know you're out of the army soon,' Alfie said, 'so you just call in to me in the Mansion House and I'll help you find a job.'

Some weeks later, Billy took up the offer and Alfie Byrne gave him a reference and told him to present himself to Brooks Thomas Timber Merchants on the North Wall at Commons Street at ten o'clock the next day. When Billy went along to Brooks Thomas, he was ushered into the offices of Mister Craig, the general manager.

'I've had a call from Mister Brooks about you, Cullen,' said Mister Craig. 'You're to start on Monday

**MANSION HOUSE,
DUBLIN.**

TO WHOM IT MAY CONCERN.

It gives me great pleasure to recommend the bearer,
William Cullen, age 23 years, of 23. Summerhill, Dublin,
as a young man of very high character, strictly honest,
industrious and intelligent, and certain to give entire
satisfaction to his employers. He served in the National
Army, and was discharged with excellent references. He
has had a fair education, and is now anxious to secure a
suitable position. I am hopeful that this reference will
help him in his efforts.

It is with the utmost confidence that I strongly recommend
him, and shall be very pleased to hear of his success.

LORD MAYOR   Alfie Byrne

28-10-1932.

---

morning in the timber yard, reporting to Mister Lanigan. With that pair of shoulders on you, it'll be no trouble at all. The wages are two pounds a week and you've a six-day week, from eight in the morning to six o'clock in the evening, with a half-hour lunch break. You get Sunday off, for yourself and your family.'

*

So Billy had Alfie Byrne to thank for his job sixteen years before and now he was on his way to look for another favour. Billy was a proud man and he hated having to seek help from anyone.

'You would starve rather than ask a neighbour for a

slice of bread,' Mary once said. 'Well, Billy Cullen, I've no stupid pride when it comes to surviving and I'll beg or borrow to keep meself and the kids.' But he knew he needed help to get out of the tenements, and out he must get before he cracked up.

Alfie Byrne had an office in Kildare Street, and when Billy presented himself to the secretary she was hooshing him out because he had no appointment.

'Mister Byrne is the busiest man in Dublin. Don't think you can just walk in here off the streets to have a chat without a by-your-leave,' she said, looking at Bill's working clothes, which were worn through.

'But I've a letter here for Mister Byrne, and he does know me, miss. Tell him it's Billy Cullen from the Phoenix Park,' he said, holding out the letter.

The secretary moved around the desk, waving her hands. 'Sure every Tom, Dick and Harry in Dublin knows the Alderman, so that's nothing new. And I suppose you're in the Park in Áras an Uachtaráin as well,' she said, as she pushed him towards the door. But she stopped when she glimpsed the strong, impressive handwriting on the envelope he was holding. 'Who did you say this was from?' she asked curiously.

'I have to give this personally to Mister Byrne. It's very important and it's from me, Billy Cullen,' he said.

She hesitated and said, 'Okay, sit down there and I'll see if the Alderman is still at his meeting.' She walked through an inner door and within seconds out came Alfie Byrne with a big smile on his face and his hand outstretched.

'Billy me boy, will you just look at the size of ya,' he said, and he shook hands warmly, 'and them boots of yours shined like a mirror as usual. Come on in here to my office for a chat while Noreen drums up a pot of tea and some cakes. Won't you look after that now, Noreen,' he said, as he brought Billy in past the dismayed-looking secretary.

So Billy had afternoon tea with Alfie Byrne, who listened intently to Billy, having read the letter seeking help for the Cullens to get out of the tenements.

'Six kids, Billy, and you and Mary still in one room in Summerhill. I can't believe it,' Alfie said. 'Well, take it from me, I'll be over in the Corporation next Monday morning and I'll get them off their arse. It's a disgrace. Those Summerhill tenements will be knocked down, if it's the last thing I do on this earth. We've new houses being built in Donnycarney and Crumlin and Ballyfermot and I'll make sure your name goes top of the list. Leave it to me and just call over here in two weeks from today and I'll have news for you.'

Billy left, floating on air, thanking Noreen for her tea and cakes. He couldn't wait to get home to tell Mary about Alfie's promise. She gave him a big hug and sat down on the chair holding her tummy.

'My God,' she said, 'even this wee one in here is jumping with excitement. We've three kids in each of those single beds and the next one will be on the floor if we don't get out of here.'

At four o'clock the next day Mary Darcy came home early from the street, wheeling her pram with the fruit still in it on top of baby Angela. She was feeling poorly. In the tenement hall she shouted for Liam, who was just in from school. 'Come down here, son, and give me a hand up with the pram,' she said. It was the first time she'd ever asked for help with anything, and Liam saw

The magnificent Alfie Byrne, Lord Mayor of Dublin for eight years

she was tired when they paused on the landing after hauling the pram up step by step. Rita had already got the turf burning in the grate and the stewpot filled with water for boiling. Vera had the floor scrubbed, with old copies of the *Herald* spread out over it.

'God bless yiz, girls, sure ya have the place spick and span,' she said. 'Here's a bag of vegetables for the stewpot, and Uncle Jack left me down a couple of mutton chops. Will ya put on the teapot and we'll have a mug of tea. I'm just going to lie down here on the bed for a few minutes for a little rest.'

Rita cleaned the vegetables and the spuds, sliced them up and emptied the lot into the bubbling stewpot. In went a couple of Oxo cubes, plus a good sprinkling of Kandee sauce. Liam put the pram away and was playing with the three younger kids on the floor, drawing animals on the newspapers with a red crayon. Mary was snoozing on the bed with her hands around her pregnant stomach. It was unusual to have the Ma home early, and the girls were delighted to show that they could prepare the family meal. Vera was just pouring out the tea for her Ma when there was an unmerciful scream up the stairs.

MARY BEATS OFF
THE EVICTION BOWSIES

'Avicshun! Avicshun! The Corpo are here for Missus Walsh! It's an avicshun!'

Mary Darcy opened her eyes and sat up listening. 'Did I hear "avicshun"?' she asked slowly.

Rita nodded just as the roar went up again: 'Avicshun! Avicshun! It's the Corpo for Missus Walsh.' With that, there was a loud bang of a door hitting the wall, and the tramp of hobnailed boots on the stone hall.

Mary's face flushed red and she stood up, with anger in her eyes. 'Give me that poker, Rita,' she said, 'and Liam, you get that sweeping brush and come with me. You girls mind the little ones.' There was a pause as she retied her white apron around her swollen tummy and then took the poker and waved for Liam to follow her.

'I don't believe this,' she said. 'It can't be an avicshun in this day and age, in this kip of a house.' She opened the door and then leaned back to dip her fingers in the holy-water font and blessed herself and sprinkled some water on her son. There were roars and screams coming up the stairs from Missus Walsh's room at the back of the hall. 'Let's go,' she said and down the stairs she went, with Liam behind her.

The Corporation had taken over the tenements years before from the profiteering landlords who had evicted tenants left, right and centre for not paying their rent. But the Corpo had a more charitable outlook and evictions were now seldom seen. Only one had happened in the last twelve months: that had been at the top end of Summerhill, and the ould fella was moving on anyway. It was still a fearful sight to see the Corpo men throw every piece of his belongings out onto the footpath and leave him sitting there in the rain while they boarded up the doors and windows of the room. His brother arrived later that night with a horse and cart. They loaded up his bits and bobs and off they went, never to be heard of again.

When Mary turned the corner of the stairs, she saw three Corpo lads in the hall, with Missus Walsh's table and chairs already being handed out from man to man. Some children were standing barefoot in the hall crying and she could hear Missus Walsh's voice from the room pleading tearfully: 'No, no, don't throw us out.'

Mary let out a roar – 'What's going on here, ya bowsies!' – and she smashed the poker on the banisters with a loud crash that brought the men to a halt.

'Who's in charge here?' she shouted, and out from the room came a big, red-faced man, followed by Mister Sutton the rent collector.

'I'm in charge here, missus,' said the big man, in a country accent, 'now you just buzz off and mind your business. This is an official Corporation eviction, and you'll be in the clink if you're not careful.'

Mary gave the banister another bang with the poker. 'Well aren't you the big brave culchie now, threatening women and children, sneaking in here when our men are out working to pay your rent? If it's trouble you want, you've come to the right place and I'm telling ya to leave Missus Walsh's things alone or you'll have me to deal with,' she shouted without taking a breath.

'And as for you, Mister Sutton, come out from hiding behind that culchie and speak up for yourself. Don't you know Mister Walsh was in hospital for a few months with the kidney stones. And he's back working now and they'll clear off the arrears. Don't ya know all that and why are ya here with these latchicos doing your dirty work?'

Mister Sutton just blinked behind his glasses as the big man did the answering. 'Listen, woman, it's none of your business. He's had plenty of warnings. When any tenant falls behind by more than six months' rent, it's out. That's the policy and there's no discussion.'

Turning to his men, he said, 'Right, me lads, let's get on with the job', but before they could move Mary smashed the banister again with the poker.

'So that's the policy is it, now? Let's throw the sick man and his family out on the street is the policy, because they owe the Corpo a few lousy pounds. Let's get a big brave culchie up from Cork with his pals to dump them on the road. Sure they're well used to this job. Didn't some of ya help the English landlords during the famine days. Turncoats and informers ya are, who take on only the women and children. We'll leave the room there empty and put Missus Walsh out in the rain. Well that's the policy we had when the Brits were here, and many's the brave Irishman's blood was spilt to get them out and change that policy. Is this what Michael Collins fought for? Of course, he was a great man from Cork and he was shot in the back by one of his own. The like of you. Let me tell you this, me boyo – the first man that moves a stick of furniture out of this hall will get my poker over his head.'

What a tirade. The big Corkman was kicking the wall, saying 'Feck ya! Feck ya! Feck ya!' Mary Darcy stood halfway up the stairs in her white apron, heavily pregnant, waving the poker, her face flushed with anger. Her young son stood beside her, with a sweeping brush held across his chest.

Mary came down the stairs into the hall and took a chair from one of the men, without resistance. 'Now, Mister Sutton,' she said, 'why don't you get these men out of here and let's see how we can clear off Missus Walsh's arrears. Sure I've two pounds here in me pocket. Wouldn't that be a better thing to do than have some of these culchies in hospital.'

The big man was livid with temper at the insults that had been heaped on him. He would have killed any man who used those words to him, but he was helpless and frustrated when faced with a pregnant woman.

The rent collector broke the tension. 'Well, are you saying, Missus Cullen, that we can have the arrears paid?' he asked.

'Of course I'm saying the arrears will be paid, Mister Sutton,' she replied. 'Get rid of these boyos and we'll sit down on these chairs and work everything out.'

'Right then,' said Mister Sutton, turning to the big man. 'You go on back to the office, Shamus, and I'll sort this out.'

The big man kicked the wall in frustration. 'Bejaysus, I'll go back to no feckin' office,' he said. 'I'll go down to Conway's pub and you'll meet us there to pay us for our day's work, so you will.' And down the hall he went, with the sparks flying from his hobnailed boots. The other men put down the furniture and trailed out after him.

'Bring that stuff in now, Liam,' said the Ma, 'and why don't you put the teapot on, Missus Walsh. I'm sure Mister Sutton could do with a cuppa tea while we talk business.' Twenty minutes later, Mister Sutton left, with the promise of six shillings a week payment off the arrears as well as the rent from next week on. Missus Walsh didn't know where she'd get the extra money from.

'Don't worry about that, Missus Walsh. We've won the haggle today, and we can win it again if need be,' said Mary, as she left to go back upstairs.

Vera and Rita had been watching the commotion from the landing. When Mary arrived back, it was to a steaming mug of tea and a slice of toast ready for her on the table. She smiled at them all and sat down. 'Isn't it a great bunch I have here now. The girls looking after the house and this young fella standing in for his Da,' she said, ruffling Liam's curly black hair. 'You can put this poker and that brush of yours away now, son,' she said.

But as she sipped her tea, she grimaced and said, 'Liam, run down and tell Mother Darcy to come up here quick, and Vera, will you put that big pot of water on the stove.'

That evening, Carmel was born in the tenement room. The children had all been hooshed down to stay in Molly's. When they trooped back for bed, Mary was sitting up with the new baby and Billy was there beside her. Mother Darcy was having a mug of shell cocoa; she had a proud look on her face and her sleeves were still rolled up. 'Mother Darcy brought the new baby up from the chapel in her shopping bag,' was the story Rita gave.

The Da was back in Brooks Thomas, but only part-time. He got the odd few days' work with his brother Jack in Granby Pork Products. Granby were up in Granby Lane at the back of Dominick Street Church, beside the rear of Walden Ford Dealers. At other times, he worked as an usher in the picture houses: the Plaza in Granby Row and the Rotunda Cinema at the Parnell Monument. His military training was great for keeping the queues of children under control, and he was meticulous in his cleanliness for the butcher's. But he'd no work coming up to the Christmas, and the markets had a lean spell for Mary, who was still nursing her new baby, Carmel. The rain was seeping in around the tenement windows and Billy had used up bundles of *Herald*s plugging the cracks to keep the draughts out.

One day his old army pal Johnny Coleman had dropped in with six army greatcoats. 'You have to keep these children of yours warm in bed, Mary,' he said, 'and these are just the job.' The coats went over the thin blankets and were a godsend for the kids.

'Snug as a bug in a rug you are now,' said Mary.

'Don't mention bugs, Mary,' Billy said. 'I've spent the last week fighting the clocks and spiders coming in these damp walls. The powder I got down in Con Foley's Medical Hall seems to be working. It's certainly done the job on the oul' mattresses, because I haven't seen a hopper since I doused them.'

Mary was quiet as she rocked the baby's cot. 'We'll have to get out of here, Billy, before this bloody place takes another of our babies. Have you heard anything from the Corpo? Mick Mullen put in a word for us and he told me that with seven kids now, we should be getting an offer of a place soon.'

Billy looked at her and said, 'No, I haven't seen Mick, but I'll go and find him in Liberty Hall tomorrow. And I've to see Alfie Byrne next Tuesday.'

Mary didn't respond. She just kept rocking the baby's cot.

'Jack has promised me some corned beef and pigs' feet for Christmas,' Billy continued. 'It'll make a fine dinner for the kids. They love the trotters.'

It was no use. She was away somewhere else. So he just undressed and went to bed. Hours later, he woke. Mary was at the table darning some of the children's gansies, singing her song in a low voice as she rocked the cot with her foot:

> *Somewhere over the rainbow, skies are blue,*
> *And the dreams that you dare to dream, really do*
> *come true.*

Hiding the Mountjoy Jailbreaker

That Christmas evening, Liam and Vera left Mother
Darcy's at four o'clock with a basket of freshly made
fairy cakes from Molly. Out they went the back door
of Number 17 to slip up the farmyard to their home at
Number 28. It was just getting dark and they heard a
noise from the old air-raid shelter. The children stopped
in their tracks. Vera put her finger to her lips. Then they
all moved slowly forward and peeped in the air-slit. A
man was lying on the ground of the shelter. At first they
thought it was a spunker in his ragged clothes with a
sack round his shoulders. But then Liam gasped when
the man moved and turned his head and they saw the
blood all over his forehead and face. Vera tugged Liam's
arm, holding her finger to his lips again and giving him
a warning look. But with that, out came Mother Darcy
in her white apron with an oil lamp in her hand, heading
for the privy at the back of the house. She saw the
children and over she came. 'Are you pair not gone
home yet, with your Mammy waiting for those cakes,'
she said, before seeing Vera's warning finger on her lips.

But there was no fear in Mother Darcy. 'Is there
some–thing going on in that shelter?' she asked, as she

moved the children aside and held the oil lamp high. 'Jesus, Mary and Holy Saint Joseph,' she said, and blessed herself, with the children hurriedly doing the same. 'What happened to you at all? You're in a terrible state.'

The man looked at Molly and tried to raise himself off the ground, but he fell back.

Molly gave Vera the oil lamp. 'Hold that, child,' she said, and moved in beside him. She looked at his head. 'That's a nasty gash you have, son,' she said. 'We'll need a doctor for a right few stitches.'

But he waved his arm. 'No doctors, missus, or they'll have me back in Mountjoy.' Mother Darcy stood back, while the two children froze at the dreaded word.

'So you're one of the jail-breakers they're looking for?' said Molly, and the children's eyes were popping.

'Have a bit of pity, missus. We just wanted to get home to the family for Christmas,' he said.

'Well, it could be a coffin you'll be going home in if we don't get something done with that head of yours,' Molly replied, and she picked up the oil lamp. 'And if anyone finds you here, they'll be on to the guards in Fitzgibbon Street, because the fifty pounds reward would be a nice Christmas box. Now, Vera, you hold this lamp and stay here while I go and get some things for this poor unfortunate.' And off she scurried to the house, clearly visible in the twilight in her white apron. The children stood hand in hand looking at the man, with Vera holding the oil lamp.

'Are you going to die, mister?' asked Vera.

He looked at her in her flowery Christmas frock and the twin ribbons holding her plaits in place. Then he looked at Liam holding the box of fairy cakes. 'Not at all, girl,' he said. 'It'll take more than a gash like this to give Mick Laverty a wooden overcoat.'

Molly was back quickly, with a sack in one hand and a big teapot in the other. 'Now we'll sort you out,' she said, and set to work. From the sack, she took an enamel bowl, and poured hot water from the teapot. With a clean linen cloth, she gently washed the blood from his face and bathed the wound. Then she took a big lump of bread, wrapped it in the damp hot cloth and held it to the wound.

'This yeast poultice will clean out the bugs,' she said. 'You hold this yourself while I make a mug of tea.' Out came an enamel mug, which she filled from the teapot; then she added two spoonfuls of tea leaves. She produced a sauce bottle filled with milk to add to the tea and then a little naggin of whiskey.

'Nothing like a few mouthfuls of Jameson whiskey to give a man strength,' she said. 'Here, I'll hold the poultice while you get that drink into ya.'

With Molly's help, he raised himself up to a sitting position, and sipped the tea while Molly freshened the poultice and continued to bathe the wound.

'There's a corned-beef sambo in the sack too,' she said.

He quickly found it. 'Jaysus, that's as thick as a plank,' he said.

'It's Big Bob's sambo, and he has a big mouth, so just get it into ya,' she said, as he wolfed down the food. After a few minutes, he'd finished, and was obviously in better spirits.

'Now I'll put some Germolene on this,' she said, and quickly salved the wound. She took out a big army bandage and had his head bound neatly in minutes.

'I got plenty of practice at this work when the Black and Tans were around,' she said, pouring him another mug of the spiked tea. Out from the sack came an army coat. 'This will keep you warm, and I'll leave you the rest of the whiskey. It would be best if you got out of here tonight.' She gave him a sharp look and flicked her eyes at the children.

He looked at her and said, 'God bless you, missus, for your Christian charity. I'll pray for you and these children and I'll head off in the morning at first light.'

Mother Darcy gathered her things into the sack and hooshed the children out. She took them up the yard to Number 28, but under the light of the oil lamp she paused. 'Now listen to me the both of ya now,' she said. 'You don't say a word to anyone about that ould spunker down in the shelter. Ya hear me now? Not a word to your Ma or Da or anyone. If ya open your mouth about our secret on Christmas Day, you'll be opening the door for the devil himself to take you and we don't want that to happen now do we?' The children shook their heads fearfully from side to side.

'Okay so,' she said. 'Let's go up to your Ma and give her these fairy cakes and we'll have a little party before you go to bed.' And up the stairs they went.

It was about ten o'clock the next morning when the quiet of the morning was broken by shouts and roars of anger from the yard at the back of the tenements. Looking out the window, Bob Darcy saw two figures wrestling on the ground. 'It's a ruggy-up out the back, and bejaysus that's like a soldier and a policeman out there,' he said, as he dashed down the back stairs in his vest, with Molly following behind.

Just as Bob got out into the daylight, he saw one of the men jump up off the ground with a big bloody rock in his hand; the man quickly dropped the rock. Then the man turned and ran off down the back of the yard and disappeared past Lourdes Chapel, with his army greatcoat flapping around him. Bob got to the other man, who was lying dazed on the ground, with blood pouring from his hair. It was Guard Byrne, his helmet lying on the ground beside him. Molly Darcy came up and pushed Bob aside.

She took off her spotless white apron, folded it and put it under the injured policeman's head as a pillow. 'Will ya move, Bob,' she said, 'and get someone down here with a basin of hot water and run someone over to Lynch's for them to ring the police station for help?'

A crowd had gathered around the scene and, looking up, Molly saw young Liam pushing between the legs of the adults, staring wide-eyed at the guard. By this time, her white apron was dyed a bright red by the guard's blood. The young fella looked at Mother Darcy, then turned and ran home as fast as his legs would carry him.

The ambulance and squad cars arrived and Guard Byrne was taken away, after pointing out the direction his attacker went. The crowd were questioned by a couple of plain-clothes detectives while a big group of uniformed guards set off in pursuit of the fugitive. No one had any information to give.

'What did you see, Mister Darcy?' the detective asked Big Bob. 'You were first on the scene, we believe, and you do know it was one of the cowardly jail-breakers who hit Guard Byrne with a rock. Could have killed him. Didn't you recognise him? Was it Laverty or Nolan?'

'Well now, sir, to tell you the truth, all I saw was the poor policeman on the deck here with his life's blood pumping out of him,' Bob said. 'Only for Mother Darcy, he might have bled to death. The other fella was long gone.'

'And what about yourself, Missus Darcy?' the detective asked. 'You seem to be handy at looking after bloody wounds. Byrne said Laverty had a bandaged head. What did you see?'

'Well now, young man,' she replied, 'let me tell ya, the only thing I saw this morning was an injured human being that needed care and attention and that he got from me. Guard Byrne knows that, and has gone off in the ambulance with my bloody apron as proof.'

While Bob added, 'And that's a fact', Molly looked around the crowd and then focused on the detective. 'As for the other fella,' she continued, 'he seemed hale and hearty to me as he galloped around Lourdes Chapel. So if someone did fix him up, they did a good job. But from here where we were standing, I thought he had a cap on his head, but Guard Byrne was the one who saw him close up. So now, if you please, I'm off to look after me family and I'll leave you to do the detecting.' She walked back towards Number 17 with Bob in tow.

The detective shrugged to his partner and said, 'We won't get a peep out of them. Sure Mick Laverty is a hero in this street. Let's go.'

It was four weeks after Christmas. The guards got a tip-off that Laverty and Nolan were hiding out in the Mount Street area. After a shoot-out the convicts escaped but they were later surrounded in the Hammond Lane iron foundry. In another fusillade of

WANTED
For Escape from Mountjoy Prison—

JAMES NOLAN

24 years, 5 ft. 7 ins.; 11 stone; complexion fresh; hair dark brown or black; eyes blue; bushy eyebrows; scars on forehead and corner of left eye;

WILLIAM LAVERTY

26 years, 5 ft. 7 ins.; 10 stone; complexion fresh; hair fair; eyes blue; moles on both forearms; scar ball of right thumb;

shots, Laverty was wounded and captured. But Nolan escaped again. He put on a pair of worker's overalls, with 'Hammond Lane' in big letters across his chest, and casually walked past the whole police blockade with a toolbox in his hand. After the gun battle, the leader of the police, Chief Superintendent Sean Gantly from Toomevara in Tipperary, was found shot dead. Friendly fire. A tragic accident. Shot in the dark of the foundry by a police bullet.

Mother Darcy cried when she heard the news of Gantly's death on the wireless. She went down to Lourdes Chapel. Liam had to go down for her hours later. In front of the statute of the Blessed Virgin he found her. With every candleholder filled with a lighted candle. She looked at her grandson with red-rimmed eyes and saw how upset Liam was. He started to cry.

Molly hugged him to her in the blaze of the candles. 'God's will be done, son,' she said. 'We have to pray to the Virgin Mary for peace of mind. We can't undo what's done.'

Some weeks later Jim Nolan was captured in a Talbot Street café. A new incantation in the family Rosary: 'God bless Widow Gantly and take care of her children.' Response: 'Lord, hear our prayers.'

For months afterwards, Liam had strange dreams, in which a policeman fell off the rocks onto the snow. The whole field of snow turned bright red, which spread slowly outwards, and as the red touched the rocks, who was standing there with her black shawl and a sad face, only Mother Darcy herself. She waved to him, put her fingers to her lips with a shush and then turned and disappeared through the doors of a church. But the dream faded away and the children kept their secret.

*

Alfie Byrne came up trumps. Billy didn't have to go over to his office at all, because Alfie came to Summerhill. A black Vauxhall Wyvern motoring car pulled up outside Number 28 and out he popped, resplendent in a light grey pinstriped three-piece suit, the gleaming watch-chain on his waistcoat, and a dark grey cravat contrasting with his starched, snow-white shirt collar. The patent-leather shoes sparkled on his feet and the finishing touch to the ensemble was a pink rosebud in his lapel. Within seconds, half the neighbourhood was out on the street.

'Who's the fancy Dan in the car? He's like a film

star!' was the question from the young girls swinging on a rope around the lamp-post at Hutton's Lane. But the group of oul' ones gaustering outside Lynch's knew who he was, and the news went up and down the street like wildfire.

'It's Alfie Byrne, it's the Lord Mayor, Alfie Byrne is here!' was the cry. The car was surrounded, and Alfie, a small man, jumped on the car's back bumper for a bit of height. He was swamped by black-shawled women and young children, some of them barefoot, while the men gathered in a separate group across the street.

Everywhere up and down the street the opened windows were jammed with heads looking down on the scene. Mary, Billy and all the kids were looking out right at Alfie, as his car was parked outside their hall door. Alfie waved at Billy Cullen.

'I've come to give you the good news!' Alfie shouted. 'The Dublin Corporation have made the decision to demolish the whole of these tenements in Summerhill within the next twelve months, and there's a new house for every family.'

A huge cheer went up from the crowd. Alfie took out a handful of coins and threw them across the street; the crowd scattered after the money. 'It's a grush! It's a grush!' was the cry as Alfie threw another handful of glittering silver coins down the street in the other direction. Tanners, shillings, two-bob bits and even half-crowns went spinning in the air and landed on the paving slabs with that unique clink of money. After a long career in Dublin politics, Alfie knew the way to distract a crowd and had come prepared. As the crowd scattered, he was into the hall of Number 28.

'Are you up there, Billy?' he cried, and up the stairs

he went confidently, ignoring the smells and decay. 'You're in the two-per-front, aren't you?' he shouted, as Billy threw open the door of the Cullen room and Alfie walked right in.

Mary was standing at the window with the new baby under her shawl. Her six children were standing around her with the two smallest, Brian and Angela, clutching the Ma's apron. They were astonished at this man, who seemed to sparkle, both in his dress and with his enthusiasm.

'This is your lovely new baby,' he said, and held out a red ten-shilling note, which he put into the baby's hand. 'But this little one won't have to spend long here, Mary, and you have my word for that.'

He turned to Billy and shook hands, saying, 'I'm glad you got me worked up about the tenements, Billy. The whole Corporation agreed that we have to get rid of this squalor, and Seán Lemass has given the green light.'

Billy was smiling while he pulled his braces up on his shoulders and buttoned his shirt. Mary laid the baby on the bed and said, 'Will ya have a mug of tea, Alfie? The kettle's boiling.'

Alfie looked at her with a glint in his eye and said, 'Is that a pot of coddle I smell in the fireplace, because if it is, there's nothing I'd like better than a bit of Dublin coddle.'

'Bedad, it is a coddle,' said Mary, 'and you just sit yourself down there, because it's on the boil and ready to eat.'

'Okay, and could someone keep an eye on the car at the door,' said Alfie, as he sat down at the table. Billy went to the window and leaned out, to see Tommy Farrell smoking a fag at the railings.

'Tommy,' he shouted down, 'you've to keep the kids away from Alfie's car. He'll be down in a minute.' Tommy sprang to attention, dropping the cigarette and squashing it under his foot.

'I'm yer man, Billy,' he said, and then started hooshing the kids. 'Now get yourselves away from the car, you lot – I'm in charge here for the Lord Mayor.'

Mary was a bit flustered to have such a fine gentleman sitting at her table. The room was tidy but nothing could hide the damp, squalid walls and ceiling. Alfie didn't seem to notice at all and was chatting away to Billy about how he had been sailing with Mister Brooks in Dun Laoghaire recently. Brooks was optimistic that the timber yard would be back on full-time working very soon. That was Alfie Byrne: always enthusiastic, always positive.

Mary served up the plates of coddle and the three adults sat at the table to eat it. The children sat on their bed and watched through the curtain.

'You know, Mary,' said Alfie, 'that's the best coddle I've ever tasted. There's a delicious tang in the soup that I've never got before. Have you a special recipe?'

'Not at all, Alfie,' she replied. 'That's the way Mother Darcy taught me to make the coddle. What you taste is this,' she said, holding up a brown bottle. 'It's Kandee sauce that I always sprinkle in the soup.'

'Well it's gorgeous, so it is,' said Alfie, as he picked up a lump of bread, used it to wipe up the last coating of the soup on his plate and popped it into his mouth. 'So I have to head off now but let me tell you that Billy Cullen's name is top of the list in the Corporation for rehousing. You'll probably get a choice of Ballyfermot or Donnycarney, but just head over to the Housing

Office on Tuesday at ten o'clock and ask for John Hogan. He's my man and he'll take care of you,' he said, as he stood up. 'I'll say goodbye now to you, Mary, and to you too, Billy', and he shook hands with both of them. 'And bye-bye too to your lovely children,' he said, as he reached into his bottomless pocket and gave each of them a shilling.

Billy opened the door. 'I'll see you down, Alfie,' he said.

Mary came over and held out her bottle of Kandee sauce. 'Won't you take this with ya, Alfie, for your next coddle?' she said.

Alfie looked at her and, experienced campaigner that he was, he knew it would hurt her dignity if he refused. 'Now isn't that very decent of you, Mary. Sure I'd love to take it home with me,' he said, accepting the bottle with a big smile. 'And the best of luck to you and your family.'

Off he went down the stairs with Billy beside him, out to the car, where the crowd had grown even larger. 'We want a grush!' came the chant from the crowd, and Alfie obliged with another handful of coins thrown up the street away from the car. The crowd dispersed, chasing the coins. Alfie shook hands with Billy, hopped into the car and away he went down Summerhill.

Billy waved after the car, while Mary watched from the window. She blessed herself and Liam heard her low voice saying 'May Jesus and his Holy Mother bless you and keep you safe forever, Alfie Byrne.' Billy looked up from the street and saw her blessing herself and joined her silently in his own prayer of thanks.

The news was still being absorbed by the street. Clusters of women were on the footpaths and Killane's pub was jammed with men drinking and toasting Alfie Byrne.

'It's goodbye to Summerhill!' was the roar from Bob Darcy, who started up the singing. The chorus rang out from the pub and up and down the street. *'Goodbye, goodbye, I wish you all a last goodbye'* was sung by every man, woman and child. Women joined hands and spun in a circle, singing *'Ring-a-ring-a-rosie'*. A group of men drinking bottles of stout outside Lynch's started up Alfie Byrne's electoral song: 'Vote, vote, vote for Alfie Byrne, here comes Alfie at the door eye-oh, Alfie is the one who will bring us lots of fun and we don't want de Valera any more.'

The celebrations went on until the pubs closed and then the cry of 'ruggey-up' brought the crowds down to the corner of Gardiner Street and Summerhill. Two men stripped to the waist and squared up to each other, one of them with a bloody nose. With all the excitement in Number 28, Liam and Vera were still out playing, and they perched on the railings to watch the fight. The roads were completely blocked off and the cars and buses stopped on the four roads leading to the junction. The people on the buses had a bird's-eye view and car drivers came out to join the spectators. In the centre the fight continued. It was Spike McCormack against Sugar Corbally.

Spike McCormack had been the professional middle-weight champion of Ireland. He was one of Dublin's great heroes, even though he was a Kerryman. Since retiring from boxing, he had lived in Seán MacDermott Street. But he'd been drinking in the pub and there was always someone who'd push into him, or spill his drink, to provoke a fight. Always some hard shaw who wanted to take on Spike. And there had always been bad blood between Spike and the Corballys. Now, Spike wasn't a tall man, but he was built like a brick shithouse. Corbally was a much bigger man, about six foot two, and a huge bull of a man altogether. So this was a vicious battle, with the two men in turn taking and giving severe blows. Spike was in his bare feet and dancing around Corbally, having kicked off his cumbersome work boots.

'Stand still and fight like a man!' Corbally shouted at him, but Spike paid no heed. Then, quick as lightning, he was in with a left hook that put Sugar on his back. Spike moved away – there was no kicking. It was man-to-man until someone couldn't stand up. Sugar got up, with blood seeping from his split lip. He chased after Spike and caught him with a swinging blow which Spike shrugged off and he gave Sugar another left hook to the face that nearly took his head off and down he went again with Spike backing off.

'Have you had enough, Corbally?' he said, but Sugar struggled to his feet and came at him again. His left eye was closed and bruised, his mouth and nose were smashed and bleeding, but he was still swinging wildly. Spike stood back and measured the distance. He hit Corbally with a right to the belly that brought his head down. Then Spike's left hook caught him again on the side of the jaw just under his right ear and he dropped like a brick, out for the count. The crowd cheered wildly as Spike stood over Corbally, his barrel chest heaving after his exertions. Out came Killane the publican with a bucket of water and threw it over Corbally, just as the sirens sounded and two garda cars and an ambulance pulled up at the edge of the cheering crowd.

'Here come the rozzers!' went up the cry, and sure Spike was off doing his training routine, dancing around in his bare feet and shooting out his fists like pistons.

'Let them come!' he roared. 'I'll take them all on, one by one or all together, I'll bate them good-looking.' Ten policemen broke through the crowd, their batons poking anyone who didn't move out of the way.

'It's Lugs Brannigan!' the crowd shouted. Now Lugs Brannigan – called Lugs because of his cauliflower ears – was a fearless man who had even beaten up some of the animal gangs. At six foot five he towered over everyone and he was tough but fair. As far as he was concerned a good box in the ear and a kick in the arse was punishment enough for a first-time offender. If that didn't straighten you out he'd give ya a good hiding with his fists for any wrongdoing. But a third offence and it was up before the judge with a recommendation for a visit to Mountjoy Jail. It was rough justice but it was a fair enough system, and fear of Lugs Brannigan prevented a lot of tough young fellows from acting the bowsie.

Lugs knew Spike and said, 'Well, Spike, have you been hitting the whiskey again, disturbing the peace and blocking up the traffic all over the city?' Spike just looked at him and Brannigan turned to his men. 'Break up this crowd and let the traffic through.'

And the guards roughly shunted the people off the road. 'Okay, break it up here, off you go, get on home, the fight's over!' they shouted.

Sugar Corbally was on his feet and disdainfully pushed the St John's Ambulance men away. 'Ger outta dat,' he said through his swollen mouth, 'sure, it's only a scratch.'

Spike came over with his hand out. 'Shake hands, Corbally. That was a fair fight, ya bollix, ya nearly got the better of me.' But Corbally wasn't having any of it.

'Piss off, McCormack,' he said, and turned away.

But Lugs got hold of him and dragged him face to face with Spike. 'Well now, lads, I'm telling the both of ya to shake hands now, or you'll spend the night in the 'Joy and face the judge in the morning.' His big arms were around both men and he shouted, 'I said shake hands' intimidatingly as he squeezed their shoulders. They quickly shook hands and he pushed both of them away. 'Now get off home with ya and if ya start another fight here, it's the clink.'

The crowd had moved off up the footpaths and the guards were moving the traffic on. Order was restored. Two of Corbally's brothers had arrived to help Sugar. They were enraged when they saw the state of him with his face in bits. Only for Lugs and the gang of guards, World War Three would have broken out. As it was, they hustled off down Gardiner Street shouting threats. 'You'll fecking well regret this, McCormack, and you're in for a right hiding when these police pals of yours aren't here to protect ya. You'll be a sorry man when we're finished with ya.'

But Spike scorned them. 'I'm here for yez anytime and bejaysus I can take on the lot of ya,' he shouted, waving his mighty left fist after them.

Lugs Brannigan grabbed him again. 'That's enough, Spike. Shut your gob or I'll shut it for ya,' and he pushed Spike into the pub doorway. 'Will you behave yourself awadat or I will have to put ya in the paddy wagon.'

Spike let out a long sigh and looked at Brannigan.

'Okay, Jim, okay,' he said. 'I'm going home. I've had enough for tonight. But I'll tell ya this. I'll never back down to a Corbally. So if it's trouble they want, I'm the boyo for them. And you know this left hook of mine. It's a hammer that'll break any man. So that's it, Jim, I'm outta here.' And he pushed away.

'Do yourself a favour, Spike,' Brannigan said, 'and stay off that bleedin' whiskey.'

Spike smiled and said softly, 'Now, now, Jim, remember your Gaelic. It's ishga baha (*uisce beatha*) and that means the water of life. You should try it some. time.' And off went Spike with his head high, giving a few bob to some of the hangers-on about the pub.

'Well done, Spike', 'God Bless ya, Spike', 'You're a mighty man, Spike' were the accolades ringing in his ears as he walked down Gardiner Street.

'Aye, that's me,' he thought. 'Champion of the whole bleedin' world. This is my town, and this is my street.'

Gardiner Street was a fighting street. The kids came out of the cot fighting. Known as 'The Street of Champions' it was, after so many fellas had built a worldwide reputation and won titles everywhere. They had their own North City Boxing Club in a tenement basement. As a kid, the Da had learned his boxing in this club. 'The best in the world they were, son,' he told Liam. 'I was taught by Paddy Hughes, a man who held eleven titles. Beat the best of the American Golden Gloves champions, he did. Fast he was, with a wicked left hook that would knock your block off. I was there for the hooley the night the lads came home from Soldiers' Field in Chicago just before the war. Our three heroes. Spike McCormack, Blackman Doyle and Peter Glennon.

They had beaten the three American champions. On the same night, in just an hour. Imagine that. Three lads from Gardiner Street and they all world champions together,' the Da said.

'You know, son,' he continued, 'isn't it a pity they can't get a job now at all. Good men, strong men, men with heart. And they live in the poverty of the tenements. Gardiner Street. Named after an English landlord. Sir Hugh Gardiner. He also had the title of Lord Mountjoy, and Mountjoy prison, which he built, was named after him too. Sad, isn't it. So many kids spend their lives as his tenant. From Gardiner Street to Mountjoy prison. One day, please God, they can knock both of them to the ground, if they only give the kids the opportunity of a decent job.'

10
—

LOUIS COPELAND
MAKES THE COMMUNION SUIT

The Ma was out selling fruit most days and had con-
solidated a permanent pitch at the bottom of Cole's
Lane outside Boylan's shoe shop and opposite the main
entrance to Arnott's department store in Henry Street.
It had been a tough winter, with Mary weaning her new
baby, Carmel. Liam was drafted in to help with the
household's earning power, once he had made his First
Holy Communion – the Catholic Church's membership
rite. It was also the end of his days with the nuns, as
his new summer term would be with the Christian
Brothers in St Canice's School. So the Holy Communion was a big day for Mary's eldest son, and she was
determined to kit him out up to the nines. Money was
scarce, and it was only with Mother Darcy's help that
she kept food on the table for the eight of them. She
had just finished paying off the moneylender for the cost
of the previous year's double kit when she'd had Rita
for Confirmation and Vera for Communion in the same
year. She swore she'd never get into their clutches again
– borrow twenty pounds and pay back a pound a week
until you could give them the twenty pounds back in

one lump. That was five per cent interest every week and poor Missus Corcoran could be paying the pound every week forever since her husband died on her at Christmas.

As it happened, a good Samaritan came to the rescue. As Mary and Liam were bringing the fruit from the markets on her pram every morning she passed up by Louis Copeland's tailor's shop in Capel Street and Louis would often give Mary a shout and buy bananas. 'They make great sandwiches for lunchtime,' he'd say.

Now, Mary could only dream of ever buying clothes in Louis Copeland's – sure, wasn't he a master tailor, with all sorts of gold medals for tailoring hanging in the window. And no prices on display.

'If you have to ask the price, you can't afford it,' was what Nanny Kelly said. 'Don't you see the toffs pulling into Louis's in their motoring cars – Mister Findlater and Mister Noyek and ould Alex Mitchell himself for his pinstriped handmade suit. That's what Louis Copeland is – "Bespoke Tailor to Ireland's Gentry since 1930", as it says in the papers.'

But as young Liam started helping Mary in the markets, old Louis began giving him the odd copper when he delivered the bananas. 'There you are, son, a shilling for the six bananas and a penny for yourself,' he'd usually say.

But it was Louis himself who made the approach, surprising Mary one day. 'Well, Mary, I hear Liam is making the Communion soon. Are you not giving me the business for his suit?'

And Mary replied, 'Well now, Louis, how in the name of all that's holy could I afford a suit from the great Louis Copeland?'

Louis took her by the arm and brought her into the shop while Liam stayed outside with the fruit. 'Just look at that suit there,' he said, pointing to a lovely white short-trousered suit hanging on the rail. Mary was gob-smacked, it was so beautiful. 'I can guarantee it will fit him, and I've left lots of material in the seams so we can let it out to fit him for his Confirmation in a few years' time, too,' said Louis.

Mary realised that Louis had made the suit specially for Liam and said a silent prayer to the Virgin Mary for giving her such a lucky child.

'You get the family discount too, Mary,' Louis said. 'You just have to pay me three shillings a month for twelve months. And that includes these shoes as well,' he added, pointing to a lovely pair of black patent-leather shoes on the floor under the suit. Mary could only look at him as she fought to hold back the tears.

'Now off you go, Mary,' said Louis, 'and I'll do the final buttonholes on the suit and you can pick it up tomorrow.' And he fussily hooshed her out the door.

Mary told Mother Darcy all about it that evening and they both went around to Lourdes Chapel and said a Rosary for the tailor who had a heart of gold. Mary paid off her bargain debt to Louis Copeland and his famous suit served her six sons in unique style for Communion and Confirmation over the next fourteen years. In between it was always the best of security for a five-pound loan from O'Toole's pawnshop in Amiens Street. Liam and his siblings never understood why Mary Darcy always instructed them to leave a bag of fruit into Louis Copeland's shop every Saturday morning. 'And it's already paid for, so you just leave it for Louis,' she'd

The late Louis Copeland Senior outside the old shop in Capel Street where he made Liam's First Communion suit

say. And Louis would just give a big smile and say, 'Tell Mary I was asking for her.'

The Holy Communion was a big occasion, with Liam getting his First Confession from a special priest who came to the school. In the quiet of the Mother Superior's office Liam confessed to 'disobeying my father once, being lazy twice, and being bold once as well,' as the nuns had instructed him. The priest gave him a Hail Mary and an Our Father for his penance and that was an easy job altogether. He was tucked into bed early that evening with no supper as he had to fast for twelve hours before he took Christ's body in Holy Communion.

The children were now in two small single beds with another floursack curtain between the boys and the girls. As the eldest, Liam slept at the top of the bed with the two younger lads at the bottom. He was awake early and Mary had the steel bath on the floor with water boiling on the gas stove. Into the bath he went to be scrubbed pink with Sunlight soap. One by one the children were bathed and dried by Mary. Then Billy trimmed their hair with an army scissors and dressed them. By seven they were all spick and span and they set off for Gardiner Street Church for the eight o'clock Mass. All the schoolchildren for First Communion were ensconced in the first rows of the church with the girls on one side and the boys on the other. The girls were all dressed in white with tiara-held veils covering their hair. The boys were all in suits but Liam was the only one in white and he stood out a mile to the parents and relations in the back of the church.

After the Mass the family and friends gathered round and Mary got all the compliments on Liam's lovely suit ('and made by Louis Copeland, I'll have you know'). Liam was the recipient of numerous coins – Mary had conveniently given him a small pouch purse to collect the money. The Communion children went around to the school, where a special photograph was taken in Our Lady's Grotto, and then all went home.

In the Cullen room that morning the children had a hearty Irish breakfast for the first time. All scrooched around the table together while Mary fried rashers, onions, tomatoes, eggs, and black and white pudding. The smell from the pan alone was scrumptious and the children's first 'fry' was a special treat. Everyone ate with a soup spoon, even the Ma and Da. The Da had got a dozen big spoons and sharpened the outer edge on Mister O'Brien's grinding stone in the bike shop. You could use this spoon as a knife by cutting with the sharp outer edge and then as a spoon to shovel the grub into your mouth. Only Brian upset the apple-cart because he was left-handed. So his spoon had a big blob of red paint on the handle. This warned everyone else not to use it or the sharp inner edge would cut the mouth off ya. There was no doubt about it, in later years, when Mary Darcy was telling stories to her grandchildren, it was no joke when she said, 'We were so poor in Summer–hill that your dad thought that knives and forks were jewellery.' So they ate everything off the enamel plates, eventually mopping up the juices with a crust of bread, and this was washed down with slurps of tea from the enamel mugs. The warmth from the turf fire and the smiles and laughter of the Ma and Da made the occasion Liam's happiest memory of the Summerhill tenements.

Mother Darcy arrived to examine the star of the show and gave him a half-crown for his purse. Then Liam and Mary and Vera set off on the rounds while Billy changed the other children into their normal Saturday clothes. Mary took Liam down Parnell Street, Moore Street and Henry Street, where all the dealers and shopkeepers who knew Mary Darcy popped a three-penny bit or more into the boy's hand. Then she moved into her usual pitch beside Nanny Kelly on Henry Street and Vera took Liam up to Cafolla's for a feed of fish and chips followed by vanilla ice cream. Then it was home to play.

That evening there was a bit of a hooley in the Cullen room with the Darcys at it. Uncle Bob brought his shiny accordion. He played a medley of Irish tunes. Mother Darcy sang 'Danny Boy' and Mary sang her own favourite, 'Over the Rainbow'. Uncle Martin and his sister Angela did a duet of 'When You're Smiling'. But the hit of the evening was the usually quiet Billy Cullen. Out of his army kitbag he brought a pair of shiny black patent-leather shoes with metal pieces on the toes and heels.

'Bejaysus, Billy, I never knew you were a tap-dancer,' said Bob.

'Well now, Bob, it was more than foot-sloggin' I learned in the army back in the twenties. And that's not all,' he said, taking out four short sticks. 'What about these bacon-rib rattlers.' With two in each hand he started off a tap rhythm as he hummed the tune of 'Phil the Fluther's Ball'. Bob picked up the tune with his accordion and Billy kept in time with his tap shoes on the scrubbed floor and both hands flicking the rattlers in cadence. Bob moved into fast Irish jigs and reels with Billy's lightning feet keeping up a staccato reverberation that had everyone in the room gasping. They'd never seen anything like this before. It was sheer magic for the children to see their Da spinning and leaping and dancing to the music. The whole evening was great craic altogether, but eventually Mary called a halt, putting the children to bed, while the adults gathered around the turf fire with mugs of tea.

The happy talk was interrupted by Billy's loud voice saying, 'Bob Darcy, I told you before there will be no drinking of alcohol in my house,' as he caught Bob taking a swig from a naggin of whiskey.

'Sure, it's only a baby Power for the flu in me chest, Billy,' Bob said.

'Then off you go to the doctor with yar flu and take that whiskey with you.'

There was silence in the room as Bob stood up to his full height. A giant of a man. He looked down at Billy. 'You shouldn't be breaking up your lad's happy day, Billy, over a wee drop of whiskey.'

But Billy wasn't to be turned and he shot back with, 'And now, Mister Darcy, when I want advice from you under me own roof I'll ask for it.'

Bob's face went red with anger. 'So that's it, Mister Superior Cullen. You think you're better than us because you can't stand the drink. Well let me tell you, that sister of mine would make ten of ya and I'd knock your block off, only that Mary would have to look after the kids without ya. Not that your few shillings help much – sure, she's doing the man's job in this house anyway.'

Billy let out a roar of anger and grabbed for Bob, but Martin and Ned came between them. There was uproar in the room with the children all bawling behind their curtains, the women shrieking at the men to behave themselves, three men holding onto Bob's arms while Billy danced on the floor with his taps, fists held high. 'Come on, Darcy, ya boyo, sure you've never fought a man in yar life. Poofters is all you ever slapped around. See this,' he said, lifting his right arm high in the air, 'Twenty-four knockouts to win the Irish Free State army championships. Let's see who'll knock whose block off.'

Mother Darcy threw the bucket of water over Billy. There was silence as he stood in the middle of the floor, drenched and spluttering.

'It's time for you all to go home,' Mary said firmly. She pulled her husband down on the edge of the bed and put a towel around his shoulders, as the relatives all filed out. Bob was last to leave, with his accordion slung over his shoulder. He paused and said, 'I'm sorry, Billy, it was the drink talkin'.' And he held out his hand.

'Keep your sorrow and your drink, Darcy,' said Billy, 'and never darken my doorway again.'

When they'd all left, Billy put on his coat and went out the door, saying, 'I'm going for a walk.' He didn't return for hours; then he packed away his tap shoes and rattlers and went to bed. The children never saw their father tap-dance again.

11

THE WIDOW WOMAN
MOLLY DARCY

Rita said that Mother Darcy had been born in a gypsy caravan. Raised by the gypsies but fostered as a ten-year-old. That's how she knew so much. It wasn't a subject that the Ma ever wanted to talk about, but the Da was always ready to confirm it, and it was from the gypsies that Molly had heard all the legends of Ireland.

Mother Darcy lived in Number 17 of the Summerhill tenements, beside the archway to the Twenty-seven Steps that led down to Gloucester Diamond. Her husband, Sheriff Darcy, a baker in Johnston, Mooney and O'Brien, had died of consumption. She had two rooms and three of her seven children still living with her: Big Bob, who was in his late twenties, and the two youngsters, Martin and Angela. Liam and Vera loved to drop in to Mother Darcy's in the evening to hear her stories. It was here, while he sat beside the turf fire, that the granny gave him a thirst for the history of Ireland.

As a young girl of ten at the turn of the century, Molly was taken in as a downstairs maid by Madame Barrington, who lived in an aristocratic townhouse on Mountjoy Square, a four-storey-over-basement mansion with a stable mews at the end of the back garden. Molly worked twelve hours a day, seven days a week, for half-a-crown, scrubbing and cleaning and polishing all the kitchen utensils. She helped the gardener, she cleaned the stable, she polished and oiled the horse harness. She was never allowed up the stairs from the basement. That was for the butler and the two upstairs maids only. She became friendly with the old butler, Michael McDonagh, a Galwayman who had lived through the famine years.

'That dark desperate chapter of our history that left a million Irish people dead on the land and another two million who left for foreign shores. Many of them died in the coffin ships.

'Michael McDonagh had been twelve years old, living in a small stone cottage with his parents, two brothers and one sister outside the little village of Cong on the banks of Lough Corrib when the blight came on the potato crop in 1846. When the potato crops failed again in 1847, it was a catastrophe. They had only the potatoes to barter for vegetables and other supplies, and they owed ten months' rent on the cottage after using all their savings.

'The winter of 1847 saw his younger sister die of the consumption, and a few days later the landlord arrived with his bullyboys and the whole family were evicted onto the roadway with the snow on the ground. The family loaded their pitiful belongings onto an old farm cart and headed off to walk the twenty-five miles into Galway town. On the journey they were joined by some more families in similar circumstances. But they were shocked to find that Galway was crowded with homeless people living on the streets. The workhouse was full, and it seemed that a cart of dead bodies left the hospital every hour for the paupers' graveyard. They found a soup station set up by the Quakers, God bless them, where they got a bowl of soup and a lump of bread each – their first food in three days. That night they huddled together under the cart with their mother saying the Rosary that the Virgin Mary would see them safely through the night.'

Molly paused to sip her cup of tea.

'Can you just imagine that, Liam? We had them English villains come over here and rob our best land, shunting the Irish off to the barren rocky ground of Connemara. And when ya couldn't pay them the rent they kicked you out on the side of the road, and burnt down old cottages to make sure no other Irish family would live on their land. Oh my God, eviction is a terrible thing, not to have a roof over your head. And listen to me now, there was no need for anyone to die of the famine 'cause it was only the potatoes that were hit. Wheat and barley and vegetables all flourished in the pasturelands of Ireland, but all owned by the English, who shipped it out to the English markets, to feather their own nests. They owned the fish in the lakes and an Irishman would be flogged for poaching a salmon. They didn't mind the Irish peasants dying like flies and that old reprobate Lord Trevelyan encouraged the export of grain.

'He was delighted at the potato failure, which doubled the value of wheat. It's what they call genocide today, because they were happy to see the Irish dying off. As bad as Hitler killing those poor Jews. The English allowed nature to do their dirty work without lifting a finger to help.

'Michael McDonagh lived to tell me the tale of his family. They survived on the streets of Galway until his father got a job for himself and the two elder boys, guess what, crewing on one of the famine ships that journeyed from Galway to Quebec. The fare was seventeen pounds a head, so his Da reckoned they would save that in three trips over the following six months and one by one they would be able to settle in America or Canada. When the ship sailed, Michael was left minding his mother, and by this time they'd both got a job in a tavern on the Tuam Road. No pay but a roof over their head and a good feed every day.

'The weeks flew by and the ship returned to Galway with Michael and the mammy waiting on the quay. But no daddy and no brothers. A crewmate told them the story. Halfway across the Atlantic one of the lads caught the fever and was buried at sea. That's why they call them coffin ships, you know. And three nights out from the American coast the daddy was lost overboard in a storm. So the last lad jumped ship when they reached dry land at Quebec. Jumped over the side onto the quayside and away like a rabbit. The musket men didn't catch him and that's it.

'"The captain gave me this envelope for you, Missus McDonagh, with his sympathy," were the crewmate's words. In the envelope were two silver crowns. Michael stayed with his mammy in the tavern but the winter of 1848 brought terrible sleet and snowstorms. One morning he found his mother's bed empty. On the pillow was the envelope and the two silver crowns. An hour later he found his poor mother stone-cold dead in the snow at the bottom of the field. She couldn't take it any more.

'So Michael left Galway and walked to Dublin, where

he worked his way up to a good job as a butler on the Square. Never married. Never talked much except to meself, pouring it all out about the famine and his lovely family. Always remember that story when you hear them sing, "Danny Boy". The Irish mother waiting for her son to come home to Ireland just to see him one more time. Those millions of Irish lads who were forced to leave the poverty of Ireland just to stay alive. But survive they did; in other countries they survived, but the mothers here just faded and passed away. We all know it's a true tragic story and there's never a dry eye in the house when someone sings "Danny Boy".'

She looked at Liam and Vera and said, 'So now, children, off you go home and be glad you have a mammy and daddy to look after ya. And here, take a lollipop each before ya go.' And she gently hooshed them out the door. Liam and Vera ran up the street. Liam stayed awake long into the night, thinking of the starvation of the famine story. Nothing to eat. Sleeping on the streets in the snow. Dying of the fever and being thrown into the sea for the sharks. What happened the young McDonagh boy who ran off into Canada? And Missus McDonagh lying in the snow with someone singing 'Danny Boy' in the distance? Was it true the English made all this happen by keeping the food? Must be. Sure, Mother Darcy knows all things, he thought, as he fell asleep.

*

'It's hard to believe, son,' Mother Darcy said over the turf fire, 'that Ireland was once known throughout the world as "The Land of Saints and Scholars". A proud warrior nation filled with the love of Christ that St

Patrick brought to our shores. Druids and holy men who lived like hermits in monasteries all over Ireland. In Glendalough, Clonmacnoise, in Skellig Michael off the coast at Ballinskelligs. One monastery on the island of Innisfallen in the middle of the Lakes of Killarney was renowned. The young princes of Europe came to that place to be educated by the scholarly monks. Known today as the oldest university in the world. Where St Brendan the Navigator taught as a professor, before he headed off across the Atlantic in a leather boat to discover America. Hundreds of years before Columbus got there, and came home to tell the tale. You should be able to find all that in your library books.'

She paused for a sip from her mug of shell cocoa, the turf light flickering on her face, framed by a mane of jet-black hair. Liam was hanging on every word. 'The great Brian Boru went to Innisfallen for his schooling, where he gained the wisdom to become High King of all Ireland. But the Normans came to Ireland in the twelfth century, so they did, and took over the country. Our warriors couldn't cope with a secret weapon they had never seen before. The simple bow and arrow it was. Strength and bravery were useless when you couldn't get near your opponent. Picked off our lads from a hundred yards. Only took three years for them to take Leinster and Munster and that was the beginning of the eight hundred years of tyranny of the English. Wiped out our schools and monasteries, killed our priests, destroyed our churches, took our lands and banished the Irish people to the rocky fields of Connaught in the barren west of Ireland. Gave our most fertile land to their soldiers and generals. Used the natives as slaves, peasants, and farm workers.

'Rebellions were many but the might of the British Empire was too much. Too much for the bravest of men – Red Hugh O'Donnell, Patrick Sarsfield, Wolfe Tone and many more that you will read all about. So many brave Irishmen tried so hard. And we had that Antichrist Cromwell, who came in and travelled the length and breadth of Ireland with his army of villains, who set fire to every town they went into. Murdered men, women and children all over the country. Condemned to death we were, for being Irish and Catholic. May the sweet Virgin Mary, the Mother of Christ, protect this little country of ours from the likes of that ever happening again.' And she paused for another sip, looking forlornly into the fire. Liam was overawed by the tragic stories, and blessed himself as she recited the prayer.

*

Mother Darcy had seen the Easter Rising. 'You know, Liam,' she said, 'you won't read much in your school books about the 1916 Rising. But I saw it all with my own eyes, so I did. 'Cause meself and your grandfather, Sheriff Darcy, were only just married and we'd a little flat in Sackville Place. Right across from the General Post Office. Beside Clery's, we were, which was the Imperial Hotel at that time. We were blockaded in our second-floor flat by the British soldiers, who were shooting straight across the road at our lads in the GPO. For a week it went on. We nearly starved and your mammy was a baby in the cot. We got bread and milk hauled up to the window in a bucket, taking some for ourselves and swinging the bucket on to the next house. And the soldiers gave us some of their rations too, they did. Odd lumps of hard meat to chew on but it kept us going.

'When the gunboat *Helga* arrived at Butt Bridge and started lobbing bombs onto our lads it was all over. We were evacuated out of the house because their aim wasn't too good. Demolished half of O'Connell Street, that gunboat did. The GPO went on fire, the survivors got out into Moore Lane, and eventually Pádraig Pearse surrendered to the British outside Conway's pub in Parnell Street, opposite the front door of the Rotunda Hospital. An uncle of Alex Findlater took his gun off him, Harry De Courcey-Wheeler. Double-barrelled name. Very posh.

'Our lads were rounded up in O'Connell Street and I saw them marched off to Kilmainham Jail. Poor old James Connolly was dying on a stretcher. And that's when I first clapped eyes on Michael Collins. A big young fellow. A ragged gang they were. Led off surrounded by armed British soldiers and me watching every bit of it with your mother under me shawl chewing the left tit off me.' She paused and looked at Liam with a grin. The lad was wide-eyed with excitement. 'And then the English bowsies went and shot our lads. A firing squad in Kilmainham Jail. The two Pearse brothers, Joe Plunkett, Seán MacDermott, and even the half-dead Connolly was dragged out strapped to a chair and shot like a dog. Inhuman it was, to treat brave men like that.

'But Michael Collins wasn't shot. They thought he was just a misguided young Corkman, thanks be to God, and shipped him off to jail in England. And though de Valera had been in command in Boland's Mills, they didn't shoot him either because he was an American.

Born in New York, Dev was, and the Brits didn't want to annoy the Yanks who had come into the First World War only when the *Lusitania* was torpedoed off the coast of Cork nine months before the Rising. Collins was back in Ireland by Christmas and set about putting the fear of death into every British officer in Ireland. He had his men set about murdering the Brits and their spies. Hit them quick and run away. Then them Brits sent in the Black and Tans. Hooligans gathered from the slums of England. Dressed in uniforms half-army and half-police, which is why they were called Black and Tans. Flew around the country in armoured cars, beating up and killing anyone who looked crooked at them. Terrible it was.

'But Collins succeeded in getting the Brits around the table in London, talking about giving us our own country back. The cute old de Valera stayed home here, 'cause he knew the Brits would never walk away. And though Collins got us twenty-six of the thirty-two counties, and insisted half a loaf was better than no bread, de Valera pulled out the hairy chestnut.

'"No Irishman will ever swear allegiance to the British Crown. Is that what the IRA have fought and died for? Is that what the heroes and martyrs of 1916 wanted? Never," he said.

'So we had a civil war, brother fighting against brother, and poor Michael Collins was shot in an ambush. Shot in the back of the head, he was. Ireland's greatest warrior killed in cold blood by a sneaking coward. Oh, I'll never forget it, he was such a great man.' And the tears were in her eyes as she rocked herself gently on the chair. Liam realised he was crying too, and brushed his face with the sleeve of his gansey.

Molly produced two white handkerchiefs. 'Here you are, son,' she said, 'we're not the first and we won't be the last to shed a tear for Mick Collins. So now that's a mouthful about our history tonight that ya should remember. And read up on the books in the library and you'll see what I've told you is the truth. As your Uncle Bob would say – that's a fact. Go on home now with ya and I'll see ya tomorrow, please God.'

Liam blessed himself with the holy water from the font at the door and turned to look at his granny sitting at the fire. She had lived so long and seen so much. 'May God bless you and protect you, Mother Darcy,' the young fellow said. 'And may God bless you too, son,' she said, and she smiled and blew him a kiss as he ran out the door.

12

‘WILL YIZ GO TO BALLYFERMOT
OR DONNYCARNEY?’

Molly Darcy burst into the room one morning waving a white envelope. ‘Mary,’ she said, ‘it’s goodbye to the Hill. The postman just gave me this letter for ya, and he says it’s the notice for one of the new houses. The first one to be delivered here in Summerhill, he says. The boyos in the sorting office have seen these envelopes before and know the routine.’

Mary took the envelope and saw it was addressed to her husband, William Cullen Esquire, 28 Summerhill, Dublin. ‘That’s how they know it’s a Corpo housing notice, cause they give you this fancy "squire" title,’ said Molly. ‘Will you go on and open it?’

‘Do ya think I’m nuts?’ said Mary. ‘Sure, Billy would go raving mad if I opened this envelope, sealed and addressed to him as it is. Don’t you know how fussy he is?’

Liam came in the door just then, his face red, breathing hard, having run all the way home from the Ma’s stall at Cole’s Lane.

‘There ya are, son,’ said Mary. ‘How did you get on in the markets?’

'Great, Ma!' the youngster replied. 'Two boxes of apples, one orange and a pear, and got a pound reduction on the pears because the boxes were damaged but I'm sure the pears are okay. Got the four boxes up to the Lane on the handcart and brought Missus Kelly's stuff up on the same run. She gave me sixpence and that's all it cost me for the handcart at Kehily's of Granby Place. So your drop cost nothing, Ma. Wouldn't it be great if I could organise that every day?'

Mary looked at him proudly but it was Molly who said with a smile, 'Well now, isn't it the clever busy young fellow you are, and all that before you go to school in the mornin'.'

She turned to Mary and again appealed to her to open the envelope. 'Will ya go on out of that and open it up, because you might have to go over to the Corpo today.'

Mary showed the envelope to Liam as he ate his porridge. 'The mother thinks it's the news of a new house for us, but it's for your Da.'

Molly was watching carefully. Here was her daughter, a tough streetwise woman, putting a tricky question to her seven-year-old son. And she could see the lad understood the nuance. They had played these games before.

'What do you think, son?' asked Mary.

Liam put down his spoon and looked at the envelope. 'Now that's very formal, Ma,' he said. 'Surely a letter addressed to an esquire should only be opened by the esquire. I mean, that's posh, and anyway, you know the Da would hit the roof.'

'You see, Mother,' Mary said, 'even this young fella knows we'd better leave it for himself to open when he comes home from work tonight.'

Molly looked at the two of them and realised just how her daughter was testing the young fella. And she knew too that they were both right. There would be no opening this envelope until Billy Cullen came home.

Talking to Nanno Kelly at the Lane that day, Mary said, 'Where is this Ballyfermot, anyway, Nanno?

'I went out there a few months ago with Sadie Caffrey,' said Nanno. 'Got the bus from Nelson's Pillar, all along the Liffey and out to Chapelizod. We went up a big hill. So big that the bus nearly stopped and the conductor was only short of asking us to get out and push. Lovely houses they are. Mansions, gardens for yourself in the back as well as the front. You could feed a dozen cows, there's so much garden. Three bedrooms and a bathroom and a lavatory upstairs and three rooms downstairs for ya as well. There's a kitchen, another big room for eating in, and another big room for whatever else. You could lose some of those kids out there, Mary. But I have to tell ya, the bus only goes every hour. And when we were coming home the bloody bus came along and didn't stop. Full it was. Had to wait an hour for the next one and it looked full too, so Sadie stood out in the middle of the road. He had to stop and we hopped in. Big row with the conductor but we were on and we weren't getting off. So ya'd better figure out that one. And as well as that, it's sixpence each way for adults and threepence each for the kids.'

Mary had her mouth open. 'How much on the bus? Do you mean to say it could cost me a pound a week for bus fares?'

'Now now, Mary,' said Molly, 'sure you'll get the keys tomorrow and out ya go yourself to the house for a look. Isn't Missus Walsh's son from Number 23 moved out to Ballyfermot Road. You can have a chat with her and she'll give you the info.'

'Well, we'll go and look but I won't be giving a week's wages to any bus conductor,' Mary replied.

Mother Darcy headed off and Liam gave the Ma a hand with the selling, delighted when he was able to coax the extra sale as the Ma had shown him. 'Yes, missus, the apples are twopence each, but I'll give you four for sevenpence, now isn't that a great bargain?' To bring home some apples, and be getting them at half price, was a sales pitch that worked twice for him.

At six o'clock the street was slackening off and the Ma dashed off home with the babies in the pram. Liam tidied up the litter and went down the rear of Cole's Lane where the Ma shared a storage space with Missus Kelly in a very old hucksters' shop that was empty and had fallen into disrepair. But a young couple lived overhead and it was secure enough for storing the boxes and stall for a shilling a week. Up he went then at about half past six to the Rotunda picture house where Mother Darcy had the pitch right outside the entrance door. It had a limited capacity for selling fruit, as the only customers were the people going into the pictures. But that was enough for Molly to sell a hundred apples and oranges every night. Liam sat with Mother Darcy, keeping her company and learning his trade. Letting her take the half-hour off to head to Lourdes Chapel for her Rosary.

Molly had some great selling tactics. She knew everyone's name. She was sixty years old at this time and had lived all her life in Summerhill. Knew every shop, business and residence for a mile around the north side of O'Connell Bridge. Had been selling on the streets all her life. And she worked at remembering names. And then gave a practical demonstration of how to do it. 'Find out the name and keep saying it while the person is with you. Hello Missus Foley, how are ya tonight? Is Mister Foley not with you? I see it's girls' night out. And isn't this young Mary and Teresa O'Brien from Gardiner Street? Kathleen O'Brien's daughters. And will yiz have these three lovely Jaffa oranges, Missus Foley. You won't taste better, and for you, Missus Foley, they're only eightpence. The family discount for regulars. There you are now girls, tell your Mammy I was asking for her, and enjoy the picture. Goodnight, Missus Foley.'

This was Mother Darcy at her best, a soft pleasant voice and a smile on her face. 'Always have a smile, son,' she told Liam. 'I met a man today who didn't have a smile so I gave him one. That's the way, and you don't just give a smile, you'll get one back for yourself. It's good for your spirit, remember that, to give a smile.'

They finished up at about half past eight..Sometimes Mother Darcy would go in to see the film, but most nights she'd walk home with Liam, wheeling the fruit boxes in a pram. Before he left her, she reminded Liam about the Corporation letter. 'Go with your Ma tomorrow and look at this mansion in Ballyfermot,' she said.

'We can't afford that kind of bus fare, Mother,' Liam replied, 'so I have me doubts. But wouldn't it be great to have a bath and electric light bulbs that go on with a switch.'

'Yes, son,' said Molly wistfully, 'it would be great. But it's too far for me so this old widow woman won't be going out there. We'll have to see about somewhere

else for me. See ya tomorrow.' And she vanished into
the dark hallway of Number 17.

Liam went on to Number 28 and ran quickly up the
staircase. He hated the smell and you never knew what
was in the hall. If there were no spunkers mooching
around you'd usually see the red eyes of a rat or two
on the prowl. So you just drew a deep breath and
charged up the dark stairs as fast as you could. The odd
time when the girls came home on their own after dark
they wouldn't come up the stairs. They'd stand at the hall
door and shout loudly into the hall – 'Daddy, we're home.
It's Rita and Vera, we're home, Daddy,' and the Da would
drop his *Herald* and down the stairs he'd go to pick them
up in his big arms. He'd carry them up the stairs, swinging
them in the air, all laughing and squealing.

'There's a drop of water in the basin for you to wash
your face and hands, son,' said the Ma when Liam came
in the door, 'and I have a nice plate of rabbit stew for
you that'll make ya smile in your sleep. You did a great
job today at the Lane. Well done.' The Da said nothing
as he read his *Evening Herald*.

Liam washed himself as the Ma loaded the steaming
food from the big black stewpot hanging over the fire onto
a chipped enamel plate. As she put the plate on the table,
she exchanged a glance with her son. He felt the tension.
There was something up. As he dried himself with the
towel, he felt himself tingling and knew instinctively what
it was. The Corpo letter. Lowering the towel, he looked
at the mantelpiece. Bingo. The Da was playing games.
Letting on he hadn't seen the letter, which was still in the
same spot, unopened. He glanced at the Ma and she pursed
her lips slightly. Say nothing till ya hear more was what
she meant. The other children were in the bed already.

Vera, Rita, Noel and Brian, all fast asleep. The two babies were in the pram. All quiet.

Liam picked up his spoon and got stuck into the stew. Carrots, potato pieces, celery lumps, and chunks of lovely tender rabbit meat. Then a big chunk of dry turnover bread washed down with a mug of tea.

'That was a grand job, Ma,' said Liam. 'Can I stay here under the globe for a bit? I've to do some sums for school tomorrow.'

The Da looked up and said, 'Of course you can, son. Education is the only way forward. The reading and writing has to be spot-on if ya want to get a good job when you grow up. You don't want to be slaving on the docks all your life like me, now do ya.'

Mary wiped the oil cover on the kitchen table with a cloth and spread an old *Herald* on the table. 'There you are,' she said, 'you can work there.' Liam took out his exercise book and started his sums.

Not a word as Mary started her knitting. Another gansey for the new baby. She glanced at Billy a few times. Liam spotted her and she knew he knew that the Da was playing the game. Eventually she said, 'Aren't ya going to open that letter, Billy? It could be about a house.' He looked at her and looked at the envelope. It seemed to be shining in the glow of the gas globe.

'Do you think so?' he said.

'I do, I do, Billy,' Mary replied. 'Didn't Alfie Byrne give you his word? You'll be first on the list, Alfie said, and it's only the Corpo calls people squires, so will ya go on and open it.'

He paused thoughtfully, and looked from her eager face to the envelope and back to her again. He looked at Liam, who kept his head down to the books, thinking it was between the pair of them.

'Maybe you're right,' said the Da and stood up, slowly folding the *Herald* and placing it on the chair. Over to the mantelpiece, but first bending over to toast his hands on the fire. A master of suspense he was, dragging out the drama. His minutes of importance had to be nurtured. Mind games.

He took down the envelope and read aloud, 'William Cullen Esquire. You know, Mary, it sounds like the King of England. William Cullen Esquire. The lads on the docks would have a laugh over that.'

As he continued to examine the envelope, Mary said, 'Ah, will ya open the bloody envelope, Billy, and give us the news, for God's sake.'

'Okay, okay,' he said, then pulled the flap apart and removed the letter. Reading it he gave a big smile and did a little tap dance. 'This is it,' he said. 'A new house in Ballyfermot, thanks to Alfie Byrne. Gimme a hug, Mary, because as true as Christ is in heaven, this is definitely goodbye to the Hill.'

They embraced in front of the fire for a long minute. Liam slipped quietly from the table and went between the curtains to the children's bed, unnoticed. The memory of that evening, the Ma and the Da in a loving embrace, would always bring a warm glow of happiness to him.

The next day Liam and Rita got down to the Lane after school at three o'clock. The Ma had the two babies lying in opposite ends of the banana box. 'Right,' said the Ma, 'Rita will stay here with the stall and the babies. You can finish up about six, Rita, and take the children home. Nanny will look after the stuff for me, won't ya, Nanny.'

Missus Kelly nodded. 'Of course I will, Mary.'

'Then myself and Liam will hike it out to Bally-fermot. Let's go, son.'

Off they went down Mary Street to Capel Street, onto the north quays and out by the River Liffey, west to Chapelizod. It was a long walk to Ballyfermot – about five miles. It was half past four when they came to the con–struction site on Ballyfermot Road. Up along the road counting off the numbers, across the roundabout, blessing themselves as they passed the church and there it was – 245 Ballyfermot Road.

A gate into the front garden, your own hall door with a letterbox and a bell. The Ma turned the key in the lock and into the hallway they went. A stairway led upstairs. There were two big rooms off the hall, plus a kitchen with presses and sinks. The Ma was smiling as they went upstairs. Three bedrooms, one with a built-in wardrobe, and then they opened the last door and there it was – a bathroom. In fact, it was a toilet as well. A loo, a handbasin with a mirror over it, plus a bath the whole length of the wall.

'There's two taps on everything, Ma,' said Liam.

'Yes, son, you get hot and cold water in these fancy houses,' she replied. Outside they found a big back garden, plus an outhouse. 'Not a loo, mind,' the Ma warned.'That's for storage – bikes and turf and stuff.'

'What do you think, son?' the Ma finally asked.

'Ah, Ma, it's really great. Lots of room for us all and a bathroom too.'

'Okay, let's head home,' she said, 'and this time we'll get the bus; there's one at five.'

Sure enough, they got a five o'clock bus and were in at the Pillar in thirty minutes. But on the bus the Ma was doing the sums. 'Well your Da can make it to work on his bike, so he's okay,' she said. 'But I'll have to go in and out twice each day, so that's twelve shillings a week for me. Even if you and the girls move to the Ballyer school it'll be six shillings a week for you to get in and out to the Lane every day. Then there's the girls coming in to give us a hand, say another three shillings a week for them. Ya know, Liam, we could buy a box of apples for all that bus fare,' she said.

'Well, Ma,' Liam replied, 'it's more than just the money. How would we get in to the morning markets and get home again in time to make the breakfast and get me to school? Same in the evening. Sure, I wouldn't get into the Lane till five and the business is nearly gone off the street then.'

As each day went by the Ma got more stubborn. 'It won't work for us, Billy,' she argued. 'The bus fare costs too much, the rent's double, and those electric bulbs cost a fortune to light. And we'd lose half the money from the Lane.'

'So,' he shouted at her, 'give up that bloody Lane then. Do ya think I like seeing my wife out on the street with them dealers?'

The Ma went mad. 'And how do ya think we feed these seven children of ours? As it is, I can hardly make ends meet. Will you pay the extra for rent, and light, and bus fare to go to that Ballyfermot mansion, will ya? *Will ya?*'

'Don't give me that, woman!' he roared at her, shoving his face angrily close to hers. 'I give you every single penny I earn. From the day we married, I've given you every ha'penny I ever got. I never opened a pay packet, when others spent it all in the pub and their poor wives didn't get a bob. So never ever say to me I don't pull me weight in this house.'

The Ma usually backed down from these angry scenes when the kids were around. She'd hold her speak until they were alone to have a go at him later. But not this time. Even though she knew Rita and Vera were sobbing, seeing the Ma and Da having a row, she retaliated. 'Yes, ya give me every penny you earn, Billy Cullen,' she said, 'and that just about covers half of what we need here in Summerhill. Who do ya think keeps this family in clothes? Who do ya think paid for that Sunday suit of yours you wear every week? Do ya know each of these kids wear out a pair of shoes in a month? Do ya know how much the rent and gas bill are? No, ya bloody well don't and like all men ya don't want to know. You sort it out, Mary, and that's why Mary is out on the streets, with her son, keeping a roof over your head, Billy Cullen.'

The Da reared up to his full six foot two with his fists raised and his face twisted with anger. Liam ran in front of the Ma. 'No, Da, stop the fighting, stop the fighting, stop the fighting and leave me Ma alone,' he cried.

The Da stopped. 'Sweet Jesus in heaven. I've never hit a woman in me life but you'll drive me to it one day. No matter what I do it's not good enough for ya. The great Mary Darcy.' He sank onto the side of the bed, his chin on his chest, breathing heavily. 'You sure know how to pull a man down. Run him down in front of his own children,' he said.

Mary slumped onto a chair with an agonised look on her face.'No, Billy,' she said softly, 'it's just that you won't listen to the sense I'm talking. 'Course I want to get out of this kip, but Ballyfermot would kill us, can't ya see that for yourself?'

He looked up at her, defeat in his face, then looked hard at his son standing with tears in his eyes, then turned and looked at the girls, who were holding hands, still sobbing. The two young ones were crying in the bed, while the baby was fast asleep in the pram, sucking a soother. He looked around the miserable dark room and let out a sigh. 'I just want a better place for our kids to grow up in, Mary. Alfie said they're pulling these tenements down, and I don't know where we can go if we say no to Ballyfermot.' He stood up and picked up his coat. 'But you're right,' he said as he turned and walked to the door. 'I don't have much say about it, do I, when it's yourself that pays the bills.'

Mary stood up and put out her hand towards him. 'Don't go, Billy. I have your tea ready,' she said.

He paused at the door, put both hands on the wall and leaned there with his back to her for a long while with his head bowed. Then he put his finger in the holy water font, looked up at the picture of the Sacred Heart and blessed himself slowly. Aloud he said, 'May God forgive us both for the angry words spoken here tonight, and let His Blessed Mother protect us and guide us at this time. God bless our lovely children and keep them from all harm. Amen.'

Mary responded, 'And may the Sacred Heart of Jesus look after you, Billy. Amen.'

He turned and looked back at his family, gave a sad smile, and said, 'I'm just going down to the Pro-Cathedral for a rest, Mary. I won't be long.' And he slipped out the door.

Mary went to the window and saw him come out the doorway. He paused and she saw him give himself a shake, then he marched off down the road with his head up and chest out. That's my Billy Cullen, she thought.

But the Da never forgot her humiliating tirade.

The Ma went back to the Corporation the next day and they offered her an alternative house in Donnycarney, another new housing project to the north-east of the city centre. Again she and Liam did the walk, did the bus and did the sums, and it was still the same, a replica of Ballyfermot. Back to the Corpo and this time she waited for a meeting with John Hogan, whose name Alfie had given her.

Mister Hogan was sympathetic. 'And you're right, Missus Cullen,' he said. 'There's no way you could work your stall in Henry Street from either Ballyfermot or Donnycarney. Not with seven children to look after. Let me see what I can do.' He ruffled through a batch of cards in a filing box. He pulled out two or three for a read and dropped them back.

'This looks interesting, Missus Cullen,' he said, 'a two-bedroom apartment in Portland Row. In fact, there's a choice of two in houses we've just renovated. And Portland Row is only a few hundred yards from where you are. Why don't you take these two sets of keys for Number 48 and Number 42, and go and have a look.'

The Ma took the keys. 'The blessings of God on you, Mister Hogan. We'll go straight there. Sure, it's only around the corner from us.' And off they went.

Portland Row was a nice row of two-storey houses running from the Five Lamps at the North Strand up to the junction of Summerhill and the North Circular Road. Although it was beside the Summerhill tenements the houses were smaller and nicer. Number 48 was a little gem. Two rooms on the ground floor, two rooms on the second floor and another small room, high in the dormer attic. When Mary and Liam opened the hall door, the door of the ground floor opened and an elderly man came out. 'Here to see upstairs, I suppose,' he said. 'I'm living here on me own. Danny Farrell's the name.' The Ma chatted with him and he showed her down the back hall.

'We've an indoor toilet here,' he said proudly, 'and electric lights in every room', as he flicked switches on and off in the hall. He opened the back door. 'And look at this huge back garden out there,' he said.

And huge it was, about sixty feet wide and a hundred feet long. The Ma was chuffed as they went upstairs to see the second floor. Two lovely rooms and the front room was really bright with two windows. All freshly painted and wallpapered. Lino on the floors. A big sink in the corner of the front room.

Mary's eyes were sparkling. 'This is the job, Liam,' she said. 'Front room for me and Billy, plus the kitchen, and we'll fit two beds in the back room. Boys and girls will have a bed each and an indoor lavatory downstairs. Electric lights and a water tap in the kitchen, plus a gas stove. And all within walking distance of the Lane.'

They said goodbye to Danny Farrell and went down to Number 42. A bigger house. Two big rooms on the ground floor and two on the second floor. There was already a family in the ground-floor flat and the lock on the front door was broken.

'No,' said the Ma, 'we'll go for Number 48, but these

two rooms will be fine for Mother Darcy. That'll keep the whole family together, and we're beside the people and the places where we were reared. Not out in the empty fields of culchie land.'

So back to John Hogan in the Corporation and the Ma went into action. John knew he had the nod from the Lord Mayor on this, so after an hour of discussions, the Ma came out with a jackpot. The Cullen family had signed a rent agreement on the two-roomed flat at Number 48. The Ma also had a rent agreement for the two rooms at Number 42 to be signed by Mother Darcy. And she had an offer for her upstairs neighbour, Mister Carey, on the dormer flat in Number 48 as well. Plus the rent payments were the same as the tenements. What a deal. The Ma was over the moon. Home they went and that evening Mary and Billy went down to have another look.

'Well, it's not a mansion, Mary,' he said, 'but you're right, it's far better for us.'

Within a week, everything was finalised and the Cullens, the Darcys and the Careys moved down to Portland Row, right opposite the Convent of St Joseph's, and that first evening all the families went over to the small private chapel and joined the nuns in their Rosary and evening prayers. A new era dawned for the Cullens as Ireland was leaving the 1940s behind.

13

GOODBYE TO THE HILL

Liam and Vera went to Mister O'Riordan's Horsestone Dairy for the messages. As Vera went down the list, Liam was looking at the Jacobs biscuit tins. The tins with the see-through glass tops. One of them was wide open, the lovely spring-sprong marshmallow-and-jam biscuits within inches of his nose. Fluffy coconut pieces sprinkled on them. Quick as a flash he had two in his pocket. Vera finished the list and gave Liam the two bags to carry. Everything was okay as Mister O'Riordan agreed the change with Vera. Then the other assistant whispered in his ear. He turned and looked at Liam. Came around the counter and stood towering over the little fellow. 'Did you rob my biscuits?'

Liam wanted the ground to open up and swallow him. The two biscuits were burning a hole in his pocket. He couldn't answer. Shook his head slowly from side to side.

'Empty your pockets out then,' said the shopkeeper, putting his big hand on Liam's shoulder.

But Vera came to the rescue. 'You leave my brother alone,' she shouted and gave Mister O'Riordan a push on his thigh. He stood back in surprise as the young girl motioned with her head for Liam to leave. Liam moved to the door, carrying the bags. Vera stood there defiantly. Pink spots on her cheeks to match the colour of the twin bows in her hair.

'He'd never take your biscuits, Mister O'Riordan. Can I have my change please?' she asked, holding out her hand. Mister O'Riordan looked at the young girl, the pleading but challenging look on her face. He gave her a grimacing smile and handed her the change.

'Okay, Vera. Don't get upset. Just a mistake,' he said, and closed the lid on the biscuit tin.

Vera turned and walked out, taking one of the bags off Liam. Out and down the street they went together. Vera stopped and looked at Liam. The biscuits still burning a hole in his pocket.

'You wouldn't let your family down by robbing a few biscuits. Sure ya wouldn't?' she asked. Again Liam couldn't find words. His throat dry. He shook his head again from side to side.

'That's good,' she said, 'so let's go home for tea.' She gave him a big smile, and ran off down the road.

Liam took the biscuits from his pocket. Threw them as far as he could over the nearest garden railings. Then ran after his sister. With a huge sense of relief. A huge surge of love for his sister. Always looking after him.

*

The move to Portland Row opened up new business opportunities for young Liam. At the corner of the junction there was a busy pub called the Sunset House. Outside the pub a long skinny fella called Lanky Lowry sold newspapers. The corner was very busy in the evening with the workers from Pearson's steel factory pouring out. Liam got a job assisting Lanky with the paper-selling when he came up from the Lane at six o'clock. So from six o'clock to seven o'clock he practised his paper-selling vocals: 'Get yer *Herald* or *Mail*', which were the two Dublin newspapers at the time.

Lanky was amazed at Liam's dexterity with the coins, all gleaned from years of practice at Cole's Lane. The papers were carried under the left arm. *Herald*s to the right, *Mail*s to the left. In his right fist, Liam held a selection of coins for a 'float' all lined up in order of descending size with pennies and florins at the rear, moving down to shillings and hapennies, sixpences and threepenny bits. No matter what coin was tendered, for what combination of newspapers, the young fella worked out the change and had it into the buyer's palm in a flash. Just using the thumb of his right hand to slide the coins out. Lanky was mesmerised and told Big Bob what a genius young Liam was. 'You're right, Lanky,' said Bob, 'he's a bleeding walking calculator, he is, and that's a fact.'

Lanky gave Liam threepence for his hour's work helping him at the pitch. But it soon became clear that Liam could handle the rush-hour volume on his own. So Lanky decided to let Liam handle the pitch for sixpence while he reclined in the snug of the Sunset House for a few pints. This monkey didn't need any help from the organ-grinder.

But Liam got bored. 'We'll have to branch out, Lanky,' he said. 'Why don't I go up to Gill's pub at Russell Street where I'll catch the Phoenix Laundry workers?' he suggested. 'We'll sell thirty per cent more papers.'

'Ya can feck that for an idea,' Lanky said. 'Then I'd

be back to square one, having to work the rush hour here at the Sunset meself.'

'Yes, that's right,' said Liam. 'But you'll make more money.'

Lanky shot back with irrefutable Dublin working-man's logic. 'But I'd be drinking fewer pints, wouldn't I?'

Liam continued selling for Lanky but he began to mooch around the *Herald* printing works in Prince's Street at the back of the Adelphi Cinema. He watched the wholesalers buy the big bulk of newspapers as they came off the conveyor belts. These 'shoppers' split the bundles and sold them off in smaller lots. So the Independent Newspaper Group had a small number of customers who took their volumes and sold them to numerous street sellers. There was also a fleet of Commer Vans to deliver to the train stations at Amiens Street, Kingsbridge and Harcourt Street, to supply the rural networks.

This was where Lanky bought his fifteen dozen 'readers' every afternoon. He brought them up to the Sunset House on his messenger bike which had a big wicker basket mounted over the small front wheel. The Ma got involved, checking the price structure of the newspaper business, and discovered that Lanky bought the newspapers off the shoppers for a penny ha'penny each, and the printed selling-price was twopence a copy.

'Ya make a ha'penny on each paper. And you sell a couple of hundred for Lanky,' said the Ma to Liam. 'You get sixpence and he gets eight shillings for sitting on his big fat bum drinking pints. Sure, you could sell them for ourselves every day.'

'Only thing, Ma, you'd have to be at the *Indo* to get the papers at two o'clock, and then I wouldn't be at the

Lane to help with the fruit-selling if I went selling papers,' said Liam.

'You're right, son, it's a trade-off. You can't be in two places at the one time.'

But Liam left Lanky anyway, as Mary started buying a few dozen papers each day, which Liam sold between six and seven o'clock outside Gill's pub. He could sell six dozen in the hour, making three shillings a day for the Ma before he headed down to the Rotunda to do the cinema queues with the apples for Mother Darcy.

It was at Gill's that Liam met Brendan Behan. Brendan's granny lived in Russell Street and Brendan rambled into Gill's of an evening for his pints of Guinness. Always gave the youngster an extra few pence for a tip.

'It's great to see ya out helping that wonderful mother of yours, son. A beautiful girl she is, the star of Summerhill. That Billy Cullen was a lucky bastard to win her hand. Tell Mary I was askin' for her,' he said. And Mary blushed when Liam told her.

'Sure, Brendan was always a smooth talker,' she said. 'When he lived up in Charles Street. But even at that time his pint of Guinness came before anything else. Many's the girl he left waiting under the clock at Nelson's Pillar while he got ossified in the pub.'

St Canice's Christian Brothers' School was only a stone's throw from the Cullens' new house at 48 Portland Row and young Liam settled easily into the school. At the Christmas and Easter exams he always finished in the top three in his class. He was good at the mathematics in particular, but the fact that all subjects were taught through the medium of Irish was a problem for all the pupils. When you learned history and geography in Irish with cities like New York referred to as New-Auw-Rock (*Nua Eabhrach*), you had to relearn a lot of things outside school hours.

It was at this time that Liam joined the Charleville Mall Library beside their new parish church – St Agatha's in William Street. He began by getting a book every evening and he'd read in the bedroom at night when the other kids were asleep. But the Ma went bananas when she found her electricity bill had doubled and discovered the culprit reading into all hours of the night. The remedy was simple. Electric bulb removed from children's bedroom. But Mary smiled at her son's response.

'Bought a flash-lamp for himself, he did,' she told Nanny Kelly. 'Ya couldn't keep up with that young fella, you know. But I have to give him ten out of ten for persistence.'

And Liam continued, getting two books some evenings as he learned to skim through the contents very quickly. The Charleville Mall Library was his bedrock for the future.

Liam liked the Christian Brothers, even though he started off on the wrong foot with Brother Pierce. On his first day, the Brother displayed his habit of lifting any lad who got the answer wrong up out of his desk seat by pulling up on the lock of hair in front of the ear.

'So you think that Barcelona is the capital city of Spain, now do you?' he said, as he gripped Jimmy Molloy by the hair and slowly pulled the squealing young fella up onto his tippy-toes. Then he quickly hauled him down into the seat again. Jimmy's face was contorted in pain but the Brother quickly pulled him up again, saying, 'Well, it's not Barcelona, it's Madrid, you fool.' Then he quickly pulled the young fella up and down in time with his reciting of: 'M for Mary, A for Anthony, D for Dublin, R for Rome, I for Ireland and D for Dunce, which is what you are, Molloy, a big dunce.' He eventually let go and the youngster dropped back in his seat, tears squeezing from his tightly closed eyes as he tried not to cry.

It took a good few minutes for Jimmy to regain his composure and during the break all his classmates gathered round to examine the red swelling on the side of his face. They all agreed the hair pulling was worse than the cane on the hand, which was the standard punishment for wrongdoing. In the first afternoon a few lads went through the same procedure for error-correction, and it was clear to Liam that the Brother's intention was to draw tears. When a lad cried he'd be dropped back into his seat, but if you resisted the Brother would pull you up and down faster and with extra venom until tears came. Then he'd let go.

Liam was watching all this carefully and luckily enough he got his answers right. But the questions were getting harder for the eight- and nine-year-olds. When it came to a third punishment for Molloy he was shaking with anxiety, and the good Brother smiled and smacked him on the head.

'Sit down, Molloy, and just remember to get the answers right in future,' he said, satisfied he had this lad in his power. And that's what the routine was all about, Liam decided. Fear. Get it right or you'll be hurt. But it was impossible for the lads to know the answers to most of the tougher questions. It wasn't punishment; it was sadistic power play. Inevitably it was Liam's turn, as Brother Pierce realised this fella was resisting. He gave Liam two hard questions and Liam got the right answers. But then came a third one.

'Who is the English Chancellor of the Exchequer?' No one in the class could even understand the question. 'What's a bleedin' "chancer of the lets-check-her"?' Georgie Curran asked later.

But Liam had seen enough to know the tactics. 'I'm sorry, sir, I don't know the answer,' he said. As Brother Pierce came around behind him and reached for his ear, Liam stood up quickly and moved away from the desk. The Brother squinted at him, and Liam saw the surprise and hesitancy in his eyes.

'You sit down at that desk,' said Brother Pierce, 'and don't move an inch without my permission.'

Liam didn't budge and replied, 'I will, sir, if it's clear that you won't put a hand to me, sir, which my mother says I'm not to let anyone do.'

The Brother ground his teeth and his face reddened. He marched up to the front of the class, opened his desk and swished his cane in the air. 'And what, Master Cullen, did your mother say about the cane, tell me,' he said. Liam looked at him and was afraid at the anger spitting from his eyes. He tried to think of a way out of this. How would his Ma negotiate it? He knew the word 'mother' had hit home.

'The mother has no argument with six of the best for wrongdoing, sir,' he replied, trying to emphasise the words 'six' and 'wrongdoing'.

'Well, you were wrong, Master Cullen, so up you come here and hold out your hand for six of the best,' said the Brother.

Liam did as he was told and took six lashes across

his right hand, looking steadily into Brother Pierce's eyes after every lash. Don't show pain, but don't show triumph. Just play dead. Indifference. Ignore what's happening. It's someone else's hand. You're not here. You're chasing Noel across the sandy beach at Dollymount.

And it worked. The Brother stopped after six, breathing heavily, and waved Liam back to his seat. Indifference, not triumph, Liam thought, as he walked slowly back, hands by his side. Show some pain. Leave him in charge. Sure enough, the Brother was smiling in satisfaction. But Liam had sensed his hesitancy and knew the word 'mother' had had its effect, so that he got only six lashes. He knew lads who had got twenty-six of them, so planting the six as a maximum had worked.

For the rest of the year, Brother Pierce continued to rule by fear in that class with his hair-pulling trick, but for Cullen it was always the cane, and only six of the best. And for all his younger brothers who followed after him, the stage had been set by Mary Darcy's dictum: 'Never let anyone put a hand on ya.' Even when a neighbour would admonish them. 'No, ya never lay a hand on a child of mine. If they do something wrong, just let me know and I'll chastise them.'

And she did beat her children. Regularly. But, as she said herself, 'And you know what that bashing was for, so don't do it again.'

It was Liam's obvious thirst for knowledge that saw him safely through St Canice's. The Brothers responded positively to the young fella's perceptive questioning and hard work, and he won his way into the scholarship class. This contained the cream of the crop. Most of the class was made up of lads from Phibsboro, Glasnevin and Drumcondra, relatively affluent areas on the north-side of Dublin. He was the only Summerhill boy but he was readily accepted in the school. The incident of him standing up to Brother Pierce was well known, and in the schoolyard during the breaks he showed his strength in the hurling and Gaelic football games. He showed a great aptitude for sport; he had no fear and would wade in with his hurley swinging like an axe.

Although he was good enough, he never made the school team because he was unable to attend the team practices after class ended. He was always first out of the blocks when the schoolday finished. He would run down the road to leave in his schoolbag, grab a cup of tea from Vera, then off through the streets of Dublin to help the Ma at Cole's Lane. So he couldn't join in the team practice and he wasn't available on Saturdays either for the games against the other schools.

Anyway, he much preferred to play soccer, which was the only ball game on Dublin city streets, for the obvious reason that in soccer the ball was mainly played on the ground. Sure, if you started kicking a football or hitting a hurling sliotar into the air you'd be bound to break windows in the narrow streets. So soccer was the inner-city game and young Liam always enjoyed playing with his Da's handmade paper balls.

One day, Liam got home from school at three o'clock to find the Da's bike in the hall. What's up, he thought to himself, as he quickly slipped down to the lavatory to tidy up and give his shoes a wipe. You were always on in-spection with the Da around. He walked up the stairs, whistling, to find Vera setting the table and the Da fiddling with the wireless.

Vera winked and said, 'Howaya, Liam, will ya have

a mug of tea? The Da got off early to listen to the match.'

Liam nodded and sat down at the table as the Da fiddled away. Say nothing till ya hear more. Vera poured the tea and Liam picked up the tin of milk. He knew the words on the label off by heart. 'Condensed Machine Skimmed Milk Sweetened' is what it was. He took a spoonful of the gooey substance and stirred it into his tea. The Ma kept the real milk for the babies.

Suddenly the wireless hit the spot and an excited but cultured English voice filled the room. 'And we're here in Everton's ground at Goodison Park for this friendly match between England and the Republic of Ireland. The first ever match of this kind for England with the newly created Republic team. A makeshift Irish team, whose players have never even met each other until this morning, are taking on the cream of English soccer. With Bert Williams in goal and our centre-half Billy Wright playing brilliantly for Wolves, the Irish attack looks puny. And with Wilf Mannion and Tom Finney pushing down the left wing, Ireland's only known player, Jackie Carey of Manchester United, will have his hands full at left back. The odds are 100–1 against Ireland and the Irish will be lucky to get out of here with less than a half dozen goals against them. But it's nearly time for the kick-off and yes the referee blows his whistle and Farrell miscues his tap back to centre-half Con Martin who is hurried into booting the ball into touch as Mannion rushes him.'

The Da had his ear glued to the wireless, ignoring the tea beside him. 'Come on, lads,' he said, 'get stuck into these guys.'

Liam and Vera went outside to the landing. 'I'll have to head for the Lane,' said Liam. 'I won't tell the Ma he's home, 'cause he's probably losing the afternoon's pay, so you say nothing either.'

Vera nodded. 'Not a word, sure he loves the football.' Another secret between brother and sister.

That evening when Liam got home, the Da was in great form. 'Did ya hear the score at the match today, son,' he said as Liam walked in, and gave him a wink. 'Ireland hammered the might of All England. Won two to nil; the English never got a smell of the ball, I hear. What do ya think of that now?'

'Great stuff altogether, Da. Who scored our two goals?' Liam asked.

'That giant of an Irishman, Con Martin, scored a penalty in the first half when Desmond was chopped down in the box. Bert Williams got a hand to it but Con Martin had really smacked that ball and there was no stopping it. And Tommy Farrell got another goal in the second half.'

'Ya know what I'm going to tell ya, Billy Cullen,' said Mary. 'Ya'd think you were at the match, the way you're talking.'

Billy blushed. 'Sure, we were able to hear bits of it from the wireless in the manager's office, and oul' Lanigan was keeping us posted too. But listen to me, the English threw everything at us but Freddie Goodman in goal was like a stone wall. Nuthin' got past him. We beat England on their own ground. Never been done, son. No one has ever beaten England before. Bejaysus, they'll never live this down,' he said, and ducked as Mary threw the dishcloth at him.

'Billy Cullen,' she said, laughing, 'will ya ever watch your language in front of the children!' It was obvious she was delighted to see him so full of beans.

'Tell ya what, Mary, how about we go to the pictures on Saturday? *Gone With the Wind* is on at the Savoy and we'll catch the Pathé News and see the goals scored in the match. What do you say?'

'Well now, Billy Cullen,' she replied, 'how could I pass up the chance of seeing Clark Gable. I'm on, and Mother Darcy will come up here to mind the kids.'

'That's great, that's great,' squealed Vera. 'Mother Darcy has lollipops for us.'

'And she tells us great stories too,' said Liam.

So the Da's day off stayed a secret. He worked overtime for the next two nights to balance his wages. The Ma dressed up for the Savoy and the Da wore his Sunday suit. They walked down Summerhill with Mary linking Billy's elbow, 'looking like film stars themselves,' said Cric Neary when he met Big Bob in Killane's pub that night. What a great start in the new house.

Every evening after tea the Ma cleared the table and the family all knelt on the floor and said the Rosary together. Then it was school-exercise time with the Da always delighted to help the kids with their handwriting. Billy Cullen was known for his copperplate writing, and Liam developed a clear bold handwriting style. As for Mary, she was a genius with the sums. This was way before the metric system hit Ireland and the currency calculations were complex.

'If you make your living on the streets, then you'd better be able to do the money sums in your head,' said Mary. So with 240 pennies in a pound, with tanners, shillings, florin, half-crowns, with twelve pence in a shilling and twenty shillings in a pound, it wasn't easy. But Mary took Liam in hand every night and went through the drill until he could do the money sums in his sleep. He could look at a list of monetary amounts and give the total answer in seconds. He delighted in showing off this talent and tested himself continuously in adding, subtracting and dividing.

And as he learned from the Ma, he realised how difficult it was for her with the handwriting and reading. So later in the evening when the kids were in bed and the Da at his Sodality duties in the Pro-Cathedral, Liam took the Ma through his old English books, helping her to spell and pronounce the words correctly. Slowly but surely, she grew in confidence, until one evening with him she read a full page of the *Evening Herald*. It was December and Mary ruffled Liam's hair, saying, 'This is the best Christmas present I've ever had.'

Mary got an opportunity to show off her reading skill just after Christmas. The family had finished the Rosary when Liam said, 'Okay gang, all quiet now for a few minutes because the Ma has something important to say to you all. Go ahead, Ma!' He was turning into a cocky young impresario, was our Liamo. Mary picked up the *Evening Herald* and started to read.

The headline story was about a ship called the *Flying Enterprise,* which had been severely damaged in an Atlantic storm. The crew had abandoned ship but the brave Captain Kurt Carlsen was still on board, trying to nurse the ship home. Sixteen sailors had perished in the stormy seas. The family were all fascinated, as much by the dramatic story unfolding as they were by hearing the Ma reading clearly for the first time.

The Da was all smiles. 'Well done, Mary me girl, and how have you learned to do all that?'

'It was Liam,' said the Ma. 'He taught me the words bit by bit over the past few months.'

The Da smiled at the young fella, but it was a bitter smile. He shook his head. 'Isn't it a pity now you wouldn't let me teach ya, and all the times I tried,' he said.

'Well now, Billy,' Mary replied, 'don't you know you've no patience for that stuff. Sure, you lose your rag if someone doesn't tie their shoelaces properly.'

The Da grimaced and stood up sharply, slapping his right fist into his left hand. 'That's always the way, Mary,' he snarled. 'I can never please you, no matter how hard I try.' And he grabbed his coat and out the door to cycle off down the street to the Pro-Cathedral.

There was silence in the room. Mary bit her lip. 'Off you go to bed now,' she said, hooshing everyone out of the room. Liam came back in some time later to see the Ma sitting by the fireplace with her face in her hands.

'Are you all right, Ma?' he asked.

She turned to look at her son. 'It's not your fault, Liam,' she said softly after looking at him for a while. 'Meself and your Da have a habit of annoying each other, haven't we?'

Liam felt the sadness in her and saw she'd been crying. 'The Da doesn't mean it,' he said. 'It's just that you can do more things than him. But he was better than you at the reading. So he was annoyed. He knows you won't need his help now with the *Herald*.'

She ruffled his curly hair. 'You've a wise head on them young shoulders, son. Go on to bed and we'll get our Mass in the morning.'

Liam never forgot the picture of his forlorn Ma, tearful, sitting looking into the turf fire.

For Big Bob Darcy, the *Flying Enterprise* was a great

story. Into the Sunset House he went every evening to catch up on the news from the wireless and give his own spin to the tale.

'This Captain Carlsen is some man altogether, with himself now tied to the steering wheel of the ship,' said Tommy Farrell. 'They'll give him the Victoria Cross for that.'

Bob looked at him with a smile: 'Sure, you don't know the real story at all, Tommy. This Captain Carlsen is staying for the money. If he abandons the ship then the crew of that salvage tug the *Turmoil* will claim the lot for themselves. So he's hanging on for a big pay day, and why not?'

The drama was being reported hour by hour on the wireless, with newspapers buying photographs of the listing ship for their front pages. 'Have you heard the latest?' said Tommy. 'The tug has got another man on the deck of the *Flying Enterprise*. It's a relation of yours, Bob, name of Kenneth Darcy. Begob, you Darcys are everywhere.'

As the ship was slowly towed towards the Irish coast, it was anticipated she would be hauled into Baltimore in County Cork. But rather than share the salvage reward with an Irish shipyard, the *Turmoil*'s owners decided to take her on the couple of hundred miles further to their own salvage yard in Falmouth, on the south-west coast of England.

'You know,' said Bob, 'they'll be pushing their luck getting across the tides of the Irish Sea. It's going to be all duck or no dinner for Captain Carlsen.' And as if he'd put a curse on the ship, the next day, Friday 11 January 1952, the *Flying Enterprise* capsized and sank, just thirty-five miles off the coast of Cornwall. The brave Carlsen and Darcy climbed up the funnel of the ship as she very slowly sank stern first into dark waters – a dramatic photograph for newspapers around the world. They were picked up by the *Turmoil* and taken into harbour to a hero's welcome.

'There yar,' said Big Bob with a new twist to the tale. 'There's a story from a sailor on the docks that the bloody ship had gold bullion on board, loaded in the dark dead of night in America it was. That's why ould Carlsen hung on for dear life. That's why they couldn't bring her into Ireland. And sure they'll have no trouble now getting the gold up with their deep-sea divers. Sure Buster Crabbe and his men could be down there now as we speak,' said Bob, leaving everyone in the pub flabbergasted.

'Do you know what I'm going to tell you?' said the barman. 'You should be writing the fairy tales of Ireland.'

But Bob gave him a wink and a nod. 'The truth is often stranger than fiction,' he said, as he took a slug from his pint, 'and that's a fact.'

*

The tenement women used Tara Street Laundry to wash the family clothes. As well as Tara Street there were two other laundries for the women of the north inner city. Phoenix Laundry in Russell Street was in the shadow of Croke Park, right beside the rear of St Canice's School. So it was handy. The Ma would give Liam a flour sack full of dirty clothes and he'd drop it into the Phoenix bag wash on the way to school on Monday morning. Collect it on Tuesday evening after school. It cost about two shillings. Charged by the weight of the bag. Clothes were washed and dried only. No ironing.

The other laundry was in Seán MacDermott Street. Run by the nuns. Over the gates the big metal sign said, 'Sisters of Charity. Magdalen Laundry.' It was dearer than the Phoenix, but the clothes were ironed. Much better job altogether. So Liam would drop a bag in there as well on Wednesday morning. Mainly the Ma's and Da's clothes. Rita and Vera were getting fussy too. Collect it on Friday. The nuns were not as friendly as Sister Bernadette and Sister Patricia in Gardiner Street, and the laundry was a very forbidding place. Dark shadows everywhere. Very noisy, with the big washing machines hammering and clattering. Steam spewing and hissing out everywhere, with the ironing presses sizzling.

The nuns looked grim, seldom smiled. Cranky if you had misprinted the weight or if they couldn't read your address on the deposit form. The workers were all women. Every bit as dour as the nuns. They were called Maggies.

'Why are all the girls called Maggies?' Liam asked the Ma one day. 'Are there no Marys or Bridgets?'

'It's after Mary Magdalen,' the Ma said. 'Maggie is a nickname for Magdalen, that's all.'

'Oh,' said Liam, 'and is that the Mary Magdalen from the Gospel? She was a prostitute, Ma, wasn't she?'

He got a box on the ear. 'Don't let me hear you using words like that in this house. Go out and wash your mouth out.' The Ma chased him out of the room.

Later that night they were in the kitchen. Just the two of them. He felt her looking at him. 'I'm sorry I lost me rag, son. But "prostitute" is a bad word. You can't use it in front of the girls.'

'I've checked it in the dictionary, Ma,' said Liam. 'It means someone who sells their bodies for sex. Vera and Rita know all about it too. We see them with the sailors on the Quay. But the Maggies aren't on the game.'

The Ma blessed herself. 'Jesus, Mary and Holy Saint Joseph protect us. Children talking like this. What's the world coming to? You're not supposed to know about all that stuff,' she said, shaking her head. Liam said nothing. Just looked at her as she murmured her prayers under her breath.

Then she said aloud, 'Well, son, the girls in the laundry are called after Mary Magdalen because they've had babies and they weren't married. A mortal sin. But the nuns take in these girls and the babies are sent for adoption when they are born. But the poor unfortunate mothers stay with the nuns, working in that laundry. No pay. Just a roof over their heads and food on the table. Their parents at home won't take them back. They are outcasts. Shamed their parents, you understand. And some of them Maggies are in that place all their lives, God help them. Shush now, here's your father. There yar, Billy, will ya have a cup of tea?' Liam could see the Ma was relieved to get away from the embarrassing conversation.

On his trips to the Magdalen Laundry Liam became more inquisitive. Watched how the girls were very strictly supervised. Even saw a nun kicking one of the Maggies in anger. Another nun walked with a big stick. Like St Patrick's crosier. And he saw her using the stick to hit and poke the girls. There was an office for the customers and there was a big wooden gate for the truck entrance to the laundry. The hotels and restaurants of Dublin used the Magdalen Laundry and the collections and deliveries were done by the truck.

One evening Liam asked Molly Darcy about the Maggies. Molly was very upset. 'You see, son, these poor girls are in a terrible predicament,' she said. 'Scarlet women in their home towns so they can't go back. They know no one in Dublin and it's hard enough for anyone to get a job these days. So they are now slaves. Slaving for the nuns. They get no pay for all the work they do. Just bed and board for a sixty-hour week. Worst of all for them is the fact that they've given their babies away. In the height of their shame, the nuns give them protection and sanctuary. But before they are allowed to enter the convent they have to sign the forms giving the babies to the nuns for adoption. When the baby is born the nuns take it after a few weeks and away. For adoption. Always someone looking for a baby somewhere. Even to America, they take them. To the shame is added the guilt. And the Maggies stay with the nuns. Free to leave whenever they want. But only a few brave ones walk away. The rest are down there in slavery for the rest of their lives. All because of a moment of human weakness.'

Liam could see the tears in her eyes. She took out her Colman's mustard tin and sniffed her snuff. 'To clear out the auld tubes.' And she wiped her eyes with the cuff of her gansey. 'So you see,' said Mother Darcy, 'while the nuns are helping, you often wonder how much harm is done as well. Mothers who will never see their children. Never know what it is to nurture and rear their child. To see them grow. And always feel empty and guilty that they abandoned their own flesh and blood.'

For the family Rosary a new incantation was introduced by the Ma: 'God bless all the Maggies. Give them peace of mind, and the reward of a special place in heaven.' Response: 'Lord, hear our prayers.'

*

The women in Summerhill had lots of babies. Some even had 'Irish twins' – two children born in the same calendar year, ten or eleven months apart. One in January, one in November. Some of the fathers were barred from visiting the mothers in the maternity wards. Over-anxious. Such was the dictum of the Catholic Church on contraception. No way, José.

There was another sinister side to the baby population in Summerhill. Most Friday evenings a van would be parked at Hutton's Lane. From the Cadden Nursing Home. Mothers were offered ten shillings a week to foster a newborn baby. A lot of money for a tenement mother with rent to pay.

'It's a little like the Maggies,' Mother Darcy responded to Liam's and Vera's questions one night. 'Unmarried girls do get pregnant and wealthy parents can pay to have their daughters cared for in a nursing home. "Gone away for an educational tour of Europe" would be the story for the neighbours. And young girls do go to Europe from the rich houses on the southside. But this girl has her baby quietly in the nursing home. And the nursing home takes the baby for fostering. Gives it to a new mother to raise. And they pay two pounds a month to the new parents who raise the baby as their own, while the real mother returns to the comfort of her home. Older and wiser she is. Not like the poor Maggies, who have been disowned by all except the nuns. Goes to show ya what money can do. There's rules for the rich but different rules for the poor.'

She paused and gave her nose a good blow. "Course, you must also realise that the nursing home works both sides of the street. Nurse Cadden is often there in the van looking for to buy a baby for a childless couple. Paid twenty pounds I heard she did, recently.' And she blessed herself. 'Sure, there's a lot of misfortune in the world and all we can do is pray to the Virgin Mary to protect us from evil. Go on now, you pair. Time for bed. Home yez go and bless yourselves on the way out the door.'

It was years later that the famous Nurse Cadden story broke in the *Herald*. The body of a woman named Helen O'Reilly was found dead in Hume Street. A botched abortion. Nurse Mary Ann Cadden was charged, tried and convicted of the murder. During the trial, it emerged that Cadden had been questioned about the similar death in 1951 of a young dancer from the Olympia Theatre. Edna Bird had been found dead on a doorstep in Hume Street, where Cadden lived. It also came out that Nurse Cadden had served twelve months in jail for abandoning a baby in a ditch in County Meath back in 1939. And even prior to that, when she lived in Rathmines Road, running her nursing home, stillborn babies had been found in the area. She had been questioned but never charged. Nurse Mary Ann Cadden was the last woman in Ireland to be sentenced to death by hanging. But she died in 1960 in the Dundrum Mental Asylum.

How many Maggies' babies grew up to a better life in America? How many children of wealthy Irish parents were raised in poverty in the slums of Dublin?

14

A CHRISTMAS BONANZA

Mother Darcy had a perpetual street trader's licence for a sales pitch in Henry Street for the month of December. She'd been selling there since she was a girl. Tinsel balls, coloured streamers, plastic toys and Christmas decorations. It earned a meagre few shillings in the wettest month of the year. Near drowned she'd be from the rain.

But after the war, business started to pick up and the street became much busier. Mother Darcy's pitch was one of the best, outside the Henry Street side of the General Post Office. The side door to Number 4 Post Office Buildings, home at that time to the fledgling Radio Éireann. In fact, the pitch alternated daily from one side of the street, at the GPO, to the other, outside the Monument Creamery. The 'No Parking' signs were switched to 'Parking' every second day, so that the shops on each side of the street could have a break from the traders. Both pitches were only a few paces from Nelson's Pillar and it was here where the weekend shoppers left Henry Street for the bus stops on O'Connell Street for the trip home.

It was here with Mother Darcy that young Liam

spent the month of December. Straight down after school, not to the Ma with the fruit at Cole's Lane, but to Mother Darcy in Henry Street. Learning the spiel. 'Get your bells, balls, balloons and tinsel. Get your monkey on a stick.' This was an exciting and glamorous time in Dublin. The street was decorated with brilliantly coloured strings of lamps from one side to the other. Giant flashing Santa Clauses. Carol singers, bell-ringing, crowds of people. The war was long over and people's optimism was showing in the laughter and gaiety of Henry Street. It was still a poor country, money was scarce, but the warmth of the Irish people came shining through at Christmas. Laughing and joking and buying, up and down the street.

It was in Henry Street that the young fella got a thorough grounding in economics and marketing. A business course on the streets it was, a practical compendium of the law of supply and demand. It started with balloons, which at the time were sold for a penny each. They weren't a great seller, lying inert in a box on the tray. Until Liam brought down the Da's bicycle pump and some sticks. He became an expert at blowing up the balloons exactly right and tied the neck with a thread to a stick. With a dozen balloons blown up, in a wide spectrum of colours, he'd be off to the bus queues and no bother selling the balloons. The kids loved them. Bawled for a balloon. And if you accidentally let them grab a stick it was a definite sale because they would never surrender it. Explode it with a bang, maybe – and that was still a sale – but never give it up. On the stick Liam could get threepence for two balloons and even twopence each for the popular orange colours. Perception. Added value.

Most of the sales items were purchased either from the Northlight Razorblade Company at the back of Walden's in Granby Row or from 'Hector Grey, Wholesaler of Fancy Goods', who had a store in Liffey Street. Hector scoured the Far East – Japan, Singapore and Taiwan – during the summer months, ordering goods for the Christmas rush. He became a mentor of young Liam.

'No, Liam,' he'd say, 'them dolls are selling slow on the street this year. Try these fluorescent Santas instead. Great value too.' And in this way, he guided the young fella to the best-sellers.

'You're selling loads of balloons,' Hector said to Liam one day. 'I hope you're making a good profit.' The ten-year-old youngster looked up at him.

'What's profit, Mister Grey?' he asked.

'Profit, my son,' said Hector, 'is the difference between the price you buy the balloons for and the price you sell them for.'

'Yes, Mister Grey, I think we're doing all right there with the profit,' Liam replied quickly.

Hector raised his bushy eyebrows and said, 'Well you have to do better than all right, Liam, you have to make sure you get your one per cent. You buy these balloons for sixpence a dozen. Ha'penny each. So you must sell them for a penny each. Get your one per cent profit, d'ya see what I mean?'

'Yes, I do, Mister Grey,' said Liam. 'Double your buying price is the price to sell for. Buy for a penny, sell for twopence, buy for a shilling, sell for two bob. That's the one per cent profit, is it?'

'Yes, me son, that's it,' said Hector. 'That's what ya need to make it worth your while with all the work you

do. As for me, here in this shop with overheads to pay
. . . ' and he paused at the young lad's quizzical look.
'Overheads, Liam, is me expenses: the rent on the shop,
the rates to the Corporation, the electricity bills, the
shipping costs on the goods, the import taxes, the staff
I employ, that's me overheads,' he explained as the
young fella nodded.

'With my overheads to pay,' Hector continued, 'sure
I have to get two per cent if I want to clear a few pounds
at all.'

So Liam continued the balloon-selling and never
forgot the wise teaching of Hector Grey, and even
managed to get his own two per cent on some sales items
over the years.

It was with Hector too that Liam learned about negotiating, and credit terms, and bulk discounts. The first year
buying from Hector, Liam saw Mother Darcy paying for
her purchase on the spot. Cash up front. But the following
December, after some experience with the Ma in the
market, Liam watched Molly buying the stock.

'That's four pounds, seventeen shillings,' Hector said,
'but we'll round it off at four pounds fifteen shillings
to you, Molly.' It was the first Saturday morning and
Liam was with Mother Darcy all day because school was
closed.

'Are we not good customers now, Hector?' Liam
asked. 'With a track record? We must be your best buyer
for balloons and we've Aunt Julie with us this year.
With three of us selling on the street, we'll be your
biggest customers.'

Hector looked at him. 'And that you are, Liam,' he
said. 'That's why I just knocked two shillings off the
price for Molly.'

Liam smiled and said, 'That's great, Hector, and thank you very much. But at the fruit markets the Ma gets an extra bit off when she buys all her apples from the same supplier for a month. Suppose we didn't buy off Northlight and gave you all our business this year, would we get a better price?'

Hector smiled and looked at Molly. 'Now isn't this fella learning fast, Molly me girl,' he said. 'You can be sure I'll make it worth your while to buy exclusively from Hector Grey. If you buy a hundred pounds' worth off me this month, I'll refund you eight pounds. No few bob here and there. We'll add up everything you buy, and if ya go over the ton I'll give you back eight quid, and we'll run a credit line, so you don't have to pay me until Christmas. How's that?'

Before Liam could respond, Molly said, 'Well, the blessings of God on ya, Hector Grey, but aren't you the dacent man. Sure that's terrific, isn't it Liam, and I'll shake hands on the deal.' And they did indeed shake hands.

Outside the shop, Molly said, 'Well done, Liam, that's a great deal ya got. Only now we'll really have to get working, to sell a hundred pounds' worth of stuff before Christmas.'

'We might have got a bit more off him, Mother Darcy,' Liam said.

Mother Darcy stopped her pram and looked at him. 'Son, you did a great job in there with Hector,' she said, and she smiled at him. 'And if we get the eight pounds, half of it is yours. But I also want you to remember that I've been a customer of Hector Grey for a long, long time. It's friends we are and he's helped meself and your Mammy when we needed it. So you don't squeeze a friendship. You take the price a friend gives you, so that's why I took his eight pounds when you could have squeezed him to ten. Maybe. For us, you see, a friendship is more valuable than a little money. So yes, always push for a good deal, but never push for more from a friend. You support your friends. Business is a two-way street between the buyer and the seller. We need each other and there's more to life than money. Didn't you enjoy the man's jokes and the cup of tea he gave us and the help he's given you?'

Liam looked at his granny and nodded. She was smiling gently at him. Even her eyes were smiling. And he smiled back at her, this small woman with her hair tied up in a bun and her black shawl wrapped around her, over her white coverall. Smiled at each other privately, they did, as the swarms of Saturday-morning people rushed up and down past them. Molly put her hand out and tousled Liam's hair.

'Come on now, son, let's get up to Aunt Julie and get to work. We've a busy month ahead if we're to make that bonus of Hector's.' She grabbed the handle of the pram and away with her up the street. Liam looked after her for a long minute. He was learning to buy, he was learning to sell, and he was now learning about people and friendship. And Molly Darcy had the wisdom of the ages.

That Christmas was terrific on the street. Really busy. Liam even took a few extra days off school to help at the stall. The eighth of December was the busiest day of all. A church holiday. The Feast of the Immaculate Conception. No school. Dublin was hit by customers from all over rural Ireland heading for the bargains in

The Henry Street girls selling the Christmas decorations, December 1950.
Left to right: Jenny Foster, Mary Ogsbey, Molly Darcy and Julie Ann Jolley.

the big smoke. By train, by bus and by car. They poured
into the big northside department stores – McBirney's
at O'Connell Bridge, Guiney's in Talbot Street, Clery's
in O'Connell Street, Arnotts, Woolworths and Roches
Stores in Henry Street, Todd Burns and Edward Lees
in Mary Street. Lenihan's Hardware and Louis Copeland, Master Tailor in Capel Street would be crowded
too. And Walden Motor Company in Parnell Street, for
a new car to go home in, for only three hundred pounds.

All the Cullen family were on duty, with Rita and
Brian helping the Ma with the fruit. Vera, Noel, Liam
and Aunt Julie manned the Henry Street pitch with
Mother Darcy. The babies were stuck in a banana box
beside the Ma, with a Primus stove on standby to make
the tea and keep the babies' feeding bottles warm. All
hands on deck, with even the Da showing up for
'security duties'. He even ran around to Hector's for
more stock when Liam sold out of balloons.

Coming up to the final weekend in December,

trouble broke out on the street. The normal setting-up time at the pitches was about seven o'clock in the dark of early morning. Prams, handcarts, boxcars, even horses and carts would arrive to unload the wooden trays and the boxes filled with stock. Some of the dealers balanced the display tray on a tall wooden leg. Liam, Molly and the Ma went straight to the street after six o'clock Mass in William Street, with Liam pulling his boxcar and the Ma pushing her pram. They arrived before seven this Saturday to find that a number of strangers had already taken over a few prime pitches, including Mother Darcy's. Mary, coming across from Nelson's Pillar, immediately tensed when she didn't recognise the dealers.

'Who might you be?' she asked of a big stout woman, dressed in a tight brown overcoat, not a shawl. 'And what do ya think you're doing here on my mother's pitch that she has a licence for since before you were born.'

The woman was taken aback and glanced at a tough-looking man on the footpath. It was he who replied. 'We're the Barrys from the Liberties and we've a street-trading licence so we're entitled to sell here if we want to,' he said brusquely.

The Ma looked at the group one by one. Five of them, two rough-looking men and three women. She knew it was still a bit early for the regulars to arrive.

'Well listen here to me now, Mister Barry,' she said. 'I'll only say this to ya once. This six feet of footpath is licensed to Mother Darcy here for the last forty years. She's been here every December, come hail or storm, all her life. She was here when the GPO was a shambles after the 1916 Rising. And she'll be selling here today and every Decem-

ber day as long as God spares her. So it's very simple. I
don't care what licence you have, but you'll move them
boxes of yours out of here. And Mary Oglesby and Jinny
Foster have the next two pitches and they're friends of ours
too. So I hope we're not going to have any trouble and
that you'll just move on, Mister Barry.'

Barry was undecided. One woman, one young fella
and an ould granny. What could they do, he asked
himself. They couldn't push him around, but then again
he couldn't hit the woman. Bejaysus, he thought, it
would have been ten times better if the menfolk had
arrived and he and his brother with a knuckleduster in
each pocket. His wife Bridget was a stout enough girl
but he could see this Darcy woman was mad for road.
She had a wild look in her eye that spelled trouble.

'Well, Mister Barry, I can see you're a Liberties man
all right,' said Mary, as she took off her shawl and
slowly rolled up the sleeves of her gansey. 'Ya take all
day to make up yer mind. I've done all me explaining
and ya still think you can take advantage of a poor
defenceless ould grandmother.'

She paused and looked at him slowly from head to
toe. 'To think that The O'Rahilly and a hundred brave
Irishmen fought and died here at the GPO for the likes
of you. Well I'll soon teach you manners,' she said, and
she reached into Liam's boxcar. Out came her poker and
she took Mother Darcy's walking stick and handed it
to Liam. She swished the poker through the air with a
vicious swipe and Barry jumped back.

'Well, Mister Barry, is it walking out of here you are
or will they have to carry ya,' she said fiercely through
clenched teeth as she walked towards him. Barry made
his mind up.

'No, Missus Darcy, it's all right,' he said quickly. 'Sure we never knew you had permanent licences for these pitches. We thought our street-trading licences were good enough for here or anywhere else. We didn't mean no harm. Come on, Bridget, Thomas, load up the prams. We'll move down the street.' And move on they did.

Jinny Foster arrived just as they were pushing off. 'What's going on here, Mary?' she asked. 'Did we have visitors?' She knew by the look on Mary's face and the poker in her hand exactly what was going on.

'Yes, Jinny,' said Mary. 'Tourists from the Liberties who got lost on the northside. But we've given them directions home and I don't think they'll get lost over here again.'

Mother Darcy had her rosary beads in her hand – she had started praying even walking across from the Pillar. 'Well we can thank Jesus and his Blessed Mother for sparing us from trouble on this dark morning,' she said.

Jinny looked at her, turned and looked at Mary with the poker and Liam with the walking stick and broke out laughing. 'I think, Molly,' she said, 'the bould Jaysus got a bit of help from your Mary in this particular row.' Even Mother Darcy joined in the laughter.

Mary knew the street was now a place to make a few bob and the likes of the Barrys would be back. So Big Bob Darcy was put on early-morning duty to mind the Christmas pitch. He came down with Liam and the boxcar at five o'clock and stayed till the women arrived. The Liberties people came back again but they set up down on the Mary Street footpath, well away from the mad Darcy woman. But slowly, year by year, they moved in on established pitches where weak owners weren't prepared to get into a fight.

The guards did nothing because they weren't trusted by either side and no one would think of getting the rozzers for this type of problem. Eventually, minding the Christmas pitch became an all-night vigil. During Liam's last year on the street, he and his brothers Noel and Brian took turns to sleep all night in the doorway of the Monument Creamery, wrapped up in army coats, as they guarded the family pitch for Mother Darcy.

'Like the homeless on the streets of Dublin, your Dad was, to make sure that we had a dinner on the table for Christmas', became a proud boast Mary made telling the story to her grandchildren many years later. Of course, Liam knew it was Mary Darcy who was the real hero of those tough times.

The yearly bonus from Hector Grey was a windfall. Mary squirrelled it away in a shoebox under the clothes in the wardrobe. 'That'll do nicely for the Holy Communions and Confirmations. We have two next year and it's costing a fortune nowadays. As for all those school books for Liam and the rest of them, it's a disgrace they can charge those prices for us to educate the children,' she said. So while the profit from Cole's Lane paid the weekly family outgoings, the Christmas money from the street became the savings account.

'For future expenditures,' Mary would say to Molly, 'and who knows, one day we might save enough to buy a house of our own.'

Molly herself lived from day to day. A frugal woman. One pair of shoes would last her for years. Bought them in Clery's at the January sales. Black suede fur-lined bootees they were, real snug and comfy. 'Always keep your feet and your head warm, son,' she said to Liam, 'and the rest of ya will be warm as toast. And sure you don't need a cap with the mop of hair that you have.'

Liam was the financial controller for Mother Darcy. Count all the takings on Saturday evening. Park the next week's outgoings in the mugs on her dresser. Four pounds as a float for her fruit and fish purchases. Two pounds for the gas and light bills, two pounds for food and groceries, two pounds for the rainy-day mug. Always a couple of pounds over. Into an envelope with it and: 'I'll take that over to the Mother Superior in Saint Joseph's.'

'Why do ya give the money to the nuns, Mother,' Liam asked.

'For to help the poor, son,' Molly replied.

Liam looked at her. 'But aren't *we* poor, Mother Darcy?'

She looked at him. Gave one of her twinkling smiles. 'Not at all, son. You're not poor. Haven't you a roof over your head. Clothes on yar back. Kossicks on yar feet. Good food every day. As healthy and as strong as a young bull, you are. With a mammy and daddy who minds ya and loves ya.' She paused, smiling at him. 'No, son, we're not poor. We're very rich.'

*

All the Cullen children wore 'Kossicks', a Dublin name for the black rubber wellington boots they wore through the winter. It was ironic that wellingtons were named after the riding boots of the famous Duke of Wellington who defeated Napoleon at Waterloo, who himself was a born-and-bred Irishman. And Dubliners then called the boots

Kossicks after the Russian boots worn by the Cossacks and referred to in many speeches by James Connolly.

To keep your feet warm in the Kossicks was an art in itself. First you needed the *Evening Herald*s, which were saved in every Dublin home. You placed three sheets of newspaper on the floor, stuck your foot in the centre and brought the paper off the floor around your ankle and shin. Squeezed the paper tight on the leg and foot, then stuck the lot, foot wrapped in paper, into a long woollen sock. The sock came up to the knee, now lined with the paper, an elastic band around the top of the sock, on with the Kossicks, and you had one leg ready for the wet and cold of the day ahead. Repeat with the other leg. A morning ritual for all the kids. Guaranteed to keep the feet warm all day.

But in the evening all Kossicks had to be left in the hall. 'Like them Japanese yiz are and that's a fact,' said Uncle Bob. This practice was necessary because of the decomposition of the paper. Between the rainwater that dripped into the top of the boot and the sweat from all the running around, the newspaper just broke into wet lumps by the end of the day. And they were very smelly lumps. So Mary left a bucket in the hall. The boots were removed, and then with your foot over the bucket you took off the sock, shaking the remains of the paper into the bucket. Out to the backyard to wash your feet under the tap, shake out the Kossicks as well, on with a pair of fresh socks and you were ready to go up for the tea.

'Sure where would we be without the *Evening Herald?*' Molly Darcy would say. 'We get the news, especially the important hatch, match and dispatch info. But we also have it as foot-warmers, and we cut it up into toilet paper too. It's a tablecloth and a floor cover. That's all on top of the fact that we make a few bob selling the paper as well. So God bless the man who invented the *Herald,* 'cause he's keeping body and soul together for a lot of us.'

When the weather got really bad – and in December the rain could pour down in bucketfuls – Liam would wear the sacks. Two potato sacks. One to hang on a thick piece of twine from the front of his waist down to his shins, like a butcher's apron. The second sack would go over his head, pixie style, and drape over his shoulders down to his bum like a cloak. And the rain would bounce off the greasy sacks as he went about his business on the street.

The street gave Liam his first lessons in marketing. The word hadn't even been invented then, but he learned to find ways of selling slow-moving stock. Started with the dolls that Hector Grey couldn't sell. Nine inches high they were, made of skin-coloured plastic. Hollow and easy to squash, but they had a pretty face with painted lipstick and a brown stick-on wig. Liam spotted that Hector had boxes of them in his rear storeroom.

'Three years lying there now, son,' he said to Liam. 'Cost me a right few quid, and it looks like I'll have to give them away.'

The young fella thought about it all weekend, and came up with an idea. 'How about giving me two dozen of them dolls, Hector, and I'll try to move them for you. You had them marked at a shilling each; I suppose you'll give them to me for threepence each,' Liam said to Hector one morning.

'Ah come on now, Liam, is it trying to rob me ya are?' said Hector. 'Sure, they cost me more than treble that to buy. I'll let ya have them for ninepence each and that's a great bargain.'

'Now, Hector, you told me you'd be giving them away to the hospital for nothing, only the nuns wanted you to put clothes on them. To cover the bare bums, et cetera, et cetera,' Liam said. This 'et cetera' was the new cool word on the Street, made famous by Yul Brynner in his part as the King of Siam with Deborah Kerr in the first big hit musical in Dublin, *The King and I*.

Hector looked at him. 'Don't give me your et cetera, et cetera nonsense,' he said, smiling. 'If you want the dolls I'll give ya them. But you take six dozen of them and you'll give me sixpence each. Up-front, cash on the nail, that's one pound sixteen shillings, take it or leave it.'

Liam looked at him and said, 'It's a deal. I'll take the six dozen on Wednesday and pay for the lot. Give me one of them now – here's me tanner for it – and see ya Wednesday.'

Off he went with the doll, with Hector looking after him wondering what he was up to. Bejaysus, thought Hector to himself, this young fella is as sharp as a razor. You'd need to keep all your wits about ya when you're dealing with him or he'll walk away with the whole place in his pocket. Good as his Ma and even better, he is.

Liam took the doll home to his sister Vera. 'How can we make up this doll to look cute?' he asked her. 'Can you make a little frock for her, something nice, and maybe put bows in her hair?'

Vera was enthusiastic and spent all the next day with Aunt Julie, who had a Singer sewing machine. She trans—formed the doll into a proper young miss. Large light-blue bow in her hair. Soft pink dress to the calves, with a light-blue cotton belt around the waist and white bobby socks.

'Now that's the business,' said Liam. 'Can you make up six dozen sets of that gear for me, and how much will it cost? Talk to Aunt Julie.'

The price was twenty-five shillings for the lot, the whole six dozen. Liam quickly figured that the dolls would stand him less than ninepence each finished, ready for the street. Sell them for one shilling and sixpence to get his one per cent. It should work, he thought, looking at the doll. Now all prim and pretty like Judy Garland in *The Wizard of Oz*. Now there's an idea . . .

That Wednesday he walked into Hector Grey's. 'Okay, Hector, here we go, me boxcar is outside and here's your thirty-six shillings,' he said.

Hector took the money and pointed behind the door. 'And there, me boyo, is your dolls. All six dozen of them, and the very best of luck to you with them,' said Hector.

Liam loaded the dusty boxes into his boxcar and off he went home, where he had Rita and Vera with the dress gear all ready. They spent the next Thursday after school fitting out the seventy-two dolls.

On Saturday morning Liam had a Kennedy's Bakery bread tray with a thick leather strap nailed to each side. The strap went round his neck with the tray in front of him and he had two dozen dolls on the tray. He tied a doll by the neck and ankle to each side of the leather strap, giving them a high-profile position. He could now stand beside Mother Darcy's stall without taking any of her display space, and he was mobile if he wanted to roam. Find the customers if you have to. 'Go to them if they're not coming to you', was one of Molly Darcy's sayings. But he didn't have to move. From the first minute he started his spiel, he knew he was on to a good thing.

'Get your Judy Garland,' he shouted. 'She's come over the rainbow from *The Wizard of Oz*. Only one and sixpence each.' They sold like hot cakes. The first two dozen before eleven o'clock. And one woman came along and bought three.

By this time the spiel had improved to, 'Only two bob each. Yes, only two shillings for the famous Judy Garland', and they still flew out. Liam knew he had a winner. He gave the tray to Vera, saying, 'You mind the pitch. I'll be back in twenty minutes, and remember they're two shillings each now.'

He grabbed his boxcar and down the street he ran, smiling and joking with the dealers on the way.

'Howaya son, isn't business great today.' 'Bejaysus, isn't Mary Darcy's young fella in a hurry this morning.' 'Hey, Liam, can ya bring up some decorating chains for me from Hector's?' were some of the shouts he waved and responded to.

He stopped at Cole's Lane to talk to the Ma at her pitch outside Boylan's Shoe Store. He pulled her away from the stall so Nanny and a few other dealers couldn't overhear. 'The dolls are selling, Ma. Half of them gone already, and I'm getting two bob each for them. We should go down and clean out Hector before the word gets round. He must have about fifty dozen in the store.'

'Do ya think you can sell them all, son?' said the Ma. 'That's an awful lot of dolls. And at ninepence each to cover the dress costs, sure fifty dozen would stand us twenty-two pounds ten shillings – a lot of money, son.

Why don't ya be on the safe side and buy another six dozen?'

'Ma, I'm telling ya,' said Liam, 'this is a certainty. Everyone is buying them. Ould ones, young ones, little children. They all want a Judy Garland. There's two weeks yet to Christmas and I know they'll sell. Ask Mother Darcy – even she can't get over it. They're flying out,' he said persuasively. 'And selling them at two shillings each, Ma, it doesn't matter if we have some left over for next year. We'll have our money back with profit in our pocket. And buying the lot off Hector, I'll get them even cheaper.'

Mary looked at him. Only eleven years old and he's covered all the angles. Knows the business inside out. Mind hens at a crossroad, he would.

'Okay, son, I'd better leave Hector to you. If he sees me, he'll know something's up. And you'll do better paying him cash for these obsolete ould dolls of his – now there's a good phrase for ya. And cash he can put in his back pocket. You'll need fifteen pounds for Hector and I've no fifteen pounds here. Come on over and we'll ask Tom Kelly for a loan,' she said, walking across the Lane.

Tom Kelly sold books from a triangular mobile kiosk outside Roches Stores. A fine gentleman he was. Always neat and well-groomed, with a pencil-thin moustache. Smoked a pipe, and Liam loved the fragrance of the smoke swirling around the Lane. The Ma had a word with Mister Kelly, who took a wallet from his inside pocket and quickly handed her three five-pound notes.

'I'll give it back to you this evening, Mister Kelly, and God bless ya,' said the Ma, as Mister Kelly smiled and nodded to Liam. Liam took the money, stuck it in the money pocket that Vera had stitched inside his trousers with a zip on it, and off around to Hector he went. Planning the words in his head as he went.

'Howaya, Hector,' said Liam, walking into the shop. 'Mary Kavanagh asked me to collect some decorating chains she'd paid ya for.'

'Bedad she did, Liam. They must be going well if you wants this lot up already. And how are the dolls selling for you, son?'

'Well, we've only got going today, Hector,' Liam said casually. 'Sure, money is tight enough and it'd be better if I could lower me price. Hard to get the oul' one per cent, ya know, Hector. Couldn't ya make the price a bit better for me?'

'Sure, it's giving them away I am at sixpence each,' Hector answered. Liam said nothing. Took the boxes for Missus Kavanagh out slowly, one by one, to his boxcar. Say nothing till ya hear more. Hector was writing in his ledger.

As Liam picked up the last box, Hector said quietly, without even looking up, 'I suppose I could drop a penny each if ya come back for another six dozen next week.'

Liam paused, staring at the top of Hector's bald head until he looked up. 'How many have ya got out there Hector?' he asked. 'Give me a real good price and I might clear the lot out for ya. Sure, you must be sick and tired of looking at them, and it would clear out space for new stuff.'

Hector sprang up, and around the counter he came. 'Bedad, I'd love to see the end of them dolls. Biggest mistake I ever made. Let's have a count.' They counted a hundred and two boxes, with six dolls in each box.

'That's six hundred and twelve dolls at fivepence each. How much is that, Liam – you're good at the figures,' said Hector.

'It's exactly twelve pounds fifteen shillings, Hector,' said Liam, 'but there's a few of the dolls squasharooneyed and you did say you'd give me a deal.' Hector scratched his cheek and looked at the young fella.

'Tell ya what, Hector,' said Liam, 'let's round it up to even figures. I'll give you ten pounds for the dolls. The whole lot. Good ones and bad ones. Dirty boxes and all. Clear out your store. Today. And I have cash. Right here and now. Isn't that a good deal for ya?' Liam pulled two of the five-pound notes out of his pocket. He spread the two big white English fivers on the counter, smoothing them out with the palm of his hand.

'And those two fivers are a lot better in your back pocket, Hector, than a clatter of obsolete dusty oul' dolls taking up valuable rent-paying space in your store.' Leaving the money on the counter, he carried out Missus Kavanagh's last box, and when he came back, the money was gone. Hector had his hand stretched out.

'We've a deal, Liam, me man,' he said, and they shook hands on the first of many a deal between them. 'And I like the way you round up the figures. That's a new one on me. Rounding up twelve pounds fourteen shillings to ten pounds. You made it sound like you were doing me a favour. But fair play, you've got lee-a-roady, that's for sure, and the best of luck to ya with them dolls.'

'Okey-dokey, Hector,' Liam said. 'Can you get Charlie to bring the lot up to our house on his horse and cart? He knows where we live. After seven o'clock, and I'll be there to unload them. There'll be a pint of

Guinness in the pub for him as well, when he's finished.'
And off he went with the boxcar.

Hector looked after him. 'Ya think of everything,
you do. Even a pint for Charlie. Sure, he'll always be
on time with them deliveries where there's a Guinness
waiting.' Hector thought to himself: That lad is a real
entrepreneur. Could take him with me to the East. He'll
make a great dealer. Six hundred dolls in one swoop and
I've had them looking at me for three years. Lee-a-roady,
that takes. And he's got them.

That same Saturday Liam sold the last of the first six
dozen Judy Garlands. He'd already sent Vera off to get
the necessary materials for the new batch while Auntie
Julie was alerted to the dressmaking ahead.

'Do it assembly-line style we will,' she said, 'with
Rita and Vera and Molly Darcy helping me.'

'Okay,' said Liam, 'but there's only twelve shopping
days to Christmas. And with fifty dozen, you'll need
to do fifty dress sets a day. Can ya do it?'

Mother Darcy showed she'd been down similar roads
before. 'Sure, we'll draft in Missus Carey, she has a
Singer machine, and my Angela will work with her.
We're not selling on the street on Sunday but we can
beaver away indoors on the machines. Twelve selling
days but fourteen dressmaking days,' she pointed out,
'so ya needn't worry about our end. We'll have them
ready for ya, you just have to sell them.' And sell them
they did.

Tom Kelly got his fifteen pounds back on the same
day, with a block of John Players plug tobacco as a
thank-you. Liam got another Kennedy's tray for Vera
and left her with Molly while he moved across to the
other side of the Pillar outside Bests Fashion Shop For

Men, where the Number 30 bus terminus was. The bus for Howth. The spiel rang out.

'Get your Judy Garlands, home from the wonders of Oz. Came to Ireland over the rainbow, and only a few more left. Only two bob for the Judy Garlands.' They flew off the tray. It was magic. After the first week they had seventy boxes gone. Over four hundred dolls.

The dealers on the street hadn't really noticed because the Darcys were the first pitch from the Pillar, and Liam was out of sight over in North Earl Street. A few asked Hector had he any Judy Garlands but he hadn't heard about them. Check with the Northlight. It was just before Christmas when a neighbour of his in Raheny showed him the Judy Garland doll he'd bought off a young fella at the Pillar. Hector realised what had happened. He looked at the doll in amazement. Bleeding simple. Bit of cloth. A few pence spent. Adding value, it is. Three years lying there. You're getting old. Have to use your loaf. That young fella has a head on his shoulders.

Just to show it wasn't a fluke, Liam pulled another stroke with some of the last dolls. Uncle Bob was a Marilyn Monroe fan. 'We'll make a Monroe doll for Uncle Bob for Christmas,' said Rita, and they gave it the treatment. Dyed the wig blonde. A white dress. Short and low-cut. With padded inserts for cleavage. Dress blowing up over the thighs. Starched to hold it up. Fishnets stuck on to the legs. Extra red touch-up to pout the lips. It was terrific. Like the famous shot in *The Seven Year Itch*. So terrific they made fifty of them.

'Get your Marilyn Monroes and give your man a flutter. Brighten his day this Christmas. Only half a crown for the Marilyn Monroes, we're selling out today.' It was naughty and it worked.

That Christmas Mary Darcy salted away a right few pounds. The best Christmas ever on the street. And the other dealers had woken up. So had Hector. We'll show ya added value. Over the next few years all sorts of dolls made an appearance on the street. Marilyn Monroes and Judy Garlands were the favourites, but you had Charlie Chaplins lifting his top hat when you pressed a rubber bulb, Doris Days, Jayne Mansfields, Grace Kellys, and Elizabeth Taylor as Cleopatra. Marketing had come to Henry Street and you had to stay one step ahead of the posse.

15

MISCHIEF AT THE PICTURE HOUSE

The Rotunda Cinema had a fourpenny entrance fee for the kids. Sixpence for adults. All sitting on wooden benches. And a shilling for a plush individual cushioned swivelled seat in the back. With five plusher rows up in the balcony for two shillings each. Lovers' Row, the balcony was called. Privacy guaranteed.

When you paid your money at the ticket box you got a two-inch square of light metal with a half-inch circular hole in the centre. The metals were stamped with the price. Four pingin, six pingin, scilling, florin. You went to the usher, who took the metal token and slid it onto a long iron poker which was notched in tens. Held a hundred tokens, the poker did, so the ushers knew how many people were in the picture house. Simple, yes. Foolproof, no.

Wide open to fiddles it was. Sure, a little chiseller's hand could reach through the glass slit when the cashier's attention was distracted and grab a handful. The chiseller got into the pictures, plus his Da and the pals. And it went further than that. The lads in Smith and Pearson Iron Foundry made the tokens. Some for the Rotunda Cinema order. And some for themselves.

But they killed the golden goose.

The usher, Patsy McCormack, was demented. 'The bleedin' picture house is jammed to the rafters. Standing at the back an' all, they are. We had nine hundred people and Maureen only sold six hundred and twenty tokens.'

The boss arrived. Mister Johnston. Big meeting in the manager's office. New system brought in. Patsy McCormack was plonked right beside the cashier's ticket box. When a punter bought tokens, Maureen shouted the order.

'Two fourpenny and two sixpenny,' she'd shout, and wait until Patsy echoed the order, as he took the tokens, before serving the next customer.

'Two two shillings,' she'd shout. 'Two of the best in Lovers' Row,' Patsy would shout back, pointing the red-faced couple to the staircase. And so the fiddle was silenced. For a while.

The new fiddle was in the lavatory, which was located inside the auditorium. Window in the back of the lavatory looked out on to a laneway at the back of the Rotunda Hospital. The McKeon lads were carpenters and one Sunday morning they were called to replace a broken pane of glass in the lavatory window. They came and they did. Replace the broken glass.

Replaced the whole window frame as well, they did. This frame had a sunken hinge. Swivelled to open. With a clever hidden lock on the outside so that the window was always solid for a security check. One of the McKeon lads spent the evening in the lavatory. The pals came in through the window and paid McKeon half price. The McKeons made a few bob. But they got greedy. Patsy McCormack was doing his nut again.

'Maureen, you've got paid for five hundred and ten,' he said. 'I've checked in your five hundred and ten. I've got five hundred and ten tokens. But the place is jammed in there. And I saw young Kevin Lawless sitting in the plushers at the back. Now you know and I know that young fella never went past us today. Did he now?'

Maureen was definite. 'Ya don't think I'd miss that fella if he came in, sure he's gorgeous he is. Ya couldn't forget him. It's weeks since we saw him,' she said.

'Well I'm telling ya that he's sitting in there in the plushers, bould as brass, laughing at me, he is. Coming in somewhere they are, and not past us. They're on the fiddle somehow, and we'd better get Mister Johnston', was Patsy's opinion. Another big meeting. Windows, doors and roof checked inside. Everything A-okay.

A different kind of meeting took place in Killane's pub. Big Bob Darcy had the chair. 'There's going to be trouble down at the Rotunda,' he said. 'Even Mother Darcy is under suspicion. They won't even let her into the lavatory now herself. And she's looking at more people going down the side lane than there is going in the front door, and that's a fact. Patsy will get the gate too over this. So I vote someone talks to the McKeons. And quick, because they could get a stretch.'

Pat Cluxton knew the McKeons and volunteered to meet them with Bob. The meeting was successful. It was agreed to scale back the operation to no more than fifty a night. That wasn't really noticeable. A good business decision. But the fiddles had sent the cinema-owners to America to search for new ideas. How did they overcome these problems in the States? They came back with some new paper-ticket machines which coincided with the new government taxation on cinemas. A penny a head they wanted for every ticket sold. Books and records to be kept. Audit spot checks. A new system.

The new system was very clever. Modernisation it was called. Into the cashier's box went a ticket machine with pre-printed numbered tickets. Matching numbers on the top of the ticket and on the bottom of the ticket. The usher tore the ticket in half, kept only one numbered half. Customer went on in with his matching half. At the interval the ushers checked any suspicious character. 'Let's see your ticket,' they said, and if you hadn't got your ticket in sync with the current day's numbers, it was out to the manager's office. They eventually cornered Waxy Higgins, a Gardiner Street lad whom Patsy knew well.

'You didn't go in the front door today, Waxy. You never passed me. You don't have a ticket. Maureen never sold ya a ticket. You are in deep trouble, me boy, and you can stop slobbering that you lost your ticket. Ya never had one,' said Patsy. 'You can tell me now how ya got in, and ya walk out of here. No one the wiser only me.' He paused, looking at Waxy. 'I'll even let you back in to see the big picture, and no one will even know we were talking. I'll do nothin' with the info ya give me for a week. You'll be safe. No one will know a thing. That's the deal. If you don't take it, you'll be talking to the big boss, Mister Johnson, and he'll have the rozzers down here. Like a flash. This is fraud and robbery we're talking about on a big scale. It's not just you bunking in, Waxy. This is putting yer hand in the till big-time. It's your choice,' he said, persuasively. 'Just give me the quiet nod and back ya go. A great film, too. Burt Lancaster as the Crimson Pirate, best action film you'll ever see. So is it a night on the ocean wave or is it a visit to Mountjoy Jail ya want?'

Waxy was frightened. 'I'm no squealer, Patsy, and I don't want to get anyone in trouble. You're giving me your word to do or say nothin' for a week?'

Patsy nodded. 'Not a dickie bird to anyone,' he said.

'Okay,' said Waxy. 'No names. The way in is the window in the gents' jacks. From the lane behind the hospital. Simple as that.'

Patsy closed his eyes and shook his head slowly. 'Under me feckin' nose all the time. I knew they were coming out of that lavatory like cows from a barn. And I checked that window a dozen feckin' times. Right. Out of here with ya, and you haven't said a word,' he said as Waxy slipped away.

Patsy did nothing. A few days later he had a chat with Mother Darcy. 'Tell me, Molly, do ya know anything about this bunking in that's going on?' he asked.

Molly was chewing an orange. 'Have a piece of orange, Patsy, they're only luvly,' was her reply.

He took the half-orange, and sat down beside her on the granite step.

'Keep yer bum on the rug, Patsy, or the cold stone will give ya the piles,' said Molly, giving him a nudge with her elbow, and they both had a laugh.

'Come on now, Molly, what's the story?' he asked.

'Now, Patsy, ya don't expect me to go squealing on what the men get up to, do ya?' she said. 'I can see you know the story yourself now. Boys will be boys. They're always ready to make a few pounds if they can. It doesn't seem like robbin' to them. Just a bit of a stroke. What are you going to do?'

'I've got to put a stop to it, Molly, and I don't want

anyone to go to jail. I'm not a squealer either, ya know. I've no time for the feckin' rozzers.'

Molly looked into his eyes. 'Well, just fix the window, Patsy. Lock it up. Get a dozen big six-inch nails and a hammer early tomorrow morning and lock that window up good. No one gets caught. And no one gets in for free any more. You can check the window every day. But the lads will know you've rumbled them and they'll keep away. Simple, Patsy, isn't it?'

Patsy looked at her. 'Ya know what I'm going to tell ya, Molly – there's bleedin' nuthin ya don't know. You're a genius. Sure, that sorts it all out. No one gets into trouble. And every ticket gets paid for.' And he leaned over and kissed Molly on the cheek.

Molly squealed and laughed at the one time. 'Get away out of that, Patsy McCormack, taking advantage of a poor widow woman.'

Patsy locked up the window with two dozen six-inch nails. Sank the nails. Covered the nail heads with filler. Repainted the whole window frame. Not a sign of the nails. But that window would never open again. He walked into the lavatory that evening, to find one of the McKeons there. Breathing heavily. Sweat pouring down his forehead.

'You're a long time in here, son, and you're wasting your time on that window,' said Patsy, and he squeezed the lad's forearm. Hard. The young fella grimaced. 'I'll say this once, son. The scam is finished. The window is locked. And you're lucky it's not in jail you are. You're no longer welcome in the Rotunda Cinema. Nor are any of your family. Ever again. Never let me see a McKeon's face on my queue or it's the toe of me boot you'll get.' He gave the arm one last squeeze. The lad howled. 'Now

out of here ya go before I change me mind.' And out
the door McKeon scarpered, never to darken the Rotunda's doorway again.

16

WHERE DO YOU SELL FLOWERS?

The family were outgrowing the two rooms in Number 48. Nine children now in one bedroom. Five boys in one bed, all under eleven years old. Four girls in the other. A curtain separating the beds. Rita was fifteen and growing up fast, so she stayed most nights in Mother Darcy's. She was working now with Aunt Angela in Alex Mitchell's rosary-bead factory in Waterford Street beside the Pro-Cathedral.

And the Ma was pregnant again. She'd already had two miscarriages and she spent a lot of time with Mother Darcy. Liam worked the Lane as best he could. He loved the Fridays when he'd go with Mother Darcy for the fish. Vera would be with them sometimes. Down to Amiens Street train station with the pram for the five o'clock train to Howth. The pram into the goods wagon and Molly with Liam sitting on the floor beside it.

Molly just nodded and smiled at all the conductors and ticket inspectors. 'Old-age pensioner with me little grandson,' she'd say. There was never a question of paying. Sure, Molly Darcy was an institution on the Howth train.

Off the train at Howth Station still in the pre-dawn

darkness and down along the quayside where the fishing trawlers had tied up. The holds under the trawler lights sparkling and flashing with the quivering fish. Some still jumping, still alive. Molly wasn't a woman to bargain but Liam knew better than to intervene. The fish were bought Molly's way. On trust. She bought from a couple of skippers whom she knew and liked. She paid the price they asked. And Liam soon understood she got a good deal without haggling. Not the best price. But a good price. And she got the best fish because they let her pick her own.

'Now, Liam, me son,' she said, after agreeing the price, 'down ya hop into the hold and toss me up the biggest, fattest Howth herrings you can lay your hands on. Sixteen dozen we own; that's one hundred and ninety-two of the silver beauties.' The sixteen-dozen purchase was a dealer trick that Liam knew well. The seller either voluntarily or by verbal pressure always ended up rounding up the one hundred and ninety-two to the two hundred. Eight extra fish would feed a family.

And the skipper shouted, 'Ya can make it the two hundred, Molly, for luck. Sure you're me first customer of the day.' And down Liam would go on the ladder into the hold and toss up the herrings to Molly on the quayside, counting as he went. Molly had two flat fish boxes across her pram and she lined up the fish in the boxes, sometimes rejecting a fish. 'Will ya open your eyes, son? Sure that's a pinkeen you threw up,' she said, tossing it back into the trawler. 'It's big fat fish I want for me customers.' So Molly got the biggest and the best.

They had a cup of tea and a scone at Wrights Fish Brokers' little canteen, where Molly would buy a few bags of prawns and some ice powder to spread over the top of the fish. Then back to the station for the train home. Using the goods wagon, of course. Liam could see the crowds of commuters were avoiding the fish pram, some even holding their noses. On occasion a brave cyclist would sit with his bike in the goods wagon, but the smell of fish was overpowering and he'd eventually withdraw to the passenger wagon.

And if the smell of fish didn't do it, Molly's snuff-taking habit would. She always carried her little tin of snuff. Ground-up powdered tobacco. In a small Colman's-mustard tin. Open the lid. Shake a small line of snuff onto the back of her left hand, put the hand up to her nose and snort. First the left nostril, then the right nostril. A common practice among the older tenement women, but it raised eyebrows when performed in public. Liam was well used to Molly's little habit, and 'Sure, won't the good Lord forgive me this little weakness when never a drop of the drink have I taken,' Molly would say.

The Amiens Street train station was not customer-friendly. No lifts. To ascend from the train level to the street with a pram was a problem. You could take the vehicular-traffic route, down a big long road that ended up at the Customs House on the quayside, and traverse back up to Talbot Street again. Or you manoeuvred the pram and the fish down the pedestrian exit, which was a flight of sixty-six granite steps. If it wasn't raining, they used the road. Took fifteen minutes. If it *was* raining, Liam unloaded the fish and Molly would bounce the pram down step by step with the help of a courteous stranger. Liam would get a porter to help him down with the fish boxes. And the porter got a juicy herring in a greaseproof bag for his trouble.

They would take the fish up to Summerhill, where Molly would sell from the fish boxes on the pram, beside her Number 17 tenement door, under the archway of the Twenty-seven Steps. From there she sold her fish for thirty years. But then the tenements were pulled down. New houses being built. Big five-storey replicas of the old tenements. So Molly and Liam would head down to O'Connell Street, with Liam doing the spiel.

'Get the last of the Howth herrings. Caught fresh for ya this morning. Only tuppence each. Healthy Howth herrings with the blessings of Archbishop McQuaid himself.' The fish were always an easy sell. They were big and fresh and looked succulent. Liam would duck and dive with the price. Holding out for threepence each when a fur-coated lady hand-picked the three biggest herrings in the box.

'The bigger the size, the bigger the price, Mam. I can give you these ones here for twopence each,' he'd say, pointing to slightly smaller fish. 'But tell ya what, you can have the three big ones there for eightpence, and that's a bargain for ya.' Sales like that balanced up Molly's generosity when she was giving six herrings to a neighbour for free.

'Sure I know you've a dozen mouths to feed, Missus Walsh, and may God bless you and all yours,' she'd say.

By the end of the day they'd get down to the Ma at Cole's Lane with a few fish still kept for Mary and Nanny Kelly. You could tell it was Friday, walking home that evening. Seán MacDermott Street, Gardiner Street, Buckingham Street, Joseph's Mansions, Fatima Mansions, the whole of Dublin's inner city had the scent of fried fish hanging in the air.

There was nothing like an evening meal of crispy

turf-fire-grilled Howth herrings or mackerel. A sprinkle of vinegar. Potatoes roasted in the fire. The Ma would make some white lemon sauce for the Da, and the kids would get a dip. Lots of small, easily chewed bones in the herrings. Ate them with bread washed down with a mug of tea. Flat ray was another favourite fish, which all the Cullen boys loved. Ate the ray fishbones and all. 'Lots of calcium to help your growth,' Mother Darcy said. Between the apples and bananas, the vegetable stews and the fish, the inner-city youngsters had a meat-free, healthy diet growing up.

It was about this time that Liam discovered flowers. It all started when Mother Darcy slipped on the stairs of her new flat in 42 Portland Row. Rushing over to the Rosary in St Joseph's, she was, when she fell and broke her hip. She spent three weeks with the nuns in the Mater Hospital and it was here that she learned how to make artificial flowers out of crêpe paper. The day she came home she got Mary and Liam up and showed them the flowers. Big pink paper roses.

'What do ya think, Mary?' she asked. 'Will we be able to sell these on the street? Paper roses, a shilling a bunch. You try that spiel, Liam, see how it sounds.' Liam practised the words with various inflections till he got it sounding good.

'Get your lovely roses, only sixpence a bunch,' he said.

'Ah no, son,' said Molly, 'we'll have to get a shilling for a half-dozen of these. They take a lot of making, and we have to buy paper and wax and gold paint, so you won't make any money selling a half-dozen of these boyos for sixpence.'

'I didn't say a half-dozen, Mother,' said Liam. 'I said

a bunch, and that'll be the little bunch of three here at the back of the stall. If ya want the big bunch of six at the front that you have in your hand now, sir, well they'll be going cheap for a shilling to you, sir,' he said.

Mary smiled at him and said, 'Well now, Mother, that's the lad you trained yourself, sure he'd put legs under hens, so he would. But okay, the proof of the pudding is in the eating. Let's see how we can make them, for how much, and how we can sell them, and for how much.'

'I think this might work, Ma,' said Liam. 'You can't get fresh flowers in the markets. It's only fruit and vegetables our farmers grow. To bring the flowers from Holland costs a fortune, and they're nearly dead and withered in the five days it takes to get them here.'

They set to work. Bought sheets of crêpe paper and cut them into four strips. Cut the edge of the paper into a series of curves, then press a spoon along the edge of the curves and they curl back into petals. Fold the paper into a bun and with the curled curves spread out you had the petals of the pink rose. Tie the stem with a light piece of wire. Dip the rose into a bowl of hot melted candle-wax, which hardened quickly, to preserve the rose and give it longevity. Then a dab of gold paint on each petal. Tie the rose with its stem wire to a twig of green-leaved hedge, and bingo, you've got an artificial rose.

The first evening they made four dozen between them and gathered them into four bunches of three, giving these smaller bunches extra greenery to fluff them out in the greaseproof wrapping paper. Plus they made six bunches of six roses, which looked really well. The next day they brought them to the Lane, with Mother

Darcy trying her best. Not one bunch did they sell. Nor the next day. Nor the next.

'Well, I suppose that idea didn't work,' said Mother Darcy at the kitchen table that night. 'We've lost nothing except our time, which would be gone now anyway. So we've learned something, son, haven't we. We've learned that the Irish won't buy artificial flowers.' Liam was thinking about what she'd said. The Ma was looking at Liam. Liam looked at the Ma.

'You pair are at it again, Mary,' Mother Darcy said, 'playing them games of yours.'

'What are you thinking, Liam?' asked Mary.

'That Mother Darcy is very wise about time: once it's gone, you never get it back,' he replied. 'But she might not be right about the flowers. Look at them there in the vase on the window. They look terrific. You'd swear they were the real McCoy from a distance, and they'll last forever. Just to replace the greenery every few weeks, and that's easy. We'll keep trying.' Liam even brought the flowers in his fruit basket along the cinema queues but still no takers.

But then it happened. He was walking back up O'Connell Street to Molly at the Rotunda Cinema one evening when he was bumped from behind by a young man in a hurry.

'Oops, I'm sorry,' said the guy, 'I didn't see . . . ', and he stopped. He was looking at the flowers. 'Are they for sale?' he asked.

'They are of course,' Liam said, taking the big bunch out of the basket. 'Pure handmade roses, with specially scented wax preservative, gilded petals, and guaranteed to stay as fresh as they are now for at least three months, sir.'

The fella was pulling his money out of his pocket. 'Just what I need to save my bacon. The wife just had our new baby today and she likes roses. Didn't know you could get something like these at this time of year. They look terrific, she'll love them. Will this two shillings be enough?' he said.

Liam couldn't believe his ears. He was tempted to say just about but instead said, 'It is, sure, and you get sixpence change as well.' But the fella took the flowers and dashed off, saying, 'Ya saved me life, so just keep the change.' Liam got back and Mother Darcy spotted the bunch of flowers missing.

'Did you give them away, or did someone rob a bunch on ya?' she asked.

'No, Mother,' said Liam. 'I have sold the first bunch after two weeks and I think I have an idea to sell the rest of them.'

There was a meeting around Mother Darcy's kitchen table that evening. The Ma was smiling. 'Well, Liam, the Mother says you have an idea for the flowers,' she said.

'Yes, Ma,' Liam said. 'No one is buying flowers from us at a fruit stall or on a picture-house queue. So we have to think of a place we could sell them.'

The Ma was looking at him. 'Go on,' she said.

'A place, Ma, where the only thing on your mind is someone else, not yourself,' he said. 'A place where someone you love is, and you want to make them feel better.'

The Ma laughed. 'I don't believe it,' she said, 'you're right. Why didn't we think of that before?'

Mother Darcy was perplexed. 'You're at your mind games again. Where is it you're talking about?'

And Mary answered. 'Outside a hospital, Mother.'

'Let's make it one better, Ma,' Liam said. 'How about outside a maternity hospital? How about the Rotunda Maternity Hospital beside us?' They laughed together.

'Under our noses and we couldn't see it,' said Mary. 'A great idea, son.'

'For a minute I thought you were talking about a cemetery,' Mother Darcy said.

Mary looked at Liam. 'Now, Mother Darcy,' she said, 'why didn't we think of that? Of course, and they'll last forever at the graveside, just need the greenery changed. I think we're just starting a new line for ya, Mother.'

And right she was. Mother Darcy took her basket of flowers down to the door of the maternity hospital for visiting hour every evening. Sold the lot. Twenty bunches one evening. Liam got down from his paper-selling to the picture house in time to let the Mother handle her flower business. On Sunday morning she rambled up to Glasnevin Cemetery, where she sold another thirty bunches.

Every one of the Cullen children joined in making the flowers. Like a production line. Rita cut the wire into lengths, Vera cut and curved the crêpe paper, Molly dipped the wax and gilded the rose, Liam twisted the rose stem on to the green-leaved twig, and the Ma made up the bundles. Big Bob wasn't too happy about his drinking table being confiscated every evening.

'Begorra, I'll turn into a culchie so I will, coming home every evening to green twigs and flowers all over the place. Might as well be in a field,' he said. But for a number of years Mother Darcy's flower business thrived, until refrigeration trucks came along and real flowers arrived in Dublin.

The Mitchell's rosary-beads girls, with Aunt Angela Darcy,
Liam's godmother, on the extreme right

*

Alex Mitchell's rosary-bead factory had hundreds of girls
making rosary beads to help Christians pray all over the
world. There was a terrible smell from the factory when
the girls were boiling the cows' horns. That's right.
Made out of cows' horns the beads were. The boiling
softened the horns so the cutting machine could extract
little round balls of horn. Then the spike machine stuck
a hole through the middle of the ball. The balls were
run through a dying machine. Different colour every
day. Some left natural. The drying machine hardened
the beads. The polishing machine gave them a shiny
gloss. The machines in rows worked by the girls, who
wore white coveralls with a big loose white hat over
their heads to keep the smell of the horns off their hair.
Hundreds of coloured shiny beads with a hole in the
centre poured into the collecting vat.

Buckets full of beads were given to the 'decade girls', who lined up at the workbench with their pliers and a roll of fine wire. Thread the wire through the bead, then cut the wire and make a little hook with your pliers. Attach another piece of wire and thread another bead. Cut and hook again. Until you had a string of ten beads. A decade of the Rosary. Drop the decade into your finishing tray and start again. You were paid by the decade, at twopence a pop. Rita was able to do sixty decades a day and could make about three pounds a week. The really fast, experienced girls could do double that. They were like lightning with the pliers.

The decades were collected every hour and taken to the finishing room, where five decades were attached together in a circle. One larger single bead separated each decade. Attached to another five-beaded string with a silver or horn crucifix dangling from the end. All designed to help the faithful meditate on the Mysteries of the Rosary. The Five Joyful, the Five Sorrowful and the Five Glorious Mysteries. Ten Hail Marys in each decade. The one Our Father in between, Hail Holy Queen at the end. The Rosary was said every day in every Catholic home in Ireland, so lots of rosary beads were needed. And Mitchell's were into exports too.

The work was boring. So the girls gossiped. About who was doing a line with whom. Which girl was seen in Lovers' Row at the Rotunda last night. Monica was seen with a fella who lived out in Donnycarney. Kissing and cuddling in the doorway at the bus stop in Abbey Street.

'I saw ya saying goodnight to him, so I did. And him with his hand up yar blouse. And it wasn't yar rosary beads he was fiddling with.'

And they sang. Every song ever written. Taking it in turns, with everyone joining in the chorus. Old man Mitchell was a gentleman. Always smiling. Always stopped to have a word with the girls. Knew most of them. Gave a few pounds' bonus at Christmas.

Young Alex Mitchell came in to learn the ropes. Tall, blond and handsome, he was, with lovely white teeth. Great charmer. Drove an Austin Healy open-topped sports car and dressed impeccably in Louis Copeland suits. Handmade shoes from Barry's of Capel Street and handmade shirts too from Charvet in Paris. Nothing but the best for the young Mister Alex.

The girls were all in love with him. The oohs and aahs and wolf whistles would bring the factory to a halt when he walked through. He was a good businessman too. Brought in new equipment and got new business from all over the world. Developed contacts with the Irish missionaries everywhere. The factory was working flat-out.

One day Liam went down to Mitchell's with the lunch bag for Rita. Late she was getting up that morning, so she'd run off without it. Liam saw the busy factory. All go, go, go.

'We've never been so busy, Liam,' said the van-driver to him. 'I'm delivering double last year, so I am. We're all run off our feet. It's crazy.'

'That's good news, Mister O'Leary,' Liam replied. 'Means more jobs for more girls.' O'Leary shook his head.

'No it doesn't, Liam. They've no space to expand here. And the Corporation won't let them put in another boiling vat for the horns. The Peggy Dell, ya know. Everyone is complaining about the smell. And Alex is not moving out to them new factories in the suburbs. Cost too much, he says. We just have to keep getting a quart out of a pint pot here.'

Liam got thinking about it. Came up with an idea. Ran it past the Ma. They went over to have a chat with Aunt Angela and Rita in Mother Darcy's. Liam made the spiel.

'I was down in the factory last week,' he said, 'and it's bursting at the seams. Too many orders and not enough girls to make the decades. Factory's only working from eight to six because of Corporation regulations in the inner city. They need to produce more beads but can't put in another smelly boiling vat. So there are two answers. First, get the abattoir that supplies the horns to do the boiling. Deliver the horns softened ready to cut into beads.'

'So what then,' said Aunt Angela. 'We'll have double the beads but we can't fit in any more girls. As it is we're jamarooneyed. How can we make more decades? That's the real question.'

'And the answer to that is simple too,' said Liam. 'We've just put the boiling vat somewhere else, so let's put the decade-making somewhere else. Somewhere else like right here at this table. You only need a bag of beads, a roll of wire and a pliers. The five of us could be working here tonight at twopence a decade. Six shillings an hour between us, we could get. Bring the decades into the factory every morning. No extra factory cost for Mister Mitchell.'

So Aunt Angela had a chat with Mister Alex. And Mister Mitchell said yes. Give it a go. And every evening Molly's table became a rosary-bead factory. Cut and hook. Cut and hook. Even with gloves, the pliers and wire cut into your fingers. Cuts and calluses. Everyone had a go at making the rosary beads. If ya had nothin' to do, it was over to Mother Darcy. Put ya on the beads or the flowers, she would.

Big Bob wasn't amused. 'Between the rosary beads and the bleedin' flowers, this house is like a funeral parlour. Afraid to have a sleep, I am, in case I wake up in Heaven, and that's a fact. And we all want to go to Heaven – but not yet,' Bob said, as he headed off to the pub for a few pints of Guinness and left the inner-city cottage industry working away.

17

ALFIE BYRNE
A FRIEND FOR LIFE

Alfie Byrne pulled up on his motor scooter at Cole's Lane one Saturday. 'Lovely apples, Mary,' he said. 'Let me have a dozen. I hope they're sweet.'

'You wouldn't get nicer in Dublin, Alfie,' said Mary, 'and you can ask your pal Mister Nesbitt in Arnotts – his missus just got her second dozen a minute ago. How are ya keeping, Alfie?'

'Couldn't be better, Mary. By the way, do you know that the new flats on the North Strand are nearly finished? Beautiful, they are. Built on the old bomb-site where I stood with Billy Cullen and your brother, Big Bob Darcy, back in 1941. A terrible night that was,' he said, shaking his head. 'But I've just come from the new flats, Mary, and they're the business. Even nicer than the houses. Right here in the city, Mary, as close as Portland Row for you. Would you look at them?'

Mary was pleased. 'You know, Alfie, I hadn't given it any thought. I was so busy with this fella,' she said, pointing to the new baby, Frank, asleep in the banana box. 'He's my eleventh child, Alfie. Doesn't time fly. And with Rita fifteen now, we'll have to get more bedroom space for the children.'

'Well, Mary, you'll find these flats are great,' Alfie said, 'and I've got a hold on a few of them to keep especially for some of you girls here on the street with lots of kids. These flats have three bedrooms and a bathroom. I know you'll like them. The caretaker's already living there. Jimmy Slattery is his name. Drop down tomorrow and he'll show ya round. If you want one, over you go to me pal John Hogan in the Corporation and he'll do the paperwork.'

Mary slowly shook her head, a smile on her face as Alfie took the bag of apples and handed her a pound note. 'Not at all, Alfie,' she said, 'sure how could I take money for your apples when you've been so good to us. That's a little thank-you for all your kindness.'

He looked at her with a grin. 'But didn't I hear that young Liam is going to secondary school? Won't he be needing clothes and school books? So this pound isn't for the apples, for which I thank you. It's for the Liam Cullen Education Fund and you haven't any right to decline it, Mary,' he said. Leaving the pound on the board, he hopped on to his scooter.

'God bless you, Alfie Byrne,' said Mary, 'and my son Liam thanks you too. He'll be a credit to us all, so he will, Alfie.'

Alfie gunned the scooter. 'And don't we know all your children will be a credit to you, Mary,' he said, and away he went down Henry Street.

Liam and the Ma went down to the building site the next morning after Mass. Not a soul around as they went down by Shamrock Cottages right across from St Agatha's Church. The site was still protected by a hoarding but, sure enough, everything was at the final-finish stage. Grass seed and shrubs planted. Mary was impressed. I didn't realise they were four storeys high,' she said, 'and no lift. So it's a ground-floor job we'd want. I'm not able for pulling prams upstairs any more.' Liam was excited. The flats looked great.

'Pram sheds over here, Ma, loads of room for the stock and even my boxcar,' he said. Dawn was just breaking as they walked around, peeping in windows.

'You must be Mary Darcy,' came a voice from behind them.

'And you must be Jimmy Slattery,' said the Ma. 'Alfie Byrne said you would show us around.'

Jimmy gave them the tour and the Ma fell in love with Number 11. Ground floor. Near the entrance gate. Beside the pram sheds. Three bedrooms. Indoor lavatory. Bathroom. Hot water. Hot drying press. Fitted kitchen. Electric lights. Built-in cupboards and wardrobes. And only a twopenny bus ride to the city centre, and on the routes out to Dollymount and Howth too. Beside the church, the schools and her friends. A straight walk to the Lane. Still only a few minutes' walk to Mother Darcy's. Beside St Agatha's Church and the Charleville Mall Library.

The Da and the kids were over the moon. John Hogan got the papers ready. The Ma's pal, Lena Redmond from Moore Street, got a flat. Her pal Mary Sherlock, a Parnell Street dealer friend, got one. And Missus Boland got the last available flat on the top floor. Old neighbours together. They all moved in within a week. A separate bedroom with two beds for the boys. A bedroom with two beds for the girls. And even closer to the docks and Brooks Thomas for the Da. The flats were opened officially and given the name James Larkin

House after the militant workers' leader of the great 1913 Lockout.

The families didn't know themselves in the new flats. A playground on the front green for the kids. A quiet street at the back for football matches and skipping. A big factory wall for handball, courtesy of Harrington's Paints. The canal for fishing for pinkeens and for swimming in the summer. Loads of new pals. The whole mysterious wonderland of the Spencer docklands, acres and acres of railway lines and carriages ready to be explored.

Summer Sundays in Dublin were great days. A visit to Hector Grey at the Ha'penny Bridge in the morning. Home for dinner. Then over to Stephen's Green to feed the ducks. Sometimes the Da and Ma came. Most times Liam and Vera would take the children. The eight kids were a handful and they had to go the long route too. Over Butt Bridge, left into Townsend Street, over to Westland Row, up Merrion Square into Ely Place, into the Green. No way could they take the simple route down O'Connell Street and up Grafton Street to the Green. Why? Because you'd have to walk along the front gates of Trinity College. Last bastion of English Protestantism in the Republic of Ireland. Perverse English schooling. Hadn't Archbishop John Charles McQuaid decreed that no Catholic could go near the place. Excommunicated you'd be if you looked at it. So the family took the scenic route. The Ma and Da would have a snooze at home. Little rest. *Sos beag.* Door locked.

In the really hot weather it was out to Dollymount for the day. Straight after Mass. The family walking along the Clontarf promenade thronged with working-class people on the way to Dollyer. Liam ran ahead with his boxcar of fruit. Set up the Ma's stall on the grass patch just at the entrance to the wooden bridge. Apples, bananas, oranges and pears. No trouble selling juicy fruit on a hot Sunday.

When the Ma arrived, Liam went over the bridge, right down to the dunes on the back beach. Here he had a forty-five-gallon oil drum stashed. The inside of the drum he had polished and burnished. Set it up on two big stones. Filled it with buckets of water from the toilet tap and lit a turf fire under the drum. Boiled in about two hours.

'Threepence a quart of hot water. Enjoy a pot of tea by the sea', was the spiel.

The Dublin housewives brought their teapots and a

Liam, as a sixteen-year-old, holding baby Aidan as he organises the kids for a walk up to Stephens Green. Noel is in his Army Reserve uniform.

packet of tea with them to Dollymount. Liam supplied the hot water. Fill a need. Go where the people are. Most Sundays he'd sell about twenty gallons of water. At one shilling a gallon it was another pound for the Ma, and no cost output. Liam had the younger ones picking winkles on the rocks and cooked a couple of buckets of winkles in the last of the hot water. Home with them in the boxcar. Sell the winkles easy in the pubs for twopence a glass and make another five shillings out of that. Fruit, hot water and winkles. At Dublin's best-known beach.

It was also Liam's first introduction to the formalities of the golfing fraternity. Royal Dublin Golf Club was also located on the back strand at Dollymount. Very prestigious building. Lots of fancy cars in the car park. Gentlemen playing golf. One sunny Sunday Liam was approached by two men at his water drum.

'Excuse me, my man,' the tall one said, 'we have a problem with your smoke blowing across our garden patio.'

'I'm only boiling water for the tea,' Liam replied.

The short guy was impatient. 'Listen here, Mac,' he said, 'this is a nuisance you're creating. It's on private property. You have no permission for it, so pack up and get lost. Understand?' He was hopping from one foot to the other. Very excited. Very upset.

Liam stayed cool. 'Well, you're wrong about that,' he said politely. 'Firstly, this is public property – so public that every Tom, Dick and Harry in Dublin is sitting here today. Secondly, I have here in my pocket my Dublin Corporation street-trader's licence. Thirdly, I am not his man and my name isn't Mac. It's William.'

The short one blew a fuse. 'Cheeky pup. If you don't

get this junk out of here this minute, the police superintendent will move you himself. He's in the clubhouse.'

The tall one was calmer. 'Hold on, James, this is my
responsibility,' he said. 'I'm the Hon. Sec. of this club,
and it's my function to resolve commercial problems.'

The short fellow got angrier. 'And I'm the club
captain, so I'm getting the flak with this horrid smoke
blowing into the players' eyes on the eighteenth,' he
said.

The tall fellow was having none of it. 'Well, you're
encroaching on my responsibilities and I won't have it.
You stick to the golf and I'll sort this out,' he said. The
little fellow was hopping mad.

Liam had stood back out of the way. Let them at it.
'Here you are, Mam. Trupence a quart of water for the
tea. There ya go. Thanks very much,' he said, as he
served a customer.

'This gurrier's rubbing our nose in it and you're
letting him away with it. Artane is the place to put
manners on him. I'm getting the superintendent,' said
the little fellow, and off he went.

Liam looked at the tall fellow. 'Is he calling me
names?' he asked.

'No, no, no,' was the response. 'He's just upset that
he lost the match this morning. Missed a three-footer
on the last green. Has to blame someone. And you're
that someone. Anyway, is there somehow we can
prevent the smoke blowing across the club gardens?'

'Of course there is,' said Liam quietly. 'If we got the
wind to change direction we'd be okay, but I don't
know how to do that. Even if I move somewhere else,
it could still blow your way.'

As he spoke, the wind did change direction and the

smoke started to blow towards the city. 'There yar, mister. A miracle you've worked.' The long fella smiled, just as he saw the captain coming out of the clubhouse door with another very tall very large gentleman.

'Okay, son, I'll head them off. But if the superintendent does come over to you, you'd better stay polite. Give him cheek and you'll be in trouble, licence or no licence,' he said, and headed over to meet them. Brief conversation, with the captain laying down the law, and the Hon. Sec. refusing to withdraw. The superintendent wisely hooshing both of them back to the club. Then he approached Liam himself.

'Afternoon, young man,' he said. 'Let me see that licence of yours.' He examined it carefully. Liam stood quietly. The superintendent looked him up and down. 'I don't think a street-trader's licence covers you for boiling water on Dollymount Strand and creating a nuisance,' he said.

'I'm very sorry about the smoke, sir,' said Liam, 'but the licence does allow me to sell goods in the borough of Dublin City. Selling water here seems to qualify. And the smoke is blowing the other way now, sir.'

The superintendent smiled. 'You're some boyo all right, and you might be right,' he said, looking at the licence again and giving Liam a closer look. 'You're not a son of Billy Cullen, by any chance? Free State army corporal, he was.'

'And that I am, sir. Liam Cullen from Summerhill. The Da was in the army, a boxer, works on the docks in Brooks Thomas.'

The superintendent laughed, and handed Liam the licence back. 'Isn't it a small world? I worked with your father on the Eucharistic Congress job in the Phoenix

Park twenty years ago. A mighty man altogether. And sure it's the spittin' image of him you are. Tell your father that Tom O'Donovan was asking for him. Garda Tom O'Donovan, as I was then. Good luck to you, son, and keep that wind blowing the other way and we'll all be all right.' And off he went chuckling back to the clubhouse.

Told the Ma and Da the story that evening. The Da remembered Tom the garda. The Ma looked intently at her son. 'What is it, Ma?' Liam asked. Games again, thought the Da. The Ma said nothing. 'Ah now, Ma, come on,' said Liam. 'I did very well. Stayed calm. Very polite. Even called the superintendent "sir". Got the other pair fighting among themselves. What did I miss?'

The Ma gave a big smile. 'You didn't miss a trick, son,' she said, 'but you learned a great Irish lesson. Some of the time it's not what ya know, it's who ya know that counts.' And she ruffled his hair.

18

CAN PIGS SWIM?

Mary Darcy's three brothers all drove a horse and cart. Big Bob worked delivering and collecting furniture for Pat Cluxton on Summerhill and for the pawnshops. Always plenty of work for the three brass balls. O'Toole's on Amiens Street, Frank Rafter's in Gardiner Street and Brereton's of Capel Street. Very busy establishments.

Uncle Martin had pigs. Kept them in the horse stables in Charles Lane. Back of Hutton's Lane off Mountjoy Square. Had about thirty pigs, and his and Bob's horses stabled there as well.

Uncle Ned worked for the Post and Telegraphs. Government job, it was. Driving one of the big twin-horse express carts. Fifteen feet long and six feet wide. Four-feet-high creels around the side of the cart to contain the bulging post-office letter bags. Uncle Ned sitting in the high seat like a stagecoach driver, wearing his big standard-issue high-collared raincoat. Big long whip by his side. Collect the mail from the post offices all day. Up to the mail-yard in Summerhill for sorting.

Every evening about five o'clock Uncle Ned would come clattering out under the mail-yard arch. The kids would gather on the footpath, all excited by the thundering noise of the horse's hooves and the banging of the iron wheel-rims on the cobblestones. Uncle Ned standing up in his seat, flicking his whip at the horses, calling them by name. Towering high against the evening sky as the horses neighed and snorted and pulled against the reins. Like Laurence Olivier in *Wuthering Heights* he was, as horses and wagon took off down Summerhill, heading for the Amiens Street train station with the bags, to make the mailboat to Holyhead. The kids would run after the cart and grab the rear end, sliding their feet along the ground as they scutted. A dangerous game. Easy to fall under a wheel. Angered the driver, who could flick his whip back.

'If I catch any of ya scuttin', it's into Artane you'll go', was every mother's cry. The threat of Artane would strike fear in every boy's heart. They'd all heard the fearsome stories. Held your bare feet to the fire if you were late for class. Took off your trousers and lashed yar bare bum with a cat-o'-nine-tails. Till you bled. Wrapped the smelly wet sheets around ya all day if ya wet in the bed. So only the bold and foolish scutted on the mail carts.

Uncle Ned Darcy was a handsome figure as he dashed through the streets of Dublin. Won the heart and hand of a dark-haired beauty in Moore Street: Anne Shiels from Cabra, who sold outside Hanlon's the fish merchants. Uncle Ned always had a few pence for Liam and the kids when he visited the Ma.

It was with Uncle Martin that Liam spent most time. Martin did his own bit of furniture-collecting during the week. But Noel and Brian started to work the street with the Ma once Liam had to stay in O'Connell's School until four o'clock. Late for the Lane. So he

An express coach like the one Uncle Ned drove

joined up with Uncle Martin to collect the pig feed in the residential suburb of Marino. Uncle Martin would head out at two o'clock to get the after-dinner slops. Irish people then had a full dinner at midday, with a light meal in the evening. Liam would follow on out after school with his boxcar to do a second trawl and continue collecting after tea. On Saturday and Sunday he'd be on the horse and cart all day with Uncle Martin. Out to Marino, driving the horse himself. Dashing around the rear of the houses. 'Any food slops today, missus,' he'd shout at the open kitchen window. Collect the slops in two buckets. One on each arm. Beating the competition to the punch. Matt and Des Kelly knew the ropes and they had pigs to feed too. (The Kellys went on to establish a carpet empire.)

The buckets emptied into two big metal oil drums on the cart, and when they were full it was back to the stables. Martin got a turf fire going and the barrels were rolled on to the two long stones with the flames under the barrels to heat and boil the food. Water and bran meal added. Stir it all up as it boils. While Martin organised the food, Liam had the shitty job of cleaning out the pigs. The pigsty was in two halves. Liam moved the pigs into the empty half, locked them there and shovelled out the pig-shit from the half the pigs had been in all day. Up to his Kossicks in the smelly stuff, which he heaped in the manure bay. Sold that to the oul' ones in Marino for garden fertiliser. When he had the shit out, he hosed and swept out the stable. Got the sack of wood shavings from the loft to spread on the floor of the clean stable. Wood shavings courtesy of the Rehab Sawmills in Portland Row.

While all this was going on, Martin was getting the food cooked, unyoking the horse, cooling and wiping her down and giving her a feed of oats and wet bran in her stable. Already cleaned and fresh with shavings since morning. The pigs made unmerciful fierce noises while all this was going on. They smelt the food, and the grunting and snorting grew to fever pitch. Attack the stable walls they would, trying to get at the grub. Eventually it was ready to serve. Empty it by the steaming bucketful from the barrel into the pig trough. They bate each other to get at the food and the grunts and snorts ceased as their snouts went into the food. Only sucking and chewing to be heard in the now-silent stable. Some of the timid pigs needed special attention and were fed separately from a bucket. You could always tell the timid pigs, the smallest, the runts of the litter.

Fires out. Pigs fed. Food all gone. Let them back into the fresh clean shavings to bed down. Check the horse. Wash down the Kossicks and brush the trousers. Bring in the cart, shafts up in the air. Douse the oil lamps.

Lock up the stable door. It was half-past eight, just in time to make it down to the Rotunda Cinema. Grab a fish-and-chip on the way. Patsy McCormack would give Molly Darcy's son and grandson the wink. A nod from Maureen. Slip inside, with Patsy handing you two half-tickets just in case. Just in time for the big picture – Audrey Hepburn and Gregory Peck in *Roman Holiday*. The Rome of Spartacus.

They didn't notice the people beside them slowly moving away until they were sitting in the middle of an empty circle as they finished their fish and chips. 'Mustn't like the smell of chips, Liam,' said Uncle Martin, who never noticed the smell of pigs. Who would, when you were up to your eyes in it every day? Into the milk bar on the way home. A pint of milk and a cream doughnut. Martin home to 42 Portland Row, Liam on over to the flats with the two shillings Martin gave for his day's work. Into bed dreaming of driving around Rome in an open-top Austin Healey.

Uncle Bob bought some bonhams. Young pigs. Housed them in a stable on the North Strand at the bottom of the cottages under the railway arches. 'Great stroke these pigs are, Liam, ya know. You could call them shit factories when they're alive, 'cause all they do is take in food and push out shit. We sell the shit for fertiliser. After sixteen weeks of feeding we get our one per cent. Buy for five pounds. Sell for ten pounds. With twenty of them here we can make a hundred quid. Less the price of the food. Ya can keep the money ya sell the shit for and I'll give you ten pounds for yourself. Is it a deal?'

'Sounds like I'm doing all the work and you're getting all the profit, Uncle Bob,' said Liam.

'You, my son,' Bob said, 'are forgetting about my expenses. My overheads. I've to pay the Widow Moran ten bob a week for the stable. I've to borrow half the investment money from the moneylender, and you don't want to know what he charges. But I'll tell ya. Twenty pigs at a fiver each is a hundred quid. I've got fifty quid. When ya borrow fifty quid ya pay interest of two pounds a week until ya can give him the fifty quid back. You're the figure man. Add all that up and I'm nearly working for nothing. And that's a fact.'

Liam liked Uncle Bob. A real tough guy he appeared to everyone, but the family knew he was a softie. 'Tell ya what, Uncle Bob, cut me in on the deal, fifty-fifty. No, no. Hold on a minute till I tell ya,' Liam continued as Uncle Bob raised his eyebrows and opened his mouth. 'Just listen and you'll see it's even better for you. We'll get twenty-four pigs, not twenty. We've twenty quid extra profit on the four extra pigs. You kick in fifty pounds and I'll kick in twenty pounds. You borrow the fifty pounds. After all your overheads, and not paying me for the feeding, we'll get about thirty quid profit each. You get your fifty back, plus thirty for your trouble. I get me twenty back, plus me thirty profit, and we've the fifty for the moneylender. Is that a deal?'

'Well now, son, ya have me confused and that's a fact,' said Bob, 'but if you have the twenty, I have my fifty and the moneylender gives me the fifty. I'll buy the twenty-four bonhams tomorrow morning and away we go. I'll leave everything else in your capable hands,' said Bob. And he got the pigs.

Liam borrowed the twenty pounds from the Ma and got out on his boxcar every day. The Ma put Noel on the run with Uncle Martin. Liam did his own collecting.

Not on Martin's patch in Marino but out further in Clontarf. Harder grafting. Had to do a bit of poaching on the Kellys. Duckin' and divin'. Wet winter it was too, so he had his sacks on. One on his head, one around his waist, and he was still drenched.

The pigs were growing and time was flying. Only one more week left before they went for sale. Twenty-four big fat pigs. Would make at least two hundred and forty quid on the Christmas market. Liam would be rich. But . . .

Then the feckin' bridge fell down, and he was bankrupt. A twelve-year-old bankrupt.

*

Liam had the day off school on Wednesday 8 December. A busy day on the street with the Christmas decorations. Liam was there all day. He'd got in extra pig feed the day before so he didn't have to do his collecting. Just went down to feed them when he got home that evening. Clean and bed them down. All quiet as he locked up. Still raining. Rain, rain, rain.

Home, off with the sacks and tumbled into a warm bath. Luvly. The Ma had a big mug of tea ready for him with a banana sandwich. He wolfed it down. The Da was saying nuthin'. Bit of a hump on, this week. Say nothin' till ya hear more. Liam headed to bed. 'Night all,' he said, leaving the room.

'Good night and God bless ya, son,' said the Ma, watching him leave. 'Night, son,' said the Da, not lifting his eyes from the *Herald*. Liam winked at the Ma. She winked back. Thinking, he's only a chiseller, but he never stops, working morning, noon and night. Liam crawled into the warm bed beside his brothers, toasty. Grunts and moans, feeling his cold feet as they settled down again. He got his torch out and read his book, the big army coat wrapped round him. *Dear and Glorious Physician* by Taylor Caldwell. Story of Saint Luke, who, Liam discovered, had never seen Christ. Lived in Rome, he did. A doctor. Only went to the Holy Land a year after Christ's death. Yet he wrote a Gospel. From the stories of witnesses, and it was identical to the other Apostles' Gospels. That just proves it's all true, doesn't it. And he fell asleep.

But not for long. It was the sound of fire-brigade bells that woke him. The Da was up and dressed. 'Come on, son, something's going on. Like the bloody '41 bombing all over again. Get dressed. Bring the flashlight. Let's go,' he said. It was about three o'clock in the morning. When they got outside, it had stopped raining. There were four fire-brigade units on Newcomen Bridge. Liam and the Da went over the railings.

'That's Nicky Bohen,' said the Da, and shouted, 'What's the story, Nicky!'

The uniformed fire officer came over. 'Howaya Billy,' he said. 'We've big trouble. The Tolka river has burst her banks. Pulled down the railway line at East Wall. Everywhere over the Newcomen Bridge out to Clontarf is flooded. Just getting reports in on the phone. Houses flooded. It's up to six feet high in places and lots of old folk in danger. The army lads are over there, some of your old mates if you want to give a hand. Have to go,' he said briskly, and walked away.

'Liam,' said the Da, 'I'll see what I can do over here. Why don't you check at the lock-keeper's gate. Can ya get a loan of a boat? I think there's a few down there.

A boat left stranded after the flooding in North Strand
in December 1954

That's Herbie Ellis up on the bridge. He'll give ya a
hand.' The Da went over to the army truck, where he
got kitted out with waders and rubber jacket.

Liam went up to the bridge. 'Howaya, Mister Ellis.
The Da thinks we can get a boat from the lock-keepers.'

'Yes, there's three boats I see down there,' said Ellis.
'How do we get down there?'

'Just follow me, Mister Ellis,' Liam said. 'Down the
side of the flats here and in through this gate. There's
Mister Cochrane. Can we borrow a boat, Mister Cochrane? It's for the army — the houses are flooded.'

It wasn't long before the army lads came down. The
three boats were brought up to the bridge, and off into
the waters. Liam was told to stay on the bridge. Too
young for the boat. The Da was in one of them. Herbie
Ellis was rowing the other, and he knew the streets. Bill
Murphy from Tara Street Station went off in the other.
The boats returned at intervals with rescued people on

board. Old people first, who were taken up to the
ambulances for hot tea and blankets. Off to hospital.
Other people came walking up to the bridge, wading
through the waist-high waters. Young men carrying old
people. A son carrying a mother. A father with his
young daughter on his back. Exhausted. All in bad
shape. Liam helped them to the ambulances.

He met the Da for a mug of tea at the canteen set
up by the Red Cross. 'It's bad down there, son. Houses
ruined. Old people in trouble. You'd better slip home,
check the Ma and the kids. I'm off on another run.' And
he hopped into the boat with a young army private and
off they went into the floods.

Liam realised it was getting bright. After eight o'clock
it was when he went home to the flat. The Ma had got all
the news. Sure Missus Sherlock could see everything from
her penthouse flat – a bird's-eye view of the proceedings –
and had popped down to keep the neighbours informed.
The Ma was coming out to have a look herself. As Liam
and the Ma walked up to the bridge, who pulled up on
his scooter, only Alfie Byrne. The Da was pulling in with
two more women in his boat.

'Well, this is some state of affairs, Billy,' said Alfie.
'Good morning to ya, Mary. Are you all right in the flats?'

'Yes, Alfie, we're grand on this side of the bridge.'
The army sergeant was over with a smart salute and gave
the Lord Mayor a full rundown on the situation. Alfie
decided to have a look himself.

'Sure, Billy Cullen here will take me in the boat,' he
said, and off they went in the boat. Mother Darcy and
Uncle Bob arrived.

'What about the feckin' pigs, Liam?' asked Uncle Bob.
'Are our pigs all right?' Liam had thought about the pigs

but wasn't going to ask the Da to check them out.

'Don't know, Uncle Bob. They won't let me on the boat. You'll have to get a lift down. Can pigs swim?' he asked.

Uncle Bob shook his head sadly. 'No, son,' he said, 'pigs can't swim. They can't feckin' fly either. So unless someone stuck a balloon up their arse for them to float up here, we are the proud owners of twenty-four very big and very dead feckin' pigs, and that's a fact.'

Bob was right. The pigs tried to swim but they ripped their necks with their front hooves. Drowned. All dead. Floating on the water. Some cows and hens as well. Army men loaded them into a truck. 'Have to be dumped to prevent disease,' said the army sergeant.

Big Bob sat in his sister's kitchen with a mug of tea in his hand. 'Well, you've lost twenty pounds, Liam,' he said. 'I'm down fifty quid, and I owe the money-lender fifty quid. That's the story.' The Ma went to the wardrobe and took out her shoebox, took out some notes, replaced the box and locked the drawer.

'Here's fifty pounds, Bob, for the moneylender. We'll have to pull together on this, so make sure you pay him off today.'

Bob pulled a face. 'Fair play to ya, Mary. I'll make it up to you and that's a fact,' he said.

'There's no making up at all, Bob. Sure it was the will of God. The whole city flooded. Another week and you'd be home and dry.'

Mother Darcy laughed. 'That's a good one. Home and dry how are ya. Listen Bob, we's better move before Billy Cullen gets back. We're in enough trouble without him having a row over you being in his house. Let's go.' And out they went.

The Ma looked at Liam. Disconsolate.

He felt her looking. 'What went wrong, Ma?' he asked.

'Wrong question, son,' she replied. 'God works in strange ways. Maybe he's telling you something. Try again.'

He paused. 'How could I have avoided the disaster?'

'That's better,' the Ma said. 'You tell me.'

He looked up at her. 'Could have sold them last Saturday, or I could have got a stable this side of the bridge.'

'If you'd known, son,' the Ma said. 'You didn't. Learn from this setback. But don't worry about it. It's better to try something and fail than never to try anything at all. That's what life is about. Trying out new things. Remember that, and never stop trying. Come on now, we'll go over to Mass before we hit the street. Thank God that we're safe and well and healthy.'

That Saturday Liam went on the Marino run with Uncle Martin. Saw the disaster area. People mopping up everywhere. The East Wall Bridge gone where the Tolka river entered the sea. Funniest thing of all was one of Mister Cochrane's rowing boats lying high and dry on the footpath beside a telephone box at Fairview. That night, Uncle Bob was philosophical. Had a good few pints on him. 'Two things to learn from this, Liam,' he said. 'Number one is insurance.'

'How does that work?' asked Liam.

'Simple. You pay a small fee – a percentage of what you're insuring – and the insurance company pays you the value of the goods if something like this happens. That's one to remember, isn't it?'

'I'll remember that, Uncle Bob. What's number two?'

'Number two, son, is perishable commodities. Fruit, pigs, cows, things that can die or rot on ya. Keep far away from them. Maybe it's them motor cars a young fella like you should be looking at. They even pay ya good money to fix them all the time. But them feckin' pigs are too much trouble, and that's a fact.'

It wasn't a good Christmas on the street. The weather was bad. The floods knocked everyone out of their stride. But the Ma hit the January sales anyway with a little bundle of notes out of her shoebox. She took Liam and four of the young ones over to Clery's on O'Connell Street. She was looking for the bargain winter gear to hold over for next winter. She never went in the front

Uncle Ned's wife, Anne Shiels, with Missus Mac-Donnell selling outside Hanlon's of Moore Street

door of Clery's. Like a railway station there, it was. In the side door from Sackville Place.

'Liam, you mind the kids here till I check the prices. Don't any of youse move from here,' she warned them. Liam knew this spot well. Beside the two roundy glass cases. Full of shiny silver pieces. The Ma always parked him here. He knew every scratch on the mahogany legs. The kids were amazed at the cash canisters flying through the air. Cables ran from every cash point on the sales floor to a glass control tower high in the ceilings. The cashiers then took the cash and the sales docket from the canister. Sent back the official receipt and the change. Cash control for Missus Guiney, who owned Clery's. A wonderland for the kids. The Ma came back, satisfied with the prices, and brought them upstairs. They all got new Kossicks. Two sizes too big, 'So you can grow into them.' When they got home, the sack of boots was put on top of the wardrobe. The kids wanted them to wear now, but the Ma insisted that the old ones would see the winter out. They did.

19

WHISTLE A HAPPY TUNE

The paper-ticket machine had been installed in all the Dublin cinemas. But it was phase two of the system that opened up the era of the ticket tout. Pre-booked tickets for Sunday night. Seventy per cent of the tickets could be booked on a permanent basis by writing in to the cinema agreeing to buy a year's supply for every Sunday night. Paying a deposit as security. The other thirty per cent went on sale on Thursday at three o'clock for the general public to queue up and purchase. Restricted to a maximum of four tickets per person. The word was soon out on the street. You could buy these tickets on Thursday and sell them outside the picture house on Sunday. For a premium. Not Hector's one per cent. You could sell the two-shilling tickets for three shillings. Liam and the Ma had a chat about it and decided it was worth a try.

It was a disaster. Liam went down to the Carlton after school on Thursday. Queued and got four tickets. Back of the queue. Four more tickets. Back of the queue again. Tickets all sold out before he got to the ticket box again. Two hours to get eight tickets. Then down on Sunday at five o'clock.

'Get your tickets for tonight. Only two left,' he shouted out, with about twenty other voices in competition. At half-past eight he had only sold four of the tickets. For face value. He eventually cleared the last four at half-price with the big picture about to start. He had a mug of cocoa with the Ma.

'Invested sixteen shillings for eight tickets, sold them for twelve shillings. Lost four bob. For six hours' work,' he said.

'You can't win them all, son. It takes a while for these things to settle down, and there's too many at it, that's what's killin' the opportunity. They all lost money tonight so they'll all give it a miss next week. Licking their wounds. I say we have another go,' the Ma said.

And they did. This time Liam cut down the queuing time. Mother Darcy got down at two o'clock. Liam, Vera and the Ma joined her at the top of the queue just before three o'clock before the ticket box opened. Four tickets each, please: sixteen tickets in one go. Thank you very much. And the Ma was right.

No competition on Sunday night. Softly, softly. No shouting or roaring. Watch out for the fellas enquiring for tickets from the ushers. Slip over quietly. 'Want to buy two tickets for six shillings?' Deal done. The tickets sold in twenty minutes. Bought sixteen tickets for thirty-two bob. Sold them for fifty shillings. Nearly a pound profit for the Ma. Not bad. Additional business to the street. Liam studied the whole Hollywood scene by buying two magazines every month, *Silver Screen* and *Screen Stars*. Read up all about the new films. Who starred in them and what the critics had to say. Helped him make the call on what pictures to go for and which to avoid.

The biggest winner he had was the blockbuster *From Here to Eternity,* the story of the Japanese bombing of Pearl Harbour. Bare-chested Burt Lancaster was the girls' cheesecake. The macho man. But it was singer Francis Albert Sinatra, in a career-saving part, who stole everyone's heart. His role as Maggio won him an Oscar for the best aupporting actor. A new talent. He had taken the part for a nominal fee of one dollar. Sinatra was back in the big time. No achievement without opportunity.

With his reading research, Liam was ahead of the posse with the teenage-revolution films. The sultry Marlon Brando in *On the Waterfront* and *The Wild Ones.* The sulky James Dean in *East of Eden* and *Rebel Without a Cause.* All sparked a new teenage dress style. Tight jeans. T-shirts. Worn under open-necked shirts with collars turned up. The demand for tickets was crazy. One per cent all the way.

Then there was the epic-film cult. Led by bearded Charlton Heston. *The Ten Commandments, The Robe* and *Ben Hur.* Three-hour-long films, premium pricing. *Ben Hur* won eleven Oscars, including best picture, best actor and best director. And a new Irish hero burst onto the scene in that film. Stephen Boyd from Belfast in *Ben Hur.*

The ads for *Dial M for Murder,* with Ray Milland, pleaded for viewers not to reveal the bizarre ending to their friends. Let them come along and guess for themselves. The musicals were great hits. *Showboat, Oklahoma, Seven Brides for Seven Brothers, South Pacific.* They ran for weeks and weeks. The glory days of Hollywood, helping the Cullens make a few bob.

The rock-and-roll craze was switched on by a school film. Story of a teacher trying to control the unruly, pushy kids. The world was changed forever when Bill Haley and the Comets sang 'Rock Around the Clock' in the film *Blackboard Jungle*. Then came Elvis Presley, followed by Tommy Steele in London. The teenage revolution. Teddy boys with long coats and drainpipe trousers. Duck's-arse hairstyles. But while the Cullen kids learned to rock-and-roll, 'There won't be any Teddy boys in this house,' the Da said.

Molly Darcy's favourite film was *The King and I*. First shown in Ireland at the Savoy. Bald-headed Yul Brynner exuding sex-appeal and regal masculinity as the King of Siam. Deborah Kerr the genteel English schoolteacher hired to educate his gansey-load of kids. The arrogant king brought to heel by the wits of a woman. Molly loved it. Went to see it dozens of times. And took a song from the film as a confidence-builder for her grandchildren. Got them to learn it off by heart. Words Liam carried in his mind for the rest of his life:

> *Whenever I feel afraid*
> *I hold my head erect*
> *And whistle a happy tune,*
> *So no one will suspect I'm afraid.*

> *When shivering in my shoes*
> *I strike a careless pose*
> *Whistle a happy tune,*
> *So no one ever knows that I'm afraid.*

The result of this deception
Is very strange to tell,
For when I fool the people I fear
I fool myself as well!

I whistle a happy tune,
And every single time
The happiness in the tune
Convinces me that I'm not afraid!

The Rotunda Cinema closed. Bought over. Got a complete restructuring. Got a new name. The Ambassador. Opened again, to a celebrity première of the Danny Kaye film *Knock on Wood*. The female star was Mai Zetterling. 'Showing off too much of her chest to let the kids see it,' said Mother Darcy. Too dear now for children. The end of the four–penny rush. A shilling for the cheapest seat.

Worse again, Molly was ejected from her perch at the door. Out onto the footpath she went. Indignant at first. 'Stuck me beside the bloody horse trough, they did. One of the horses got a mouthful of me apples,' Molly said. But she found her business increased. The Ambassador customers bought more apples and could pay more too. The customers going into the nearby Gate Theatre could see Molly now. More business. When change comes, you go with the flow. Every problem is an opportunity.

The opening night of the new Ambassador was a big affair. Tuxedos for the men and glamorous dresses for the ladies. Looked gorgeous in the new foyer, they did, drinking champagne, in the dazzling light of a huge, sparkling chandelier. First chandelier ever to be made by Waterford Crystal. And who came over to buy a bag of apples off Mother Darcy? The man himself. Alfie Byrne.

*

The Ma always worked to *the list*. Every night before he went to bed Liam wrote out a list with the Ma. A list of all the things they had to do the next day. Written on a page from Liam's schoolbook. Always started with the same things:

Mass
The markets
Kids to school

Always ended with the same things:

Mother's dinner
Rosary
Knitting

In between you had the daily differents to do:

Laundry
Electricity bill
Savoy tickets
Da's shoes
Pay Mister Keeling
Kossicks for Brian
Et cetera, et cetera, et cetera

The Ma believed in ticking off the list. Items marked

with an 'X' were the must-dos that needed her attention. Most of the other items could be delegated. Every day she took great satisfaction in having everything ticked. If not, the unticked item started the next day's list. Write it down and you won't forget it. She wrote down her day's takings at the Lane, in her little cash notebook, and her payments. Liam later learned that this was her cash flow. Income-and-expenditure account.

Liam took over Mother Darcy's dinner. The dinner of the day was put in a big soup plate, covered with another plate, and wrapped up in an old *Evening Herald*. And over he'd go with it to Mother Darcy. Stayed if he could, to hear her stories. Sometimes she'd read from her prayerbook. She knew every page of it off by heart. Pick a page, and Molly could recite it word for word. Looking at it without her eyeglasses. Taking the odd pinch of snuff. Cosy and comfy by the turf fire.

When he got home, the Da might be snoring, but the Ma would be working away, nursing a baby, darning, knitting, washing, ironing. Never done. Didn't seem to need more than four hours' sleep a night. A mighty woman! Said that 'Sleeping was the nearest thing to death you'll ever get, so don't do too much of it.'

The Ma had another trick with Liam. She taught him to remember every Dublin street by quizzing him at night. He had to name every street he passed going from home to the markets via Parnell Street. And the same thing for the route back via Abbey Street. Name every street you pass going from home to Clontarf. From home to the Phoenix Park. Watch the green nameplates everywhere you go. Remember it. Street quizzes every night. Where's Horseman's Row? Where's Fownes Street? Give me street by street on both sides of Abbey

Street from Capel Street up to Gardiner Street. Liam became an expert on the streets of Dublin. Got the Dublin street map in the library. Nowhere he didn't know.

*

The *Evening Herald* newspaper was already a great contributor to the Cullen household, with Liam selling them at Gill's pub. So it was a pleasant surprise to find the newspaper again coming to the family's aid. Selling predominantly on Dublin's northside, and positioning itself as the voice of the working man, the newspaper had a marketing support scheme, which emphasised its social responsibility.

One day Brother Gallagher came into the classroom and introduced 'Mister Tom O'Rourke, from the *Evening Herald* Boot Fund, who is giving a pair of boots to the six most needy lads in the class. And thanks be to God, we don't have any shoeless lads in St Canice's these days.'

'Yes, Brother Gallagher, not like the old days when you and I went to school in our bare feet, sure these lads have it easy,' said Mister O'Rourke, 'so if you call out the six names, I have six *Herald* gift vouchers here for a nice pair of leather boots to be collected at Guiney's shop in Talbot Street. Free, gratis and for nothing. With the compliments of the Independent Newspaper Group, publishers of the *Evening Herald*, Dublin's favourite evening newspaper and the paper that all you lads should make sure you read every night to get all the sports reports and keep up with the current-affairs news that is so important for your success here in school. So make sure the Da gets the *Evening Herald* every night as part of your learning programme.' Young Liam admired the flowing spiel and how O'Rourke managed to fit in the name of the paper four times. He was a seasoned campaigner. But Liam was even more excited when Brother Gallagher announced the first name.

'And sure our first recipient has to be young Liam Cullen, his father on the docks, his mother selling fruit on the streets, and him one of ten children', and up Liam went and took his envelope and shook hands with Mister O'Rourke, who was smiling warmly and said, 'And I believe that you sell newspapers yourself, Liam, so make sure it's the *Herald* not the *Mail* you're pushing.' Liam understood. The difference between selling and marketing. O'Rourke was marketing. Preparing the ground. Planting the seed. Nurturing the young minds. Different from the hard sell on the street but all part of the selling game. And six kids in the class got Guiney's boot vouchers, which became a yearly ritual for Liam, and continued for his brothers following on behind him in Canice's.

The *Herald* Boot Fund was a great support for the Cullen family and, of course, Mary Darcy knew how to maximise the boot gift vouchers. 'Yes, sir,' she said to the young shop assistant in Guiney's shoe department, 'I know it says children's boots, but I can't help it if my young fella has size twelve feet now, can I?' And after a half an hour of cajoling the store manager, she ended up with a beautiful pair of black hobnailed boots, size twelve.

Outside, she said to Liam, 'Now ya see, your father gets a pair of boots that for the first time didn't come out of the back door of the Griffith Barracks quartermaster's store. These are the real McCoy, and worth thirty shillings any Monday morning at O'Toole's pawnshop. May Jesus, Mary and Holy Saint Joseph always look after them wonderful people in the *Evening Herald*, and never let me see any other newspaper in my house again.' And so it went on for many years. The Ma became adept at changing the vouchers for all types of goods – trousers and shirts, blouses and skirts for the girls. Even cash on some occasions. And the *Evening Herald* became the newspaper of choice for all the Cullens, clearly showing to Liam the power of marketing and giving him his first exposure to the principle of how social responsibility works for the giver as well as the receiver.

Every day when Mary bought the supply of newspapers in Prince's Street, she always got a quantity of unsold newspapers from yesterday's returns. These came up to the Cullen household, where every night Liam used his school ruler to cut them up into eight-inch squares. With a hammer and nail he made a hole in the top left-hand corner of a one-inch block of these newspaper squares. Ran a piece of string through the hole, and down to their indoor lavatory to tie the string to its hook. He always did a block of squares for Mother Darcy too. So as well as being the best-read paper on the northside, the *Herald* served another purpose in many homes, as the cheapest toilet paper you could buy.

It was Mother Darcy who first introduced Liam to the Celtic Warriors. 'You have the name, me son,' she said, 'of the greatest warrior in the history of all Ireland. The famous CuCullen. Chief and hero of the Red Branch Knights of Ulster. The bravest man ever to walk our lands, and his blood flows in your veins. His courage is in your heart. His strength is in your body.' These were wonderful words for a young boy to hear, sitting at the turf fire with his grandmother.

Mother Darcy painted the picture in his mind of Cu-Cullen single-handedly defeating hundreds of warriors with his sword and spear. How he could run faster than the wind. How he fought the troops of Queen Maeve of Connaught to win back the Black Bull of Cooley. How he was mortally wounded in battle, but tied himself to a tree rather than fall dead on the battlefield.

'For three days the enemy kept away until the raven dropped on his shoulder, to show it was a dead man they feared.' She spoke slowly and with great emphasis and Liam was quivering as he listened, seeing the faraway look in her eyes. She put her hand on his shoulder and looked piercingly at the young fella.

'That's why you need never fear any man. Always remember that. You'll never meet a man better than ya because you are strong in mind and body. You have a great heart and you must always do what's right. You're named William after your father, and that name means 'protector'. Your second name is Patrick, after the saint who brought Christianity to the Irish people. You have the responsibility to protect your family, your brothers and sisters, because you are the eldest son and you have the warrior blood in ya.' She raised her right hand and dipped it into the black embers in the fireplace, and with her thumb made the sign of the cross on his forehead. Like the priest on Ash Wednesday.

'When God is with you, Liam, it doesn't matter who is against you,' she said, and she sat there with the boy, holding his hands in hers in the flickering firelight for a long few minutes. Then she ruffled his curly black hair. 'Now off ya go and look after your Ma for me,' she said, and Liam silently left her and ran all the way home.

He couldn't wait to get to the library the next day, and read up everything he could find on CuCullen. Mother Darcy was right; all her stories, and more, were true. The young fella became a student of Irish heroes, adding Finn Mac Cool and Brian Ború to his list of Celtic warriors. He learned how Brian Ború had become High King of All Ireland and lived in a fairy-tale castle on the top of the Rock of Cashel in Tipperary. How he fought the Vikings and drove them from Ireland and died at the Battle of Clontarf a thousand years ago. As his knowledge of Irish history increased, the list expanded to include more modern-day heroes – Patrick Sarsfield, Robert Emmet, Daniel O'Connell, Padraig Pearse and Michael Collins. All great Celtic warriors who had left a legacy of freedom for the Irish people.

Liam's avid interest in Irish history gave him a strong republican bias. The school history books ended in 1916, when 'a group of Irish Volunteers took over the Dublin General Post Office in defiance of the British-government rulers. An act of treason, with the British army of the day fighting against the German Kaiser's troops for Europe's freedom. The Irish rebels were overcome and disbanded.' That was it. In the early fifties the Christian Brothers' version of Irish history ended with those words. And again it was Mother Darcy by the turf fire who filled in the blank spots, in her own inimitable style.

20

THE BELVO AND THE BRÚ

It was Tommy Sherlock who told Liam about the Belvedere Newsboys' Club. Tommy was one of the sons of Missus Sherlock, who lived in the same block of flats. Top floor beside the Bolands. Missus Sherlock was a Parnell Street dealer with a gang of kids. Had lived beside Mother Darcy in Portland Row. Always smiling. A great neighbour. Tommy was Liam's age and they played football together behind the flats.

'Ya should come down, Liamo,' Tommy said one day, 'and join up in the Belvo. There's table tennis and snooker, loads of comics and games. Come on down tonight and I'll get ya in.'

The Ma was reluctant. 'There's a lot of bowsies from the Buildings down in that club, up to all sorts of divilment,' she said. It took a few weeks. The Da was the way round her.

'They teach boxing in the Belvo, Ma,' Liam announced one evening. As if the Ma cared. But the Da did, and his head came up out of the *Herald*.

'Well, now, what could be better than that? Every young fella should be able to box,' he said, and hopped up from the chair. Taking up a boxing stance, he shadow-boxed around the room, both fists swishing as he flashed at imaginary opponents. Breath whistling out of his nostrils. Feet dancing, like the tap-dancer he'd been. Showing all the style of his champion days in the Free State army. Liam jumped up.

'Get your mitts up, son,' said the Da, and Liam shuffled around the room, with the Da's clever footwork cutting off his escape every time. The Da's punches stopping just short of target. Ducking and weaving and easily avoiding the young fella's wild swings.

'Bedad, Mary,' said the Da, 'he can move okay. I think we should let him get some lessons in the Belvo. Why not?'

The Ma had her hands on her hips looking at the pair of them, smiling. 'Is it Jack Doyle ya think you are, Billy Cullen, an ould fella like you?' she said.

The Da was laughing. 'Ah now, Mary, you always had a fancy for Jack Doyle ever since he bought the box of pears off ya for Movita that night outside the Theatre Royal,' he teased.

'It was the fiver he gave me that I fancied,' Mary replied, 'and sure you couldn't take your eyes off the tits of her nibs, popping out of her frock at ya.'

Billy flushed a deep red. Still smiling. 'Now, Mary Darcy, that's terrible language altogether in front of the young ones. Ya'd better tell Father O'Reilly all about this in Confession', and they both laughed heartily.

There was never any bad language in the Cullen house. The children never ever heard the big 'F' word. In a row, the worst adjective was 'feckin',' and the same situation applied on the street and in the Lane. The dealers were all Christian women whose Mass and Communion were the bedrock of their faith. And it was that faith that helped them through the poverty and deprivations of their daily lives. There was bawdiness at times, yes, but never obscenities, and never, ever when children were around.

'Anyway, Mary,' the Da said, 'sure it would be a good thing for Liam to learn the boxing. He will have to use his mitts some day on the street. The club is next door to the Pro-Cathedral in Marlborough Street, so I can drop him down and bring him home with me after sodality work. He can't get into trouble then; sure it's run by the Jesuits from Belvedere College.'

The Ma hesitated and Liam moved in with the ace card. 'And Ma, he said, 'the Jesuits have a great library in the club. Shakespeare, George Bernard Shaw, all the classic books that I'll need in O'Connell's. Able to use them for free, I'll be.' That was enough. The following Tuesday night the Da walked Liam and Tommy down to the Belvo. No trouble to Tommy to get his pal in.

'Liamo lives in the flats with me,' he told the Brother in charge. 'His Ma is a dealer on the street, and he sells *Herald*s himself every day.' Three qualifying credentials for a membership of the Belvedere Newsboys' Club. A club for helping the kids of the inner-city slums to get some sort of basic life skills.

But Liam saw straight away that the Ma was right. A number of the lads around the ringside in the gym were real tough nuts. Some he recognised as shoplifters from the Buildings and a couple he knew had been in trouble with the police. But the facilities were fantastic – snooker room, table tennis, reading room, two arts-and-crafts rooms, social workers in charge, a priest in the reading room. Some young students from the college were also on duty. Liam and Tommy were co-opted for the boxing class and found themselves togged out in white shorts and singlets, each with a pair of huge boxing gloves. The trainer was a young red-headed fella from the college, big as a house, who put them through their paces with the speed ball. It took a while to get the knack of hitting the ball, as it swung back to hit you if you weren't quick on your feet.

Big Redser was terrific at it. Tap, tap, tappity tap — he hit it on the button every time. The punchbag was easier. Big and heavy it was and Redser got them at it. Punching until they got tired. Then it was into the ring. Three two-minute rounds with another fella. Tommy was first, boxing Guggy Walsh, a small lefty they knew from Gardiner Street. Tommy was good, a very solid boxer who gave as good as he got, although he found it difficult coping with the left-hander. After the three rounds, Redser, as referee, held up Tommy's hand.

'And the winner is Tommy Sherlock from the North Strand.' Cheers from the fellas who knew Tommy, whose quick wit had already made him popular in the club. Liam was drawn against a guy called Dixie Dunne from Cumberland Street. He'd heard of him, as Mother Darcy sold clothes on the Cumberland Street market every Saturday. He had played football with him too on the street at Gloucester Diamond. It was an easy name to remember and young Dunne was a well-built boxer. Smaller than Liam, but heavy through the shoulders, and it wasn't long before Liam was feeling the power of his punches. Liam tried to keep him at bay by jabbing out his long left, but Dunne was very fast on his feet and with a feint ducked inside and caught Liam flush on the face with a quick one-two and away again. For three rounds Liam did his best, jabbing and swinging and back-pedalling, but Dunne was too good, too quick. And he jabbered away non-stop.

'Here ya go, Liamo, watch the left hammer,' Dunne shouted, as he ducked and hit Liam with a right to the chest. Then he smiled as he danced away, with Liam swinging after him.

'Watch me feet, Liamo, like lightning I am.' And in he'd come again with a one, two, three and away.

'Jaysus, ye nearly caught me that time', after Liam missed with his own right hook.

'Mind your language, Dixie,' said Redser. And Liam caught Dunne high on the forehead with a left jab.

'Is it two of ya I have to fight, Brother, with you on his side distracting me?' said Dunne, and in he came again, bang-bang to the head, and ducked away. Liam was exhausted for the last round. He couldn't believe that two minutes could last so long. He blocked and held on as much as he could. Till at last the bell rang. Liam had to hold on to the ropes at the end of it, totally out of breath as Redser held up Dunne's hand.

'And the winner is Dixie Dunne.' Dunne was fresh as a daisy, still skipping and dancing on the balls of his feet as he came over to tap gloves with Liam.

'Well done, Liamo,' he said. 'Ya gave me a few good digs but you're slow. Real slow. Ya need to work with the skipping rope.' Liam still hadn't got his breath back. Still gasping, he was, as he touched gloves and nodded his head, with blood on his face and singlet.

'Come on, Liam,' said Redser, 'next bout is due. Over you go to Brother O'Connor for a bit of first aid. You'll be better next time. Plenty of guts you have to hang in with Dunne.' Liam got cleaned up and washed and dressed. He had a bruised lump under his eye, a plaster on a cut on his forehead, and a ball of bloody cotton wool hanging from his nose. He was sore all over. The boys were gathered into the gym for the Rosary at nine o'clock.

Outside, the Da was waiting. 'Well you're a sorry sight,' he said. 'That was supposed to be a lesson, not the real thing.'

Tommy was quick to help. 'Liamo did a great job, Mister Cullen,' he said. He was in with one of the best and nearly took him out, so he did. He has a great left hook, just like yourself, Mister Cullen, and he only got caught with a few belts in the last round, when he was worn out. Needs a bit of hard training and he'll be as good as yourself.' Tommy Sherlock was one of the best spielers around. Butter anyone up, he could. Had the Da in his pocket. But it was a different story when they got home. Tommy slipped off up the staircase of the flats and Liam walked in to his Ma's kitchen.

'Jesus, Mary and Holy Saint Joseph, what happened to you?' the Ma asked. 'Were you not minding this young fella, Billy Cullen?'

The Da was taken aback. 'Now, Mary, it's only a few scratches; you can expect that in boxing.'

The Ma was having none of it. 'Don't you "Now, Mary", me,' she fumed. 'That young fella is black and blue all over. Ya should be ashamed of yourself, bringing him home to me like that.' The Da got the blame. Didn't get his mug of tea that night either. And Liam didn't get back to Belvo.

The following Tuesday, the Ma insisted he wasn't going to Belvo. Still had a black eye, she told Tommy. 'Anyway, he has a load of work to do on his new schoolbooks.'

The Da had bought home a rope and he had Liam skipping every night. 'You'll be fit for anyone the next time ya go into a ring,' he said, as he pushed Liam from twenty to fifty to a hundred skips. 'Ya have to aim for a thousand skips without a break, and not a bother to the breathing either.'

Liam started to run everywhere, to school, from school, to the Lane, to the market, back to the Lane, to the flats. Running, running, running. On Sunday morning he ran out to the Clontarf Bridge and home. And before long he was running to the wooden bridge at Dollymount and back. Fit as a fiddle. Called himself 'Taza, son of Cochise', as it was a common practice in the tenements for the young fellas to take the names of Indians from the cowboy films. Sitting Bull and Crazy Horse were the popular names. It seemed the tenement folklore was to empathise with the American Indians whose land was taken by the British, just as Ireland had been colonised. Support the underdog.

Liam had seen Jeff Chandler starring as the great Indian Chief Cochise in the movie "Broken Arrow". But lots of guys called themselves Cochise. Rock Hudson played the starring role in *Taza, Son of Cochise* where Taza could run fifty miles a day for weeks. Across America. While he was running, he talked to himself. 'Come on, Taza, your tribe is depending on you to save them. Faster, Taza, faster.' This was his way of pushing himself.

'Come on, Taza, you've to beat the bus to Nelson's Pillar. Come on, Taza, you've to get home before eight o'clock.' Liam burst into the hall of the flats gasping for breath. 'Well done, Taza, you did it,' he'd say to himself, with the Da giving him a wink.

'Did ya hear the news, Liam,' Tommy said. 'There

was a row outside Belvo last night. Someone broke a window and the rozzers came down. The brothers were upset.'

The Ma had heard about it. 'Now, ya see, the police an' all down. That's not very nice. I think you should go up to the other club in George's Street. The Brú Mhuire – the House of Mary. I know Missus Larkin's son is in there, and it's smashin'. Got him a job and all, they did,' the Ma said.

Mother Darcy was listening. 'Yes, I heard that too. They take the young fellas on summer holidays to the country as well,' said Molly.

The next week Liam and Tommy were enrolled in the Brú Mhuire Boys' Club, a Catholic Youth Council project in North Great George's Street. And it was here that Liam came under the wing of Sean Moran, a volunteer social worker and a schoolteacher by day in St Mary's School in the East Wall.

*

The Brú Mhuire became a second home for Liam. Up there three nights a week. The chaplain, Father O'Neill, was the administrator for the Catholic Youth Council, a plump, smiling man who managed the business with a team of voluntary workers: Sean Moran, operations director; Brother Cleary, Brother Kirwan and Brother Collins. The lads had aero-modelling classes, made leather wallets and lampshades in the crafts class, played table tennis, snooker, draughts and chess on house-night. There was a library as well.

Sean Moran was the dynamo in the Brú Mhuire. In his forties, tall and well-built, with a little paunch and baldy head, he looked a typical headmaster. Stern of face but with a great laugh and always ready to smile. As a bachelor with no family ties, he would jump on his motorcycle and go straight up to Brú Mhuire from school in the evenings. Organised the house-nights, kept the boisterous lads in order, taught kids to play chess. Hopped from room to room all night. Brother Moran saw that Liam had an interest in the books.

'I see you're living in the North Strand Flats, Liam. What school are you in?' he asked. Raised his eyebrows at the reply. 'Well, fair play to you,' he said. 'And you'll sit for the Dublin Corporation scholarship this year for a place in O'Connell's Secondary School?'

'I will, Brother,' said Liam. From that conversation Sean Moran took an interest in the young fella. Checked out his progress with the Christian Brothers. Got a copy of his curriculum and made sure the necessary school books were in the Brú's library.

Liam took up table tennis, with Brother Moran as his trainer. Moran was a great player. Loved the game. Used the Chinese pen-grip himself. All attack, never left the table to defend. The harder the ball was hit at him, the harder he blocked it back. No one ever beat him, from in the club or outside. He brought an English champion, Johnny Leech, up to the Brú to give an exhibition. When the world champion, Jan Kaminsky from Czechoslovakia, arrived in Ireland, got him up one evening a week giving lessons, with Moran acting as interpreter. Liam, Tommy Sherlock and Sean Treacy became the Brú's table-tennis team, playing in the club leagues. Liam and Sean eventually went on to claim the Leinster Championships in singles and doubles, with Sean Moran as coach and solitary cheerleader. And made the Irish development squad with Tommy Caffrey of Balbriggan and the Gibney brothers.

But it was the soccer that Liam loved. Started playing with the Brú straight away. His strength, size and enthusiasm made him a good defender, and he was thrown in at centre half against the Belvedere Newsboys' Club for his first game. It was Liam's first soccer match on a real football pitch. Played at noon on Sunday in the Dublin Jewish Maccabi Ground in Terenure. Kitted out with real gear, matching jerseys and socks with white shorts. Brother Moran supplied a loan of a pair of football boots. Newsboys versus Newsboys. All knew each other, all came from the same streets of the inner city. Bit of trouble to be sorted out. But it was shoulder to shoulder. No sneaky stuff. The match ended in a two-all draw. Liam had shown his fitness with some match-saving tackles and never-say-die chases. Shouting encouragement to the end. Brother Moran came up to him after the match.

'Well done, Liam, and you've just got yourself a job. Captain of this lot from now on, you are. Get them training in the gym with you, and keep up that roaring on the pitch. Just what they needed. A kick in the bum.'

Liam had to dash when the match was over. Bus to O'Connell Street, then run home to grab his boxcar and out to Marino after Uncle Martin for the lucrative Sunday after-dinner pig slops. Didn't get into the house until eight o'clock that evening.

The Da was delighted when he heard the news. 'Team captain. Great responsibility, son,' he said. 'Sure we could have another Jackie Carey in the house, Mary.'

'Ah no, Dad,' said Liam, 'you know I'm a Charlie Hurley fan. The King of Roker Park, he's the greatest.'

The Ma smiled to see father and son having an adult
discussion. Then made a face as she added the mucky
football gear to the sack of laundry. Extra work for her
at the Tara Street laundry on Tuesday. And five more
boys coming along behind. Liam noticed the wistful
look on her face. Felt her flush of sadness. She knew
he noticed. Stupid. She looked up at his concerned
glance, smiled and winked at him.

*

Liam was doing well at school. Even though the Ma had
arranged for his days off on Wednesday and Friday,
some of the Brothers resented his absence. But they
knew he worked hard at the reading. And it showed.
Great at Mathematics and English and History and
Geography. Good at the rest. Now he was in the
scholarship class. The cream of the crop. Preparing for
the Dublin Corporation examination. Entries from
every school in the country.

Only one hundred and ten winners. The prize for the
lucky boys was six years' free secondary education.
Unheard-of for a tenement lad. They finished school
with the Primary Certificate at best. Maybe got a place
in the technical school for a two-year carpentry or other
trade training course. Secondary school cost thirty
pounds a year. With the Da earning a hundred pounds
a year, and ten mouths to feed in the Cullen house, there
was no way Liam would be going to secondary school
unless it was on a scholarship. So he would have to win
it. He was released from duties helping Mother Darcy
at the Rotunda Cinema. Noel and Vera stood in for him
that year. Once he finished his paper-selling at about

seven o'clock, it was into the corner with the books.

It was in this last year in St Canice's that Liam discovered gymnastics. The physical-education instructor usually ran the lads through some callisthenics, after which it was a free-for-all football match. But a new PE instructor arrived, with new ideas. A vaulting horse and parallel bars appeared. Everyone was invited to participate. Liam was good on the bars. Strong arms from the Lane. But he loved the vaulting horse. Charge down the runway, hit the springboard and soar over the horse. Learning aerial somersaults. Full of enthusiasm.

At the school sports day that year, the team gave a gymnastics display in Croke Park. Liam was chosen for the spectacular finish. The seven-foot-long wooden horse with six lads sitting on it. About eight feet high to their shoulders. Heads bent down. Clear them with a dive, hit the shoulders of the last man with your hands, flip into a somersault and land on the mat. He had done it in practice. But it could go wrong. On the day, he waited as the lads got in place on the horse. The Artane Boys' Band was there. The drums rolled a fanfare. Sweaty hands. The crowd cheering. The Ma and Da didn't make the sports day, but his sister Vera did. He could see her in her blue frock, waving at him, the white bows in her hair swinging from side to side.

Don't think about it. Just go for it. He charged down the runway, hit the springboard, up over the lads he dived, with his arms stretched out, bent his elbows as his hands landed on big Jimmy Molloy's shoulders, over went his legs, pushing off into the somersault, to land feet-first on the mat. At attention. Don't move a muscle. Perfect. The crowd cheered. The lads dismounted and the whole team moved into the final tableau, with Liam at the centre, fellas on his shoulders, on his thighs, hanging out of him. The crowd applauded and cheered, with the band playing 'A Nation Once Again'. Out of the corner of his eye, with Derek Keogh's big foot on his shoulder, Liam saw Vera cheering, jumping up and down, waving a green-and-yellow Canice's scarf. What a great day!

Mister Stack was the English teacher in St Canice's. Not a Christian Brother but a lay teacher. A quiet, smiling man who loved his books. He took Liam under his wing. Unlike most of the Brothers, who were stern-faced and severe in their teaching, Mister Stack was friendly and funny. Always in good humour. Introduced Liam to Richmal Crompton's series of *Just William* books. About a bumbling schoolboy who gets into the funniest of scrapes. Reading them out loud in dramatic form, Mister Stack would have the class in tears with laughter. But he also did the classics. The Charles Dickens and the Shakespeare. It was Mister Stack who developed Liam's public speaking.

'Up here now, Liam,' he'd say, not using the impersonal surname, like all the Brothers did. 'Read out this chapter of *Oliver Twist*. Where Fagin is teaching the kids to pickpocket. And let me hear you put some real feeling into it. I want the class to close their eyes and listen. See the words; paint a picture in your mind. Come on, Liam, it's about tone, inflection. Put feeling into it.'

It was here that the young fella developed his love of Shakespeare, the wit, the drama, the wisdom. Mister Stack took the whole class one afternoon to the Metropole Cinema to see the Hollywood version of Shakespeare's *Julius Caesar*. Liam learned most of the play off by heart. But it was in *The Robe* that Liam fell under the spell of a great new star from Wales. Richard Burton. What a voice. Of thunder or of velvet.

Even when he moved on to O'Connell's Secondary School, which was just down the road from Canice's, Mister Stack would often wait for him after school. 'How's it going, Liam? I thought you might like this,' he'd say, handing the young fella a hardback edition of the *Reader's Digest* condensed books. Great reading. And one day, when he'd left school, Liam got a prepaid three-year subscription notification from the *Reader's Digest*. With a little note. 'It pays to increase your word-power and realise your potential. With fond affection, M. Stack,' the note read. And Liam continued his *Reader's Digest* subscription for a long, long time. A wonderful teacher, Mister Stack. A great man.

Examination time came. Nothing left to do except go do it.

'You've put the work into it, son,' the Da said. 'Up half the night with the books.'

The Ma gave him a half-crown. 'That's for your dinner. You'll get some fish and chips in Cerasi's chip shop,' she said. Big time this is, a ray and chips in Cerasi's. The exams were held in O'Connell's School. A big classroom. Hushed atmosphere. Strict instructions from the supervising teachers and Brothers. Exam papers given out for the first subject. Arithmetic. A doddle for Liam. The timeframe to finish five questions out of eight was two and a half hours. He did the eight and finished in one hour. Had to wait and look busy until time up. Checked and rechecked his answers. The bell rang, papers were handed in, and the lads burst out into the schoolyard, checking answers with one another. And so

The St Canice's scholarship class. Liam is at the extreme left in his gansey and corduroys. The proud teacher, centre, is Brother Gallagher, with Jimmy 'Elvis' Molloy to his left. Dermot Keogh (now CEO of Aer Rianta) is in the front row, in his Scouts uniform, next to Liam.

it went on for the week. Liam thought he'd done well in most papers, except the Religious Knowledge had some quare questions and the Irish paper was tough. But he was confident he'd done well.

Two months later, the results came through. Young Liam Cullen from the Summerhill tenements had got his Dublin Corporation Scholarship to O'Connell's School. Thirty-first place out of the top hundred and ten.

Molly Darcy gave him a pound. 'The first Darcy to get an education,' she said, smiling.

The Ma took the pound. 'We'll be needing that to buy school books for ya,' she said. The Da took him to the Palm Grove in O'Connell Street after Hector Grey's on Sunday. Got him a Knickerbocker Glory – a huge vase of ice cream and fruit topped with cream and melba sauce. Could hardly finish it. The Da stopped to chat with Harry Cavan, the giant uniformed doorman out-

side the Gresham Hotel. An old mate from his Free
State army days. 'Got a scholarship to O'Connell's
School, he did,' said Billy Cullen proudly. 'Education
is the way forward, son,' Harry said to Liam. 'Get an
education and you'll be able to eat here in the Gresham
Hotel one day. Now wouldn't that be something, Billy!'

*

Monday night was PT Night in the Brú. Physical Training.
Where Liam met the famous Tony Myles. *'Mister* Myles,
to you lot,' he arrogantly introduced himself on the first
night, 'and famous in the gymnastic world, which you
know nothing about.' Myles was a small man. Five feet
four inches. Black hair worn very long, like a Russian ballet
dancer. Built like a wedge. In his tights and singlet he had
wide shoulders, massive arms, tiny waist. The real McCoy.
The gym was equipped with a vaulting horse and parallel
bars, plus a boxing ring and punchbag. And Liam soon
showed the skills he'd got in the Canice's vaulting team.
With his new fitness, he could last the three rounds in the
ring with anyone.

Myles appointed him class leader, leading the way in
the exercises and going first with the new jumps. Myles
was a superb gymnast. In his personal workouts he did
back flips, double somersaults, one hundred press-ups.
He drove the lads on with his sarcastic disparagements.

'Come on Sherlock, you're like an old grandmother,'
he'd say in his posh accent. 'Give me fifty sharp push-
ups. One, two, three, come on, faster,' he'd say, and
drop on the floor and do push-ups beside the unfortunate chosen one at ten times the speed. Up and
down like he was weightless. Then hand-spring up with

a back flip, leaving his victim collapsed in a breathless heap on the floor.

Liam worked hard. One night Myles gave them a lecture on positive thinking. 'It's your mind that dictates your achievements. You can do anything you believe you can do, although I know I'm wasting my time with some of you idiots,' he said. 'Come out here Cullen, Morton and Sherlock. Line up here in front. Here, take this ten-pound weight in your right hand. By your side. Now lift slowly sideways to shoulder height. Hold it a second. Lower to your side. Slowly. Again. Controlled. Up. Hold it. And down,' he said. 'Just keep at that for as many as you can. And down. Slowly. Up again. Hold.' After six, seven and nine lifts the lads were goosed.

'Okay,' said Myles. 'Out here, anyone who thinks they can do better.' Kevin Lawless hopped out. Full of confidence. But finished at eight.

'Now, my young friends, the power of positive thinking. Next Monday night I want you to be able to do fifty lifts,' he said. Everyone laughed. 'That's all you useless lot are good for. Foolish, childish laughter. Not prepared to listen and learn from your betters. But before you go, let me say there's a pound note for anyone who does fifty lifts next Monday. Maybe money will motivate you,' he said. 'Dismissed.'

The lads headed for the shower. Liam hung back. 'Well,' said Myles, 'it's a laughing matter for you too, Cullen. I thought you had brains. Was I wrong? Wasting my time, was I?'

Liam looked at him. 'I do want to learn, Mister Myles,' he said.

Myles took a deep breath and sighed. 'Okay. Here's the secret. Listen very carefully. You did seven lifts and stopped. You didn't believe you could do more. You focused on how hard it was. I want you to come up here every second evening. Three times before we meet again. First time you will do fifteen lifts. Second time thirty lifts. Third time fifty lifts. That's it. It's easy. You've got to believe it's easy. Watch me.' And Myles picked up the weight and, counting to a one-second cadence, lifted the weight one hundred times.

'Don't even think you have a weight in your hand. Pretend you've no weight. Pretend your hand is empty. Convince yourself there's no weight. Don't stop. Just keep lifting your arm. Slowly, controlled, to the beat. There's no weight. It's simple. Just do it.' He slapped Liam's face. Hard. Looking fiercely into his eyes. 'Just do it, you little gurrier,' he said, and strode out of the room. Threw his cashmere coat around his shoulders, his white silk scarf around his neck, and swaggered from the club.

The next Monday night Liam did sixty-five lifts. Myles took the pound note from his wallet and handed it to Liam with a flourish. 'That's for milk and dough-nuts in the milk bar, Cullen,' he said, 'and I want someone in this class to do that every Monday. And get a pound,' he added. Eleven other guys won the pound before the summer break. Tony Myles, Ireland's gymnastic entrant for the 1948 London Olympics, had certainly showed some Gardiner Street gurriers the power of positive thinking. With his own brand of personal motivation.

*

The Brú had swimming lessons for the lads in Tara Street Baths on Tuesday evening at seven o'clock. Liam got home from school at four and loaded his boxcar with three sugar sacks of family washing. Off to meet the Ma, who came over when Noel and Brian got down to let her away from the Lane. The Tara Street laundry was a big red-brick building, full of steel washing urns, steam spewing everywhere. Long drying shelves to hang the washed clothes on that slid into heated slots in the wall. All the dealers used the laundry, paid sixpence an hour for the facilities.

Liam gave the Ma a hand, squeezing the wet clothes through the wringer, hanging them and operating the drying shelves. Helping with the ironing. The Ma took the boxcar home loaded with three bags of fresh clothes. Part of the weekly routine. Liam stayed on for the seven o'clock swimming lessons with the Brú. No problem swimming after his summer dips at the Royal Canal. But here he was learning to do it properly. The crawl, the backstroke and, toughest of all, the butterfly. He was never fastest, just like on the football pitch. But he had the stamina, never gave up, was a good middle man in a relay.

In the summer months, after the baths finished at eight, the Brú hard shaws moved down to Butt Bridge to swim in the River Liffey. The currents were strong at the bridge. But every young fella had to at least jump in off the quay wall near the bridge at the Custom House side and swim across the river to the steps at the other side on Sir John Rogerson's Quay. If you didn't, you'd better find another way home. Chicken, chicken, chick, chick, chicken. So Liam and Tommy did the jump together. A long, feet-first jump out into the current. Down, down, down into the depths of the water. Kicking out with the legs. Up towards the light above. Agonisingly slow. Kicking. Lungs bursting. Then gasping out of the water. Onto your back. Get the air in. Kick backwards, nice and steady, the current pushing across the river.

'Well done, Liamo,' said Tommy. Liam nodded, out of breath, and he wasn't rushing over to do it again. In time he did do the jump from the roof of the Guinness security hut. Graduated to jumping off the Loop Line railway bridge. Jumped. From the lowest girder. From a sitting position. Nearly drowned. Lucky to get out. Swallowed gallons of water. Cold, cold water. Never again.

But Tommy Sherlock was like a fish. One of the brave few who dived into the River Liffey from the top parapet of the Butt Bridge Loop Line. Majestic. His wet, glistening body seemed to hang in the air. Feet together, toes pointing back, arms spread wide. Like Tarzan. Diving in a majestic curve. Bringing his hands smoothly together in front of his head at the last second. Cleaved the water with hardly a splash. Came up quickly with a fast crawl and out onto the steps. Not even breathing hard. The group of onlookers clapped him. Liam shook his hand.

'Beautiful dive, Tommy. Like a bird you were in the air,' he said.

Tommy gave his grin. 'Fallin like a bleedin' stone, I was. Never want to try that again,' he said.

But Tommy went into the inner-city folklore. 'I was there the night Sherlock went off the Loop Line. The top bar of the bleedin' bridge. Dived, not jumped. He's got bottle, he has lee-a-roady.' He was the only fella Liam ever saw diving off the Loop Line. Yes, that's what he did. Young Sherlock. Tommy Sherlock. Dived off the top bar of Butt Bridge into the Liffey. Put that in yar pipe and smoke it.

*

In Tara Street Baths, having a communal shower was great fun. Gang of young lads washing under the pouring waters spewing from big overhead sprays. Pushing and shoving. Bare bums and swinging willies. Liam noticed the swimming instructor watching from behind the curtain of his changing room. Not just keeping an eye on the fooling and frolicking. Watching. Intently. It didn't seem right. Liam left the shower, wrapping his towel around him, into a cubicle to change. The instructor hadn't moved. Still watching the naked boys, with a funny look on his face.

One evening, when the lads were drying off, a big tanned man came into the drying-off room from the steam room. Very big. A giant, with a large white fluffy towel wrapped around his middle. The white towel made him look really brown.

'Hi boys, want some candies?' he said in an American accent. Real cowboy style. Just like Gary Cooper in *High Noon*. His smile was gleaming and friendly and the lads took the chocolates eagerly. Real friendly guy. Told them he was staying in the Gresham Hotel and had a taxi at the door if anyone wanted a lift. It was Paddy Walsh who broke it all up.

'Hey, mister, we don't go anywhere for sweets, right? We're going home to the flats for a football match. Now hurry up you lot, we're out of here.' The big man just smiled shyly and slipped away. Paddy Walsh had a gut instinct for doing the right thing. They quickly dressed and had a race home, which Tommy Sherlock won by a nose.

It was weeks later, after a PT class, that Mister Myles was giving the lads the usual hard time. 'Come on,

Treacy, it's power-skipping you're at, not dancing a slow waltz with a duck. Lift those legs, pump those knees, swing that rope!' he was shouting.

Then he turned to the rest of the class. 'You guys want to get yourself fit if you really want to make anything of yourselves. Look at me. No education, but I worked hard in the gym. Now I'm in films, a real movie star,' he said, and swaggered around the floor with the lads looking at him in disbelief. Sean stopped skipping.

'Yes, in the movies I am. *Captain Lightfoot* it is. Out at Ardmore Studios.' He paused for effect, examined a fingernail. 'Doing all the dangerous stunt work for the star. Spent the day falling off the rigging of a ship into the sea. Twenty-five quid a day, now that's real money. Few weeks' work on *Captain Lightfoot* and they're talking about a Hollywood contract. What do you think of that, Cullen?' he sneered, poking Liam in the chest with his finger.

The lads were dumbfounded. Could ya believe him. Myles sensed it. Took a photograph out of his pocket. 'Here, get a load of this. Yours truly and the star. A new guy called Rock Hudson.' And he showed them the photo of Tony Myles with the tanned American they'd met in the Tara Street Baths.

*

Every day someone was threatened with Artane. Mitch from school, break a window. All reasons to be sent to Artane. The Artane Industrial School, Marino. Famous for their Artane Boys' Band, which played at every game in Croke Park. Big, forbidding-looking building, run by the

Christian Brothers to discipline misbehaving young fellas. Tough. Regardless of how trivial your crime, you could be sent to Artane until you were sixteen and ready for a trade. The Artane boys were only let home for a weekend once a month.

Blinky O'Toole from up the North Strand Road was in Artane for mitching from school. When he came home on weekend leave, he was wearing a rough-haired woollen suit, big black hobnailed boots and a shirt and tie. Fierce respectable-looking. But feeling miserable, with very sad stories to tell.

'You wouldn't believe the half of it,' Blinky said. 'You get thumped with the leg of a chair every morning just to wake you up. And if you show any sign of resistance, they bate ya black and blue. They did me in on me first week. I closed the door with a bang. Disturbed a Brother who was reading. When I said sorry, he punched me. Just like that. A full punch to the ear. For nothing. Kicked me on the ground. Ya move carefully after that. Never look them in the eye. Do as yar told. Quiet as a mouse.'

The second time Blinky came home, he was in a bad way. Eyes red-rimmed. 'I can't stick it much longer,' he said. 'A beating for being bold is one thing; a vicious hammering for nothing at all is something else. Brutal, they are. They seem to enjoy hitting ya. And then at night there's other things going on. They hauled a fella off to their own room and took his clothes off and pulled the prick off him. Christian Brothers, me eye. Animals, they are. They should be shot.'

Liam couldn't believe this stuff. Unreal, it was. This couldn't happen with Christian Brothers. 'Why don't you tell the Brother Superior. He's in charge. He wouldn't let those guys do thinks like that.'

Blinky was blinking away. With tears in his eyes. He looked shattered. 'The Brother Superior is one of them. The leader of the pack,' he said. 'He chased John Joe Flanagan out of the class waving a hurling stick. We heard the terrible smacks of the hurley, with John Joe screaming. Taken away to hospital. Dead, he was. The brothers said he fell down the stairs.' Sad eyes, Blinky had. 'I'm afraid, Liamo.'

Liam was asleep in bed some weeks later when he heard a tap on the window. He swung open the window when he saw Blinky outside. In a terrible state. Black eye, blood congealed on a huge bruise on his cheek. Liam pulled him through the window into the bedroom, with Noel and Brian now awake. Liam slipped out and brought back a basin of hot water with a towel and washed his face. Put a sticking plaster on the jagged cut, with a lump of Germolene. Quietly. Don't wake the house. Talking in whispers.

'What happened to ya, Blinky?'

'They got me, Liamo,' he said. 'I was running to the chapel when I slipped and knocked over a vase of flowers. They marched me up to the Brother Superior's room. He gave me the leg of the chair.' He put his hand to his cheek. 'Nearly took the head off me. Then they held me over the couch and pulled me trousers down. Lashed me bum with the cane. Two at a time. I nearly passed out with the pain. Then that fuckin' headmaster takes out a jar of Vaseline. Here you are now, son, let me heal your sins. He rubbed the Vaseline all over me bum but then he put his finger up . . . ' Blinky broke down. Sobbing quietly.

'The three of them, Liamo, the three of them. One

after the other.' And with his arms hugging himself, he rocked back and forth gingerly on the floor. Liam didn't know what to say.

'So I ran away. Out the window. Down the drainpipe. But I can't go home. The Da will just haul me back to them. He wouldn't believe me. He doesn't want to know,' Blinky murmured through the tears.

Liam took one of the coats off the bed and wrapped it round him. 'You can sleep here, Blinky. Get in behind the bed so the Ma won't see ya in the morning,' said Liam, and tucked him in a ball on the floor. Liam didn't sleep. He could hear Blinky sobbing, but eventually the crying stopped. He'd worn himself out.

Liam was up at half-past five. Up to the kitchen past the parents' bed. Came back with two bananas, an apple, a mug of milk and a slice of Vera's apple pie. Woke Blinky. 'Here's something to eat. But be quiet. If the young ones see ya, they'll tell me Ma, and we'll all be in trouble,' he said, and as he spoke he heard the Ma at the door. Liam sat on the side of the bed, blocking any view of Blinky's corner.

The Ma walked in. 'Ready for Mass, son?' she asked quietly. 'Now you're up early, aren't ya? Janey Mac, the window's open. Sure Eamon is wheezing.' And she moved to close the window. Liam slipped in front of her and closed the window before she went behind the bed.

'It's okay, Ma, I've got it,' he said.

'Right, son, let's go,' she said, and walked out. Liam looked at Blinky cowering on the floor in the corner. Wrapped to the neck in the army overcoat. Face bruised, bloody and swollen. Blinky held up his hand with the apple in it. His thumb up. Mouthed thanks. Liam gave

him a thumbs-up, closed the door softly and went out
after the Ma. When he got back from Mass, Blinky was
gone. Never seen or heard of again. As if he had never
existed.

It was from Tommy Morton that Liam heard about
the other industrial school. Over in Galway. A pal of
Tommy's from Saint Joseph Mansions in Seán Mac-
Dermott Street was sent there for robbing a vest off the
clothesline. Sent on the train, to Letterfrack, in the
middle of nowhere. The fella was a great footballer. But
he was a tough guy. Bold as brass.

'Whacker took on the Brothers, gave them back cheek,
so he did. But they fixed him good. Used to lock him in
the shower, in the nude, with the cold water spraying on
top of him. All night. He still gave them cheek, and he
kicked the football through the class window one day.
They gave him an awful hiding with the hurling sticks.
Everyone heard him screaming. He was taken away in an
ambulance. Two legs broken. Spent four months in
hospital but the legs were broken in bits. He came home
on crutches. Now he's in a wheelchair. Doesn't talk. Just
looks at ya. Hasn't said one word since he came home two
years ago. So that's the story. Keep yar nose clean and don't
get into the clutches of the Brothers. Christian, me bollix.'
That's what Tommy said.

Liam had heard the terrible stories from Blinky's
own lips. He'd seen him battered and bloody. He'd seen
Whacker in the wheelchair. But he still couldn't believe
it. He was in school with the Brothers. One or two a
bit rough. Pull your hair. Use the leather. Yes. But
mainly decent fellas trying to knock some sense into the
lads. And a lot of unruly lads, at that. They gave you
an education. If you wanted it, that is. But Liam was

always wary. Told all his younger brothers, 'Never give back cheek. But never let them touch ya. Only with the leather. On the hand. And only six of the best. Any messing, and ya tell them you're going to get Liamo.' And they never had any trouble.

There were occasions in the church sacristy when Liam was suspicious of messing. Not with any of the local priests. Father Nix, Father Duffy, Father O'Reilly worked very hard with the community. Training the choir. Weddings. Christenings. Funerals. Confirmations. Communions. Confessions. Sodalities. Rosarys. Novenas. St Agatha's Church in William Street was a hive of activity all day every day. The busiest place in the parish. Held about twelve hundred people and was full out the doors for every one of the nine Masses on Sunday.

Liam often served at Benediction after the ritual evening Rosary. Ring the bell, serve the incense. Hold the priest's vestments as he held the magnificent golden monstrance on high to bless the congregation. The Ma always there when he was on the altar. Herself and Mother Darcy in the front row leading the responses of the congregation. Visiting priests often arrived to do this service. From a less busy parish. Or a training course for new priests. Gave the local priests a bit of a breather.

After the service one evening Liam removed his black-and-white vestments in the sacristy, said his cheerios and ran off home. He was to get a loaf of bread on the way and he realised he'd left the ten-bob note in his prayerbook at the church. He ran back but the sacristy door was locked. Liam knew where the spare key was hidden, so he opened the door and slipped in. Relief. There it was, the Ma's red ten-shilling note still in his prayerbook.

As he was about to leave, he heard a noise from the priests' changing room. 'Who's there?' he asked, went over and pushed the door open. The priest was in his street clothes, turning his back to the door. Young Jimmy Conway was standing there, still in his church robes, red-faced. Liam saw the priest adjusting the front of his trousers, pulling down his black pullover.

The priest turned to Liam. 'It's okay, son,' he said, smiling. 'Just giving Jimmy some help with his Latin pronunciations. That's all for now, Jimmy, you may go, and here's a shilling for some sweets.' Jimmy took the shilling and slipped past Liam. Liam looked at the priest. The priest proffered another shilling.

'Why don't you get some sweets too?' he said. Liam looked at the shilling lying on the palm of the priest's upturned hand. Shining. Glittering in the flickering light from the huge Benediction candle. Something was wrong here. He didn't know what. He shook his head to decline the money and turned and walked away.

Jimmy was in his street clothes. 'Are you okay, Jimmy?' Liam asked him.

Jimmy looked at him. Fear in his eyes. Red-faced. 'I'm okay, Liamo,' he said.

The priest was watching from the door. 'Goodnight now, boys. Hurry on home to your mother, Jimmy, it's getting late,' he said, and Jimmy went out the door and up the road like a scalded cat. Liamo looked at the priest. A big, tubby, smiling priest, who'd been there a few times before, from the Navan Road parish. He'd keep an eye on this priest if he ever showed up again. After that he never left an altar boy with a priest or curate in the privacy of the sacristy. We all go in together and we all leave together: Liamo's rule for the altar boys.

21

CHARLIE HAUGHEY COMES TO TEA

Around this time there was a row going on between Noel Browne, the social-welfare minister, and Archbishop John Charles McQuaid about the 'Mother and Child' scheme that Browne planned. Arguments were bandied about in the *Herald* about contraception methods, and the tenement women were gossiping. One evening, Ellen Preston, a neighbour with a dozen kids, was in the kitchen talking to the Ma in hushed tones. The Da was at the sodality. Whisper, whisper, whisper. The Ma stood up suddenly, surprising all the kids when she said out loud to Missus Preston: 'Look at these lovely children I have, Ellen. Which of them would ya like me to send back? And you can ask yourself the same question, Ellen. That's where I stand on this.' End of conversation! And the kids didn't know what it was all about.

It was Noel Browne who introduced the Infant Aid Society, with the help of the Quakers. Milk depots were established in the poorer communities and mothers with new babies could collect a pint bottle of fresh milk every morning for the two years after the birth. The Ma was a permanent customer, sometimes with two qualifying babies, getting her two bottles every day. The milk depot was in Killarney Street at the Five Lamps, and Liam would often get in the queue for the Ma. One morning the horse-drawn milk float arrived at the milk depot.

'No free milk today,' shouted the Merville Dairies driver. 'There's some row with the social welfare people and your milk is temporarily suspended. Sorry, ladies', and he clucked at the horse to move off. A big mistake, with Mary Darcy waiting for her milk. She grabbed the horse's reins.

'Do you think we can give these babies the lousy ten-year-old condensed milk syrup that's at home?' She waved two-month-old Marie at him under her shawl. 'What do ya mean, no milk? Sure you've hundreds of bottles of milk here in the float,' she shouted, with the other women gathering around, most of them with babies under their shawls, some even on the breast.

The driver shrugged his shoulders. 'There's some row, Missus Darcy. No free milk this morning. These are for me paying customers.' Like a red rag to a bull, that was.

'Paying customers!' she said with outrage. 'And you a neighbour's child, Jamesy Cleary. It's ashamed of yourself you should be. Your poor mother would turn in her grave if she'd heard them words of yours. Hold these reins, son,' she said to Liam, who took the horse's bridle at the bit. With the shawl tied around her waist holding the baby in place, she used both hands to lift a crate of milk off the float and onto the footpath. Then another. And another. She was breathing heavily. Jamsey raised his eyebrows, but said nothing. It would take a brave man to stop Mary Darcy and her in full flight.

'Now, girls,' Mary said to all the mothers, 'help yourself to this lovely fresh milk for your babies.' And they did. Nearly emptied the float. 'Jamsey, me ould flower,' she said, 'now that you've done your Christian duty and looked after the poor, ya can get your Communion at Mass next Sunday. And ya can take what's left of the milk to your paying customers.'

The rozzers from Fitzgibbon Street came to the door that evening. Tough men. The Ma denied everything. 'Sure, I wasn't at the milk depot at all this morning. There must be some mistake.' Not a witness could be found. A wall of protective silence around the community. Jamsey, the driver, said he didn't recognise the perpetrators and the free milk was back on stream for the mothers the next morning.

*

General-election time was always exciting. Banners and posters all over the place. Candidates out knocking on doors, exhorting the residents to vote for them. Pushing bundles of literature into the housewife's hand. 'Make sure you vote for me now, missus. Peadar Cowan is the name and this leaflet tells you all about me.'

And often the answer was: 'Well, yar wastin' yar money, Mister Cowan, with this stuff, 'cause I can't read.'

'That's okay, missus, 'cause all ya have to do is put an 'X' after my name on your voting card. Peadar Cowan. See it here: C-O-W-A-N, like that. And you put your 'X' after it. Like that. Thank you, mam. I'll say no more. No blather. Vote Peadar. Here we go.'

Vans and lorries and cars paraded the streets with

loudspeakers on top, from which the people were deluged with noise, music and rhetoric. Women standing on the street, gaustering under the lamp-post. The kids playing ball, or skipping, or swinging around the lamp-post on a rope. Colourful, noisy, exciting times, with the footpaths thronged with people, stopping to hear an enthusiastic candidate on the back of a lorry, roaring into a loud hailer. Hardly heard a word he was saying, with all the crackling, but it sounded dynamic and vigorous.

Haughey Boland, the accountants, had their offices on Amiens Street, opposite Tom Stafford's garage. Liam used to do the punctures in Stafford's garage some days, if it was too wet or snowy for the Lane. Got himself sixpence for helping to fix a puncture on a motor-car wheel. The mechanic took the tyre off. Liam would find the hole in the tube with a basin of water, clean around the hole and stick a big amber patch over it. The mechanic would refit the tyre. Got another sixpence for cleaning the reception windows in Haughey Boland's office every fortnight. Used a stepladder for the high parts. Got paid his sixpence from Maura in reception, who knew the Ma.

One day, Maura asked him would he put up posters on the lamp-posts for Mister Haughey. Running for election to the Dáil, he was. Liam'd get sixpence for every dozen posters he put up. Would he what?

That evening, with Noel and Brian in tow carrying the stepladder, he put picture-posters of Charlie Haughey up on every lamp-post in the area. And the next night, and the next night. All over the place. Six hundred posters.

Maura phoned upstairs when he arrived for his twenty-five shillings and a chubby accountant came down with the money.

'You'll have to sign the expenses ledger for this, young man,' he said. 'All matters of finance must be fully recorded in detail for the Revenue Commissioners, you know. I need your name and address.' Liam gave him the details, which he wrote down very carefully. He gave Liam one pound note, and two half-crowns.

'Now you must sign this receipt here, on the dotted line.' Liam signed the paper, which was captioned Expense Sheet. He noticed that under the heading 'expenditure details' it read 'replacing broken glass in reception window'.

'Thank you. This is your correct address now, is it?' he asked.

'It is indeed,' Maura said. 'I know Liam and his family a long time, Mister Traynor.'

'Well, that's all right then. I have to be sure all my records are correct. Correct to the last full stop and comma', and up the stairs he hopped, ledger in hand.

The Ma was delighted with the twenty-five shillings. 'Well done, son,' she said, 'and sure we'll all have to vote for Charles Haughey, now that he's been so good to us, won't we?'

On the last evening before the election, the candidates were out in force. A huge red lorry stopped at the footpath and a black car pulled up behind it. Out came a slick-looking young man, hair combed back and glistening with Brylcreem, wearing a shiny grey suit. Real mohair job. And up on the back of the lorry he went. One of his helpers started connecting the microphone wire to the loudspeakers on the roof of the lorry. Liam saw that there were other loudspeakers on the nearby lamp-post. Like the Corpus Christi procession day it was, when the music blared out of all the loudspeakers. Very clear. No crackling. Expensive gear. *'Amhrán na bhFiann'* they played, and every man, woman and child within hearing of it stood to attention. Not a move. All joined in the singing as the Irish national anthem rang out. Liam saw his father throw a professional army salute to the two tricolours fluttering on top of each truck door. Irish we are. Republican Irish and proud of it.

Liam saw the tubby accountant, Mister Traynor, take the microphone. 'Ladies and gentlemen, it gives me great pleasure to introduce your new Dáil member for Dublin Central. Your local northsider from this very parish. The man who will get this country on the move: Mister Charles J. Haughey.'

'Thank you, Des. Hello everyone,' said Mister Haughey, in a clear, cultured voice, and he went into his speech. Loud cheers at the great promises. More jobs, more money, more houses, more health support, more hospitals and lower rents. A great spiel altogether. Loud applause at the end.

Then he came down from the lorry and moved among the crowd, shaking hands. Liam saw Maura whisper to him. Haughey looked over at Billy and Mary standing at the door and over he came, smiling, confident.

'Hello, Missus Cullen. Hello, Billy,' he said. 'Maura tells me you are great friends of Alfie Byrne and Mickey Mullen, so I hope I can count on your votes. And here's a bag of sweets for this young fella', as he handed Liam a small white bag of Honeybees.

The Da was star-struck but the Ma was her usual confident self. 'Oh yes, Mister Haughey, this house will be voting for ya, and so will every friend and neighbour of mine, because I told them all to. Won't you come in and have a cup of tea? Ya must be parched after all that talking', and she opened the door.

He didn't even hesitate. Mister Haughey knew a leader when he met one, and he wanted votes. With Maura and Mister Traynor, he sat in the kitchen with the Ma and Da. The kids were hooshed out but the Ma pointed to a chair in the corner for Liam. So Liam listened to Mister Haughey as he thanked the Ma for her support, hoped she'd spread the gospel for him, asked the Da for his help in Brooks Thomas, smacked his lips drinking the tea, and complimented the Ma on her lovely home-made apple pie. He stood up to leave and shook the Da's hand.

'Cheerio now, Missus Cullen,' he said to the Ma, holding her hand with both of his. 'Thank you for the lovely tea and I appreciate your support. May God bless you and these lovely children you have.'

'Thank you, Mister Haughey,' said the Ma, and sure, didn't he smile and look into her eyes.

'It's "Charlie" to my friends, Mary,' he said. 'Please call me Charlie,' and he smiled and winked at her. Then out the door with the entourage. The Ma was thrilled.

'It's not often we get a charmer like that in the elections, Billy Cullen,' she said to the Da. 'I think we'll be hearing a lot more of my pal Charlie. I mean Charles J. Haughey', and she smiled, leaning her head to one side. 'Sure, that man has all the makings of a taoiseach, so he has.' She ruffled Liam's hair absent-mindedly with her fingers.

*

The Da was in charge of family preparations for Christmas. The multi-coloured Christmas paper chains hung from corner to corner of the living room, with a big paper lantern ball dangling from the centre. The electric bulb went inside the paper ball, which lit up brightly when the light was switched on in the evening. The Christmas tree went in the corner and the tree became more colourful as the slow-moving tinsel balls from the street were brought home. Santa Claus cut-outs were thumbtacked to the walls. Snow powder was sprayed over the mirrors and in the corners of the window-panes. Red-berried holly twigs were stuck over pictures: even the Sacred Heart of Jesus got his holly twig. Lots of silver bells dangled on strings of beads from silver hoops which were hung on the doors. A holly wreath was nailed to the hall door.

The Christmas pudding was made in early December. A huge thing it was, made by the Ma, with Molly Darcy supervising. Mixed in a big basin, using all sorts of ingredients: currants, raisins, flour, beaten eggs, spices, margarine, a drop of whiskey, all mixed up in the basin. The final flourish was a bottle of Guinness to brown it all up. The wet mixture was wrapped up in a muslin window curtain, placed in a big stewpot of water and steamed for hours. When it was considered cooked, it was left hanging in the muslin cloth in the wardrobe, where it remained until the big day. It developed a shiny, light crust that held the moisture in.

The Da was a great woodcarver. He made wooden presents for the kids. Cowboy guns, blackened and polished with Nugget Shoe Polish, the trigger painted silver, looked like the real thing. Wooden multicoloured spinning tops were made, to be lashed with a small whip. Hurley sticks. Dolls' houses for the girls. All were carved and painted with tender loving care. Liam got a magnificently realistic rifle one year that brought the rozzers down from Fitzgibbon Street. They confiscated it. All the boys wore army-style paper hats made from specially folded *Evening Herald*s.

Christmas Eve was one big hurly-burly shambles. Up at four o'clock. On with the Kossicks filled with newspapers to keep the feet warm. A sack around the shoulders if it was raining heavily. Bringing the stock down on the prams and in the boxcar to the stalls at the street. The dealers in the dark morning, all around the Primus stove and the huge teapot. Tea for everyone in big white enamel mugs. A hectic day at the stall, up and down to the markets for more fruit, or to Hector Grey for more toys or decorations. Selling at the stall. Up and down bus queues with the gear on a tray.

Running around the provision shops at the last minute to get the sell-off bargains. The cream-slab Madeira cake, the Oxford lunch, the corned beef, a few chickens. Turkey was a luxury, for the well-off. At about six o'clock it was slackening off, crowds thinning. Time to pack up. The Ma and the girls headed home. Liam, Noel and Brian packed up the last of the unsold stock. All the dealers shouted 'Happy Christmas!' to Mary and Molly and gave little gifts of sweets and lollipops to the kids. Most of the dealers headed into the pub for a refreshing glass of Guinness after a long day.

The Cullen convoy got home at about seven in the evening. A quick debriefing with the Ma, a rough check on the day's takings, and the money was wrapped in a sock and put into the shoebox in the wardrobe. The Ma kept a good few bob in her apron pocket. A dealer's speciality, the pocket was. An eighteen-inch square of tough sackcloth, covered with white linen, and a half-dozen pockets in various sizes sewn on the front. All the dealers wore them, with a light rope through loops that tied around their waist. Small silver coins went in one pocket, large silver in another, small copper, large copper, small notes, and 'the wad'. That's what the six pockets were for, and all dealers kept their money in 'me pocket', which they wore from morning until undressing at night. After the Christmas Eve debriefing there was always a quick prayer: 'Thanks be to God for a good day', and 'May the Blessed Virgin look after us through Christmas' when times were bad.

The older children had to head down to church for Confession, which was quick, with the extra priests laid on to take the massive crowds. The six Confession boxes in St Agatha's seemed to have revolving doors, chewing up and spitting out the faithful: doors opening and doors closing every few seconds as the priests forgave the nation to celebrate the coming of Christ. Home for the tea and a big banana sambo. One by one, the children were washed and scrubbed. The hair was cut by the Ma and trimmed using Da's old army clippers and a big scissors. The young ones were bedded down. The older ones stayed up, helping with the ironing of clothes, wrapping presents, finishing the decorations on the tree, cleaning and polishing everything in the room. Liam and the Da went out to bleach and scrub the granite door-step and Brasso the knocker, the lock and the mailbox. A big mug of shell cocoa and into bed, leaving the Ma and Da with the last-minute bits and pieces to do, into the small hours.

The household would be silent for a short while. But

in that silence there was an expectancy. The kids dreaming of wonderful gifts. The parents tired, worn out, but satisfied they had done their best. An air of peace, of contentment. Mary went around the children's beds, straightening limbs, moving the army coats up over cold shoulders. Liam was awake. She winked at her eldest boy. He winked back. Enough said! A brief, wonderful lull before the great day.

And what a day Christmas was. The kids awoke about six o'clock, squealing and laughing and fighting in the bed. The parents resisting the noise until they had to get up. The Da lighting the turf fire with balls of paper. Good ould *Evening Herald* again. The kids getting their presents. Some happy. Some disappointed. All excited. The older ones getting dressed for the Youth Mass and Communion. New clothes. Not really new. Mostly cleaned and pressed hand-me-downs. The Ma supervised the top end – the washing of hands and faces and combing hair. The Da oversaw the bottom end, knees scrubbed, cuts and scratches smeared with Germolene, boots checked.

The Da was a genius with the shoe polish. Army style. A little tin of water, wet the cloth, take some polish on the wet cloth and rub hard into the leather. Brings a lustrous shine. A Billy Cullen shoeshine was like a mirror. You could see your face in the toe of your boot. All lined up for inspection. Bless yourself before you leave the house. God bless this house and all who live here. And away to Christmas-morning Mass in St Agatha's of William Street.

Six altar boys with the priest in his golden vestments. A great Mass. Packed with children in their Christmas clothes, faces shining, eyes sparkling, all singing the hymns, led by the choir in the balcony. The long queue for Communion as everyone in the church, row by row, received the Body of Christ in celebration of his birthday. The exultation in the after-Communion hymn, 'Tantum ergo sacramentum/veneremur cernui', sung in Latin. The Mass ended with everyone joining in joyous song: 'Faith of our fathers, holy faith, we will be true to thee till death.' Indoctrination of the youth of Ireland. Give me the boy and I'll answer for the man. 'Go forth in peace, this Mass is ended', and the church emptied the children onto the street. Dashing home for Christmas breakfast. Eggs, sausages, black and white pudding, fried bread. Once-a-year breakfast. Eat slowly. Savour each mouthful.

Off after breakfast, taking the young ones to visit the aunts and uncles. Showing off the new clothes. Comparing presents with friends. Getting pennies and tanners pressed into their hands. Cake and lemonade. Be home for the dinner at two o'clock, though, for a feast. More than you could eat of corned beef, chicken, roast potatoes, peas and cabbage, followed by loads of red jelly. A feast, to be relished and remembered for another twelve months. Playing games by the turf fire all afternoon. Snakes and ladders. Ludo. Blind man's buff. The Da and Ma snoozing. Listening to the wireless. The Goons. Jimmy O'Dea, Maureen Potter, Jack Cruise from Ballyslapdashamuckery. More tea and cake. Mother Darcy arrived with a box of Lemon's Pure Sweets. The kids didn't like the Christmas pudding. Smelt terrible and tasted sour. They loved the twin-coloured layered Madeira cake with its jam and cream.

The little ones got tired. One by one they were undressed and put to bed. Molly told her stories of Ireland, of CuCullen, of Brian Ború. Of Michael Collins.

Of bravery and of treachery. Then she too slipped off home. All the children were in bed. 'Get your foot out of me mouth!' was a familiar shout. By twelve, all was quiet except for the Da's loud snores. The Ma was still sitting in the chair, darning some socks, with a baby asleep on her lap. Humming her lullabies: 'Somewhere Over the Rainbow'.

A great Christmas. Small expectations. Lots of love and friendship. Memories to cherish forever.

22

A STREET EDUCATION

On Sunday mornings, Hector Grey sold his wares himself, standing on a box outside the Dublin Woollen Mills on the north side of the Ha'penny Bridge. Liam loved to see him in action. In the summertime he'd walk down O'Connell Street with the Da after all the kids had got Mass, and breakfast was over. Along the quays, past the furniture auction houses, with the beautiful bridges reflected in the calm, deep waters of the River Liffey.

'That's one of the things that makes Dublin city a great city, son,' the Da would say. 'Our beautiful Anna Liffey, with its wonderful bridges, and we have Grafton Street, Henry Street and the Phoenix Park on our doorstep. Mountains, rivers, beaches and parks, all within a stone's throw of Nelson's Pillar. There's nowhere like Dublin, so always be proud to be Irish, and that you're a Dubliner.' Liam pushed his chest out and tried to match the head-up, chest-out, brisk military march of his father.

It was early when they arrived at Hector's pitch. A good handful of punters, but the big width of footpath could take a lot more. Hector was in full flight in his spiel, waving a box in his hand.

'Yes indeed, me ould flowers, the finest soaps of the Orient. Mystic scents for the love of your life. And I know Billy Cullen will be wanting a box of these for that beautiful wife of his,' he said, nodding to the Da as he personalised the spiel, 'and there isn't one scented bar of soap in this box, nor is there two bars, nor three, nor four, nor five. You have, ladies and gentlemen, six different-coloured bars of scented soap for the delicate skin. Leave the carbolic and the Sunlight Soap for the gurriers and try the secrets of this Mandarin Soap for yourself. And the six bars are at half-price this morning. Four shillings in Harrods of London but two bob here today. No, I won't charge you fine people two shillings; let's reduce it to one shilling and sixpence. No, I won't ask you for one and six on this beautiful May morning, nor will I ask you for one and thruppence.' Hector threw the box high in the air and gave three almighty claps with his hands before catching the box again, as he roared, 'I'm only charging you one little shilling piece for this beautiful box of soaps. Six bars for one shilling – that's only twopence each. I'm giving it away and who's first for the bargain? We haven't got many of these today. Thank you, sir,' he said as he handed two boxes to one of his sidekicks and took the two bob, which started the ball rolling. Hector had three or four assistants now going through the crowd with the soaps, doing brisk business. Even Billy Cullen bought a box.

Hector was having a quick smoke and said quietly, 'Mary will like them, Billy, and I see you've the young fella with ya. He'll be able to take over from me soon, I hear.' But no one could match Hector's spiel. When he took a break and his assistant stood in, it wasn't the same. Hector Grey had a flow about him. A way with words. A laugh, a joke, a smile, all with perfect timing. A different spiel for every product. And Dublin came to watch and wonder and to buy. And some learned. Liam Cullen learned. Bob Darcy and Mary Darcy learned, but for most people, public speaking was something they left to the likes of Hector Grey. The master of the spiel. The best of the street traders. He could move hundreds of pounds' worth of merchandise at the bridge in a few hours. And that's when a pound would buy you twelve pints of Guinness. Hector Grey – a Dublin institution in the fifties.

The Ma decided that Liam should come off the Lane and get a proper job during the school holidays.

'We're not wasting your time on a school education to have you end up like meself on the street. You have to get ready for business somewhere,' said the Ma. And it was the Ma who came up with an offer from a shop beside her. Mister McNamara, the manager of Hayes, Conyngham and Robinson, the chemists, was looking for a messenger boy.

'While you will only be riding a bicycle to deliver orders to customers,' said the Ma, 'you'll see and learn how a business works.' So Liam took the job for the summer. The pay was a joke, at a pound a week, because Liam could make that amount in a good day on the street. Okay, the street was a fifteen-hour day, compared to nine hours in the chemist's shop.

In he went at eight in the morning to wash the windows, sweep the footpath and polish every bit of wood and glass inside and outside the shop. Onto the bike to deliver a few small items to customers, mainly in the business area of the city. At eleven thirty every morning he was given the restocking order and headed over to HCR's head office in Grafton Street. A laneway at the rear of Brown Thomas's was where all the messenger boys from all twenty-two branches of HCR Chemists headed for their respective stock order every day. Liam wouldn't get back to the shop until three o'clock. A few more deliveries around the city, and he would finish at six o'clock. Easy work. But Liam watched how everything worked: how the restocking order was done up, the suppliers' invoices written up in the purchases ledger, the lodgement book made up for the bank. He even got familiar with the Latin names used for the chemists' ingredients. And he saw the profit margins.

'Ya won't believe it,' he told the Ma. 'They open an ordinary box of aspirins, price sixpence, and put it in their own HCR prescription box, put a fancy Latin name in copperplate ink handwriting on the box, and charge the poor unfortunate customer four shillings for it. Eight times the price.' The Ma couldn't believe it. But it was true. All about perception. The customer was in awe of their white coats, professional credentials, Latin names and fancy handwriting. It was how the product was packaged.

He spent two months with HCR on the bike, and got himself into trouble. He was over in head office one day, waiting for the stock order in the warehouse loft. It was a big room, where all the lads gathered while the orders were being assembled, reading comics and playing cards while they waited. It was a little after two o'clock when a tall, slim young man walked in. He was well dressed, in a grey pinstriped suit, with a white hand-kerchief in his top pocket.

'What are you lads doing, hanging around here?' he asked. Dressed well. Spoke awfully well too.

'We're waiting on the orders,' Liam answered.

'Have you no manners?' Fancy Dan asked coldly. 'Stand up on your feet when you're speaking to your betters, and you'll address your employer as "Sir". There's to be no waiting around here for you lot. On your bikes, back to the shops. We'll phone when the orders are ready for collection.'

The lads started to move out, but Liam hesitated, and said quietly: 'Well now, mister, that's another waste of time. Back to the shop, then back here, and then back to the shop again. Some of these lads are from Clontarf. And Dun Laoghaire. Why don't ya give us all different times to come in for our orders? Then we won't be clogging Tommy up, who can only serve one of us at a time. And why do we all have to come? Sure, I could collect the orders for three or four branches that I pass on the way over here.'

Fancy Dan went red in the face. 'You've some cheek,' he said, 'and I'm not a "Mister". I'm "Sir" to you.' The lads scattered down the stairs, with Liam following. 'Come back here and apologise for your impertinence!' came from behind him but Liam was moving even faster. Out to the lane, onto the bike and gone.

When he got back to the shop, Mister McNamara was not a happy chappy. 'Gave cheek to the boss's son, you did. Absolutely gross impertinence. What did you say? He wants you sacked. I've to go over to collect the stock order myself, and you'll be lucky if you still have a job,' said McNamara.

With only a week left before school reopened, Liam wasn't worried. McNamara phoned from head office.

He wouldn't be back today: big meeting. The Ma was fuming when she heard the story.

'Did you let me down in that shop? I'll kill ya!' she said, taking a swipe at him with her boot.

'Ma, will you listen to me! You told me never to tip me cap. He was insisting I call him "Sir", and he didn't know what he was talking about.'

'Okay, sit down here and tell me the full story, word for word,' she said, 'and no porky pies.' Liam gave her chapter and verse. The Da was listening.

'Well, ya were certainly cheeky, but what you said makes perfect sense to me. A stupid waste, having all the young fellas over at the same time, only to hang around waiting half the day, doing nothing,' he said.

The Ma nodded. 'Yes, it is stupid, but bosses don't like to be told they're stupid, now, do they? You could have done better than that, Liam,' she said, looking at him. 'So let's try again.' The Da watched them. Here we go with the games.

Mary put on a posh accent. 'So now, Cullen, on your bike and back to Henry Street. We'll phone when your order is available for collection,' she said, and nodded to Liam, who was thinking fast.

'You're right, we shouldn't all be wasting our time here. And if you'll excuse me, sir, we could be even more efficient if we came for the orders at different times, and not all together here at half eleven, jamming up the warehouse,' he said.

'Oh, you all arrive together, do you?' said the Ma in her posh accent.

'Them's our instructions, all over at half eleven. You can see that's not the best way to do things. And you can also see there's no need to bring all of us over, with fellas like me passing loads of your other branches on the way,' Liam replied.

'Thank you, young man. What did you say your name was?' said Mary in her posh accent, and broke out laughing. The Da shook his head. 'There's no doubt about it, it's a promotion you would be getting, not the gate,' he said. Mary ruffled Liam's hair.

'Yes, you have to think on your feet, son, and keep cool. It's too late when you've got the gate. Only you did say "Sir" once,' she said, smiling.

'It was a very little "Sir", Ma, and the way I said it, you knew I didn't mean it,' Liam replied. Mary looked at her son. Ten out of ten, she thought to herself.

The following morning McNamara was waiting, smiling like it was his birthday. 'Bad news and good news for you, Liam,' he said. 'And first the bad news. You're sacked. Today. Right now.' Liam said nothing. 'But the good news is that you get a little going-away present. There's a fiver in this envelope for you. And a reference to say how delighted we were with your service. So the best of luck to you.' Liam took the envelope. He left his apron and cap in the wicker basket of the messenger bike, shook hands with McNamara and headed off to the Ma with the fiver.

'Well,' she said, 'you have your reference, so you weren't sacked. And it's time for school, anyway. And the fiver will pay for some of those expensive school books.'

A few weeks later, the Ma brought home the news. 'Well, Billy,' she said, 'I just heard today that there were big changes in HCR. Half the messenger boys got the gate. Out on their ear. One messenger boy to work for

Bill at the Bloomsday Messenger Bike Rally raising money for the kids

two shops now. And ould McNamara promoted over to head office as production manager. Some win and some lose.'

Liam had a few messenger-boy jobs during the summers. Temporary. The lads wouldn't stay, with the low pay, and most shops had signs in the window: 'MESSENGER BOY WANTED', to which a disgruntled hand had added: 'HORSE OUT SICK'. And in some cases it would need a horse to pull the bike. Butchers' shops were the worst. Twelve-hour days in Kearns', the butchers in Parnell Street, where Missus Sherlock sold her fruit. They were opposite Kennedy's bakery. Liam only lasted a week there. The wicker basket was specially made. It was big, really big. It took two of the biggest lads in the shop to lift it onto the bike with the Saturday-morning deliveries. The front tyre would be flattened under the weight. Liam had to get Noel and Brian to help push the bike until he'd delivered enough of the parcels to lighten the load. He would plan the journey. No heading up hills until the basket was half empty. And the pay! Ten shillings Liam got, after a seventy-hour week, plus a big wrap-up of chops, bones and meat ends. It made a great stew for weeks, but the Ma gave oul' Kearns a piece of her mind. New messenger boy every week, had Kearns.

The best places to work the bikes were the grocery-provision shops. Light loads to carry. Lipton's. Monument Creameries. Home and Colonial Stores. The most famous of all was Findlater's, with twenty-six branches, all over Dublin. Liam had a few weeks in Findlater's one summer. It was a real cushy number, working in the main branch on the corner of O'Connell Street and Cathal Brugha Street. A huge shop, with a big yard at the back, and horses and carts for the wholesale deliveries. Twenty messenger boys delivered the orders that came in by phone.

Liam could spend an hour delivering a parcel of provisions out to Missus Guiney on the Howth Road. Speedy delivery was the Findlater's motto, and if a customer phoned for sausages for tea, sausages for tea the customer got. Pronto. On yer bike, Liamo. One little parcel in the basket, a twelve-mile spin. Get a suntan on the way out and back. And the pay was twenty-five shillings for a forty-eight-hour week. Decent people, the Findlaters. Scottish Presbyterians. Strict, but very fair. They built the Protestant church up on Parnell Square. Findlaters' church. It cost the great-great-grandfather ten thousand pounds back in 1840. It was a family business.

Liam was there on the morning that the boss formally introduced his two sons to the staff. Mister McGrail was in charge, and he lined up the messenger boys at the back gate. All were scrubbed, boots polished, and stood beside their bikes: the Findlater's delivery fleet. A big black chauffeur-driven limousine pulled into the yard. What a car. The uniformed driver got out and opened the rear door.

'Mind the step, sir,' he said, as he tipped his cap. The boss and his two young lads came out of the car. Mister McGrail had given his troops their instructions.

'No looking at the Findlaters, me boyos,' he said. 'Stand up straight, beside the saddle of your bike. Chin in, and your eyes looking down at the toe of your boots. When Mister Findlater says "Good morning" to yez, you'll all respond together. You'll say, "Good morning, Mister Findlater, good morning, Master Alex and Master John." That's it, with your eyes glued to the toe of your boots.' That had been the drill and that was how it went. After which the trio walked past the row of bikes through the rear door of the shop, with McGrail in close attendance.

'Merchant princes, those young lads are,' said the Ma. 'With an empire to inherit. And they are great employers. Look after all their staff, they do: good wages, wrap-ups and Christmas bonuses as well. The salt of the earth, are the Findlaters.'

'That's right,' said the Da. 'Sure I was at Findlaters' on the first morning of Easter Week in 1916. Only a chiseller, I was. No British troops had arrived, but an Irish rifleman blew the window out of Findlater's and I got cut by a piece of glass. Blood everywhere. And it was oul' Findlater himself who came down and got me taken up to Temple Street Hospital on a horse and cart. Gave me a shilling too, so he did. Good decent people, the Findlaters.'

Liam listened to the stories, but he was still thinking

of the big black car. A Bentley it was. Leather seats. Walnut dashboard. It cost nine hundred pounds, the driver had told him. He went to sleep that night dreaming he was driving his own Bentley. Driving himself, with the Ma and the Da and all the kids with him. Till Noel woke him with a kick on the chin.

'And you won't be getting a jaunt in my car,' Liam said out loud, as he pulled the coat up over his shoulder. Nobody heard him.

*

Liam's newspaper business was growing. He was selling now on the corner of Ossory Road, right on Newcomen Bridge, outside the Smith and Pearson factory, with workers pouring up as well from the East Wall Road industrial estates. Young Noel was helping, and was old enough to mind the pitch while Liam did his roaming. Go where the customers are, Molly had said, and Liam had realised where the customers were. In the pubs!

So into the pubs he went. Quietly. The publicans didn't take kindly to brazen young fellas coming in shouting 'Herald or Mail' all over the place, and taking money that could be spent on beer. So Liam's tactic was softly, softly. Not a word. Slip in the door with a paper held up in his right hand, showing the title, *Evening Herald*, and a big '2d' marked with a pen on top. He just held the paper in front of a group of lads and smiled, with his eyebrows raised. And he sold papers. 'Gimme that, till I see the racing results', and Liam always had the latest sports edition. From pub to pub. Cusack's, Humphry's, Lloyd's. When a barman shouted, 'Get yourself out of here! No kids in my pub!' Liam would wave, turn straightaway and head for the door. But he'd come back the next night, and the next. And eventually the barman would ignore him. Softly, softly.

The big night for newspapers on the street was the launch of the new *Evening Press*. There was huge publicity on the wireless. Liam took the day off school and had himself organised. Papers rolled out just after two o'clock, well before the *Herald*. The Ma paid the shopper and got him twenty dozen papers. Liam had Noel and Brian with him and he loaded the boxcar for them to push. He took a bundle under his oxter and he was off down O'Connell Street, and east on Eden Quay to the North Wall docks, with his brothers following with the boxcar.

'Get yer *Evening Press*, Dublin's latest and greatest.' The dockers bought the new paper out of curiosity. Down to the Point Depot, where he sold a lot of papers to the railworkers, back through East Wall, along the North Strand to the pitch at Newcomen Bridge. He left the brothers there and went back to Prince's Street to the Ma. The *Herald*s had now been printed. More *Evening Press*, *Herald*s, yes, but leave the *Mail*s.

'The punters want the *Herald* still, Ma,' he said, 'but this new paper is hitting the *Mail*. And there's no way the customers want three evening papers, so I think the *Mail* will go for a burton.' They had the best night ever for the papers. Got the sixteen dozen *Evening Herald*s and sold them, as well as the *Press*es. And the *Evening Mail* was to cease production after a few years.

Liamo got a surprise one evening as he was running down O'Connell Street, having glanced at the newspaper headlines. '*Herald* or *Press*. Read all about it. O'Reilly to play against France,' he shouted. 'Brilliant schoolboy gets Irish cap. Read all about it.' It wasn't until he got home that he read the paper. Headline story about Tony O'Reilly's brilliant pre-Christmas display for the Rest of Ireland at Lansdowne Road that had won him a place on the Irish rugby team. Only eighteen. And Liam smiled as he recognised the face in the picture. It was Redser. The big fella who had been in charge of the boxing in the Belvedere Newsboys' Club. Tony O'Reilly was about to burst into an international sporting and business career. And make a lot more money selling newspapers than Liamo's few shillings.

23

Working for Jam

It was a great summer. The sun shone all day, every day. Not a cloud in the sky. Liam went out for a job on the Scott's Jam fruit farms at Balgriffin, out in the country. He had to get the bus, it was so far out. He would get the six o'clock Mass, home for the porridge, grab the lunch bag and down to get the seven o'clock bus at the Five Lamps. The Number 42 bus to Malahide. But he would get off at Campion's pub, beside the Balgriffin graveyard, then walk five hundred yards down the country road, with not a car nor a horse and cart to be seen. He would turn right, in through the big gates and down the long, tree-lined driveway. About fifty kids got off the bus together – mainly boys, but some girls.

The driveway led to a circular gravelled courtyard in front of a huge three-storey mansion. It was one of Ireland's great houses, built by a British millionaire two hundred years before. Now it was owned by Scott's Fruit Jams, the whole three-hundred-acre estate, and was managed and run by Mister Rankin. At a quarter to eight, a crowd of about two hundred kids had gathered in the courtyard. The mansion door opened and the foreman came out, waving his riding crop.

'Shut up, the lot of you buggers!' he said, in a country accent, and he slapped his leather knee-high boots with his whip. Dead quiet. Mister Rankin came out. Like Dr Livingstone, he was. White shirt and cravat, with jodhpurs and polished riding boots. Small and tanned. Rotund. Moustached. Balding head, with a friar's fringe. Glasses. Very important look and stance, as he stood, whip in hand, at the top of six magnificent granite steps, flanked by two Grecian urns. He was like Napoleon surveying his troops. He addressed the crowd in a cultured voice. 'Good morning all, and the good news today is that the raspberries are ready for picking.' Cheers from the crowd.

'Mister O'Grady here has work for a lot of you people today.' More cheers. 'You'll get paid twopence a pound of fruit, cash every day, so the more you pick, the more we pay.' Bigger cheers from the crowd.

Rankin waved his whip nonchalantly in O'Grady's general direction. O'Grady immediately strode down the steps and stood, hands on his hips, looking over the crowd. He was a big strong man, with a weather-beaten brown face and a big cap on his head. He wore a red check shirt, like John Wayne in *Stagecoach*.

'I don't want any slackers on this farm,' he said. 'It's only workers I want. Work hard, get paid well, and you have a job for the summer. Slackers get the gate. So let me see,' he said, as he walked along in front of the crowd. He obviously knew some of them from the previous year. He just pointed at them and they moved forward and over to the farmyard.

'You, you and you.' They all tried to catch O'Grady's eye. Tommy Sherlock was picked. The picked gang was getting larger than the courtyard lot. Liam was apprehensive, as O'Grady had looked at him twice and passed him by. He said a Hail Mary to himself. And an Our Father. He began to stare at O'Grady. Come on, pick me, mister. I'm no slacker. I'll pick your rassers for ya. Just give me a chance. O'Grady turned abruptly and walked up to Liam, looking hard at him.

'Who do ya think you're looking at?' he said.

Liam looked him in the eye. 'I'm just a worker. A real good worker, looking for a job,' he replied. Quietly. Not aggressive. Softly, softly. It took a long minute before O'Grady nodded slowly in the direction of the farmyard.

'Okay, we'll soon see how good a worker you are,' he said, and walked back to the steps. 'That's it, sir,' he said to Rankin, tipping his cap. Rankin waved his riding crop around.

'That's our lot for this week, so the rest of you people are dismissed. Try again next Monday,' he said, then turned and walked inside. There were about forty stragglers left, and they walked disappointedly back down the driveway, dragging their feet. Too young, too small. Rejected. Heading for the bus home.

The pickers were shown where to stow their lunch bags on shelves in the hay barn. Then they went back out to the courtyard, where O'Grady announced: 'We're out to the roadside twenty acres this morning for raspberry picking. So follow me, and let's move it. I'll be watching who's last, and there's a bus out of here every hour for slackers.'

Off he went, with a long stride on the dusty foot-path. The pickers were falling over themselves to keep up with him. A horse and cart followed them, loaded with light baskets and trays. Another cart had a huge weighing scales on it. At the field, he gathered the crowd around him on the headland. Rows and rows of green bushes, miles long, stretched into the distance. Plump red raspberries were on them.

'Pay attention, you buggers!' O'Grady shouted. 'This is a raspberry bush.' He waved the leaves of the bush and pulled a stem with some raspberries on it towards him. 'And this is how you pick a raspberry. Hold the stem with your left hand, firmly. Close to the raspberry. With your right thumb and forefinger, you catch the fruit. And you turn it clockwise. Gently. Very gently. Handle the fruit gently. And as you turn the fruit, it separates from the bud. See?' he said, and held up the stem, with a white triangular bud on it, in one hand, and the raspberry, with a hole in the centre, in the other.

'That's all there is to it. Bloody simple it is, except that you have to be quick. There are millions of raspberries on millions of bushes and I want you buggers to have them all picked by Saturday. Leonard!' he roared. 'Come on out here and show them how. You too, McAllister.'

Two big lads came out of the crowd, and got a basket each off the cart, then stood either side of the bush, with the basket on the ground. Their hands moved like lightning: holding, turning, holding, turning the fruit until the right hand had about ten rassers in it, then dropping them into the basket. Up and down the bush they went, shoving the basket up the drill with a foot. They never stopped picking and dropping.

'And it's as simple as that. So one on each side of the bushes. Spread out row by row. Get your basket. It holds about ten pounds of fruit. When it's full, bring it down to the headland here for weighing and ya get paid by the tallyman. That's Seamus there, beside the scales, with the money. So let's go. Row by row. Get your baskets, it's picking time. No starting till I blow the whistle!' shouted O'Grady, his voice carrying over the field in the clear morning air. The kids scurried to get the baskets and moved to the bushes. Liam and Tommy took the same row. Baskets were placed on the earth of the drill on either side of the bush. Both tentatively removed a fruit as O'Grady had shown. Easy.

'Okay, you buggers!' roared O'Grady, 'we'll soon seen now who the workers are.' He was looking at Liam. 'We pay double for the first six baskets of the season. But it had better weigh more than nine pounds, so start when I blow the whistle. One, two, three', and then the piercing sound of the whistle scattered the crows from the treetops and the bushes were rustled by hundreds of eager fingers. Hold. Turn. Hold. Turn. Clearing the fruit on the bush. Push the basket forward. Keep picking, bending up and down to take all the fruit from the top and bottom of the bush.

McAllister and Leonard filled first and walked back down to the headland. Their baskets were hung off the hook of the scales.

'Ten pounds apiece, means three shillings and four-pence each for McAllister and Leonard. Not bad for forty minutes' work, now, is it?' roared O'Grady. One of the next four got a roasting. 'This bugger's basket is only eight and a half pounds, isn't it? No bloody use to me. What's your name? Well, Kelly, you just stand there now for half an hour, doing nothing. You won't be so quick running up here with an empty basket again, will ya?' he roared.

It took Liam and Tommy an hour and twenty minutes to fill the baskets. Not the worst. They joined the queue at the scales. The weights were checked. Ten pounds each. The rassers were emptied into a barrel.

'Name?' asked Seamus, the tallyman.

'Cullen,' Liam responded. Seamus wrote his name on the sheet in clear block letters. He had a big cash box, all coins. He counted out one shilling and eightpence and entered it on the sheet. Liam picked up the money. O'Grady towered over him.

'"Real good worker," ya said, Cullen!' he roared. 'A hundred better ones I have before ya, Cullen, so that's not what I call really good, now, is it? You'll want to be doing better than that to be staying with us at the end of the week.'

Liam said nothing, but walked quickly back to the drill. But did he start picking raspberries! Faster and faster he got, and learned to use both hands. The fruit was so ripe, it just fell off the stem. On Friday morning, he was up to the scales in the first nine. O'Grady was there, looking at him. He nodded to him. Liam nodded back. The next Monday morning, he was one of the first to get the nod. O'Grady knew a good worker when you'd proved it to him.

The work was hard – standing all day. Bending, reaching. You took turns kneeling on the hard, lumpy soil to get the fruit low on the bush, using a bit of carpet to kneel on. It was still rough on the knees. Rough and mucky when it was wet. You had a dull pain in the back all day. Twice as much was picked in the morning as in the evening on the first week. Pace yourself. Stay alert. If O'Grady came behind you and found fruit you'd missed still on the bush, he went ballistic.

'Kelly, ya little bugger, get your arse back here and pick raspberries!' he roared. 'Is it blind you are? Look at this fruit ya left behind. Handfuls of luscious fruit you're leaving to rot. Get it into your basket, or bejaysus, you'll get the gate.' The second time it happened, Kelly got the gate.

'Get out of my field and don't ever bring yer ugly face out here again. Get out now, before I take the whip to ya,' he roared, red in the face, and chased Kelly across the headland, waving the whip at him. O'Grady came back panting. He blew the whistle to call the workers to the headland.

'Listen to me, all of ya. I don't care how fast you pick, ya don't leave good fruit behind. That's a mortal sin, to leave fruit to rot on the land. Pick fast, but clean the bushes. Kelly's got the gate and so will anyone else who doesn't mind their good job,' he shouted. 'Now back to work. Let's pick raspberries.' He blew the whistle. Back to the picking. A tough man, O'Grady, but by God he was serious about his job.

Each evening at six o'clock the whistle blew and there was a frantic scramble for the tallyman. Weigh the last basket. Get your money. Into the farmyard. Wash the mud off your Kossicks, and run for the half-six bus. Three buses were laid on for the fruit pickers. If you didn't make it, you'd to wait for the seven o'clock one. Some of the lads deliberately stayed back to drink lemonade in Campion's.

Liam went home on the bus and straight down to the canal lock at Newcomen Bridge for a swim. You always had your swimmys and a towel with you. Gangs of young fellas would be in the lock, diving and swimming in the evening. No girls were allowed to go swimming with the boys. They couldn't even come over to have a look. 'An occasion of sin', the nuns called it, to see boys undressed. Except your brother, of course; that was okay. Quick drying off and into the flats for the dinner. The menu in the Cullen house never changed. Tuesday and Thursday was vegetable stew. Wednesday and Friday was fish. Saturday was rabbit stew. Sunday was corned beef and cabbage with the odd dish of pigs' feet. Monday was Sunday's leftovers fried in the pan. Bubble and squeak. That was it, except when money was scarce. Then it was only boiled potatoes – a huge basin of boiled spuds in the middle of the table. Balls of flour with the skin hanging on them. A dab of margarine. The faster you ate, the more you got.

But for Liam, the working man that summer, it was special treatment. Boiled potatoes mashed and browned in the pan, with two soft-fried eggs on top, so you could mix the egg yolk into the spuds. Four fat juicy sausages stuck into it. Or maybe two fried gigot chops instead of the sausages. A flat ray and chips from the Congress Café on Friday. Not home-made. Very fancy. All washed down with a big mug of fresh milk. Cold milk. The bottle was submerged in a bucket of water to keep it cold for Liam and the Da. The working men, bringing home a wage.

After dinner, get into fresh jeans and T-shirt and head off to the Brú with Tommy – gym with Myles, table tennis with Moran, finish the wallet in leatherwork for the Da, with his initials carved on it. Home before ten, worn out. Into bed and out like a light. Too tired to read.

Rankin had a permanent crew of about twenty women, from Donnycarney on the Malahide Road, who had been working with him for years. If you were permanent, you worked all summer long. Four pounds a week they got, every week. The seasonal workers only got paid for what they picked. If it lashed rain, you sheltered under the trees at the headland ditch. If it was a steady downpour, pickers could waste the day sitting around. No dough. Too bad.

After the raspberries came the strawberries, and the gooseberries. Then the work was finished for the pickers. Bye-bye, Mister Rankin, till next year. Liam and Tommy were kept on for tomato-picking in the greenhouse. Permo. Three quid a week. And for weeding – the toughest job of all. On your knees all day in the fruit fields, with a basket and trowel. Lift the weed from amongst the bushes with the trowel.

'Not the feckin' fruit bush, you eejit!' O'Grady would roar. 'The *weeds* you get out. *This* is a feckin' weed. *That's* a strawberry stem.' And you shuffled up the drill on your knees. Back bent. All day. The walk with a full basket of weeds back to the headland was a relief on the back. The ache set in once you kneeled down again.

Weeding the grazing fields wasn't too bad. You would walk along the field in rows behind a tractor pulling a flat trailer, pulling up the big yellow-topped ragweeds with your hands, digging out the nettles with your fork.

'Get the root out, ya buggers!' roared O'Grady as he marched back and forth across the field, smacking his riding crop off his boot. 'If ya leave the root behind, I've another weed in a week. The root with the weed. Up she comes!' and you threw your bundle of weeds into the trailer. Up and down the acres of fields. It was tough on the back, and hard on the hands. But you were paid every Friday, with a brown pay packet.

There was a distinct pause in the house that first Friday evening when Liam got home about seven o'clock. The Da reading the *Herald*. He had finished his dinner. Lovely smell of fish and chips. The Ma came out of the scullery when he walked in.

'Howaya, son,' she said. 'How did it go?'

'Great day, Ma,' he said. A pause all round, with the Da looking at him over the paper. Smiling. The Ma went into the scullery.

'I have your dinner ready. Big flat ray. And chips. And a tin of beans for ya as well,' she said, as she piled the food onto a plate and put it on the table. 'A three-course meal for the working man.' She hooshed the other kids out of the room. They had been looking enviously at the plate. 'Off ya go, and play skipping. Outside with yez,' she said.

Liam put his hand in his pocket, took out the unopened pay packet and walked over to the fireplace. He placed it beside the Da's. 'LIAM CULLEN' handwritten on his. 'BILLY CULLEN' typed on the Da's. Side by side. He looked at the Da. The Da smiled and gave him a wink. He winked back, strolled to the table and sat down. The Ma put a big mug of milk beside his plate, looked at the mantelpiece, and ruffled his hair as he shovelled the food into his mouth with a big spoon.

They only got three more weeks on the farm before it was back to school. Goodbye in Campion's on the last Friday night. Lemonade. On the bus they sang songs with the Donnycarney women:

Down on Joe Rankin's ould farm,
Where the young ones are working for jam.
You'll be slaving all day —
You might get no pay,
And knackered going home to yer Mam.

Suntanned and dusty you'll be.
You'll soon be worn out, just like me.
O'Grady will roar,
'Yez better pick more
Or no work next week will ya see.'

We'd love to sneak up in the grass
And give oul' Rankin a kick in the arse,
Give O'Grady the snot
Tell him 'Buggers we're not'
And get a real job, but we need the brass.

Liam and Tommy got a cheery goodbye and even a sly kiss from the girls as they got out at the tin church in Donnycarney. 'See ya next year, lads.' Home for the dinner.

24

CROKE PARK – AND UNCLE ARTHUR

The GAA matches in Croke Park were a major event for the Cullen family. From the time Molly had taught him to 'go where the people are', Liam recognised the potential of a hundred thousand people heading for one place on the same day.

He started his GAA Sundays selling newspapers outside Gill's pub, his old pitch on the corner of Russell Street. It was the gateway to Croke Park. The big matches in Croker were dominated by the rural teams, and their supporters flocked up to Dublin; some by car but mainly by train. While they would have read the Irish newspapers on the way up, the English newspapers had added attractions. English soccer reports. The Pools results. Titillating stories about film stars and celebrities. Crosswords and puzzles with big-money prizes. They were not generally available in rural Ireland, so the papers sold well. 'Get yer *Chronicle*, *Empire*, *Despatch*, *People* or *Reynolds' News*.'

The crowds poured up the North Circular Road from Amiens Street Railway Station, and down Fitz-gibbon Street from Kingsbridge Station, all merging into Russell Street, with Gill's pub on the corner. The newspapers sold quickly. Then Liam began to assess the other opportunities, and the obvious one was fruit. Sunday fruit-selling. The day of the match started early. Plenty of supporters had arrived by Saturday for a night on the town in the dance halls of Dublin – the Ierne, the National Ballroom and the Ballerina on Parnell Square; Barry's Hotel in Denmark Street; the Crystal, the Four Provinces and the Olympic on the southside. The lads had a great time, over-nighting in a bed-and-breakfast for six shillings a head. They were up early for Mass on Sunday, and that's where the Ma first deployed the troops: herself at St Mary's Pro-Cathedral in Marlborough Street, Liam on Mountjoy Square beside St Francis Xavier church in Gardiner Street. The Ma with her fruit in the pram, Liam using his multipurpose boxcar. After twelve o'clock Mass, they withdrew to the Russell Street pitch, one on each footpath. The fruit sold well. Noel and Vera acted as restocking couriers, bringing new boxes of fruit up from Mother Darcy. The minor match started at two o'clock, and with the stadium filling up fast, the crowds outside had thinned out to the last-minute stragglers. Then they moved into phase two – getting the fruit into the ground during the pause when the minor match was over. The stewards let the dealers in.

The Ma continued selling around the Hogan Stand while Liam took his boxcar, heaped with empty apple and orange boxes, around the back of the Cusack Stand to Hill 16, up to the back of the Hill, where the crowd were standing on tiptoes, straining to get a glimpse of the field. Liam went into his spiel. 'Make yourself seven feet tall with a two-shilling orange box. Only two bob for a bird's-eye view of the match.' The wooden boxes sold like hot cakes. Liam had Noel feeding up all the empty boxes he could get from the other dealers. And the lads saw the match, until the excitement grew and three or four of them pushed up onto the same box and smasharooneyed it into pieces. And luckily, Liam just might have another one – for another two bob. 'It'll only hold two of yez, lads, or you'll break it in bits. Take it easy,' he told them. But by the end of the game, every box had been shattered to pieces. And Liam had a few sacks to gather up all the pieces. He chopped them into even-sized bundles to sell for twopence each as firelighters outside the Horsestone Dairy the following evening. He collected all the empty porter and lemonade bottles as well, and sold them back to the pubs for a penny each.

As they expanded in confidence and expertise, the ancillary activities grew. A big earner was programme-selling, which was controlled by the GAA. They would be distributed on the Saturday evening to an army of schoolboys. You had to have a written reference from your schoolteacher to get ten dozen programmes. You sold the programmes for sixpence each – three pounds in takings for the lot, and Mister Lonergan gave you twenty-five per cent commission. So you got fifteen shillings for your weekend's work. Pretty good. It took Liam a while to figure out how Hector Grey's one per cent profit was better than the GAA's twenty-five per cent commission. Of course, the odd scallywag gave a false reference and did a Danny Boy with all the GAA programme takings. One hundred per cent profit.

'Mind your car, mister!' became a growing revenue-earner around Croke Park. 'Only sixpence to mind your car all day. Make sure no one breaks into it', was the spiel.

There was a famous story told about the Corkman who parked his car on Charles Street. Walking off to the match he was, with his red-and-white flag, when a chiseller gave him a shout. 'Mind your car, Mister, for sixpence.' The Corkman just waved nonchalantly and breezed on. But it was a persistent young fella. 'Hey, Mister, there's joyriders up here in Dublin; your car could be gone when ya come out!' he shouted. The Corkman stopped. He walked back slowly to his car. 'Be the bejaysus,' he said, pointing his flag at the window of his car, 'I don't think any Dublin gurrier will be touching *my* car. Look.' The young fella put his nose to the window. He nearly had a heart attack when an Alsatian came off the back seat and smacked off the window. Growl, growl, slobber. The Corkman laughed and headed off. The chiseler got his breath back. 'Hey, Mister,' he shouted, 'can that oul' dog of yours put out fires?' He got his sixpence. It pays to think on your feet.

There was good money in colours. Big rosettes. It was the same system as the paper flowers – coloured paper to match the team colours cut into shapes and made into rosettes. Sixpence each. But the pièce de résistance came from the *Evening Herald* again. Liam got his hands on the unsold papers and cut out all the photos of the match heroes from the sports sections. He glued the photos to the centre of the rosettes. Whose rosettes did the punters buy? 'Get yar colours of the match. Mick O'Connell on our Kerry colours.' You could get an extra twopence for the rosettes with the photos of the star stuck on. Liam learned later that this was the USP – unique selling proposition. Adding value to the product.

There was always the last-minute brigade who couldn't

get in. Turnstiles closed. Full-up signs. 'This way, sir, if ya want to see the match', was Noel's cry. He gathered a group of disappointed fans around to the lane at Clonliffe Road, then up the bank and across the tracks to Liam at the high wall at the Railway End of the ground. 'Only half-a-crown to go up the ladder to see the match,' went Liam's spiel. Up they went and jockeyed along the wall. Not a comfortable perch. But up to sixty extra fans got to see the match. Liam had to buy the ladder for two pounds, so he needed sixteen paying fans up the ladder to break even, before a steward nailed him and seized the ladder. But sometimes a 'comfort fee' could be paid to the steward so that he would look the other way.

Liam was in Croke Park for every big match from 1951 to 1964. He saw Mick O'Connell play his first game there. Even as a Kerry minor O'Connell could out-jump his opponents by two or three feet, soaring into the sky like an eagle. He went on to become the prince of Gaelic footballers, gracing the game with his brilliance and sportsmanship for Kerry into the seventies. The 1956 football All-Ireland between Galway and Cork was the game of that decade. Galway won, thanks to the magnificence of Sean Purcell and Frankie Stockwell. Stockwell scored two goals and five points that day, while Purcell will always have the accolade of being the finest ever all-rounder in Gaelic football.

In hurling, the Wexford team that won the All-Ireland matches of 1955 and 1956 has to go into history as one of the greatest ever. It contained three Rackard brothers – Bobby, Billy and the legendary Nicky Rackard. In the 1956 final, Wexford beat Cork, who had won three titles in a row in '52, '53 and '54. With the greatest hurler ever in Christy Ring, the 'Wizard from Cloyne',

Cork were favourites. But the boys from Wexford won, thanks to their goalkeeper, Art Foley, who made many brilliant saves on the day. It was in the fifties that Ollie Walsh, Kilkenny's legendary goalkeeper, introduced his *'camán mór'* – the big hurling stick. With this weapon, he could puck out the sliotar the full length of the pitch. A mighty man.

The final whistle of the All-Ireland matches was blown at ten minutes to five, and was followed by the presentations to the teams, captains' speeches in Irish and English, and the fans cheering and singing. They had an hour to clear the ground. The Ma would head home before the match ended, to check on how the girls and the Da had managed with the dinner. Liam and the boys filled the boxcar with sacks of sticks and bottles. On the odd occasion, there was the joy of finding a pound or some change under the litter on the terraces. Then they would head for home and a big feed of corned beef and cabbage. The Ma would be counting the day's revenues. The boys got stuck into the delicious apple pie that Vera had baked.

'Learning her domestic science, I'll have ya know. With Sister Louise in William Street,' said the Ma. Great feed. They didn't see much of the match. But it was a great day.

*

O'Connell's School was tough going. Liam and most of the scholarship class bypassed the first grade and went straight into second. It was a different school to Canice's. This was a top-class paying school, with well-dressed young fellas. Shirts and ties. Real leather shoes and knee-length socks. Brown leather shoes, not black, would you believe. Liam's were the only Kossicks to be seen. They brought fancy cakes for tea breaks. No prairie sandwiches here. Egg-with-mayonnaise sambos. Ham-and-cheese sambos. Rasher-and-sausage sambos. And they had so many, they shared. They gave them away to hungry mouths like Liamo. Thank you very much.

The teacher was a big red-faced countryman with a deep country accent, hard to understand. He was from Skibbereen. A good, no-nonsense guy. Do your work and he was happy. Swing the lead or mess around and you got the leather – a fearsome thing. Twelve inches long, two inches wide and an inch thick, with a nice curved handle for the teacher's hand to hold. Thick lumps protruded. Lumps of iron was the rumour. Six of the best hurt, really hurt. Your hand was swollen for a week. Brother Finn was his name; he was called 'Huckleberry' by the lads. Brother Laffan was the science teacher. Dr Carew was the principal.

Liam was doing okay in the class – top ten in the first exam. Very good in his first Latin lessons. It was easy when you knew all the Mass words and Latin hymns. And he saw the link between Latin and English. *Bene*, meaning 'good'. *Volens*, meaning 'wishing'. Benevolent – a well-meaning (good) guy. A person who was well meaning. Great help for his Reader's Digest Word Power quiz. He got into the Roman history big time. Gladiators. Centurions. Warriors. Caesar and Cassius. Mister Stack's teaching paid off, as Liam was called up first to read a Latin translation. He placed the Longmans Latin book on the master's desk as if it were a podium. Using his hands for added effect, he read the story with

Stack's advice in his head. 'Get the tone right. Hard and strong for the battles. Soft and light for the death scenes. Pause to get attention. Have them waiting for more. Inflection. Timing.' When he had finished, Huckleberry led the applause: 'Begorrah, sure it's on the stage you should be, me boyo.'

After that, Huckleberry took an interest in the young fella and gave him a loan of books on Roman history and Greek mythology. The voyages of the Portuguese and Spanish explorers. Wonderful adventure stuff that Liam read avidly at night with his torch. Warriors. Achievements. Go do it.

He played the Gaelic Athletic Association games. The GAA football. You could catch the ball in the air. Liam's height made him an easy choice for centre back. In hurling he loved the clash of the ash as the hurley sticks smashed together. In both games, strength counted, and Liam's aggressive style, using his weight to bowl opponents out of his way, got his name on the selection board for the school team. But the Ma needed him at the Lane and he couldn't attend the after-school practices. Brother Dempsey, the football coach, was not amused.

'You should consider it an honour to be chosen for the school team. Rest assured, you won't be picked again as long as I'm in charge. And I believe you've plenty of time for soccer-playing on the street. Traitor!' was his admonishment. The traitor bit referred to the GAA ban. No GAA man or boy was allowed to play soccer. Soccer was the English game, the game of Ireland's oppressors. 'Only traitors play soccer' was the GAA philosophy. No soccer or rugby was allowed in the Christian Brothers' schools. Christian me eyeball.

Liam's 'absence' routine was causing problems. The

different class structure in O'Connell's meant he actually missed out on complete subjects when he was with Molly Darcy for the fish on Fridays. No science class, no geometry class. At the Easter exam he failed science. He was up before the headmaster, Dr Carew. 'We can't have this, Cullen. Terrible bad example to your peers. The school would fall apart if we let every lad take days off for domestic reasons. I want your parents up here. They either want you to have an education or they don't. *And* you refused to play for our football team. Unheard-of arrogance.'

The Ma came up and met Dr Carew privately. It seemed to go all right. Sure, the Ma could talk Christ down off the Cross. But that evening, she was worried. 'I don't know if we can make this last, son. Five long years in school, when you could be earning a living. And the bills in this flat are something else. The electricity bill has me scourged. I've taken the bulbs out of the bedrooms and the fuse out of the water heater. And the bill is still two pounds a week. It's robbin' banks I'd need to be. That Latin schoolbook I got ya last week was twenty-five shillings. A week's wages for one buke! About a language that's dead and gone, except for the priests. Trying to keep it alive, they are, for their own importance is all that is. I told Carew you'd read up more at home on this science stuff, and he's let us away with the Fridays off till he sees how your year-end exam goes.'

Liam got a pass in the year-end science exam and came ninth in the class overall. Sigh of relief all round. Brother Laffan, the science teacher, met him in the schoolyard. 'Never attended one class and got a pass. I just have to shake your hand.' And he did, and swished away with his black robes swirling around him, laughing. Yes, Laffan laughing.

But Huckleberry Finn wasn't laughing. More and more, Liam was missing classes due to pressure at home. The Ma was finding it difficult, with eleven children, seven of them under nine years old. Liam had to stand in for the Ma at the Lane. Even though he managed to pass the mid-term exams, Brother Finn was unhappy. 'Sure you swan in and out of this school as ya please. One day this week, two days next week, begorrah, you might grace us with your presence for three days some week. We should run the flag up the flagpole and salute when you're in residence. Well I'm not puttin' up with it any more. So it's up to Dr Carew with you, me boyo. Let's go.'

Dr Carew was unhappy too. 'We can't run a school like this, Cullen,' he said. 'You've missed seventy-four days out of a hundred and thirty. That's a disgrace. The truant officers would have you off to Artane. Well, it's unacceptable, intolerable. I want your mother up here tomorrow to sort this out, once and for all.'

The Ma went up, and it wasn't pleasant. 'It's very simple,' she said at the table that evening. 'I've had to commit to four days a week. They'll concede your Friday off with the mother but that's it. So we'll just have to do the best we can.'

Liam struggled to get to school every day, but some days the Ma couldn't make it to the Lane without his help. He just about saw out the school year.

When he went back to school in September, he was called up to Carew's office on day one. 'Cullen, I just want to reconfirm that you must attend from Monday to Thursday every week. No missing out on those days, or you'll be expelled,' he said. But when November came along, it was clear that the Ma would need Liam on the street for the whole month of December. He approached Brother Gallagher from St Canice's. Would he negotiate with O'Connell's for him? Yes he would. And he did. The answer was no. A very definite no.

Liam went on the street for the month anyway. The Ma was written to by Dr Carew — a satisfactory explanation required from Missus Cullen in person for Liam's absence. The Ma went up with a sick note for a week. It was reluctantly accepted. But another written request arrived for her — a personal explanation for Liam being fit enough to be in Henry Street, selling balloons. The Ma went the sympathy route. No alternative. Twelve hungry mouths to feed. Liam a breadwinner. She got a slight reprieve. Liam was to report to Dr Carew's office when school started again after Christmas.

The Brother Superior was in bad form when Liam returned in January. 'You're not interested in an education. You have been defying authority. Undermining the whole scholastic system. Feigning illness and duping an innocent doctor to issue a sick note for the fittest young fella in the school. And to add insult to injury,' he said, waving a newspaper picture of Liam and the Brú Mhuire soccer team, 'you won't play football for this school yet you blatantly play soccer, as this picture shows. You're a traitor to your country and your school, and we have no place for you here. You're expelled.' That was the speech. End of story. Bye-bye.

The Ma was upset. She gave Liam a few thumps. She had to take her anger and frustration out on someone. But up she went the next morning to see Dr Carew. The administrator wouldn't let her into Dr Carew's office.

'Well, I'll just have to wait here until he's free,' said Mary Darcy. She waited for four hours, but eventually the good doctor had to come out of his office. He tried to walk past, ignoring her. Impossible. She stood in his way. 'Well now, sir,' she said, 'I believe you've kicked my son out. Denied him an education because he has to support his brothers and sisters. You won't make some allowance for his situation. You're a man of the cloth. Where's your charity and understanding?'

Dr Carew's face was stern, his voice cold. 'I won't tolerate any student undermining the authority of the school management. If he doesn't conform with school policy, he's out. And out he's gone. Playing soccer! He is expelled. And there will be no further discussion,' he said, getting redder in the face with each word of admonishment. He was breathing hard, an angry man.

Mary Darcy stood back and looked at him for a long minute. She shook her head slowly. 'Sure, it's to be pitied you are, sir. And I'm glad my son will have nothing more to do with the likes of you,' she said, giving him a fierce look. Then she turned and walked out.

Brother Gallagher contacted Liam some weeks later. He told him to keep on with his studies, because he had entered him for the Inter Cert examination in June. Liam did. Brother Gallagher got him into the examination. He sat for it. And passed with honours – the only Summerhill lad to get an Honours Inter Cert. Wasn't Brother Gallagher a great Christian Brother?

*

Brother Kirwan was a voluntary social worker in Brú Mhuire at night. By day, he was a clerical officer in

Guinness's – the Arthur Guinness Brewery at St James's Gate, affectionately referred to by all the staff as 'the Brewery'. If you could say 'I work in the Brewery', everyone knew you had a well-paid job, with a pension after forty years of service. And two free pints of Guinness a day, too. Brother Kirwan was a quiet man. He smoked a Sherlock Holmes pipe. He was very dedicated. He was also a republican, who played his records of rebel songs in the Brú: 'A Nation Once Again', 'The Croppy Boy' and his favourite, 'Down by the Glenside'.

One evening, Brother Kirwan approached Liam. 'Could I have a word, Liam?' he asked, taking him by the shoulder into a quiet corner of the gym. 'Liam, the Brewery will be hiring ten office messengers this year. Exams start in two weeks and I can nominate two entrants for the exam. Would you like to have a go?' he asked softly, with a smile.

'But of course I would, Brother,' Liam replied.

'Fine. Well, yourself and Paddy Walsh will present yourselves at this address in James's Street on Saturday-two-weeks,' he said, handing him a card and a large white envelope. 'This envelope contains the exam papers for the last five years, so you can get the feel of it,' he said with a wink. It's not what you know, it's *who* you know.

Liam and Paddy sat the exam. Forty applicants for ten jobs. Handy questions. They were mainly sums – add, subtract, divide. Complete easy quotations. Identify pictures of sports stars. It took half an hour. Liam was told afterwards that he could expect a job offer. Walking home with Paddy, they compared answers. Paddy hadn't known the rest of 'All the world's a stage'. It was one of Liam's favourite Shakespearean quotations, and he knew the whole page off by heart.

Paddy was impressed. 'What about the half-dead-looking geezer in the sports stars. I got the other five,' he said.

Liam smiled. 'The greatest athlete in history, he is, Paddy,' he said. 'The only man to win Olympic gold in the 5,000 metres, the 10,000 metres and the Marathon, all in the same Games at Helsinki. We'll never see that record broken. Emil Zatopek is his name. He's from Czechoslovakia. He reminds me of Taza, son of Cochise. Great warriors. Great runners.'

The letter arrived from Guinness's the following Wednesday. Clipped, structured, clinical. Please sign, accepting position as office messenger. Remuneration fifteen shillings per week, with yearly increments as per attachment A. When Liam looked at the attachment, his heart sank. Year one – fifteen shillings; year two – seventeen shillings and sixpence; year three – a pound a week. And so on, year by year, up to year forty. Year ten was four pounds; year twenty was six pounds; year thirty was nine pounds; and after forty years' service he could be earning the magnificent sum of eleven pounds thirteen shillings and eightpence per week. A lifetime gone by. A long grey beard. He might not even make it. Sheriff Darcy died at fifty-three years of age. What's the pension? Fifteen per cent of salary. Thirty-five shillings a week.

The Da read it. 'Great job altogether, son. Steady full-time employment in the Brewery. And a pension. Well done,' he said proudly.

The Ma was quiet. Say nothing till ya hear more. When the Da went off to the Pro-Cathedral, the Ma said, 'What are ya thinking, son?'

Liam looked at her. 'I'm thinking I won't be working in Guinness's. Sure, part-time at the Lane I can make two pounds a week. Full-time it would be five pounds for ya. Even in Joe Rankin's fields, I get three pounds a week. On their attachment A remuneration scale it would be thirteen years from now before I could make a fiver in the Brewery.'

'Ah yes, Liam,' she said, 'but that's only if you stayed an office messenger. Don't you know you'll be promoted? And there's no pension from Joe Rankin, nor at the Lane.'

'Yes, I'm sure I'd move up the ladder. But there's thousands of workers in the Brewery, with a lot more pull than I have. Lads with fathers and grandfathers before them in the job. And with a college education. As for the pension, it's buttons!'

'Well, my opinion is to take the job and see how it goes. You can always be looking out for something else while you're there. It's easier to get a job when you're working in the Brewery than when you're on the street, selling penny apples.' The Ma speaks words of wisdom.

The rebellious son thinks and responds. 'But Brother Kirwan would be mortified if I started and then packed it in. One of his protégés walking out on the Brewery. Unheard of. At this stage, I could decline for family circumstances. You've also forgotten how the drop to fifteen bob a week will affect yar budget.' Mary agreed.

The Da went nuts. 'Typical. Keep my son at that kip of a Lane. Pull him down into the gutter with ya.' Liam tried to reason with him. No dice. He nearly took the door off the hinges again.

Liam gave Brother Kirwan the story. Extremely

grateful. Very sorry but the Ma needed him helping at the Lane until the children got a bit bigger. He nearly swallowed his pipe. After a fit of coughing, he looked at Liam and said, 'Are you really telling me you are declining a position of employment with the Brewery? With the *Brewery*?' His eyes were wide with shock. Liam tried to back-pedal softly, but it was clear that Brother Kirwan wasn't listening. His eyes were glazed over. He reached out, took the Guinness appointment letter, stood up and walked away in a daze.

He didn't speak to Liam for twelve months. And Paddy Walsh got the job in the Brewery.

25

A Room of His Own
and Night School Too

Liam worked at the Lane all day, but answered news-paper ads every night for a job. Stock clerk, office assistant, apprentice typewriter technician, warehouse trainee. Everything under the sun. No replies. About 700 written applications in six months. Zilcho.

'Looks like James Larkin House is a no-no. Like a red rag to a bull for employers who remember the lockout strike. And North Strand Flats doesn't sound great, either,' the Ma said. 'This whole area of Dublin's inner city is a no-go zone!'

Liam expressed his frustration to Brother Moran, who came up with a solution. 'That's simple, Liam,' he said. 'Use my address. Vernon Avenue, Clontarf. You won't get a posher address on the northside of Dublin.' The first time Liam used the address, he got a response. Brother Moran handed him the letter in the Brú. It was from Walden Motor Company in Parnell Street. 'Attend for interview for the position of office messenger on Friday morning at 11 o'clock.' Liam knew Walden's well. Sold Ford cars, they did, opposite the top of Moore Street, next door to Maxie Cosgrove the vet, where he'd often been to get help for a sick horse.

Liam got Uncle Bob to go into Walden's and get some car brochures to read up on. He learned all about the new cars they sold. Ford Prefect and Ford Anglia with an E93A engine. Two- and four-door models. Price £325. He went to the library and got a book on the Ford Motor Corporation. He was surprised to find that Henry Ford was an Irishman – or at least his father was. In May 1847, the Ford family were starving in their little cottage in Ballinascarthy, County Cork. The Great Famine had killed the potato crop and the people were dying like flies. The family packed up and walked to Cobh to get the boat to the States. On the way, they stopped with relatives in the Fair Lane in Cork City, now known as Wolfe Tone Street. The name Fair Lane became a link between the Ford family and their Irish roots. John Ford and his wife Thomasina, with their four children, including twenty-two-year-old William Ford, got the ship to America. Thomasina died on the trip and was buried at sea.

They settled in Dearborn, Michigan, where young William Ford married. His son, Henry Ford, was born in 1863. This was the famous Henry Ford, the son of an Irish Famine survivor whose grandmother died on a coffin ship, a man who was now known for his cars all around the world. Fairlane became the name for the Company's head office and the family estate. It was also the name of the company's flagship car, the Ford Fairlane V8. Ford means cars, and Fairlane means Ford.

And so it was that when Henry Ford began his expansion in 1917, the first production plant opened outside America was in Ireland, in Cork, the birthplace of his father. The Irish had returned to help rebuild their home country.

Liam was delighted to know so much about Ford and went along to the interview very confidently. But Mister Cole, the company accountant who interviewed him, never asked him anything about Ford or motor cars, but instead asked about more mundane, local matters. Did he know where Jervis Street was? Did he know where Louis Copeland's was? It was like buns to a bear for Liam, who knew every shop and every street in Dublin's city centre. Mister Cole was very impressed. He couldn't trip him up.

Then it was the sums. There was a big calculating machine on the desk. Loads of buttons and one handle. Mister Cole pressed buttons. Pulled the handle. Took the paper strip of monetary sums and handed it across the desk to Liam. 'Add those up,' he said and pulled the handle one more time to give himself the answer.

Liam looked at the list of pounds, shillings and pence. As Cole handed Liam a pencil to do the sum, Liam gave him back the paper and said, 'The answer is thirty-nine pounds, fourteen shillings and eightpence.'

Mister Cole looked at him in surprise. 'How did you do that? You're right. But you didn't add up the columns!'

Liam said, 'I do them all together, just like that.'

The man was astonished. 'You just stand over at the door and I'll give you another one.' Buttons clicked, the handle was pulled, the machine clanked, and swish. 'Try this one then.'

Liam looked at the list. Longer. The answer came just as quick. The right answer.

Mister Cole couldn't believe it. He picked up the phone and summoned Bill Lambert, the office manager. 'Take this young fella downstairs for five minutes. I think he can see the answers reflected in the window behind me.' They came back after five minutes. 'Now try this one for size,' Cole said. Liam did it again. Added it up in his head. Gave him the answer. Correct.

'You've got the job,' said Cole. 'You can start next Monday at nine o'clock sharp.'

'You haven't told me the wages, Mister Cole,' replied Liam.

'Oh, yes. It's fifteen shillings a week. The hours are nine to six, with a half-hour break for lunch. Saturdays are from nine to one. We'll see you on Monday, then,' Cole said as he stood up to leave for lunch, picking up his gloves.

'I'm sorry, Mister Cole, but I couldn't work for ya for that kind of money. Fifteen shillings for a forty-six-and-a-half-hour week is no good. That's only four pennies an hour. I'd need at least twenty-five shillings a week, because the Ma has ten kids and only me Da working.'

Cole's jaw dropped open. He flopped down into the chair, looking at Liam in disbelief. Bill Lambert was standing against the wall, with his eyebrows raised, but his eyes twinkling. Cole placed his gloves back on the desk. 'But . . . but . . . but your family circumstances have nothing to do with our wages. The rate for an office messenger is fifteen shillings. To start. You will be reviewed for an increase. Aren't those the parameters?' He looked to Lambert for support.

'Well, he's good at figures, Mister Cole,' said Lambert, 'so he'll be very useful for the clock-card work and repair orders, as well as normal office duties.'

'Well, all right then, we'll make it the even pound a week, and that's it. Way over the normal wage. Okay?' Cole said, looking at Liam.

'Okay,' said Liam 'and we'll have the review after two months, to assess me for the five-shilling rise. See you on Monday.' And he held out his hand to shake hands with both men. Cole was still sitting in the chair with his mouth open, looking after him, as he closed the door.

Outside, Liam met Jimmy Ryan, the petrol-pump attendant who had directed him to Cole's office. 'How did it go, son?' he asked.

'I'm starting next Monday.'

Ryan looked at him. 'Aren't you Billy Cullen's son?'

Liam nodded.

'Jaysus, put it there! Sure, you're the spittin' image of your Da. Doesn't my sister, Josie Ryan, sell in Moore Street. Great pal of your mother's. See ya Monday and I'll show ya the ropes,' Ryan said.

The Ma was delighted. The location couldn't be better. He'd still be able to do the markets at seven, get the fruit to the Lane and slip into Walden's, only a hundred yards away. Back down after work to store the stall away. He was available for Saturday afternoon at the Lane and Sunday with Uncle Martin on the Marino pig-feed-collecting run.

Monday morning came and it was all excitement. Liam got his Mass, but skipped the markets for that day. He was getting ready for his first real job. Trousers pressed all night under the mattress. Shirt white, Persil-bright – a Kingston shirt makes all the difference. Shoes sparkling. Hair cut extra short last night by the Ma. Spick and span and ready to go at half past seven. The Da looked him over, delighted that his son was getting away from the Lane at last. Smiled. Shook his hand. 'Good luck now, son. I know you won't let us down.

Work hard, and never be late,' he said, as he left for his Mass in Saint Laurence O'Toole's Church, on his way to the docks.

The Ma looked at him and said, 'Remember what I told ya, son: you'll never meet a man better than yourself. Do yar best at everything.' He blessed himself with the holy water, said a little prayer to the Sacred Heart and off he went.

He stopped off at Mother Darcy's. Molly said, 'You look great, Liam. Now remember, son, no matter what they give you to do, do it better than anyone else ever did it before. If you've to clean windows, then clean them so well you wouldn't know there was a window at all. If you've to sweep floors, sweep them so clean a king could eat his dinner off it. Hard work never hurt anyone, so God bless you now and I'll be praying for you today. And every day.' She started whistling and he joined her in the tune, 'Whenever I Feel Afraid'. She blew him a kiss as he marched up to Summerhill, feeling great. His first real job.

Liam worked hard. Up from the markets quickly and into Walden's at half seven most mornings. He helped Jimmy Ryan on the petrol pumps, filling up the cars. There would be lots of big shots early in the morning. Mister Hardy, who owned Hanlon's fish merchants in Moore Street, drove a smashing two-tone Citroën DS Pallas. Mister Kilroy, of Kilroy Brothers in Jervis Street, had a gorgeous Jaguar – white leather upholstery and walnut interior – but it was a divil for petrol. Mister Gore-Grimes, with a rosebud in his buttonhole, was from the solicitors on Parnell Square. A Ford Zephyr, he had. Two Mister Noyeks came from the timber yard down the street. They drove Ford Zodiacs with special gold number plates.

Liam stayed on in the evenings, doing paperwork. Helping the mechanics who were working overtime. Listening. Watching. Learning. You got two eyes, two ears and one mouth for a good reason. He got his five-bob increase. He took on more and more work tasks. Bill Lambert became a close mentor, and advised him to go to night school, so he enrolled in the commerce school on Parnell Square, beside Findlaters' Church. Three nights a week, from six-thirty to ten o'clock. Book-keeping, commerce, English, shorthand and typing.

The Parnell Street Traders' Association decided to have a December promotion. For every purchase made in any shop on the street, you got an entry form for the competition to guess how many peas were in the huge jar in the window of Duggan's Pharmacy. With Liam getting all the messages for the garage-workers every day, he filled in a lot of entry forms.

Duggan's Pharmacy was owned and managed by Timmy O'Sullivan from Kerry. A dapper gentleman with a bow tie and a very busy air about him. Good business for a chemist opposite the Rotunda maternity hospital with the women rambling over for prescriptions. His lovely daughter Ciara served in the shop and all the Walden lads had a crush on her. Ciara was a Rose of Tralee and married the property developer John Byrne, who was a great friend of Charles Haughey. Liam never forgot the big sign on display behind the shop counter, which read: 'The price of everything you buy includes the integrity of the man you buy it from.' Wise words.

At eight o'clock on Christmas Eve, Mary Darcy was scrubbing the young ones in her steel bathtub when the doorbell rang. Liam came out and found Dan Sullivan at the door with a huge crate, bigger than a coffin.

'Well done, Liam,' said Dan. 'You've won this Christmas hamper.' The Da opened the box. Gobsmacked. It was filled with ham, turkey, chickens, cakes, wine, whiskey and chocolates.

And what did Mary Darcy do? She shared it out, up and down the street. Everyone got something. The Cullen family tasted turkey for the first time. And Mother Darcy took a big slab of Oxford lunch over to the nuns in Saint Joseph's. She convinced them that it wasn't a sin to eat the cake, when it was the will of God that had sent the hamper to young Liam. Lots of happy faces that Christmas.

*

Sean Moran was a great supporter of them all. Noel and Brian were now in Brú Mhuire as well. He looked after them. Football, reading, chess. Open your mind. You can get out of the tenements. You can get out of the flats. That was his encouragement to all the Brú boys.

One evening, Brother Moran called all the older lads in to see him. Great news. 'We've got ourselves an old railway carriage from CIÉ, and we've got a site on the beach in Portrane. A truck takes the carriage down this Saturday. I need volunteers to work with me for the next few weeks to renovate the carriage. It's going to be the Brú's beach house.'

Portrane was a beautiful beach, about fourteen miles north of Dublin, past Portmarnock, Malahide and Rush. You could cycle down in an hour, or a train from Amiens Street would take you to Donabate in thirty minutes. Then it was another half-hour run to Portrane.

Brother Sean Moran (extreme left) with the lads at Portrane beach in 1960

It only took a few weeks to install twelve bunk beds in the carriage – good practice for the carpentry class. There was a separate kitchen, with a fold-up dining table. A little private caboose for the Brothers in charge. Outside loo, and washing facilities.

The Brú's beach house in Portrane was used at weekends, with all the boys rostered in turn. Older boys got a week's holiday in the summer. Football, swimming, cycling and all sorts of games were played on the beach. The tenement lads now sported year-round tans. Another great amenity, thanks to Sean Moran and the Brú.

Liam always had to leave Portrane early on Sunday evening. He hopped on the bike at three-thirty to cycle home, to do the Sunday-evening ticket-selling in O'Connell Street. One evening, his pedal snapped off as he pushed up the hill out of Swords. He got a piece of twine and tied his foot to the hole in the crank. Push-pulled his way home. He got a bloody ankle, but he was in time to sell his tickets. Got a nickname for a while as a 'pedal-and-cranker'. Not nice, when you understand the Dublin rhyming slang. He left the bike with Mister O'Brien, to fit a new pedal. When Liam collected the bike, he found it was O'Brien's young son, Willie, who had done the job. Only a seven-year-old, and already repairing the bikes with his Da. They start them young in Summerhill.

Liam got another sharp business lesson in the Brú. Brother Kirwan was telling everyone all about a terrific investment. Double your money in three years. 'Everyone in the Brewery is investing. Syndicating, they are. Groups of twenty, each putting in a pound every week. Giving twenty pounds a week to Mister Paul Singer, of Shanahan's Stamp Auctions. They buy and sell used postage stamps and make a fortune.' The Brewery syndicate got nearly three hundred pounds in quarterly dividends last year, on a one thousand pounds investment. Brother Kirwan invited the other Brothers and older Brú boys to form a syndicate. Liam kicked in five shillings a week to the syndicate for six months. Six pounds. He got a pound in dividends.

Sean Moran had opted out. 'I can't believe that these stamps can make so much. Sounds chancy to me,' Sean said. And was he right. The whole shebang came down like a deck of cards when the rozzers raided Shanahans. A scam it was. Singer was using new investors' money to pay the dividends to old investors. Sometimes he invested in stamps, but it was all about robbing Peter to pay Paul. Liam lost a fiver, but the Brewery boys lost a lot more. Sean Moran laughed. Singer went to jail but got out after conducting his own appeal a few years later. Lesson learned for Liam. 'Don't give your money to another man to look after,' said Sean Moran. 'Mind it yourself. And shares that go up can come down with a bang,' said Sean Moran.

*

The Ma took Liam over to Portland Row to look at a little house that was for sale. Number 18, opposite the Rehab on Dunne Street. Four rooms plus a five-foot-high basement with two more little rooms. Water and electricity. Outside toilet. No bathroom. A big come-down from the facilities of the flats. It was in poor repair – a lot of work needed to be done. But the Ma was excited.

'I can buy it for five hundred pounds, and I have that saved now. It's a house of our own. Our own hall door – for the first time ever, our own hall door,' she said fiercely. 'Liam, look at what we can do. One big room as a kitchen and our bedroom. One bedroom for the boys, with two beds. The same for the girls. And we'll have a parlour for visitors. We can use one of the small rooms downstairs for a bathroom. Sure, it'll be terrific.'

Liam saw that she was set on it. 'Can I have the other little downstairs room, Ma? I've exams for the next few years. I could sleep and study by meself, away from the gang.'

She looked at him and ruffled his hair. 'Why not? Sure, you're earning more than the Da now, so ya are,' she said. The Da was delighted to get away from the flats. The Ma bought the house, and in they moved. A lot of carpentry, plastering, wallpapering, plumbing and painting had to be done. Liam learned another carpentry rule from the Da. Measure twice and cut once – better than the other way round. They worked on the house all through the winter.

Liam had Tommy Sherlock and Sean Treacy in every Saturday, digging out the floor in his little basement room. It took six months to take eighteen inches of earth out. They set in a new concrete floor. Then he had a snug little room, with his single bed, his library shelves, a table for a desk and his record player. And they bored a separate entrance down from the front garden. Read, study, exercise, plan, listen to records, with the pals able to slip in and out at weekends. Privacy. The outside loo was still a problem. You had to run for it when it was raining.

And the water pipes froze in the winter. That was Liam's job early every morning, with the *Herald* coming to the rescue again. Get a basin. Tear up the bundles of old papers. Light them in the basin and hold the fire under the external pipe in the yard, until the ice melted and the water flowed. God bless the man who invented the *Herald*.

*

Every summer the Brú Mhuire took the boys on a summer-camp holiday to County Kildare. Liam missed the first two camps in Timahoe and Allenwood. He couldn't afford the twenty-five-shilling cost, or the week off. But the Ma let him off the Lane for the Clonsast Camp and paid the money for the week. She gave him ten shillings in pocket money, too. Here we go, here we go, here we go. The trip started from North Great George's Street. One hundred young fellas, two buses. Singing all the way. Down the Galway road, left for

Celbridge at the Spa Hotel, to Clane, to Prosperous, to Clonsast. Out in the heart of the country. Culchie land. The Bog of Allen.

Bord na Móna was the state agency that was responsible for developing the boglands of Ireland. They cut and saved the turf for burning in the electricity-generating stations at Edenderry and Tullamore. Miles of mini-railway tracks criss-crossing the bog, taking the turf to the stations. Half a dozen turf camps dotted the bog, housing the bog workers, who worked eleven months a year. The camps were wartime corrugated-tin structures shaped in a half-arc. Dormitory space, dining room, kitchen and play area. They were not unlike the prisoner-of-war camps of Stalag Luft Seventeen.

The bog workers left to go home to their families in Connemara, Mayo and Donegal for the month of August. The young fellas from the city centre moved into the camps. Irish army quartermaster chefs volunteered to feed the lads. The social workers to oversee the boys were led by Father O'Neill and Sean Moran. It was a week of adventure from dawn to dusk. It was so exciting.

Football matches in the field. Swimming in the river. Cricket matches. Rounders. Basketball. Cycling trips. Hiking. Quiz games. Obstacle course. Up at seven. Father O'Neill said Mass. Liam and Tommy Sherlock served as altar boys. Breakfast was the usual porridge; for dinner it was rabbit stew. Tea in the evening with banana sambos, then a sing-song around the campfire, and bed at ten o'clock. The older boys were allowed into Prosperous on Friday night for the *céilí* dance in the parish hall. Only touch the girls' hands. No close encounters. Three feet apart. The parish priest walked the floor, ensuring that no occasions of sin took place.

The highlight of the week for Liam was Professor Hurley, the visiting Professor of Botany from Trinity College. He spent an hour every day walking the lads around the hedges and riverbanks, identifying the fauna, the flowers, the bird-life. He held an exam on the Saturday morning, before they packed up. Twenty bird pictures and twenty plant stems to be identified. Liam got first place and a prize of two pounds. The Ma was delighted when he brought it home. Full refund of the camp fee.

From left: Liam with Kevin Lawless and Frankie Smith at the Bord na Móna Clonsast Camp in County Kildare

—

26

THE BROTHERS FLY THE NEST

Brian wasn't getting on too well in school. Or with the Da. Headstrong he was, and quick-tempered. Resented authority. One evening he had a row with the Da, who gave him a dig and sent him to his room: 'No, you're not going to the Brú tonight.' Brian went. The Da was furious, walking the floor, waiting for him to get home.

Liam was coming from classes in Rathmines on his bike and dropped into the club to pick up Brian and Noel. He heard about the hubble-bubble. 'Okay, this is serious,' he told Brian. 'The Da will bate ya black and blue.'

Brian was stubborn. 'If he touches me, I'll break the chair over his head.' From a thirteen-year-old. And the Da with arms like tree trunks from his timber-lifting. Liam laid down the strategy. He'd go in first with Noel. Calm the Da down. Give Brian a chance to slip into the bedroom. Brian wasn't to go near the Da in the kitchen. It worked well. Liam and Noel said how good Brian was at the table tennis and at the aero-modelling. They had the Da sitting down. Calm. The Ma was supportive. Liam heard the bedroom door creak outside. Brian was in.

But the Da heard too, and raised his voice. 'But if that young fella ever talks back to me again, I'll brain him.'

Brian kicked the door in. 'Come on then, see if I'm afraid of you. You're only a bowsie, throwing yar weight around. Big man.' The Da went bananas. He caught Brian by the shirt collar and gave him a few thumps. Brian couldn't get near him. Liam and Noel were grabbing the Da's arms. Waste of time. The Ma smacked her poker across the table with a resounding crash. Silence.

'Billy Cullen, you leave that young fella down or you'll get this poker across the head. Now!' she said fiercely. The Da backed away.

'And now, Brian, you apologise to your father this minute. Go on. Say you're sorry.'

Brian's lips were blue with temper. Tears of frustration stood in his eyes. 'Never,' he said. 'Never, never, never', and turned and ran out of the room. Old bull, young bull.

The Ma nodded and Noel and Liam left and went inside to Brian. He was sitting on the bed. Kicking the wall in frustration. Wouldn't talk. Liam told him to take it easy, that things would blow over: the Da was just exerting his parental authority. Brian kicked the wall again. The Ma and Da were fighting and rowing inside in the other room. Eventually, things calmed down and Liam went down to his basement room. Brian would have to realise there was discipline in the house.

The following morning, Liam found a note under his door. 'Liam, I've taken twenty quid out of your stash. Don't worry, I'll pay you back. Mind the Ma. See ya, Brian.' Up to the bedroom. Brian gone.

Telegram three days later from Birmingham. The Ma's sister, Esther. 'BRIAN OKAY WITH ME. WORKING. I'LL MIND HIM. ESTHER.'

The Ma asked Liam to go to Birmingham. 'Talk to Brian. See how he is. You might be able to talk him into coming back home.'

Liam went over to Auntie Esther for a few days. He got the mailboat and the train. He left his overnight bag with Esther and went down to the Murphy building site where Brian was working on an apartment block. He spotted Brian climbing a ladder with a load of bricks in a hod on his shoulder. He was already bigger. Filled out. But when they met face to face, he could see Brian was haggard. He was worn out completely from carrying a six-stone load of bricks up a ladder all day. Then home to Esther, dinner, look at TV and bed before ten. Six days a week. Stay in bed on Sunday. But Brian wasn't coming home. 'And let the Da see I was beaten? Never.'

Liam got him to take a day off and they walked the city, into the Bull Ring. They went to see *Rio Bravo*, a film with John Wayne, Dean Martin and a Hollywood pretty-boy, Ricky Nelson. It was a great cowboy picture. Brian was a John Wayne fan. Give them stick, never back down. And home to Aunt Esther for a lovely pan-fried haddock and home-made chips. It was the only time he ever had a full day out with his younger brother.

Two weeks later, another telegram from Aunt Esther: 'BRIAN GONE. JOINED THE BRITISH ARMY.'

Liam eventually got him on the phone in the Catterick Training Camp. A private in the Irish Greenjackets Regiment. He had had a row with the foreman on the building site. He won the fight, but lost his job. Feck them all. He joined the army to see the world.

Brian (left) and Liam (right) with their cousin 'Joe Boy' Corcoran (centre). Liam and Joe Boy are trying to persuade Brian to come home from Birmingham.

'They're sending me to Sarawak next month. Where's that, Liam?' he asked. And he did end up in Borneo the next month. The British Vietnam. A postcard came. 'I'm only a teenage killer. Shooting gooks all day.' Two years he spent in the Far East. Didn't come home. Went to Canada. Worked as a steeplejack on the Americans' early-warning missile-construction sites. The DEW Line. Dangerous. Forty degrees below zero. But great money.

Brian returned from Canada on his first trip home since the row with the Da five years before. He checked into the plush Gresham Hotel. Rented a big Zephyr Zodiac. Top-of-the-bus stuff. 'I'll show the Da style.' He drove down to the house in the big car. The Ma ran out of the door onto the street to hug him as he got out of the car. Brothers and sisters all around. The prodigal son returns. The Ma shed a mother's tears of joy. Silence as he walked into the kitchen, with the Da standing there. Brian a husky young fella. The Da still towering over him like an oak tree. 'Howaya, Da. I brought ya this leather jacket from Canada.' A peace offering. It worked.

'Howaya, son,' the Da said. 'That was thoughtful of ya', and he held out his hand. They shook hands, toe to toe, eyeball to eyeball, man to man. The Ma smiled in relief. Time sorts out everything.

Brian stayed until his money ran out. That only took two weeks, the way he flung it around. He had a night out with Liam. Drinking Hennessy brandy, he was now. Told Liam horrific stories about killing and surviving in the jungle. The fear he felt. The bravery of his mates.

'If they're not white, just shoot them,' were the orders. Of course, Brian got himself into trouble with authority. Slapped a captain with his rifle-butt and spent six months in the Singapore stockade. Animal country. Serious assault stuff. Untold stories he carried with him forever.

'Had to kill a few more in there,' he said with a sad, tortured look on his face. Enough said. He left for the plane without a word. Never say goodbye. But there was an envelope on the mantelpiece for Liam. Four fivers. 'Thanks for the loan.'

Noel was an action man. All the fighting war films. *Back to Bataan, The Sands of Iwo Jima, From Here to Eternity*. And then a famous Irish-American World-War-Two film called *The Fighting Sullivans*, about five Irish brothers who joined the American navy. The youngest running after the older brothers, shouting, 'Hey, wait for me!' They fought through the Pacific War, and one by one, they were killed in battle. Even the young sixteen-year-old, at the Battle of Guadalcanal. The film ended with the lads marching up to the Pearly Gates in their

American sailor's uniforms. And as Peter opened up, a shout rang out and the young fella came charging up, shouting, 'Hey, wait for me!' A tribute to the thousands of Irishmen who fought for the Star-spangled Banner. For their adopted country. The country which had given hope, freedom and a new life to countless Irish families. From the time of the Civil War, after the Famine, the Irish were always ready to fight for the American flag.

Noel joined the LDF as a reserve recruit. The Local Defence Force. Teenagers in uniform who went away at weekends for training to the Glen of Imaal and the Curragh Camp. That summer, all the Irish boys got the soldier bug. There was a big recruiting drive from the British army in Irish newspapers. 'Join the Army and See the World.' Glamorous pictures of soldiers in Gibraltar sunning themselves, in Heidelberg with the *Fräulein*s, in Singapore on the rickshaws. Sport, fitness, travel, good pay. It attracted a lot of young lads from the tenements. There was little future for them in the Ireland of the fifties. No jobs, no dole. You either started a criminal career or you got the boat. Or you joined the army.

Liam sent in a recruitment form for the Commandos. Report up to Ormeau Square in Belfast for the examination. He got the train up and sat for a written test with twenty other lads, from all over Ireland.

The test was a doddle. An IQ test. Complete a sequence of numbers. Which box of dots is next. A hundred questions to be finished in one hour. Hands up when you finish. Liam finished first. Paper checked. Taken to the major's office.

Liam stood to attention in front of his desk. The

major sitting behind the desk had a quick look at the test forms. 'All correct,' he said. 'Well, that's a first for this paper.' He looked Liam over. Boots sparkling. Kingston shirt gleaming. Chin in. Chest out. Fists at his side with the forefinger knuckle pointed at the toe of his boot. Billy-Cullen trained.

The adjutant added, 'And finished in twenty minutes, sir.' The major nodded approval. He stood up and walked around from his desk. He looked Liam in the eye.

'You're wasting your talents, my boy,' he said. 'This man's army would do your head in. We cater for the lowest common denominator and you are too clever to take orders from muscle-bound idiots. Go home to Dublin. Start a business. Any business. You can't go wrong.' Not a smile. Deadly serious. 'Dismissed,' he said, throwing a salute, which Liam automatically returned. He swung on his heels and marched out the door, which the adjutant had quickly opened. He stood outside on the street in the drizzle. Stunned. The other lads were still inside doing the test. All the way home on the train, he repeated the major's words in his head. 'Start a business. Any business.' Wow. How could he do that?

A month later, Noel took the trip north and joined up as a recruit with the Irish Guards. Loved the army, Noel did. Went off to training school in England, where he graduated first in his class. All his LDF experience. Corporal Noel Cullen of the Irish Guards went off to Germany to serve with the British army on the Rhine. Football, skiing, *Fräulein*s. The life of Riley. Until he was riddled by Arab bullets in the desert sands of Aden.

When Noel and Brian both emigrated, the Ma lost

two wage-earners. Liam and the Da had the only wage packets to put on the mantelpiece on Friday night. Unopened. Frank and Eamon were recruited to the team.

*

Every year, the *An Óige* youth organisation held a big hooley in the Mansion House, in the magnificent Round Room attached to the Lord Mayor's residence in Dawson Street, just off Stephen's Green. The hooley was officially titled the Tramp's Ball, and the idea was that you could dress as you liked. Charlie Chaplin, court jesters and the Lone Ranger were the favourite outfits. No alcohol was allowed, only lemonade. Music was by the Laurence O'Toole Céilí Band. There were prizes for the best outfits.

The lads – Liam, Tommy, Sean, Jimmy and Kevin – decided to go as the Belles of St Trinians – a take-off of the English schoolgirl comedy. Vera organised the girls' school uniforms from Sister Louise in St Agatha's. Fishnet tights, green gymslips, white blouses, and high-heeled shoes. Tommy was able to wear a stuffed bra. Liam was already bursting the gymslip, but wore a sexy blonde wig.

Off through O'Connell Street they went, causing great hilarity, and ribald comments. A few drinks in Sinnotts on the Green. It was mostly lemonade, but a couple of the lads were at the pints-of-Guinness stage. The publican joined in the fun.

'Ladies can only be served in the snug. This is a gentlemen's establishment.' Before Kevin could take umbrage at this insult to his obvious moustachioed masculinity, Liam made the point that there were four good-looking girls already in the snug, and Kevin was in like a shot.

They hit the Mansion House. The four girls, all nurses from Dr Steeven's Hospital, went along with them. A great night. Dancing, singing. They won the 'best group' prize. Did the conga into the Lord Mayor's house. Finished at eleven. Time to get home. But Liam ended up in an alcove in Dawson Street, squeezing and kissing one of the nurses, who was in flying form after two lemonades. Plus, she told him, a drop of whiskey from her perfume bottle. She was dressed in jodhpurs, as Dale Evans. She found out how hard it was to get inside Liam's fishnet tights with swimming trunks over them. Liam found out she had no bra on.

It was half eleven as he ran home, and the Da was in the window, watching. But Rita and Vera were on the footpath, waiting for him.

'You're late! We stayed here, or the Da would be out looking for ya. Did ya have a good night?' Vera asked.

'Great time. Danced me head off. Fantastic,' he said.

Rita looked at him. Smiling. Knowingly. 'Hope you didn't leave your wig in some girl's blouse,' she said quietly as they walked in the door.

The wig was gone. What to say to Father Nix in Confession tomorrow? he thought. No, make it next Saturday. And then he discovered that the alcove he'd been in with Dale Evans was the entrance porch of Saint Anne's Church in Dawson Street. Excommunication, he thought. Jaysus, I'll leave it until we go on that weekend retreat with Brother Moran next month.

A weekend of silent retreat with the Jesuits in Rathfarnham Castle was an annual event for the Brú

The Belles of St Trinian's outside the Gresham Hotel on the way to the Tramps' Ball in the Mansion House. Liam is on the left in the front row, wearing a blonde wig.

Mhuire boys. Sean Moran worked hard to get all the lads to go. 'It's a great opportunity to clean out any problems. Start afresh. Set new goals. Talk through any problems with an understanding priest in a quiet atmosphere – not your local priest, who knows your mother. It's a priest who doesn't know you. Absorb the ambience of peace and contentment,' said Brother Moran.

So most of the lads went every year. Up to Rathfarnham Castle at four o'clock on Saturday afternoon. Move into your Spartan room, containing a bed, a closet, a table, a chair, a reading lamp and a wash-hand basin. Communal toilet and showers down the hall. Very, very quiet.

Once you checked in and went to your room, you read the rules. Total silence until eight o'clock on Monday morning. Two nights in the cloister. If you really have to communicate, do so by gestures or by notes.

They started with the Rosary at six, followed by a lecture until eight o'clock on the sins of youth, followed by Benediction. Confessions after that, with six priests available. Liam took a long while to work up the courage to confess his sin with the nurse. Three times he made for the priest's room and three times he passed by to the toilets. Then he saw Tommy Sherlock coming out from Confession. Big smile on his face. Gave Liam a thumbs-up. Liam took a big breath and opened the door.

The priest was sitting in one of the two fireside armchairs. 'Come in, son, and sit down here and we'll just have a chat.'

It was so gentle. Talking through the temptations of growing up. The realities of sexual desires. Respect all girls who are created in the image of the Virgin Mother of Christ. Go in peace, your sins are forgiven.

Mass at seven on Sunday morning with Liam and Tommy as the serving altar boys in the lovely church. Then breakfast, another lecture, and free time to talk with the priest in the garden. General absolution for all the sins you may have ever committed. All gone, washed away, you're pure as the driven snow. An apostle of Christ.

It was an exhilarating experience. The adrenalin surged. You were jumping out of your skin. A temple of the Holy Ghost. You read all about the life of Saint Ignatius Loyola. You renewed your Confirmation pledge of abstinence from alcohol. Mass on Monday morning. When the abbot had said grace before breakfast, you could speak.

Tommy looked at Liam. His eyes were glowing. 'I feel terrific, Liam. I feel like a new man.' Sean Moran was right. A new beginning. Go forth in peace and sin no more.

'Where's Waxy?' asked Tommy. Kevin had been next door to Waxy.

'He went over the wall last night to the Yellow House for a few pints, said Kevin. 'Ended up in the Buglers' Rest with a few girls. Got a taxi to bring him back here and he fell into the reception, pissed out of his mind. One of the priests took him home in the taxi.'

Waxy's last silent retreat in Rathfarnham, that was.

27

A NEW FREEDOM

The Cullen family were growing up fast in Portland Row. Vera was now the full-time housekeeper. She was a great cook, and terrific with the baking. She loved the kids and took care of the babies. A little mammy.

Rita was getting restless. She was processing an application to emigrate to America. 'As an au pair, whatever that is,' said Mother Darcy. 'Takes a while. Say nothing till ya hear more.'

Rita left Mitchell's. She got tired of the same routine with the same people and the smell of the cow horns. She got a job in Maguire and Patterson, the friendly match people, down in Smithfield. Similar boring job, but a different smell – sulphur. There were different people, and fresh gossip. She bought a new bike on the never-never from McHugh himself in Talbot Street. Five shillings a week for two years. She saved a fortune on bus fares.

Rita was well into the rock-and-roll scene. Tight skirt and sweater for the dances in the Crystal. She was doing a steady line with Mattie Saunders in Number 44 – a great jiver. But she was meeting plenty of fellas under the clock by Nelson's Pillar as well.

She was still restless. The wages were poor. A pal,

Nancy Ennis, had emigrated to Boston and was sending home letters with glowing reports of life in America. Rita and another pal, Ann Bowes, eventually made the trip when they got a temporary USA visa. Two years in the States as a housekeeper for $100 a week, less the deduction for the prepaid plane ticket.

The Ma didn't go to the airport, just waved goodbye at the door. She went inside to sit by the fire, looking wistfully into the flames. Liam came in. 'Well, Ma,' he said, 'that's another one off to stand on her own two feet. Give us a smile.'

Mary turned and looked at him, knowing he was cheering her up. She gave him a big smile. 'You are dead right, son.'

All the Cullen kids in 1957 in Molly Darcy's kitchen
Back row, left to right: Carmel, Angela, Brian and Noel; middle: Vera, Rita and Liam; front: baby Aidan, Frank, Marie, Brenda and Eamon

'So let's make a cup of tea,' Liam said, putting the kettle on.

Mary went to the dresser. 'And I have some Madeira layer cake here that ya like. Let's celebrate Rita going off to the States.' Putting the cake on the table, she ruffled his hair. 'And may the Blessed Virgin watch over her out there,' she said quietly.

Rita's first year in America was an unhappy one. She moved from her first employer to another. Hassle over the wages. Homesickness. But eventually she settled down with the Vidal family in East Falmouth, on Cape Cod. She came home when her contract expired, and went to work in Lemons Sweet Factory, up at Drumcondra Bridge. Same old factory routine. Poor wages. But she enjoyed the craic and the rock-and-roll scene with the showbands. The Miami, with the ould pal from St Peter's Hall, Dickie Rock. And another family friend, Butch Moore, with the Capitol Showband. Rita followed them at weekends. Herself and Kathleen Fox, hitch-hiking all over the country to the venues. Rita had a big crush on Paddy Cole from Castleblaney, who played the clarinet and saxophone. Then a letter from the Vidals arrived, and off she went, back to America, leaving Butch Moore to his Eurovision success with 'Walking the Streets in the Rain'.

Arthur Vidal had a well-known construction company. He did a lot of building on Cape Cod and maintenance work on the Kennedy compound in Hyannis. It was Ted Kennedy who proposed the visa application for Rita to go to the States. Eventually, Carmel and Marie followed, and now there are three Cullen sisters living in Cape Cod. God bless America.

LISTER HILL, ALA., CHAIRMAN

WAYNE MORSE, OREG.   JACOB K. JAVITS, N.Y.
RALPH YARBOROUGH, TEX.   WINSTON L. PROUTY, VT.
JOSEPH S. CLARK, PA.   PETER H. DOMINICK, COLO.
JENNINGS RANDOLPH, W. VA.   GEORGE MURPHY, CALIF.
HARRISON A. WILLIAMS, JR., N.J.   PAUL J. FANNIN, ARIZ.
CLAIBORNE PELL, R.I.   ROBERT P. GRIFFIN, MICH.
EDWARD M. KENNEDY, MASS.
GAYLORD NELSON, WIS.
ROBERT F. KENNEDY, N.Y.

        STEWART E. McCLURE, CHIEF CLERK
        JOHN S. FORSYTHE, GENERAL COUNSEL

United States Senate

COMMITTEE ON
LABOR AND PUBLIC WELFARE

September 15, 1966

Mr. James H Smith
207 Shore Street
Falmouth, Massachusetts

Dear Jim:

Enclosed is a report I just received from the American
Embassy in Dublin.

As you will note, Mary Teresa Cullen has not yet made
formal application for her visa, and as soon as she does
so, she will be given an appointment for her medical. Since
the quota is current in Ireland, she should be given her
visa the same day she has her medical, providing she is in
good health.

I will contact you when I receive further developments
on her case.

Sincerely,

Ted

Edward M. Kennedy

Letter from Senator Ted Kennedy regarding Rita's US visa

*

Liam was working twelve-hour days in Walden's. He
was keenly interested in the car-sales side of the business.
The Ford cars were shipped from the Cork factory to
Dublin by rail. It took about a week for them to reach
Kingsbridge. Some cars, however, were urgently needed
for important customers, so every Wednesday a posse
of Walden salesmen would head for Cork on the afternoon train and drive the cars back from Cork to Dublin.
Slowly. The new cars had to be run in. They had a
maximum speed of thirty miles an hour, so they didn't
get to Dublin until two or three in the morning.

One day the head salesman, Kingsley Long from Malahide, told Liam that he would be coming on the trip to Cork. For experience. 'To show you the ropes.' It was an exciting day for the young fella. The train journey to Cork. Fish and chips at the station. Down to the Ford plant at the Marina in Cork, where the Ford cars were lined up. Liam travelled back in the black Ford Prefect with Mister Long. All the cars were black. 'Any colour you like, as long as it's black' was the Ford motto in those days.

Mister Long had a large flask with him. 'Water it is,' he said to Liam. 'You need to drink plenty of water for this job.' The roads were slippery in the winter ice, and when the little convoy came to Watergrasshill, it was obvious the lads knew the drill. Into the lay-by, reverse the car, and nice and slowly go up the long hill in reverse gear. She wouldn't go up the hill any other way.

And Liam found out why he was drinking the water. None of the Fords had heating systems. Sixteen pounds ten shillings as an optional extra, which most customers wouldn't pay. 'Sure, what do I need a heater in the car for? Haven't I an overcoat?' Being without the heater meant the windscreen iced up. So every hour or so the convoy pulled in for de-icing. With hot urine.

'Keep drinking the water, son; it's really freezing tonight.'

Liam didn't get home to his snug basement room until after three in the morning. The Ma had left him a mug of milk and a slice of apple pie. And unlike the salesmen, who got the morning off after the long Cork excursion, Liam was in work at seven-thirty the next morning as usual.

And the boss, Billy Wallace, noticed. 'Did you not

go to Cork yesterday, Willum?' he asked.

'Yes, Mister Wallace, and back safe and sound here at three o'clock last night,' was the reply.

The boss smiled. 'It's the early bird that catches the worm,' he said, and Liam got a ten-bob wage increase that week. He was never late and never out sick in his seventeen years with Walden's.

*

Liam sat his year-end exams in Rathmines College of Commerce and got first place. He won the Usher Prize, an award presented annually to the best student by the Dublin Chamber of Commerce. The boss was delighted and gave him a rise of a pound a week. The Ma was delighted with the rise. Liam was notified to present himself at the Chamber's monthly luncheon to receive his award: the Usher Prize certificate and twenty pounds.

Mister Wallace travelled over to the Chamber's head-quarters in the Ouzel Galley in Dame Street, driving his brand new Zephyr Zodiac V6. The bee's knees. Top of the bus. Liam ran over through the streets – down Moore Street, saying hello to all his dealer pals. He stopped for a chat with the Ma and Nanny Kelly. The Ma gave him a big pippin apple. Tom Kelly waved him over, smoking his Sherlock Holmes pipe.

'Well done, Liam,' he said. 'I believe you were *numero uno* in your exams. Here's a little present for you, and the best of luck.' He gave Liam an envelope. When Liam opened it later, he found a gift voucher for five pounds from Fred Hanna's, the bookshop in Nassau Street. Good oul' Tom.

He headed for the Ha'penny Bridge and popped into Hector Grey's. 'How's it going, Hector?' Hector looked at him. Liam was all dressed up in his Louis Copeland charcoal-grey flannel suit.

'Not as well as it's going for you, obviously, swanning around like Lord Muck. Bejaysus, you're looking great, Liamo,' he said. 'Does this executive look mean you won't be on the street this Christmas?'

'Not at all, Hector,' Liam replied. 'Sure, ya couldn't do without me to keep your turnover up. And get yer one per cent, right?' They both had a good laugh. Hector watched him marching confidently over the bridge. Spittin' image of his father.

The porter at the Ouzel Galley had bad news. The businessmen were upstairs, having cocktails before lunch. Yes, Mister Wallace of Walden's had arrived. But Liam wasn't to join the group until the after-lunch presentation. The good news was that the porter was an army pal of the Da's. 'Come on, son, and you can share my lunch. I've a little caboose under the stairs.' So Liam shared a few cheese sambos with the porter. They each had a few slugs of milk out of the milk bottle, and they split the Ma's apple.

On the dot of two o'clock, the porter knocked loudly on the door, threw it open, and made his deep-voiced announcement. 'Gentlemen of the Dublin Chamber, I give you the winner of this year's Usher Prize: Master William Cullen.'

The group rose, clapping loudly. Mister Wallace came forward with the Chamber president, who gave Liam four five-pound notes. Liam was photographed getting his certificate. The meeting was over, and Mister Wallace gave him a lift back to work. In great form, he was. Gave Liam an envelope.

'There's another twenty pounds for you, Willum, and today was a great day for Walden Motor Company. Puts our name on the map for those businessmen. I got three enquiries for new cars,' he said, looking very pleased with himself. 'Can you drive this car, Willum?' he asked suddenly.

Liam looked at the sumptuous interior. The huge bonnet. The automatic gear lever. 'Well, Mister Wallace, I've only driven Anglias with a manual gearbox up to now. But I'll give it a go.'

The boss had a little think. Only four hundred miles on the clock. Thousands of cyclists in O'Connell Street. 'A better idea would be for us to get you a full course of driving lessons from Gerry Barry. Starting tomorrow. We'll talk to him when we get back to the garage,' he said.

So Liam had his driving lessons, with manual and automatic gearboxes, and got his full driving licence.

*

He was getting bigger now, and was well over six feet tall. He was selected to play for a Dublin Soccer XI against Belfast in Bushy Park, wearing the sky-blue jersey of the Dublin GAA team. It was a great game, with his East Wall pal Ben Hannigan scoring. Liam played a blinder.

He got a phone call the next day and agreed to meet Peter Keely from the famous Home Farm amateur soccer club in Dublin. He went up to their Whitehall academy and played in a trial match. Afterwards he had a cup of tea with Peter and Don Seery. Would he sign for the Home Farm Club? Yes! Then Peter stuck him

The Dublin Soccer XI that played against Belfast in 1959.
Liam is at the extreme right of the back row;
Ben Hannigan is at the extreme left of the back row.

to the floor when he said, 'You were watched by a cross-Channel scout on Sunday, Liamo. Would ya like to play for an English club?'

Liam smiled. There was fierce allegiance in Dublin lads to the English soccer clubs. 'I suppose it's Wycombe Wanderers, in the Fourth Division,' he said jokingly, to cover his surprise.

Peter looked at him hard. 'Now, son, this is no joke. I was a professional left-half, played for Ireland, marked Stanley Matthews, and I'm dead serious. We can get you a three-year contract with Manchester United.'

Silence. Liam's heart was thumping, but he didn't show it. 'What's the deal? The money.'

'It's a standard three-year contract. Six pounds a week for the three years. But you only get two pounds. Two goes to the landlady in Manchester who takes care of ya, and two pounds is sent to your mother here in Dublin.' Liam looked at him. Say nothing till ya hear more.

'Did you know the maximum wage for a footballer in England is twenty pounds a week? For the top stars. That's what Bobby Charlton and Denis Law get paid,' Peter said.

'Suppose I did happen to make the first team. Would I get the twenty?' Liam asked.

Peter looked at Seery, who replied, 'No, Liam, it's a complete three-year contract, with the wages fixed for three years. Whether you're sweeping terraces or playing on the first team, your pay is six pounds a week. That's it.'

Liam looked at the two of them. 'Well, you can raffle that,' he said.

Peter laughed. 'You're right, Liam,' he said. 'The pay is brutal. Great honour and glory if ya make it, and only one in a hundred do. But the pay is buttons. Take it from me, I know, there's no money in football. Off you go, and mind your good job in Walden's. We'll see ya for training up here next Monday.'

And that was the end of celebrity aspirations. Although he got a great surprise at training, because who was there to give a coaching week, only the great Jackie Carey. The Da was thrilled to see a picture in the paper of his son, in Home Farm colours, kicking a ball with his hero.

*

The Ma agreed to let Liam have every second weekend off in the summer, so that he could join the lads, hitch-hiking. They got the bus out to Bray after work on Saturday morning. Hitch-hiked to Arklow. Pitched the tent down on the beach dunes, not far from the Arklow

Leisure Centre. Up the town for the craic in the pubs. Most of the lads were on orange, but one or two would be into the pint of Guinness. Tommy would always start the sing-song. Into the Irish rebel songs. The Clancy Brothers and the Dubliners were all the go. Then down to the leisure centre for the dancing, to a local band playing all the Elvis and Beatles numbers.

The local girls were all ready and willing to dance with the lads from Dublin and joined in for a fish-and-chip after the dance. Kiss and cuddle as well, if you were lucky, but no messing. The lads all went back to the tents. Paddy Matthews always insisted on pumping up the Primus stove and cooking a pot of porridge, which he ate before going to bed. Always did his own thing.

The gang were up at eight-thirty on Sunday morning, in time to run up to town for nine o'clock Mass. Then it was back to the tents for the Primus stove and a big fry-up. Two lads volunteered for the cooking while the rest went swimming. A game of football then, followed by another swim, then a game of pitch and putt with rented golf clubs.

Liam would hit the road early. He had to get back to O'Connell Street to sell his cinema tickets. Great weekend. A new freedom for the inner-city young fellas.

A two-week hitch-hiking holiday was planned for the August holiday fortnight. New tent and equipment and haversacks were bought in Alpha Bargains. Ex-army surplus stuff. The lads set off for Galway city. Liam didn't make it on day one. Lifts were slow, so he overnighted in a field in Athenry. Famine country. He made it to Salthill on Sunday to link up with the pals. Ballad-singing galore in the Galway pubs, with Tommy in demand for 'The Shoals of Herring', while Frankie

Smith gave a dazzling display on his tin whistle. Then dancing to the Capitol Showband in the Hanger Ballroom, with Paddy Cole doing all his Acker Bilk numbers. They visited Barna, Oughterard and went out into Connemara. Wild country. They saw a sign for Letterfrack and thought of Whacker and Blinky. 'Wonder where they are now?'

They caught a lift on a truck, south, to Limerick. Bunratty Castle, Dirty Nellie's Pub, Shannon Airport. Some of the lads headed for Cork. Liam, Sean and Jamsey Sherlock went for Killarney. They camped in the Flesk caravan park on the Muckross road, beside the Gleneagle Hotel, where the Miami Showband were on for the weekend. Dickie Rock had the girls screaming

Liam (right) with Jamesey Sherlock on his first trip to Killarney in 1959

for more. World-class, our Dickie. They took a trip around the lakes in a horse and trap after serious but friendly negotiations with the jarvey driver. They stopped at the Muckross Hotel for afternoon tea. Real swanky.

They walked out to Killarney Golf Club to see the breathtaking views of the famous lakes of Killarney and watched the fishermen pull out in their boats from beside the clubhouse – until a club official came out with some friendly advice: 'You backpackers will have to get out of here; this is private property you're on. There's no camping allowed, so buzz off.' The usual golf-club attitude. Regulations must be obeyed, so the lads camped at the Fossa campsite before heading off home, via Cork and Waterford. They saw more of Ireland in two weeks than all their parents combined had seen in a lifetime!

Liam was a health fanatic. He didn't smoke, didn't drink alcohol and wore his Pioneer pin, like the Ma and Da. His running, cycling, football, table tennis and gymnastics kept him fit as a fiddle. He ate plenty of fruit, particularly oranges, for Vitamin C. He followed Mother Darcy's rule: 'Never eat after six o'clock in the evening. Don't have food in your belly overnight.'

On Saturday evenings, the lads went dancing, usually to the Crystal Ballroom in South Anne Street. They would jive the night away. That is, providing they got in. Frankie Smith from Cabra had a chip on his shoulder – a truculent look on his face. Bouncers would have one glimpse of him and say: 'You're not getting in. Beat it.' For nothing. Just the way Frankie would look at them. So if Frankie didn't get in, they all left.

'Let's try the Four Provinces. They'd let Franken-stein in. But for the luv of Jaysus, Frankie, will ya smile?

Just give the bouncer a smile,' Tommy Sherlock said. Frankie practised his smile in the shop window. He looked like a bear with a wasp in his mouth.

Ireland was heading into the sixties. There was a new air of excitement in Dublin. Motor cars were outnumbering the horses and carts. Liam and the pals were listening to Elvis Presley on the record player in the basement room. 'Hound Dog' and 'Heartbreak Hotel' were nearly worn out, with the lads practising the jiving with Rita and Vera.

Elvis was the icon of social revolution. The words of 'Hound Dog' were innocuous. But the rocking sound of his voice pulsated. Tight jeans, turned-up shirt collars and swivelling hips were all the craze. Parents were dismayed at this ostentatious behaviour. It undermined the conservative ethos of Christianity. Young people went out to the dance hops. Jived together. Slow-danced with the opposite sex. Lurched around the dance floor to the sensuous tones of Elvis's 'Love Me Tender'. The parish priest and his pleas about occasions of sin went out the window. The young people were enjoying their youth. Elvis Presley had set them free.

The Saturday-night dancing was great fun. Ballrooms of romance. Girls on one side, boys on the other. All eyeing each other up.

'Two nice birds at the pole, Liamo,' said Tommy, 'but I don't fancy your one.' Kevin Lawless was nicknamed Valentino. A real good-looking charmer, he was. Always away first with a cracker. Tommy could charm the birds off the trees. 'I'm wonderin' would the nicest-looking girl here tonight have a little dance with me?' was one of his opening lines.

Frankie's truculent looks attracted the girls. Little boy

lost. They felt sorry for him. All he had to do was walk over, point to a girl, nod his head towards the dance floor, and the lucky girl would follow after him. Meekly. It worked every time. Almost. On the odd occasion, when the girl stayed put, Frankie would turn back.

'I said, are ya getting up?'

The haughty reply: 'Not with the likes of you.'

Frankie's retort: 'Sorry, I didn't see your wooden leg.' Macho stuff.

Liam was shy with the girls. He had acne during his teens. But he was a good mover and shaker on the floor. Once he got one dance, he was spotted as a jiver and he'd no trouble getting his dances. The lads would meet outside after the dance. Sometimes a man was lost in battle – off leaving a girl home. It was usually Kevin. The rest of them went down to the Paradiso Restaurant in Westmoreland Street or up to the Ships' Grill for St Patrick's filet mignon, with onions, chips and a glass of milk. A special treat. Then a quick run home. There was no curfew for him now, but he always made it before midnight. He never got home without seeing a lift of the curtain as he ran up the road. Mary Darcy never went to sleep until all her brood were in bed.

*

The 1960 Olympics were in Rome – the city of Audrey Hepburn and Gregory Peck in *Roman Holiday*. The Colosseum. Spartacus and the gladiators.

Liam went to see the Pathé news in the Ambassador Cinema time and again, to watch a short clip of the boxing. The light-heavyweight winner was a coloured American. Like Sugar Ray Robinson, he was. A great

The Cullen family on Vera's wedding day in 1961.
Noel was away on Defence Forces duties.

mover. Danced around the ring, with fists like lightning. No one laid a glove on his film-star face throughout the whole tournament. Hit and dance. Hit, hit, hit and dance away. Like a butterfly. Cassius Marcellus Clay. A winner in Rome – with a Roman name. Liam opened his new scrapbook with a picture of Cassius Clay, arms aloft, white teeth flashing, smiling at the world from the Olympic ring. A legend was born. Liam had a new hero. A man from the wrong side of the tracks. A black man in a white man's country. From the segregated town of Louisville, Kentucky. Liam tracked his career from that very first film clip. The boxer went on to greatness. Liam saw him beat Al 'Blue' Lewis in Dublin in 1972. He got up close to him in the Kilternan Hotel in the Dublin Mountains, where he stayed and trained. The supreme athlete. The heart of a lion. His own man always. With lee-a-roady.

*

The Beatles came to Dublin, to the Adelphi Cinema.
Liam got twenty of the ten-shilling tickets. Got three
hundred per cent profit, selling them for two pounds
each. He kept one for himself and was enthralled by the
Fab Four. They brought the house down with their fast
medley: 'Love, Love Me Do', 'Listen Do You Want to
Know a Secret', 'I'm Telling You Now'. After a second
encore, Liam was near the stage, and spotted the lads
heading for a rear exit. The girls inside were screaming
for more. Crying. Pulling their hair. Mass hysteria.

Outside the front entrance in Abbey Street, the
police had their hands full. The street was jammed with
thousands of fans waiting to see the Beatles leave after
the show. Two big black limousines for the stars were
standing outside the front of the cinema. But the Beatles
slipped out to the rear lane, to where a van was parked
in Prince's Street. Liam laughed as they were whisked
quietly away in the back of the red *Evening Herald* van.
'Whatever it is, the *Herald* has it.' Lived up to the slogan
that night, so it did.

Other international entertainers came to town. The
Theatre Royal was the usual venue, over in Hawkins Street,
beside the Regal Rooms. The standard Sunday night at the
Royal was always great craic. An hour of variety show. The
beautiful Royalette dancers. Tommy Dando and his organ.
It was a big one. It came up on a lift into the air. Words
of his songs were on the big screen for the singalong. Sure,
karaoke was invented in the Royal. Tommy always disappeared into the pit, playing his signature song. It was
written in the depression of the war years, but always got
the huge crowd singing enthusiastically.

Keep your sunny side up, up
Hide the side that gets blue
You will find things cannot go wrong
If you keep on singing a song.

Keep your sunny side up, up
Let your laughter ring true
Stand up on your legs, be like two fried eggs
And keep your sunny side up!

The biggest visiting hit was Johnny Ray, with his number-one song 'Just Walking in the Rain'. Frankie Laine took Dublin by storm when he came out on a window balcony of the Gresham Hotel to acknowledge the adoring crowds jamming O'Connell Street. He sang 'Rawhide', with the crowd joining in. You could hear the noise up in the bishop's palace in Drumcondra. Archbishop John Charles McQuaid gave his opinion in the *Evening Herald* about the heathens adoring false gods. Liam discovered that Frankie Laine was a real brother of Jeff Chandler, his 'Son of Cochise' hero.

28

The Young Businessman

The boss told him he was to accompany him on a trip to Ford's headquarters in Cork. One hundred and seventy five miles in the big Zephyr Zodiac. They were going the following Tuesday.

They didn't leave the garage until eleven o'clock. Drove slowly. Stopped on the roadside at the halfway stage in Urlingford and spread out a rug on the grass. A big picnic hamper was produced from the boot. Smoked salmon sandwiches. Cake. Hot tea from a vacuum flask. The boss had a snooze. They entered the Metropole Hotel in Cork at six o'clock and had a light meal, then reviewed the agenda for the meeting the following day. Priority item was to procure a hundred Ford Cortinas for a fleet deal with the firm Williams and Woods, one of Walden's best customers. Early to bed.

The Ford plant in Cork was a massive industrial operation, employing fifteen hundred people on a one-hundred-acre site. They met the managing director, Tommy Brennan, in his office, where he was flanked by John Wyer, the sales director, and Jerome Daly, who was the marketing development director. A huge office, it was: a big desk with only a phone on it, four sofas for a relaxing chat, a long conference table to seat twelve people. A private secretary outside, who monitored the phone and allowed people access. And Mary Barry protected her boss.

It was a very amicable meeting – a general review of the growing car market over tea and coffee. Liam just listened. Say nothing till you hear more. When it came to the crunch issue of the hundred Cortinas, Mister Brennan excused himself. His colleagues would host lunch in the executive canteen. Liam took time out to slip down to the operations office. He had a chat with the pals: Tim Healy, Oliver Barrascale, Mossy Ahearne, Denis McSweeney and Redmond O'Donoghue. He checked out the production schedules for the next few weeks. Plenty of Cortinas being built, but they were mainly reserved for the big local Ford dealers in Cork. Liam got the production numbers fixed firmly in his head before he rejoined the group for lunch. He had a chat with the office girls, Mary O'Brien and Eve Wixted. Two Cork beauties. As for Mary O'Brien and the way she might look at ya . . . 'Dream on, boy. Them's our Cork girls. Isn't there enough up in Dublin for you jackeens?' said Oliver.

And what a lunch. Liam had never experienced a meal like it. It was served in a magnificent private dining room on a huge mahogany table, with a cut-glass bowl in the centre heaped with fruit – enough for a good morning at the Lane. Lace napkins, zillions of knives and forks and spoons. Three girls in maids' uniforms serving. Smoked-salmon starter, soup, leg of lamb carved beside you from a big round silver dish on wheels, sherry trifle, coffee with cream and biscuits. Liam had to watch everyone else at the table to see which pieces of cutlery to use. He had never seen that funny-shaped knife for the salmon before. He nearly got mixed up between the spoon for the soup and a different one for the dessert. It was the first time ever for him to taste coffee. Horrible stuff, but he drank it down. Sherries and wine were available, but Liam's Pioneer pin got the nod of approval. He drank water from the heavy cut-glass goblet. A meal fit for a king.

John Wyer told a famous Henry Ford story about the great man coming to Cork in 1917, to open his first production plant outside America, bringing two thousand jobs to his father's birthplace in Cork. He bought a hundred acres of land on the River Lee, where the ships could dock in the deep water. He signed a contract for construction, hired lawyers, accountants, and bankers, and set up recruitment and training offices. The city was buzzing with excitement. Henry Ford and his team were guests of honour at a gala banquet in the City Hall. Uncle Henry was flanked by the Lord Mayor and the local-newspaper owner. After the dinner, the speeches and the brandy, the Lord Mayor gently enquired if Uncle Henry would like to contribute to the building of a new city hospital.

'But of course I will,' Ford responded magnanimously. 'I'll have the accountants send you a cheque for one thousand pounds.' It was a lot of money in 1917.

The following morning, the motor magnate read the headlines in 'de paper': HENRY FORD GIVES TEN THOUSAND POUNDS FOR NEW HOSPITAL'. He phoned the newspaper owner.

'Some mistake. I said *one* thousand pounds.'

'Oh, well now, sir, I'll correct that mistake right

away. Tomorrow's headline will say HENRY FORD DOES NOT GIVE TEN THOUSAND POUNDS FOR NEW HOSPITAL.' Gotcha. Silence. Between a rock and a hard place. 'No,' said Uncle Henry, 'we won't do that. I will give the ten thousand pounds – on one condition. That I get a Biblical inscription carved in stone over the door of this hospital.'

'Begorrah now, sir, you are certainly entitled to that for such magnificent generosity, so you are. What's the inscription?'

'"He came amongst strangers and they took him in",' replied Ford. The inscription is there to this day. Cute hoors, them Corkmen. But Uncle Henry's wonderful contribution to Cork gave Ford the number-one slot for car sales in the country. Ford cars were Irish cars. The people acknowledged and rewarded the heartfelt gesture from a Famine survivor to his homeland. It was the beginning of a great Irish-American tradition. As Mother Darcy always said, 'You must never forget your roots.'

They didn't finish lunch until three o'clock, and then went back down to John Wyer's office. Mister Wallace lit up his pipe, while Mister Wyer smoked a huge cigar. Convivial chat. The football, the new government, et cetera, et cetera. When Mister Wallace brought up the subject of the hundred Cortinas, the response from Wyer was lukewarm. They had limited production runs, they were short of CKD (completely knocked down) kits, they had problems in the paint line. He would see what he could do. When pressed by Mister Wallace, he reluctantly conceded ten Cortinas a week for the next ten weeks. It was no good. They needed a hundred within four weeks. That was impossible. The factory hadn't even got that number of completely knocked down kits. Impasse. Liam's boss was disappointed, but pleaded for John to do his best. Another cigar. Meeting over.

Then Liam chipped in his tuppenceworth. 'Maybe Oliver Barrascale could find us a few extra Cortinas,' he said.

Wyer looked at him sharply. 'Don't think so. I've got the figures here,' he replied.

Liam smiled. 'And paper never refused ink, Mister Wyer. I've always found my physical stock checks never agree with the printed list,' he said, 'and I see a ship outside the window here on the marina unloading hundreds of Cortina kits.' He pointed out to the crane on the quayside. Wyer was taken aback.

'No, no, they are the CKD kits for the Anglias,' he said.

'Sorry, Mister Wyer, look at the kit numbers on the boxes. All 113E, they are. Cortina kits. Every one of them. The Anglias are 105E.'

'Well, I'll have a word with Barrascale,' Wyer said, getting up out of the chair. Out the door.

But Liam followed. 'I'll go with ya; I haven't seen Oliver for a while.' Oliver Barrascale could see the problem when Wyer asked him about the low Cortina production. He couldn't tell porky pies, because he'd given Liam the numbers earlier. The truth came out. Serious volumes.

'Oh, then my schedules mustn't have been updated,' Wyer said. 'Looks like we can find you those Cortinas after all.' They got the hundred in four weeks. It pays to have friends at the low end of the totem pole. John Wyer acknowledged the young fella's tenacity. 'Bejaysus, our big dealers will want to sharpen up, with you around to keep them on their toes.' And he became another mentor, always ready to help Liam with a problem.

They drove back to the Metropole Hotel that evening. The boss was in great form. He phoned Kingsley Long in Dublin to confirm the delivery date for Williams and Woods. Mister Long rang back. Walden's got the deal. Mister Wallace celebrated with a brandy and headed off to bed early. Liam went down to the Markets pub to meet the Ford lads. He couldn't get over Dominick Carey. 'What will ya have, Dominick?' Liam had asked.

'Oh, the usual,' he'd replied, with a nod to the barman. Liam put a pound note on the counter.

'You'll have to go again,' said the barman. 'It's two quid for Dom's usual. A pint of Carlsberg, with a large Rémy Martin and twenty Gold Flake cigarettes.' That would teach the young Dublin whippersnapper a lesson.

The boss let Liam drive the Zodiac home the next day. It was a beautiful, powerful machine.

'Just stay around fifty, Willum: we're not in any hurry.' Liam had a smooth drive all the way. Mister Wallace was relaxed and snoozing after a light meal in the Horse and Jockey pub. They got home to Dublin at seven o'clock and Mister Wallace dropped Liam off at the garage.

'I've some paperwork to do on this deal, Mister Wallace,' he said, and the boss drove home.

The following day, Mister Cole confirmed another salary increase of a pound a week.

*

The boss was buying up all the tenements to the rear of
Walden's. They were mainly yards and stables. But getting
Maxie Cosgrove's vet's yard next door gave additional
main-road frontage. And with business improving, a new
car showroom and Maxol petrol station was built. Liam
was given the job of coordinating the grand opening.

Customer invitations. Press releases. They needed a
celebrity for the occasion. Liam suggested Brendan
Behan, who had just returned from the successful run
of his play *The Hostage* on Broadway. It was a great idea.
Liam met Brendan. Fee of £100 agreed. Cash up front.
Liam gave Brendan the outline script of what to say. See
ya at Walden's on Friday at eleven o'clock, to meet the
VIPs before the noon tape-cutting.

Eleven-thirty on Friday and there was no sign of
Brendan. Liam made a good guess and found him up the
road in the Shakespeare Bar, which opened at seven in
the morning. And Brendan was pissed. Coffee, coffee,
coffee, and linked arms with him to bring him down
to the garage. It was after twelve, and a very unhappy
Mister Wallace was about to cut the tape, the press
photographers in place. Liam had a Kehily's handcart
ready for Brendan to use as a podium. Mister Wallace
was disgruntled at Behan's obvious indisposition.

'You are late, Mister Behan,' he said, 'and you were
paid good money to be here on time.'

Brendan looked at him through bleary eyes and said
to Liam, 'Get this baldy oul' bollix out of me way till I
make me speech'. He climbed up on the handcart.

Mister Wallace was furious. 'Willum, this is your
mistake. Be in my office at two o'clock sharp,' he said,
red-faced. Hubble-bubble. Trouble. But Behan was at his
brilliant best.

'This great new business initiative in the heart of Dublin city. Part of the living community. Mister Wallace, and his father before him, giving jobs to Dublin lads. Giving young fellas a trade. A great thing it is to be a mechanic, with motor cars now replacing the horse in Ireland. Helping the business companies of Dublin to grow. To prosper.' Like Jim Larkin, he was waving his arms around on the handcart. 'Ford cars for Irish people. Sure isn't Henry Ford our greatest Irishman. So buy Ford and buy from Walden's. The best garage in Dublin. Run by that great man, Mister Billy Wallace himself, who'll speak to you now. Where is he?'

The boss was smitten, overcome at the compliments. He was delighted with Behan's powerful and dramatic oration. In his office at two o'clock, it was congratulations Liam got, and another pay increase of a pound a week. He'd be paying income tax soon.

*

The other big development in Walden's was the introduction of the turnover tax by the Irish government. It was a forerunner of the value added tax. Every company had to add two-and-a-half per cent TOT to the invoice value of the goods sold. It was a lot of money on a four-hundred-pound motor car. But you didn't have to pay the tax if you were in business and had registered as a company. All the seller had to get from the buyer was a turnover-tax number. And some buyers just gave a telephone number as a TOT number, sold the car, and pocketed the tax themselves. Liam got the job of overseeing the administration of the tax system for Walden's and ensuring the company's collected tax was more than the company's liability. His controls worked.

Then he installed the new employees' payroll system – the hated Pay As You Earn scheme. The government ensured that all the workers who were paid weekly had their tax deducted weekly. Upfront, like. Nailed the lowest-paid people. Liam himself was caught in the net. He was allowed to earn six pounds a week tax-free. He was earning eight pounds a week. He was taxed at twenty-five per cent. He had to give ten shillings every week to Mister PAYE. Then he looked at his father's situation. Tax-free allowances of forty-five pounds a week. Earning eight pounds a week, pays no tax.

So down Liam goes to see the Revenue Commissioner in Hammam Buildings, over Kingston's Shirts in O'Connell Street. It used to be the Hammam Hotel. A Mister O'Riordan heard his case.

'Me and the Da are both William Cullens, living in the same house, supporting the same family, giving all our earnings to the Ma, Missus Mary Cullen. The Da has surplus allowances. Suppose ya take twenty pounds off the Da's, reducing him to twenty-five pounds. He'll be okay, no tax. Give Liam the twenty added to his six. He'll have twenty-six pounds, no tax. It'd still be the same combined allowances of fifty-one pounds.' It seemed an open-and-shut case. Simple logic. Fair and square.

'Sorry, son,' said O'Riordan, 'the system doesn't work like that. You both have to stand on your own two feet.'

'Not very fair,' Liam replied.

'That's right, son,' O'Riordan said. 'It isn't fair. And when you get to my age, you'll realise that life isn't fair. And governments are *never* fair.'

Still, Liam's involvement in the system's application had necessitated working closely with the boss, who became more and more aware of his abilities.

*

It was a while after his inauguration in 1960 that the Irish people fully realised that America had an Irish president. As Irish as the day was long. John Fitzgerald Kennedy. Family roots in Dunganstown, beside New Ross in County Wexford. His great-grandfather left for America to escape the Famine in 1848.

He had the Irish charm, the gift of the blarney. And he came to visit Ireland in June 1963, just as Ireland was beginning to feel the positive benefits of Seán Lemass and

US President John F. Kennedy in Dublin with
Éamon de Valera (centre) and Seán Lemass (right)

T. K. Whitaker's financial policies. The Irish economy was opening up. Tourism was taking off, with Aer Lingus, the Irish national airline, flying to America now. But it was the visit of John F. Kennedy that inspired the nation. He came from Dublin Airport with a cavalcade of black limousines, in the open-topped limo that would later become infamous. They went in through Drumcondra, Dorset Street, and down to O'Connell Street. The city was packed. Every business had closed for the morning. Hundreds of thousands of people jammed the streets, waving small Irish and American flags. Mother Darcy had been selling them on the street for weeks before the visit. Liam had got himself a terrific viewing-point on the Parnell Monument, only five hundred yards from Walden's – hanging from Parnell's arm. The cavalcade stopped briefly at the obelisk. Kennedy stood up in the car and waved with his right hand. His left hand in his jacket pocket.

'Like Napoleon, he was. An Irishman – president of the United States. He'll get Ireland on the move, and that's a fact,' said Big Bob.

Kennedy's address to the Irish parliament in Dáil Eireann on 28 June 1963 was electric. He was proud of his Irish heritage. He praised the contribution of Irish emigrants to America's success. He committed himself to helping the Irish government to fulfil its economic policies.

In his opening statement, he talked of the bravery and courage of the Irish soldiers in the American Civil War, and the vision of the Irish architect, James Hoban, who designed the White House. He spoke of the tenacity of Irishman John Barry, the first commander of the American navy, whose sword hangs in the Oval Office. He quoted George Bernard Shaw when he said:

'Other people see things and say why, but I dream things and say why not.'

He predicted the influx of American business into Ireland, when he said: 'The other nations of the world, in whom Ireland has long invested her people, will now invest their capital as well as their vacations in Ireland.' He exhorted business leaders to develop a modern Irish economy to share in world prosperity. He reminded them of their Celtic heritage, and how Ireland since earliest times had been a rich and powerful influence on the world:

> No nation did more than Ireland to keep Western culture alive in their darkest centuries. No nation did more than Ireland to spark the cause of independence in America. No nation has provided the world with more literary and artistic genius.

Liam listened to the speech on the wireless. He was inspired. Every Irish man and woman listening to that speech was inspired. An Irishman had made it to the top of the tree. All Irish people could aspire to success. That very evening, in his little basement room, a twenty-year-old young fella took out his notebook and started to write. 'The Things I Want to Do.' A long list. It included 'a house of my own, a car of my own, a business of my own, be my own boss, stay strong, stay healthy, go to the States.' It was the beginning of his lifelong habit. Make out the list. Prioritise. Go do it. As taught by the Ma and Mother Darcy. As inspired by John Fitzgerald Kennedy.

Liam decided to stay on in Rathmines College for

one more year and go for the full marketing diploma. He could fit in the gymnastics as well. He was getting really good on the vaulting horse, and could do a good handspring. He was too tall for a back-flip but was trying really hard on the high rings.

And that's where he was on the famous day, 22 November 1963. It was about eight-thirty in the evening. A teacher rushed in through the door. Kennedy had been shot in Dallas. John F. Kennedy, shot by a sniper, in his open-topped limousine. Critical. Liam showered, dressed, and walked his bike home, in a daze. He met people on the streets. Crying, gathered in little groups. Looking at the televisions in TeleRents windows. He got home. The lights were out, but there was a candle in the window. The family were on their knees, saying the Rosary. Mother Darcy was rocking in her chair. The Ma with a new incantation: 'May the Virgin Mary watch over the Kennedy family.'

The response came: 'Lord, hear our prayer.'

The Five Sorrowful Mysteries: the Agony in the Garden, the Scourging at the Pillar, the Crowning with Thorns, the Carrying of the Cross, and the Crucifixion. The wireless was on low. The word came through. John F. Kennedy's life, snuffed out, at the age of forty-six. The flame of youth and hope extinguished. Ireland's greatest son was dead. Murdered by a cowardly sniper. His body to be laid in the tomb. But his spirit, his enthusiasm, would be with the Irish forever. He had already inspired a generation. Liam never went back to Rathmines College again. It was time to move on. He was twenty-one years old.

29

FULL STEAM AHEAD

Liam put everything into the job in Walden's. He carried out his main responsibilities in the general office, controlling debtors, creditors, payroll, parts and petrol purchasing, with Bill Lambert his trainer and mentor. He also helped out at peak hours in the service reception. He controlled all car-fleet quotations and developed a direct-mail campaign for fleet-leasing business. He assisted with the car-rental operations in the summertime. He went looking for a salary increase from Mister Cole. The usual response.

'Oh, for God's sake, William, you got three increases in the past fourteen months,' he said, looking at Liam's personnel file. 'Yearly increments is all you're entitled to, and you're now on ten pounds a week. And you're only twenty-one years old. Sure, that's more than our forty-year-old mechanics are getting. I bet it's even more than your dad is being paid in Brooks Thomas,' he said accusingly. Liam looked at him. He said nothing. He had his arguments all thought out, but say nothing till ya hear more. He just kept looking at him.

'Oh, come on now, William. I know you do a great job, but I can't give you another rise. Tell you what,

I'll review you after the Christmas holidays. How's that?' Cole asked.

'No good, Mister Cole,' Liam said. 'What the mechanics and my Da get paid is their business. You didn't mention that our car salesmen get thirty to forty pounds a week.'

Cole pulled a sardonic face. 'Now, William, you wouldn't want to be compared with a car salesman, would you? You could become the accountant here. That's what you should be aiming for,' he said.

'Sorry, Mister Cole,' Liam replied. 'The car salesmen get paid a lot more than you do. I don't want to be an accountant. I want to be where the money is.'

Cole shook his head sadly. 'William, William, William. I'm a professional. A qualified accountant. You can be a professional too. You surely don't want to spend your time haggling over car prices all day.'

'Mister Cole, I don't care what I have to do if I'm learning more, achieving more and getting paid more. You know I work at least seventy-five hours a week for you. For ten quid. The car salesmen get three times that for half the hours. You're saying that I'm better than them. Why don't I get paid like them? Or like a mechanic? Yes, I'm getting the same money as them, but I work double the hours. Put me on their hourly rate, with the union overtime, and I'd be on thirty quid a week. Whatever way you look at it, I'm losing out. So if I don't get paid fifteen pounds a week for my seventy-five hours, I'm out of here. That's it. Give me that assurance by the end of this month, or I'll have to give you a month's notice. Thank you.' He stood up and walked out of the office.

It went to the last hour of the deadline on the last

day before Liam was called in by Cole. 'I've spoken to the boss. He's disappointed. His usual response to such threats is two words. Bye. Bye.' Cole paused for effect. 'However, because he respects your abilities and commitment, he's prepared to overlook your arrogance. And give you a twenty per cent increase, to twelve pounds a week. Extremely generous. I'd really advise you to take it.'

Liam looked at him and said, 'Mister Cole, I love working here, but I'm going to get fifteen pounds a week before this year is out. And if it's not to be here, I'll just have to get it somewhere else. So I'm sorry, but you now have my notice of resignation for four weeks' time.'

The Ma was upset, but kept her counsel. Liam got a ring from John Burgess, a former colleague now working for Sonny Linders in Smithfield. Linders was looking for an assistant accountant, and the wages were fifteen pounds a week. The magic number. Liam got an interview and got the job.

Mister Wallace called him in on his last day. 'Sorry to see you go, Willum, but if I gave you what you wanted, it would upset too many people. Best of luck. I'm sure we'll meet again,' he said. Liam said his goodbyes, and down to Linders' he went. But only for a few weeks.

Liam got a call from Mister Wallace. The general manger of Walden's North Strand branch had had a serious car crash. Could William meet to discuss a proposal? Could he what?

The boss asked if he could take over management of the North Strand branch. He would be responsible for vehicle sales, service, the workshop and a staff of fourteen. Liam smiled. He remembered his Ma's words as she looked at him in the mirror. 'You'll never meet a man better than yourself.'

'Of course I can, Mister Wallace. I live only a hundred yards away from the premises. Day and night, I'll take care of things for you,' he said. Liam negotiated a deal. Twenty pounds a week, plus executive car, expenses and performance-related bonus. From ten to twenty pounds a week in three months. From office clerk to general manager. Aged twenty-two. This was a quantum leap up the ladder.

In the very first week of the new job, Liam knew he could handle it. There were two good, experienced salesmen, Eddie Dixon and Tim O'Donovan. He had a good service manager, Tommy Nolan. He quickly put the control systems in place that he'd learned from Bill Lambert. Move the working capital through the business quickly. Have a quick turnover. Move the metal. Give good deals. The secret of motor-trade profitability is maximising the sales volumes.

Liam worked a hundred hours a week, sometimes well past twelve at night. He finalised all the paperwork every day. Aidan Bradshaw from the Irish Life Assurance Company gave him his first corporate deal. He bought the new showroom Cortina with all the bells and whistles. Aidan was a great ad for Liam as he worked the area in his fancy new Ford. 'Up to me pal, Liam Cullen, in Walden's. He'll look after ya.' Liam got support from the local businesses.

In March, he took a phone call from Frank Cusack of Rowntree Mackintosh, the chocolate manufacturers in Kilmainham. Could he supply thirty Cortinas within two weeks? All in one colour: white. Frank wanted his sales team to be noticed. Confirm in writing. Liam had to use all his credits with John Wyer in Cork, but he got the cars. He got the deal. The branch made more profit in three months than it had in the previous two years. Off to a flying start.

On the domestic front, Liam was doing a line with Rita Campbell, the car-hire controller in head office. She was a really nice girl from Cabra. They went dancing in the Palm Beach out in Portmarnock on Saturday nights, to the pictures on Sunday in the Carlton. They went out driving in Liam's flashy new Cortina. Got engaged on his twenty-second birthday. Went house-hunting.

The Ma encouraged him to move well out of town, to look at Howth and Sutton, out past Dollymount, on the beautiful coastline of Dublin Bay. They settled on a new housing development in Sutton Park, being built by Curtis and Farrelly. A superb four-bedroomed house for £3,950. Liam had three hundred pounds saved.

'It's an expensive house, Liam,' the Ma said 'but it's the right thing to do. Make a complete break from your old environment. You're a businessman now. You're out of the tenements. You must never forget your roots, but you must move up to a new social level. Perception.'

He knew she was right. 'The repayments will put me to the pin of me collar, Ma,' he said.

'When you're buying property, son,' she said, 'what's expensive today is cheap tomorrow. They're not making any more land around Dublin Bay. As for the repayments, just hold on a minute.' She went over to the gas cooker. She lifted the rug, pulled up the floorboard and pulled out a Woolworths plastic bag. 'This is yours, Liam,' she said. 'There's five hundred pounds in this towards your new house. That'll bring the repayments down.'

He was gobsmacked. 'But that's for the family, Ma. We've the whole gang of them to look after. Aidan is making his First Communion this month, and we'll have Marie for Confirmation as well.'

Mary Darcy looked at her eldest boy. 'You don't have to worry about that any more, because you'll have your own family to look after. Frank and Eamon are a great help to me now, stepping into your shoes at the Lane and in the street. And you've given me every penny you've ever earned, all your life. Some of this money goes back to them paper roses you made fifteen years ago, son. And your wage packet on the mantelpiece, unopened, for the past ten years. To this very day. This is a little bit of what I've been able to save for you. So off you go, and buy that house.' He took the bag.

Mary Darcy watched from the window as Liam walked out to his lovely new car. Big strapping lad. Head up, chest out. She might as well be looking at Billy Cullen marching up Summerhill to meet her. She brushed the tears from her eyes with the hem of her apron as he waved, with a big smile, from the car. She waved back and watched the car move off down to the Five Lamps. And smiled as she remembered Alfie Byrne's words: 'Of course he'll be a credit to you, Mary.'

Liam bought the house that day. Number 89, Sutton Park. He got a hundred pounds off the price. Borrowed three thousand pounds. He got a fixed-rate mortgage from the Irish Life Assurance Company. Repayments of seventeen pounds a month for twenty-five years.

'It makes you work harder to move up that ladder, son,' Mother Darcy said, 'and buying your own house is a great way of making you save. I'll say a prayer for ya,' she continued, as she went over to her Rosary in St Joseph's.

The Farrelly brothers, who were building the houses, came in and bought six new cars from Liam. Business is a two-way street.

Liam had continued playing football with Home Farm, every Sunday, until he got a call from Ben Hannigan to join Shelbourne FC. He spent a season with the League of Ireland team, playing with Ben, Freddie Strahan, Joe Haverty, Eric Barber, and another great little footballer, Stephen 'Rossi' Walsh. However, Liam was working flat out in his business career and football was a non-runner for him. He was missing training. Not available for some away matches. He packed it in after that – except for the summer when he captained the Walden Wizards in the Castrol Cup. Walden always made it to the final rounds, and at the after-match celebrations he met some of the motor-industry chiefs – Con Smith of Renault, the great Stephen O'Flaherty of Volkswagen, and Reggie Armstrong of Opel.

Liam married Rita Campbell and moved to Sutton. Tommy and Sean gave him a hand with fitting out the house, digging and planting the garden. Aidan Bradshaw and his wife, Colette, moved in beside them. Great neighbourhood. Only fifteen minutes from Walden's at the Five Lamps. He played tennis and squash at Sutton Tennis Club, but was really busy putting lots of time into developing the Walden business. He worked late

Bill Cullen, captain, pictured with ball in the
1963 Castrol Cup final in Tolka Park

into the night, building a Marcos sports car with young
Willie O'Brien from Summerhill, whom he'd started as
a mechanic. Genius with cars, Willie was. Only sixteen,
and already the best and fastest mechanic in the city.
Liam's first child, Anita, was born in 1968, and it was
in that year that he got the big break.

He was called up to Parnell Street by Mister Wallace.
Good news and bad news. The bad news was that
Seamus Phelan, the head-office sales manager, was
leaving. The good news was, he was offering Liam the
job. At double his current salary. He would be managing
a team of ten salesmen, selling eight hundred new and
seven hundred used cars a year.

Liam was aware of the nuances in the offer. He had
every confidence he could do the job. But he had to
think on his feet. He was only twenty-six years old, the
youngest guy in the company. Some of the salesmen
were in their fifties. Paddy O'Reilly had been selling cars
in Walden's for thirty years. He had his own little

empire. The service manager, Paddy O'Brien, ran his side of the business with dictatorial control. There had been rows between himself and Phelan. Michael Cole, the accountant, was the power player behind the scene, next door to the boss. He had the boss's ear.

'Sorry, Mister Wallace. I don't think that's for me,' he said quietly.

Billy Wallace was taken aback. 'What do you mean, that's not for you? You've done a great job in the branch. It's a natural progression to head up the sales team here in head office,' he said. 'I never thought I'd see the day that Willie Cullen couldn't do a job for me.'

Take it easy. Get the words right. 'I never said I couldn't do the job, Mister Wallace. I believe I could do a great job for you. But not as sales manager. Sure, the older salesmen are always running to you with their problems, bypassing Phelan. The service and parts managers run their own show. We have a finance division, a car-hire division, and a body-repair operation. We've five or six businesses under one roof, and they're pulling against one another. This company of yours could double sales and profits in the next few years, but we have to bring the team together. As managing director, you're upstairs now. I believe you need a hands-on general manager on the floor to run the show. That's what could make Walden's hum. That's the job I could do for you,' Liam said.

It was a long, careful speech. The boss looked at him intently. They talked it through for an hour. Liam knew the words 'double sales and profits' had rung the bell. He ended the day as director sales manager of Walden Motor Company, with responsibility for all aspects of the business. Reporting only to Mister Wallace. Salary doubled. But more importantly, a performance-related bonus on the profitability of the whole company.

'So go double my business, young man, and you get a slice of the profits,' Mister Wallace said in parting.

There was a big celebration that Friday in Conway's pub, as Liam toasted the birth of his first child, Anita. A new baby girl and a challenging career promotion all in the same week.

Liam spent the first six months reorganising the company's structure, getting Paddy O'Brien's service department focused on customer service. He took the new- and used-car preparation units out to a separate building. Service is for our customers. Keep them happy. Look after them. They did, and service profits went through the roof.

Liam brought in some new, young salesmen. He made Brendan Hession his sales manager, still selling on the floor, but controlling trade-in prices. As he'd learned at the Lane, you have to buy at the right price to make a profit. There was none of Hector's one per cent in the motor business. They had very small margins, but on bigger amounts. So volume sales was the key.

The older salesmen fought his authority. It wasn't easy for a seasoned fifty-year-old to be told, 'No, we'll only go six hundred on a trade-in,' by a young fella still wet behind the ears. But Liam talked to them, pushed them, cajoled them and bullied them into working as a team. He got some of the salesmen specialising in used cars; others became fleet specialists. Profits increased, and their commissions increased. Liam worked around the clock. Fifteen-hour days, seven-day weeks. He never stopped. By 1972, Walden Motor Company was the biggest Ford dealer in Ireland, selling two thousand new

Fords a year, plus three thousand used cars. And a very profitable empire it was.

*

The Nesbitt family owned Arnotts, the big department store in Henry Street, right opposite the Ma's pitch. Always bought her fruit from the Ma, did Missus Nesbitt. When she heard about young Liam, she told the Ma she'd make sure that Arnotts sent all their car and van business up to Walden's. Another community supporter.

By law, all vans at the time had to have the name and phone number of the owner's company secretary painted on the front doors, in case of emergency or police enquiries. So Jack Doody of Arnotts became one of the best-known names in Walden's. He drove a sporty new silver Ford Capri. He balanced the Arnotts account with Mister Cole every month. A great guy. He got his apples every day from the Ma. The Ma started buying all her growing-up children's clothes in Arnotts. Business is a two-way street.

Séamus Costello was a car salesman in Walden's, and supposedly he'd been interned in the Curragh for alleged IRA activities. When the Northern Ireland fighting broke out in 1969, Seamus went nuts. 'Murdering our Catholic brothers. Let's load up with guns and take up the fight.' He vanished for a few weeks, but returned to work, although he only came in a couple of days a week. He sold four or five cars a month, mainly to friends.

The Special Branch detectives followed him everywhere. But Seamus would go out of Walden's in the boot of a customer's car being driven by a mechanic on a test drive. He would be out on business all day, and back the same way, so that he could walk out the front door and drive off in his own car, for the detectives to follow. He left abruptly one day. 'Have to go, Billyo. Won't be back,' he said to Liam. 'More important work to be done.'

The papers said he had become a military commander of the IRA. He broke away from that group and formed the Irish National Liberation Army. Warring factions. He was riddled with bullets one day in his car on the North Strand Road. He had always been a nice fella. Quiet type, in Walden's. Still waters can run deep.

Noel, Liam's brother, had gone to Germany, where he was based in Frankfurt with the British Army on the

Sergeant Noel Cullen with his platoon of Irish Guards
in the deserts of Aden

Rhine. The *fräuleins*, skiing in the Alps. Learning about leadership. He was promoted to sergeant and transferred to Chelsea Barracks in London for guard duty at Buckingham Palace. Liam organised for the Ma and Da to travel to London. They walked down Pall Mall on a beautiful spring morning, to stand proudly among the tourists, looking at their son, Sergeant Noel Cullen, in full Irish Guards dress. Bearskin on top. Barking the orders for the Changing of the Guards at the Queen's palace.

But it was a different story when Noel was posted to the Middle East, to Aden in the British Protectorate, now the Republic of Yemen, where the English colonists were under attack. They couldn't match the Arabs in their desert habitat. The Guards Brigade suffered casualties as the last of the British contingent withdrew to the port to board the flotilla taking to the sea. It was the retreat from Aden. Noel's platoon came under attack. Close comrades died and Noel was airlifted to an English hospital with shrapnel wounds. He had six months' recuperation. Honourable discharge, with an army pension. He returned to Dublin, where it took a long time to put the experience behind him. Eventually, he became the production director of a logistics company. Putting his army training to good use.

*

Walden's was now the number one Ford dealership in Ireland. Aggressive marketing, car-leasing as a new tool for corporate fleets and service packages were all paying off. Walden's own car-hire fleet business was also growing, thanks to the personal efforts of Walter

Kavanagh. Credit and cash controls were tight. Cheques
were accepted only from blue-chip clients. Otherwise
bank drafts were required. If a cheque bounced, the
customer owned the car. You could only sue for payment on the cheque, which took a lot of time, while the
car was clocking up miles.

One Saturday the 'no mun no fun' rule was broken,
when a car dealer, Eamonn Doran from Ashtown Car
Sales in Castleknock, took delivery of a new Ford Capri.
It was the latest sports coupé model. It was paid for by
cheque – £898 – but the cheque bounced. Mister Wallace
was not a happy camper. Liam was angry. Doran knew
the score. He had always paid by bank draft, but took
advantage of a staff member when Liam was out of the
office.

Liam heard that Doran was selling up and emigrating,
so there was no chance of getting paid on the bounced
cheque. He decided to repossess the car, which Doran
was blatantly driving around town. He kept promising
to come in with a banker's draft, but no show. Liam
got his fastest mechanic trained to hot-wire the Capri,
in double-quick time. Willie O'Brien got it down to
twenty seconds, to jemmy the door lock, hot-wire the
car, drop the steering lock and away. They followed
Doran one evening and got their opportunity when
Doran pulled up outside the Croke Park bar across from
Gill's pub, Liam's old stamping ground. Doran and his
friend went into the pub. Liam pulled up fifty yards
behind the Capri. He took a jack handle from the car
and hid it under his jacket. Willie sauntered to the Capri
while Liam walked briskly to the door of the pub. Liam
inserted the jack handle through the two brass door
handles. Willie attacked the car door and was quickly

inside the car, working under the dash. Doran spotted him and charged to the door of the pub. It wouldn't open. He shook it, then kicked it, roaring and shouting. The Capri's engine fired and Willie went off down the road.

Liam removed the jack handle. 'Okay, lads, take it easy. I've got the car. You pay the money, you get it back,' he said.

'I'll break your feckin' head,' threatened Doran's pal. 'That's my car you've stolen, 'cause I've paid Doran for it.' Good tactics.

'Okay then, let's slip around the corner here to the police in Fitzgibbon Street station, and you can make your complaint.' Up they went. All the station police recognised Liam. They were not interested in an ownership squabble. Go talk to your legal people. How can you own this car, if Walden's weren't paid for it? Liam slipped away while the arguments were going on. He parked the Capri in a private garage.

But Mister Wallace was upset. Could Walden's be charged with car theft? 'This was your decision, Willum. You know I won't tolerate wrongdoing. If this goes wrong, it's on your head,' he said.

Luckily, Doran emigrated to America the following week. There was no further action. No legal letters. Zilch from the police. But Mister Wallace froze the car. 'We can't sell it, just in case.' He was the most honest man in the motor industry. He wouldn't take a penny that he wasn't fully entitled to. Two years later, Liam sold the car and handed one thousand pounds to the boss, who was delighted at the successful outcome.

Eamonn Doran opened a restaurant in New York which became a famous American eatery. It was a focal point in New York for all Irish visitors. Liam always dropped in when he was over. Eamonn always tore up the bill.

'Sure, didn't I run your car around Dublin for a few weeks for free before I left? This check is on me.'

30

THE BIGGER PICTURE

Ireland was going decimal. No more shillings and pence. Simplify. A precondition for entry to the European Economic Community. Twelve pence in a shilling, twenty shillings in a pound. It had to go. An Irish joke. No more 240 pennies in a pound. Decimalise. One hundred new pennies in a pound. So one new penny was worth about two and a half old pennies. It was a simple enough changeover for the business community.

But not for the ladies selling fruit in Moore Street. No sir. 'We don't join them clubs. Not the PAYE club or the PRSI club. Not the VAT club. And we're not joining this decimalisation club either,' said Mother Darcy.

Liam tried to explain the new system to a full house in Madigan's pub. But Mother Darcy blew him out of the water with simple common sense. She picked up the old copper penny, two inches in diameter, in her right hand. The new three-quarters-of-an-inch copper penny was in her left hand.

'Are you trying to tell us, son,' she said, 'that this tiny new penny is worth two and a half times this big old penny? That's nonsense. Even a baby can see that's stupid.' Cheers from the crowd. He was wasting his time after that. It was all about perception.

So the dealers continued to buy the boxes of fruit for the couple of pounds. But when it came to selling them for threepence each, it was still threepence each.

'And I don't care what Charlie Haughey says, I want threepence for me apples.' They got the three new pennies.

The Ma called Liam in after a week. 'Son, look at all this money. Me cash flow is terrific. What's wrong?' she asked.

Very simple. She was still buying for the same price, but selling for two and a half times the old selling price. Profits were up by two hundred and forty per cent. That was the day that street trading became a profitable business, not just a struggle to survive, for all the Moore Street dealers. It was a decent return for all their efforts. It applied to all businesses with unit selling-prices in pennies. Rounding up gave profits a big boost. But the end result was to contribute to surging inflation in the economy.

Liam told Charlie Haughey the story at a dinner table one evening. 'Astounding, and the mandarins blamed my budget deficits. We blamed the sheikhs for increasing oil prices. And all the time it was those poor oul' ones in Moore Street who invented the inflation of the seventies,' C.J. said with a laugh.

Mother Darcy decreed that Decimalisation Day, 14 February 1971, known by every girl as Valentine's Day, was a special day for the family. Everyone would go to a private family Rosary in St Agatha's to thank the Blessed Virgin for the benefits. The special Rosary was held every year, with a new affirmation: 'God bless the man who invented decimalisation.'

Response: 'Lord, hear our prayers.'

*

Government advisers were convinced that Ireland's economic future lay in joining the Common Market, later the European Economic Community. The EEC. Despite reservations in many quarters, it was believed that Ireland should proceed with achieving the entry criteria, and a study group was formed to lead the thrust. It combined the labour unions with the political and business federations.

Liam had been on the National Executive Committee of the Society of the Irish Motor Industry (SIMI) since 1958, and had been involved in advising on the motor industry's view on EEC entry. He had worked with Senator Jack Daly, and Con Smith of Renault.

Con Smith was appointed president of the Confederation of Irish Industry. He was a brilliant, dynamic Cavanman, very articulate. He was convinced that the EEC was the way forward, particularly because he had business connections in Europe. And he was married to the beautiful daughter of an Italian physician. Con Smith was one of Ireland's new entrepreneurs. From a small engineering business in Cavan town, he had developed the Renault, Peugeot and Citroën car franchises for Ireland. He had expanded the Smith Group into many areas. He was in the process of merging with Sir Basil Goulding's group of companies; this would make the Smith Group the second-largest industrial company in Ireland. But disaster struck.

On Sunday 18 June 1972, this group of Irish businessmen were travelling to Brussels for EEC discussions. They made their way to London and caught flight BEA 548 to Brussels. The Trident aircraft stalled after take-off and crashed in a field at Staines, four miles from Heathrow. All 118 passengers and crew were killed, in what was at the time Britain's worst ever air crash. It would have been a tragedy at any time. But for Ireland, at that time, it was a national disaster. Twelve of the passengers were from Ireland's EEC team. The cream of Irish businessmen died an untimely death. The group included Guy Jackson of Guinness, Michael Rigby-Jones of Irish Ropes, Merville Miller of Rowntree Mackintosh, Ed Coleman of Irish Steel and Con Smith, aged forty-three, the chairman of the Smith Group.

For three other members of the team, missing the flight was not the misfortune they had thought. It was a blessing that Dan McAuley of the Federated Union of Employers, Frank Dwane of the Federated Chamber of Commerce and Christopher Aliaga Kelly of the Confederation of Irish Industry were not on the plane. God does work in mysterious ways.

For the Smith Group, the death of the chief executive had grave consequences. The Goulding merger was cancelled. The spectre of death duties meant that the Peugeot and Citroën franchises were ring-fenced into the Gowan Group ('Gowan' is Gaelic for 'Smith'). The Renault franchise and other Smith Group activities were sold to Waterford Crystal, the McGrath empire. For Mrs Gemma Smith, it also meant the sale of their magnificent family home, Mount Eagle, on a six-acre site overlooking Killiney Bay, for forty thousand pounds. A full retrenchment was on the cards and the dreams of the great Con Smith lay smouldering in an English field, sacrificed in the search for a new prosperity for Ireland and all her people.

The EEC welcomed Ireland as a member some months later.

31

WHEN THE GOING GETS TOUGH

It was with Unidare Ltd that Liam did the biggest motor-deal of his life. It all came about from Mother Darcy's dictum: 'Always be willing to do any man a good turn, son.'

Liam took a phone call from a McKinsey business consultant. The consultant was doing a review of the motor industry in Ireland. Could Liam spare ten minutes to advise him? Okay, come on in. He was a nice guy. Ian Cairnduff was his name. Liam impressed him when he told him that his Scottish surname meant 'the black rock' in Gaelic. It turned out that Liam had sold cars to Ian's dad in Gilbey's, the wine merchants. They were destined to become the creators of Bailey's Irish Cream. Ian and Liam spent a few evenings discussing motor-trade operations and statistics. Nice fella. Six months later, Ian rang again. He had an assignment in Dublin to restructure the Unidare Group. This was a large engineering firm out in Finglas, beside Liam's sister, Vera, on McKee Avenue. Could Liam drop out to review their vehicle fleet?

Walden's ended up supplying a whole new fleet of Ford cars, trucks, vans and trailers to Unidare and its seven subsidiary companies. A hundred and eighty vehicles, all told. There were big celebrations in Mick Whelehan's pub across from Walden's that evening, toasting the big deal and the birth of Liam's second daughter, just up the road in the Rotunda Hospital. It was Eddie Farrelly who named her. Hilary Cullen. Hilary Roslyn Cullen, to include her godmother, Rosaleen Campbell. Liam had his first alcoholic drink. One glass of white wine. He had to stand at the pub door for ten minutes until the buildings stopped waving. He got Brendan Hession to drive him home. The Ma was disappointed to see his Pioneer pin gone, but she loved the new baby.

*

One of Liam's most effective actions was a weekly trip to Ford's in Cork. It wasn't Mister Wallace's three-day voyage. Liam left Dublin at five o'clock in the morning. He could make it to Cork in a little over three hours. He would be in early at the Ford gates – he was known by all the security guys – and up to the sales offices. He would get all the details on current vehicle availability and negotiate his forward purchases. He might pick up a few special models. The early bird gets the worm. He would set off home by ten o'clock. All business, all go. No long lunches. He'd be back in his Dublin office by two o'clock in the afternoon. On some occasions, he'd head off back to Cork at five o'clock with a team of drivers to bring home some urgently required vehicles. No need for the water bottle now, with heaters standard equipment on all Ford models.

Mister Wallace was impressed. 'How could you have

been in Cork yesterday, when I spoke to you in the office at half past two?'

'Yes, Mister Wallace,' said Liam, 'I left at five in the morning, down in three hours, one hour to do the business, and back in the office at two o'clock. Did you know we went back down again in the evening? I have that new Ford Corsair, for your friend Mister O'Riordan, to deliver today.' The boss was absolutely gobsmacked. From then on, he took great pride in introducing Liam as 'the fellow who can drive up and down to Cork twice in the same day. Mission impossible. No problem to him.'

It was on one of his early-morning trips that Liam ran out of petrol, about a mile past Fermoy. He got out the petrol can and walked back up the road. On the hill to the south of the town, a car was parked, with a guy in it drinking tea from a flask. It was his first meeting with Johnny McCarthy, who had just bought a couple of acres of land for a car dealership. They shared the tea. Johnny produced a full can of petrol. So every early Monday morning, on his trips to Ford's, Liam pulled in at Fermoy. He watched Johnny filling his low-lying site and building his dealership. Converting wet bogland into a business premises with hard work and determination. The steel came out of the ground. For breakfast, Liam brought the ham or banana sambos. Johnny supplied the tea.

The McCarthy Opel dealership opened with a flourish, but Johnny had tough competition from Tom Cavanagh's Ford operation in the centre of the town. It was a second-generation business, with a huge customer bank, loyal to the Cork product. But Tom Cavanagh decided to move his car-sales operation out beside Johnny. A bigger and better premises.

The opening of Cavanagh's new operation was the making of Johnny McCarthy, because the huge volume of Cavanagh customers who came out to the new Ford dealership were now exposed to the Opel products. And Johnny had a shop and petrol station which was customer-friendly. Before very long, Johnny McCarthy was one of the biggest Opel dealers in Ireland. Both Cavanagh and McCarthy became millionaires from their dealerships in the small town of Fermoy.

*

Mister Wallace's two sons were still in college. Young Billy had a few years to go, but Vincent was due to move into the business that summer. Liam received a few tempting headhunting offers to run other operations in both Ireland and England. He loved Walden's, and Mister Wallace was a great guy. Michael Cole and Bill Lambert were fantastic mentors. But he remembered the words of the commando major in Belfast: 'Start your own business. You can't go wrong.'

He met one evening with an old friend, Denis Mahony. Denis had worked in a competitor's Ford dealership in Smithfield Motors, until he set up his own motor business. He gave Liam the same advice.

'Go work for yourself, son,' Denis said. 'You have all the headaches anyway, you might as well have all the profits as well.'

Liam sat down with Mister Wallace and told him he was intent on leaving. He had made up his mind. He would work with Vincent for twelve months on a fast-track grounding operation. Mister Wallace was disappointed, but pleased that Liam was prepared to give the twelve months to facilitate an orderly handover. The king is dead, long live the king.

Liam had discussions with John Wyer in Ford's. Yes, they were prepared to offer him a Ford franchise in the new Dublin suburb of Tallaght. Liam had twenty thousand pounds saved after his eight-year executive stint at Walden's. The bankers were prepared to finance his new operation. There was a big hooley on the night of his departure. Another lesson in life's vagaries. Just like the pigs, it's all about timing. The day he left, the sky fell in on the motor trade. Some things are outside your control.

October 1973. The day he left Walden's, the Egyptian War broke out in the Middle East. Worldwide recession. A scarcity of petrol in Ireland for six months.

Al Williams, Brendan Hession and Bill looking worried after hearing news of the start of the Egyptian War in 1973

All motor-trade activities ground to a halt. All new Ford franchises were postponed. All bank loans for motor-trade activities were cancelled. Read the small print in the letter of offer. 'Subject to board approval. Subject to cancellation without notice.' The king is dead, all right. Now what do we do?

'Well, the one thing we won't do is worry about it. That does no one any good at all,' said Mother Darcy. 'Remember them ould paper roses, Liamo. Sure, we'll work it out, one way or another.'

So forget the big car. No more fancy title. No hundreds of staff to manage. Liam moved into the garden of a petrol station in Ballymun with two former colleagues, Al Williams and Shay Hession. It was a small site. A caravan office. They were selling used cars and new Chryslers. Al worked the corporate-fleets-for-leasing business. Shay did the retail deals. Liam processed the paperwork, the finance, the service and reconditioning operations and the car purchases. They bought a site in the Glasnevin industrial estate to build and develop a specialist car-leasing operation. They got the finance from David Hogg in Mercantile Credit, a great supporter.

Shay was Brendan Hession's brother and it wasn't long before Brendan joined them from Walden's. It was a tough year. Property companies were in free fall. Banks were tight on loans. Unemployment was rising again. Keep the head down. Work hard for every bit of business. They were working long hours, trawling the Dublin garages for used-car bargains. Liam had to meet the payroll every week. Tough going. Time for strong fingernails. For hanging in there. It was a long way from the fancy lunches in the Ford executive dining room.

He certainly had the headaches. He wondered how long it would take for the profits to start rolling in.

On 17 May 1974 they moved into the new development in Glasnevin. Nice offices and full service workshops. And on that evening, three car-bomb explosions rocked Dublin. One was in Parnell Street, opposite the Shakespeare Bar. Another was in Lincoln Place, beside Trinity College. The third car bomb went off in Talbot Street.

Twenty-six people were killed and over two hundred injured. Horrible injuries. In peacetime. At the height of the Friday rush hour. Ninety minutes after the Dublin-city bombing, another car bomb exploded in Monaghan. Seven died and forty were injured. Liam and his staff gathered in the Autobahn pub in Glasnevin, looking at the carnage on TV. All the paramilitary organisations disclaimed responsibility and condemned the violence.

Liam dropped in to see the Ma and Da. Everything was okay with them, and all the family accounted for. Said their Rosary as usual. New incantation: 'May the Virgin Mary bring peace and forgiveness to this Emerald Isle.'

Response: 'Lord, hear our prayers.'

Mother Darcy said it was the Brits. 'Just trying to stir up trouble, they are. To get the vote passed in Westminster to put more troops into the North.' How can Ireland achieve any form of economic stability with blood and murder on the streets? Liam thought.

*

Senator Jack Daly was a great supporter, a garage-owner in Killarney. Liam had met him at his first SIMI meeting in 1957. Jack was a Chrysler dealer, and he lived in Dublin during the week to attend sessions in the Dáil. He stayed in the Skylon Hotel, close to the Chrysler assembly plant in Santry. It wasn't very far from Liam's car-sales pitch at Ballymun. Jack supplied Liam with new Chryslers and Liam bought some of Jack's used trade-ins. They became very close friends.

Jack Daly had a great mind. Sharp as a razor. He was into gadgets. The first pocket calculator Liam ever saw was Jack's. He was always pushing new technology. Computers and the like. He was a great wit and raconteur.

But it was at negotiating he excelled. With Jack Daly on your side, you just remembered Mother Darcy's line: 'You got two ears and one mouth for a very good reason.' He'd say nothing. Listen to everyone. Light his oul *dúidín* of a pipe. Listen. When they were about to wrap up and vote for Plan B, Jack would make a few caustic comments, undermine the whole plan with two or three relevant factors, swing everyone against Plan B, and bingo, his Plan A was voted in unanimously. Liam saw him do it many times. He could argue black was white and convince you of it. Liam learned a lot about negotiating from Senator Jack Daly.

*

Liam got a Fiat franchise. A sub-franchise really, under a former Walden man, Johnny Forte of Sweeney and Forte. They had a big signing-up with Nicky Blume, the head Fiat man, in their massive Kylemore Road premises. They sold a lot of Fiat Mirafiori 121s, but they were always in trouble with Fiat.

As a sub-dealer, Liam couldn't pre-order cars. He had

to take from the Forte supply. This needed a Fiat executive sign-off for every car. But as a sub-dealer, Liam wasn't allowed to enter the premises for the sign-off. Catch 22. He couldn't even get into the reception area. Eventually, he found a side door to the building where the security man couldn't see him. He got a clerk there to take the paperwork in to the sales manager for the sign-off, to enable him to collect the car. It could take an hour. It was a horrible waste of time, every time you collected a car. But rules were rules, and they continued to fight to get the sign-off to sell the Fiat cars.

Through 1975 and 1976, they soldiered on. Shay packed it in and went to London, to the big-time motor-dealer operations. Business picked up, with some excellent fleet accounts. Smurfit Bunzl was a neighbour in the industrial estate, and Liam sold one of Jack Daly's Simcas to the manager, Terry Coleman. Terry was hugely interested in cars. He spent a lot of time getting his new Simca rust-proofed. Liam had an agency for the under-sealing product and Terry got a car alarm and sunroof fitted to his car. He became so interested in the car after-market operation that he left Smurfit and started his own car-care business in the estate. He worked hard. On with the overalls and under the ramp, Terry went. Day and night. He got contracts from the car distributors. He went to England and did the same there. Then he bought the car alarm company in Italy. Now he's flying his own Learjet, just like his old boss. He paid six million pounds for a house on Killiney Bay – the most expensive house in Dublin. Always had style, did Terry. It just shows what hard work and elbow grease will do for you.

*

Of course, when the going gets tough, the bank gets tougher. One Friday, Liam was collecting the wages from the bank in Cavendish Row. Six hundred pounds' worth of banknotes and change. Problem. Cashing the cheque will put you in excess of the overdraft limit by two hundred quid. They wouldn't budge. It was three o'clock. The banks were closing. Liam headed down to the Ma at the Lane to borrow the money. He got it, after a bit of a collection from the dealers. The Ma, Nanny Kelly, Jinny Foster and Lena Redmond. He would never forget the way the girls gathered the money into a brown paper bag. Laughing and joking. 'We're making an investment loan to the tycoon.' Liam paid them back the next morning with a box of chocolates each, for interest. As Mother Darcy always said, 'Never forget your roots, son. They'll always be there for ya.'

The Ma's house in Portland Row was a dry house. Even for weddings or funerals, there was never any alcohol under her roof. 'There are nineteen pubs within five minutes' walk of the door,' the Ma would say. When Brian married Alice Lemare in Saskatoon in Canada, he came home for his honeymoon. Knowing Brian was a Hennessy cognac man, Liam chanced bringing a bottle to the Ma's house for the celebration. But no way, José. The Ma confiscated the bottle. Liam and Brian eventually ended up in the pub.

Brian showed his street smarts when he tasted his brandy and called the barman. 'I ordered a Hennessy,' he said.

The barman tried to brazen it out. 'And that's a Hennessy I gave you'.

Brian gave his sardonic smile. 'Well, then, you can just bring me the same again. Only this time, bring the bottle with ya, so we can see if it's the real thing.' Gotcha. Brian knew his Hennessy. The barman couldn't produce a Hennessy bottle.

It was many years later when Aidan, the youngest of the family, returned home from a five-year stay on Cape Cod. Liam went into the Ma's house.

'Time to head down to Humphry's for a Hennessy,' said Aidan.

'Hold on,' said the Ma, producing the previously confiscated bottle of Hennessy from the kitchen press. 'You can take this with yez, if it hasn't gone sour by now.' Mary Darcy wouldn't know a pint of Guinness from a small Jameson.

32

——

'FAIR LANE' FORD

In 1976, Liam got back into discussions again with Ford, on the Tallaght franchise. He bought a three-acre site on the Greenhills Road and got the franchise. David Hogg came good with the finance package. He built a spanking new Ford dealership on the Ford Dealer Development Plan which gave Ford a shareholding in the company. Fairlane Motor Company. A name that means Ford. Fair Lane, the street where Henry Ford's father and grandparents stayed while they waited for the coffin ship in 1847. The ship his grandmother died on. The Fair Lane name was resurrected again in Ireland.

The turmoil of his career had seen Liam separate from Rita. He had spent too much time missing from his home. He was never there. He bought a house on Brendan Road in Donnybrook and moved Rita to a bigger house in Howth. The girls came over at weekends. The pictures. Tennis in Herbert Park.

The Ma was really upset. Very disappointed in her eldest son. She didn't speak to him for a long time. But he went into Portland Row to say hello most Sunday mornings, and eventually the frost thawed. 'Time heals all wounds,' Mother Darcy said.

'But what's all this I hear about you living in Donny-brook?' Molly said to him one night. 'Whereabouts are ya, over there.' Liam knew she never crossed the Liffey. She was a northsider all the way.

'I'm in Brendan Road. It's a little street off Herbert Park, Mother,' he replied. 'Sure, you don't know posh places over there.'

Mother Darcy smiled knowingly at him. 'Is that what ya think, now. Well now, son, let me tell ya, I know Herbert Park like I know the back of me hand. Seventy years ago, I spent a lot of time working at the Royal Dublin Society. Before your mammy was ever born, I worked in the bars and kitchens of the RDS. How's that for ya, now. And I know every door on Brendan Road, too,' she said, taking out her Colman's tin. Sniff, sniff, sniff to you, me boy, was what that meant.

'What number are ya living in?' she asked, during the sniffs. Liam should have known not to take Mother Darcy for granted – she who knows all things.

'Number Five, Mother,' he said.

'Ah yes, sure I know Number Five, the third door down on the right from Morehampton Road. All the uneven numbers on that side,' she said, with a smile on her face. Gobsmacked, he was.

'Dead right, Mother, and how do you know it so well?'

She looked out the window. Smiling. Dreaming. 'Back in the early days as a young girl, son, I would walk in Herbert Park during me break. From the kitchens of the RDS, that is. Watching the ladies playing bowls and the gents on the tennis court. From a distance, 'cause I was just feeding a few breadcrumbs to the ducks. With Aloysius, who was a waiter in the Shelbourne. Aloysius

Hitler, with a brother in the Austrian army called Adolf
Hitler. What do ya think of that now, I ask ya?' Liam
was stunned. Molly was still smiling, gazing out the
window, that faraway look in her eyes. He said nothing.
There was silence for a good few minutes. A tear stood
in her eye. She spoke quietly. 'And then there was the
Big Fella. During the Troubles. He'd go into Number
One and hop over the back gardens to stay in Number
Nine. I'd bring messages from Parnell Square for him.
Stuck down the leg of me drawers. The Tans were
terrible men, but they'd never touch ya down there.
Knock at the door. "Any oul' clothes to throw out
today, Mam?" I'd ask. She'd give me a gansey and I'd
hand in the envelope. Sometimes the Big Fella himself
would be in the hall. A smile and a wink for me. Lovely
man.' She was talking very low. Still smiling. She gave
herself a shake. Gave a good oul' blow in the hem of
her apron and stood up. Smiling.

'And now I'm off to me Rosary, son, and may the
Virgin Mary look after ya and keep ya safe in that house,
just like the Big Fella.' She grabbed her shawl, blessed
herself with the holy water from the font at the door,
and out she went. He followed and watched her climb
the steps to the church of St Joseph's, right across the
road from her hall door. At the church door she turned,
gave him a big smile and blew him a kiss.

Liam sat in the car. The Big Fella was Michael
Collins. He couldn't wait to get home to his bookshelves. And there it was. A picture of Michael Collins
on his bike in Morehampton Road. Details in the book
of the safe house he used in Brendan Road. What an oul'
one. Molly Darcy, sure she knows all things.

*

Fairlane started life in a warehouse on the Belgard Road, a twelve-month facility the company was to use while the new dealership was under construction. They were like the Summerhill tenements – no water, no electricity, no phones. But Liam had cars to sell and punters to buy them. Paddy Hayes of Ford saw Liam's determination in action.

He got a big ten thousand-gallon tank for water supply. A diesel generator for electricity. There were no mobile phones in those days. Paddy Lumley in the neighbouring building gave him one phone line for outgoing calls. The Belgard Inn came to the rescue for

Bill (centre) with Paddy Hayes of Ford (left) and Gene Fitzgerald (right), Minister for Finance, at the opening ceremony of Fairlane Company

incoming calls. It was about half a mile up the road and the owner rented Liam two public phone boxes. Fairlane used those numbers for advertising and customer contact, with their girl sitting in the pub all day, taking messages, which were collected every hour.

It was a funny scene for the pub drinkers. The girl sitting answering the constantly ringing public phones with, 'Good evening, Fairlane Motor Company, how can I help you?' And they sold a lot of cars and made good profits in that temporary building. The building was eventually bought by Brian Murphy and is now a high-profile dealership – Belgard Motors – for Mercedes and VAG.

The new Fairlane Ford dealership opened with great fanfare. The ribbon was cut by the Minister for Finance, Gene Fitzgerald, a Corkman helping out the Cork brand. All the Ford dignitaries were there. Ford of Europe executives. The Ma and Da were there, with all the family except Brian and Rita. Speeches, celebrations – a great night. Liam went back to the Burlington with the Ford executives.

One of them, Hank Rowley, got sentimental. 'Great speech you made tonight. Off the cuff. Nothing typed. From the heart. And fair play, you gave great credit to your family for all their support. And what a mother you have. She's a great lady.

Liam laughed. 'I didn't know you were talking to the Ma. What was she on about that impressed you?'

Hank looked at him. 'When you finished your speech,' he said, 'I turned to your mother and said, "You must be very proud of young Bill tonight." I'll never forget her answer. She said, "Well now, sir, I'm not waiting till tonight to be proud of that young fella." And then she smiled and looked across the showrooms and added, "but there's ten of his brothers and sisters here tonight. Housewives, printer, soldier, mechanic, one on the dole, and I'm just as proud of every one of them. Great kids, they are." What an answer. I felt so humble. What a woman. What a mother.'

Albert Williams had decided not to go along to Tallaght. 'A three-way partnership is one too many.' Liam bought him out. There were just two partners now. Brendan Hession had moved to live in Templeogue, only five minutes from Fairlane. Peter Ennis joined them from Walden's to run the fleet-leasing operation. George Brennan and young Aidan Cullen ran the parts division, with Shay O'Reilly and Gerry Glennon on the service end.

Business boomed for Fairlane Ford in Tallaght. The area was a new dormitory town for Dublin. Houses were popping up everywhere. Industrial estates, a shopping mall, a huge hurly-burly of activity. But Tallaght was a low-income area – social housing and first-time buyers coping with high mortgages. Liam had to use marketing tactics to pull the punters from the higher-income, lower-mortgage, settled areas of Templeogue, Terenure, Churchtown and Rathfarnham.

The first successful tactic was on-the-spot delivery. The established city-centre Ford dealers were very much union-controlled. If you walked into Archer's Ford showrooms and put your hand on any car and said, 'I'll buy this for the sticker price', they could take your money. 'But you can't get this car for two weeks, sir,' you would be told.

'Here's my money, why can't I have it right now?'

Simple reply. 'It's the union, sir. The mechanics only

process five new cars a day. We've fifty before you in the line. That means your car gets inspected, plated and ready for delivery in two weeks. It's the union, sir.'

Liam had a new union in his new garage. Flexible. They wanted jobs for local kids. Fairlane trained them, paid well, and got cooperation and flexibility. So the Fairlane strapline was: 'No delay, you drive away today'. It worked. They came. They bought. No waiting. They drove home in the new car.

Liam met Jackie Lavin at the Royal Dublin Society's Spring Show of 1979. She was a fashion model. Separated, with two young boys. They had dinner together one Thursday evening and Liam invited her to the show at the Gaiety Theatre the following Tuesday. They agreed that Jackie would get the tickets. On the night, Liam was waiting for her to arrive. At seven o'clock, his doorbell rang. Jackie was on the doorstep. Fire and brimstone.

'You didn't ring me once since we had dinner last week. Here are your tickets. Enjoy it.' She threw the two tickets into the hall and away in her car, smoke coming from her ears. 'Janey Mac, does she not realise I'm a busy man in Fairlane?' Liam thought. He picked up the tickets, drove down to the Gaiety and sold them. He got double the face value. The law of supply and demand. Old habits die hard. He eventually mended the fences. Liam and Jackie have been together ever since. They moved from Brendan Road to a house in the Dublin Mountains – Stepaside Lodge – with a beautiful view of Dublin Bay.

*

The second successful car-marketing strategy, he learned in America. Liam tried to get to Cape Cod every year, to visit the sisters and have some fish in the Flying Bridge or the Boathouse in Falmouth. Have a jar in Bobby Byrne's and the Sagamore Inn. He stayed in Daniel Webster's or the Coonamesset Inn. Sometimes he flew to New York instead of Boston to enjoy the drive up Highway 193 to the Cape. On the way, he passed through Providence, Rhode Island. He saw a Ford dealership and dropped in, to Bob Tasca Ford. He met Gene McCarthy, the greeter. Bob Tasca had the biggest and best Ford dealership in the north-east, selling five thousand new Fords a year. Bob gave him a lesson he never forgot.

'Gotta sell something different than the other Ford guy up the road,' Bob said. 'Get yourself fifty or a

Bill and Jackie in 1981

hundred Ford cars. Put an option pack on. Sunroof, alloy wheels. Doesn't really matter what it is. But make sure you give it a name. The Fiesta Bobcat. And the trick then is to say in all your adverts, big and brassy: "The Fiesta Bobcat, exclusive to Bob Tasca Ford, with the free this, that and the other for only so many dollars".' He paused. 'The word "exclusive" is the key to this.'

Liam went home. He bought a hundred new Ford Fiestas. Sunroof, stripes, rear boot glider, tape player. 'The Fiesta Flyer, exclusive to Fairlane.' The dealership was stormed. They sold out in a week. Next, they had the Escort Falcon. And so on. The Flyer sold six hundred in one year. Fairlane become Ireland's number-one Ford dealer, from listening to the experts. 'You got two ears, two eyes and one mouth for a very good reason,' says Molly Darcy, 'and isn't it exactly like the Judy Garland and Marilyn Monroe dolls we sold on Henry Street?'

*

The bubble burst in 1982. The market collapsed. The Irish economy stuttered and stopped. Zero growth. Interest rates went through the roof. Twenty per cent on overdraft loans, calculated daily. You paid interest on interest. Liam moved fast to cut the overheads, which meant cutting the staff in half. It wasn't easy. A lot of decent, hard-working guys lost their jobs. But there was no choice. If some didn't go, the whole place would close. The Ford chairman, Paddy Hayes, was very supportive, but it was up to Liam to keep the ship afloat. He just about managed to keep the head above water.

Bill (centre) at the launch of the Ford Escort with his partner Brendan Hession (left) and Enda Hogan of Ford Motor Company

David Hogg in Mercantile Credit was sensible and adjusted repayments to suit the cash flow. Although England, Europe and the States were buoyant in the Reagan–Thatcher era, Ireland remained in the doldrums.

*

In 1985, all car manufacturers ceased assembly in Ireland. The production lines were too small, at a hundred cars a day, to compete with the economies of scale of the European plants. Valencia could produce two thousand cars a day. So Cork lost Ford's and Dunlop's. There was a famous story told about the week the Ford plant closed in Cork. The men got large redundancy lump sums. But it's fair to say that the dole wasn't a nice thing to have ahead of you. The components in the parts division started to vanish. It got so bad that when one of the lads was struggling to walk out the gate, one of the security guys quipped: 'Will youse look at Mossy, lads. He's got so many car parts under his coat that if ya pushed him, he'd start.'

Paddy Hayes of Ford got the job as chief executive of Waterford Crystal and he brought Redmond O'Donoghue with him as marketing director. He needed car expertise to sort out the now loss-making Renault division owned by Waterford Crystal.

In 1985, Liam sensed an improvement. A slight uplift. He got bank support to buy a garage property in Rathmines. Then he heard that Waterford Crystal were selling some of their Renault garages. He rang Paddy Hayes to see if he could buy Renault's garage in Templeogue. Hayes invited him to discuss it with Brendan Reville, a retired motor-trade executive whom Liam knew well, who was a consultant to Renault. Reville came and met Liam, suggested a price, and Liam felt it was too high. He made an appointment with Paddy Hayes.

33

RENAULT FOR A QUID

Paddy Hayes was in the Shelbourne Hotel. He stunned Liam with his opening statement, in his lovely sing-song Cork accent. 'Have you no lee-a-roady at all, Cullen? You only want to buy one miserable garage off me. Why won't you buy the lot?'

Liam knew the Smith Group had twenty garages. 'So it's the twenty garages you want to sell,' he said, playing for time.

'Not just twenty Renault garages. The whole Smith Group you can have. There's forty-seven companies in the group, from cars to tractors, to wallpaper, to paint, to finance houses, et cetera. But it's going for a bargain price, because it's losing its shirt at the rate of two million pounds a year,' Hayes responded. 'So now, Cullen, you Dublin jackeen, have you the lee-a-roady for all that? 'Cause you can have it for one pound, to take it off my hands.'

Liam was shocked into silence by the aggressive, challenging tone. His hand reacted automatically, by placing a pound note on the table. Hayes laughed. 'It's not that simple, boy,' he said.

Liam looked at him. Smiled. Say nothing till ya hear more.

'There's a little matter of an eighteen-million-pound bank debt to pay off. Can ya borrow that anywhere?'

There had to be a catch. There was no point in going down to the girls at the Lane. He looked at Hayes. 'We can try,' he said.

'You've three months, then, if you just sign this confidentiality agreement.'

The ball was in play. Liam got his auditor, Des Peelo, a former Haughey Boland accountant, to act as financial consultant for the project. Des Peelo was great. He got the balance-sheet numbers and drew up the business plan. He knew all the inner circle of Dublin's banking fraternity. Liam and himself made the rounds. They had great business plans. Great restructuring ideas for the Smith Group. Lots of assets as security. They only needed a loan of *eighteen million pounds*. The reception was negative.

'A couple of noughts too many, Des. Sure, the motor trade is going down the tubes. If this recession gets any worse, it's walking we'll all be,' was the reaction.

Des and Liam got an appointment with the corporate director of a big bank. An old pal. Of Des's, that is. Great chat in his sumptuous office. The football game last week. How's the tennis. Ever see Charlie since you left Haughey Boland's? Finally, Jim walked around behind his huge desk.

'So now, Des, me ould pal, what can I do for you today?'

'Well, Bill is buying the Smith Group. We need an eighteen-million-pound loan. Bill will show you the proposal.'

Des was a fast talker. Jim's hands were on the desk. His knees were bent. He froze. His bum hadn't reached the chair. His face went white. He straightened up. 'Run that up the flagpole again,' he said. Bankers' speak. Des repeated his three sentences verbatim. With Jim shaking his head slowly from side to side. Liam had opened his briefcase. Pulled out the magnificently printed, very extensive and expensive business plan.

Jim waved his hand. 'I don't need to see that,' he said. 'The motor business is drowning in red ink.' He picked up a thick folder from his desk and waved it at Des. 'Twenty-two pages of loan defaulters in the car business, I have. Top of the hit list in every bank. Des, I couldn't loan you eighteen pence, never mind eighteen million pounds,' he said. Silence. Broken by the door opening, with Jim's secretary pushing it in with her knee as she carried the tray of cups, teapot, coffee pot and plate of biscuits. She froze at the door as Jim waved the defaulting folder at her. 'We won't be needing that, Michelle, the lads are just leaving. Sorry, Des, I'm really very busy!'

Des grimaced. He was let down and a bit embarrassed. 'Thanks very much, Jim,' he said, and marched out, past the frozen Michelle with the tray in her hands, her back stiffened against the open door.

Liam stood up to his full height and replaced the business plan in his briefcase. He looked at Jim. 'You know, Jim,' he said, his first words since the introduction, 'you shouldn't have done that to your friend. You could have taken the plan. Had a cup of tea. "I have to study this with the credit committee. Get back to you soon." Then send a "very sorry" letter. It doesn't cost anything to be nice to a friend.'

Jim looked at Liam. 'When I need advice, I'll ask for it. Goodbye,' he said.

Ouch! Cool it. Liam walked to the door, with his open briefcase in his hand. 'And we don't get a cup of tea,' he said to Michelle, who had her eyes fixed on the teapot.

'No, you don't,' answered Jim.

Liam nodded, picked up the plate of biscuits, and shook them into his briefcase. 'Well I'll just have an oul' biscuit, so. Cheerio,' he said, and walked out past the cups rattling on Michelle's tray. Nice biscuits. Poor ould Jim must be stressed out by all his red ink. Should give a thought to the poor fellas on his default list. They've good reason to be stressed.

*

It was David Hogg of Mercantile Credit who came to the rescue, a good friend who had supported Liam in Fairlane from the beginning. Over ten years, he had got lots of retail-finance business from Fairlane, and this was an opportunity for Mercantile to get all the retail paper from the Renault-dealer network. A two-way street. Mercantile were owned by Barclays Bank in England. They had one corporate branch on Dublin's Stephen's Green.

David liked the business plan, and Paul Shovlin of Barclays Bank in Dublin was supportive. Des went to London with David and Paul for a presentation to Barclays' head-office team. They came back with a positive. Subject to a few covenants, of course. Personal guarantee from Liam, full security on all his personal assets, too. If this doesn't work, we're on the street again. You need lee-a-roady.

During the months it took to get the financial

backing, the Renault franchise suffered. Newspaper headlines reading 'Smith Group up for sale' and 'Waterford Crystal to offload Renault'. It wasn't helping people to buy Renault cars. The dealers in the network were despondent. Sales fell away. In France, Renault were struggling to survive as a car manufacturer, having sustained huge losses withdrawing from the American market. Liam had to move fast to finalise the deal before confidence in the car brand evaporated.

The next job was to convince Renault to give him the franchise. He went to Paris with Des to meet the Renault finance team – Christian Estève and Kathleen O'Neill. The Irish are everywhere. Kathleen O'Neill is a descendant of Owen Roe O'Neill, who left Ireland after the disastrous defeat by the English at Kinsale in 1601, to settle in France. Like the Wild Geese, who were forced to leave Ireland too, after the Treaty of Limerick. The wines of Chateau Lynch, the Hennessy cognac. The French were friends of Ireland. The two countries had been in constant battle with the English. The enemy of my enemy is my friend, as Mother Darcy would say.

Estève was positive on the business plan. He brought in the French Export Guarantee Board, who supported the finance package. The next hurdle was the approval of the Renault export director, who needed to assess Liam and his plans. Pierre Herrmann came to Ireland for a weekend.

*

Liam and Pierre met for dinner in Dunmore East, with Paddy Hayes and Gerry Dempsey of Waterford Crystal. They were hidden away in a magnificent coastal retreat.

Liam spent the weekend discussing the motor business, which he loved and knew so well: the American market. The withdrawal of Renault, who sold out their American Motor Corporation to Lee Iacocca of Chrysler fame. Pierre had been on the French negotiating team. The history of the European car brands. The success of the Japanese brands in Europe and America. Liam showed his knowledge of the French car market and the latest statistics on the progress of Renault and its competitors. He knew the complete history of Renault, down to the little publicised fact of how the owner, Regie Renault, had died mysteriously in a French prison just days before the end of the Second World War. De Gaulle confiscated the Renault empire for the French government and nationalised it. Liam's intimate knowledge of the Irish car market reflected his thirty years' experience.

Monsieur Pierre Herrmann was very impressed. They even got around to discussing Liam's family. The Frenchman was interested in the Da's and Brian's military careers. Pierre had been in the French navy. He had fought in the Asian War at the famous Battle of Dien Bien Phu in Vietnam in 1954. The French Foreign Legion were defeated by the Vietnamese. It was the beginning of the end for the French colonial empire. Pierre was one of the few who escaped. He spent four months swimming down the Red River. Swimming by night. Staying underwater by day, breathing through a hollow bamboo reed. He made it to the port of Minh Binh, stowed away on a freighter and eventually got back to France. The Americans followed the French into Vietnam the following year, and the horrors of that war scarred a generation. Pierre was a big man. He became known in Ireland as the 'French Legionnaire' after that story.

Pierre approved Liam for the Renault distribution franchise in Ireland. 'You are a real motor-man,' he said. Another Mister Con Smith. We are delighted to continue our 1958 agreement into the future with you.' And intrigued him with a further comment. 'You know, we have had two approaches for the Renault franchise. Two rich Irish industrialists, who have eyes for our brand. But they don't know cars, and don't have your passion for this complex business.' Liam knew that the Smurfit Group director, Howard Kilroy, was on the board of Waterford Crystal. Michael Smurfit had shown his interest in the motor trade when he'd taken a twenty-five per cent holding in the Irish Nissan distribution company. Maybe? Then again, Tony O'Reilly was also on the Waterford board. A collector of global brands. *C'est la vie.*

Then to finalise the due diligence and agree the takeover balance sheet. Des Peelo took control. He was a brilliant accountant, sharp as a razor, and a superb strategist and negotiator. A rare combination. With the sales of Renault collapsing in Ireland that summer, it was agreed to parachute Liam into the Smith Group as chief executive, while the accountants and lawyers finalised the details.

34

THE MA LEAVES HER LEGACY

The Ma was in the Mater Hospital. 'Arthur Itis in me hands.' A very painful condition. From the rain and snow at the Lane. But she was depressed too. She'd been mugged by a neighbour's son. One of the ever increasing number of drug addicts. The local TD, Tony Gregory, had worked so hard to protect the community, but the government only paid lip service. They never gave the police the resources to do the job. Drug barons flourished, addicted the kids and turned them into pushers to pay for their fix.

Mary Darcy couldn't come to terms with the disintegration of her community, where everyone had helped each other. Where the front door had always been open and unlocked, so that friends could drop in and help themselves. They all had so little, it was easy to share. Now there was no respect. Doors and windows were barred and locked. Old people lived in fear. Break-ins, burglaries and beatings. The Ma was mugged and her purse stolen. She was shaken up. Very upset. Liam and the brothers had no problem getting the purse back. Intact. A mistake, didn't realise it was Missus Cullen. But the Ma took it bad. She had taken care of the lad's family while his mother was in the Rotunda giving birth to him, eighteen years ago. Helped to get him started safely in the world. Now he was a drug addict. No sense of right or wrong. 'May the Virgin Mary protect my children from them drugs. Lord, hear our prayers.'

Mary Darcy was tired. Disillusioned. All the children had grown up and gone. Mission accomplished. No need to sit up half the night darning. No ganseys to mend. No one to wait up for at night, to make sure they got to bed safely. Didn't go to the Lane anymore. She was tired of all that, after seventy years at it. An empty house. Just herself and Billy. They were poles apart at this stage. She would drop over to the Mother in the evening. They'd go to the Rosary together. Like the early days before she was married. Billy at home reading his *Herald*. The cycle of life. And death.

Liam using all his powers of persuasion to win the Renault franchise

Liam was wrapped up in the Renault deal all that year. He dropped up to the hospital most weeks. The papers were speculating. 'Cullen moves into Renault'. Early in September, he was walking in the hospital grounds with the Ma. She was chatting and very lucid. 'The *Herald* says you're doing some big deal, Liam. Borrowing a lot of money,' she said.

'That's right, Ma,' he replied. 'It looks like the bank will put up the money. What do you think?'

She looked at him with a puzzled expression.

'They said you're borrowing eighteen million pounds. How many noughts is that?' she asked.

Liam wrote it out for her on his notebook. She looked at it. Eighteen and six zeros. Eighteen million pounds.

The Ma gave him a big hug. 'You're my lucky son,' she said, 'so just go and do it. You remember when you were a kid, I used to smack ya when ya got into divilment. With the gang of yiz, I didn't have much time for explaining things. So you just got a dig to make ya behave.'

'That's right, Ma,' Liam said into her hair, 'you could be rough when you lost your rag.'

The Ma moved away and looked up into his eyes. 'And every time I hit ya, I was telling you I loved you.' Her eyes were misty.

Liam remembered the nights he'd spent teaching her to read. The *Flying Enterprise*. The Da doing his nut. Walking out to Ballyfermot. At the Lane in the rain and snow. Handing him the five hundred pounds from under the floorboards. He knew she knew. They were thinking the same things.

'Eighteen million. Not much when ya say it quick.

The cover of *Aspect* magazine on Bill's takeover of the Smith Group in 1986

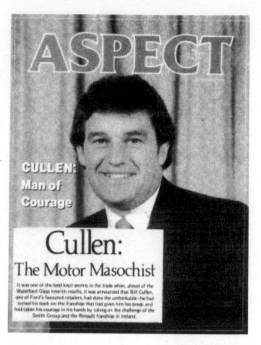

ASPECT

CULLEN:
Man of
Courage

Cullen:
The Motor Masochist

It was one of the best kept secrets in the trade when, ahead of the Waterford Glass interim results, it was announced that Bill Cullen, one of Ford's favoured retailers, had done the unthinkable – he had turned his back on the franchise that had given him his break and had taken his courage in his hands by taking on the challenge of the Smith Group and the Renault franchise in Ireland.

Go for it, son. You'll work it out. Always did. And you know what Mother Darcy says: "Better to try and fail than never to try at all." She paused. 'You've borrowed eighteen million pounds. God bless you, son. That's a long, long way from penny apples.' She reached out and ruffled his black curly hair.

Liam went up to the hospital a few days later. As he opened the door of the ward, John Jolley was just coming out. He looked at Liam and said, 'I'm sorry, Liam', stepped around him and went out. What's that all about? Liam thought, as he walked into the ward. The Ma? Was she okay? He looked up the aisle and saw his sister Vera sitting on the side of the bed. The Ma was looking at him. Smiling at him. He was relieved and walked up the ward, nodding to a 'Howaya, Liam' from one of the patients. When he got to Vera, he realised she was crying softly, stroking the Ma's left hand gently.

The Ma was still smiling, but her eyes were closed. He saw the wet sheen on her skin.

Vera turned to him. 'You just missed her, Liam, she was asking for ya.'

The next few days were a blur. Organising the funeral. Sisters and brothers returning from America and Canada. Looking after the Da. The churching and the long evening. Friends and visitors pouring through the house, only a few yards from St Joseph's Church. Where the Ma lay. It went on into the wee small hours. Everyone had gone. Da was in bed. Liam and Vera were left sitting by the turf fire in what was now the kitchen. It had been Liam's old room, in the basement. The bookshelves were still there on the wall. Still with a multitude of *Reader's Digest*s. His learning manual of the fifties. Out of the blue, Vera spoke quietly. 'Liam, do you remember the day of the messages in Mister O'Riordan's?'

He knew exactly what she was talking about. Forty years before. The biscuits he nicked from the glass-topped tin. The fluffy coconut marshmallow biscuits. His face reddened as he looked at her. But she was gazing into the flames of the fire.

'Of course I remember,' he said.

She didn't look up. 'I always think of them biscuits when me kids do something wrong. You didn't mean any harm. You weren't taking anything. Kids do foolish things without thinking. We just need to be around. To let them make some mistakes and correct them. Teach them. Help them. Support them. That's what the Ma taught me. What Mother Darcy taught me. It's what I teach me own kids.' She looked up at him.

'You see, you never really took them biscuits, did ya, Liam?' she said with a big smile. Liam walked over and they hugged each other. Standing there by the fire in that low-roofed room. Holding each other. The spirit of Mary Darcy all around them.

Liam knew a priest. He was a Brú boy, younger than Liam. A pal of Noel and Brian. He agreed to say the funeral Mass in St Joseph's. On the morning of the funeral, he spoke to Liam. 'You're not going to your Mass and Communion any more, Liamo,' he said.

'Now, Father, don't you know I broke the rules when I separated from Rita. I still drop in to the chapel. Catholic or Protestant. Say sorry to the Man Above. Have a quite little think. Peace and serenity is still there for me.'

The priest put his hands on Liam's shoulders and looked straight into his eyes. Not one of the younger chisellers any more. Man to man. 'I want you to come to Communion this morning, Liam. For the Ma. She'd want you to do that.'

Yes, she would, Liam thought.

'And you don't have to worry about it,' the priest continued as he raised his right hand and made the sign of the cross over him. He made a similar mark on Liam's forehead with his thumb, gently. 'The good Lord forgives you. Forgives you any sins you might ever have committed. It's not about rules, Liamo. It's about goodness. The goodness in your mind. The charity in your heart.' Liam took his Communion that morning, beside his sister, Vera, who put her hand on his as they knelt together at the altar rail. He felt the elation. The joy of his Rathfarnham retreat. He knew the Ma was smiling at him. Happy for him. God bless you, Father.

It was a long day. Shaking hands. Smiling thank-yous. Old friends everywhere. The burial in Balgriffin cemetery, beside Campion's pub. Liam remembered the Ma rushing him out the door in the early morning to make the bus for Joe Rankin's farm. He looked at the fields where the rassers and strawberries had been. Now they were the new Balgriffin cemetery.

When the evening was coming to a close, he said his goodbyes to the family and took Mother Darcy home, to Number 42 Portland Row, where they sat together at the fireside. Her little black pillbox hat still on her head. Big mother-of-pearl hatpin sticking in it. Out came her little Colman's mustard tin, and she took her pinch of snuff. She looked at Liam.

'Clears out the ould tubes, son,' she said. 'You know, there's no smoking allowed in the Houses of Parliament, but ya can have yar snuff anywhere.'

Kicking for touch, she was. Liam knew her. He held her hand. 'Mary is up in Heaven now, Mother,' he said. 'Getting a rest from all the hassle we gave her.'

Molly looked at him. Seeing the confident business-man but remembering the young fella. Always running everywhere. Great on the Street. The gift of the blarney. Mary's lucky child. Born in the caul. 'You know, Liam, that's the fifth child of mine that I've buried. It's hard for me. Ninety-four years old, I am, and He still won't take me. But that's God's will. Must still have something He wants me to do down here.'

'Of course he has, Mother,' Liam replied. 'He needs you to teach the kids. To talk to your grandchildren. My pair. Vera's gang. Sure, they love to come in to you on Sundays. Look at the picture on the wall. Yourself, the Ma, Vera, her daughter Karen, and Karen's daughter Tara. That's five generations together. Five generations of Darcy blood.'

Molly looked at the picture and smiled. 'Great

woman, your Ma was, son,' she said. 'Never stopped working. Like yourself. Always on the go. But ya know what I always say, Liam', and she paused. Holding hands by the fire, they repeated it together – a phrase he knew well: 'It's better to wear out than rust out.'

He felt happy as he drove away, Molly Darcy watching him from her window. The Ma smiling down on both of them. From over her rainbow.

> *Somewhere over the rainbow,*
> *Way up high,*
> *There's a land that I heard of*
> *Once in a lullaby.*
>
> *Somewhere over the rainbow,*
> *Bluebirds fly,*
> *Birds fly over the rainbow,*
> *Why, tell me why, can't I?*
>
> *Sometimes I wish upon a star*
> *And wake up when the moon is far behind me*
> *Where troubles melt like lemon drops*
> *Away up on the chimney-tops*
> *That's where you'll find me.*
>
> *Somewhere over the rainbow,*
> *Skies are blue,*
> *And the dreams that you dare to dream*
> *Really do come true.*
>
> *If happy little bluebirds fly*
> *Above the rainbow,*
> *Why oh why can't I?*

—

35

BUSINESS AS USUAL

Back to work the next day with the accountants and the legal teams. Six weeks of fine-tuning the deal. The credit lines. The final meeting in the Smith Group headquarters on Fitzwilliam Square. Des Peelo head-to-head with Gerry Dempsey. After three full days, they were still a million pounds apart.

Gerry and Liam went into the oratory of the magnificent house. It was the former home of the lord lieutenant of Ireland in the bad old days. Gerry was firm.

'It's Hallowe'en and this is the day we finish the deal, 31 October. If you don't sign off with these balance-sheet figures, we're all done, we walk away.'

Liam looked at him. 'Des says the assets need a million written off, Gerry. He's the accountant.'

Gerry Dempsey gave him a cold, flinty look. 'You're the man who can make it work. Renault have said yes. We're giving you the best deal we can. We've got to get moving fast or the whole thing goes down the tubes. It's seven o'clock, and I'm going home in half an hour. So take it or leave it,' he said, and left the room.

Liam followed him. 'He won't budge, Des,' he said.

Des shrugged. 'The numbers are tight. Very tight. It's up to you, Liam.'

Liam went for a walk. Head down, collar up, hands in pockets. A dark, cold evening. Light, misty rain. Thinking. A million-pound gap. But that's only six per cent on eighteen million. Take a chance? Or hold out? Car sales in the pits. The country dying a death right now. We'll need every bob to keep this ship afloat.

'Looking for action, Mister?' A cockney accent.

He broke out of his reverie to see three short-skirted females. Under an umbrella. Under the lamp-post. High skirts, low tops. Liam smiled. 'How's it going, girls. Wet oul' night for business.'

Red lipstick flashed. 'Bleedin' right. Punters home with the kids for Hallowe'en. Bleedin' rain will give us newmonia. Are ya on?'

'Afraid not,' he replied. 'We've a business meeting to finish, and her indoors is waiting at home.'

'Jaysus, that's the third straight tonight. I'm headin' home. Hey, mister, if ya have a car, ya can have it for nuthin' for a lift home.'

He moved on, smiling. Head up, chest out. Marching back to business. He was a lucky man to be getting this chance. Meet the market. The way the poor oul' street girls have to.

'Okay, Gerry,' Liam said, back in the oratory, 'let's do a deal. You want to unload the Smith Group. I'm happy to take it on. Put something into the pot, and we'll shake hands here and now.'

Gerry smiled. 'You're right. It's Hallowe'en. We've better places to be. Another two-fifty and we're done.' He held out his hand.

Liam stepped forward. 'Make it three hundred grand, and we shake hands. The luck penny.' The two men shook hands.

Gerry opened the door. 'Deal done!' he shouted. 'Get that paperwork moving; we've done a deal. Where's the phone?'

It was eight o'clock. It took five more hours to finish the paperwork. Brendan Reville came on the board of the new company. Des, with his hawk-eyed attention to detail, checked every piece of paper. Liam and Brendan signed their names four hundred and eighty times. Done deal, all right. Liam guaranteeing all the loans. Putting the house deeds and every shilling he'd ever made into the pot. He signed a cheque for fourteen million pounds and handed it over to Gerry Dempsey. Last thing before they left, Liam signed and kissed the one-pound note – the purchase price.

The first two years were pretty horrendous. The Smith Group was in disarray. The first thing was to reduce the overheads, which meant losing people. Redundancies. The whole country was suffering from unemployment, but Liam had to let a few hundred people go to keep the business afloat. Not easy. Tough times.

The Renault dealer network were not amused by the stringent new financial controls that had to be introduced. They had already issued legal claims against the company before the takeover, for a million pounds. So with legal claims flying around, it wasn't a very good basis for teamwork. They boycotted the first official launching of the new operation. It took six months of stand-offs, meetings and negotiations to bring them around. Some disillusioned dealers left for competitive

Paddy Hayes, chairman of Waterford Crystal, smiles as Bill Cullen takes over Renault, with its £18 million worth of debts, in August 1986

franchises. The Renault accountant, Jerr Nolan, was a rock of support during that time, travelling around the country, meeting dealers in the cold, snowy weather. Jerr became the company's chief executive. Great guy.

Liam needed to unload the non-motor activities and focus on the core Renault franchises. On the first day of the new operation, they received an order for twenty railway carriages from the national carrier, CIÉ. When the costings were examined, they found they were losing about fifteen grand on each wagon. They had to cancel that deal. They folded the commercial vehicle company. Sold the CRV works depot on the North Wall docks to Harry Crosbie. It wasn't worth much then. But Harry had his dreams for the docklands. Now it's part of the resurgent Dublin quayside developments. All about timing, isn't it?

The Smith Group had a company in Wexford town making car-wiring systems for Renault. Smith's Engineering. It had been an assembly plant for the old Renault 4L car. When car-manufacturing finished, they had converted the factory to this component supply operation. It was losing money hand over fist. It had been earmarked for closure, but with two hundred workers it was the biggest employer in County Wexford. It wouldn't be right to close it down. They had to let the workers know how serious their position was. No Waterford Crystal cheques were around now to cover losses, so they had to stand on their own feet. Make profit, or we'll all be out of a job. They needed some positive thinking, some motivation.

In the first week, Liam decided to drive down himself to assess the Wexford factory. He left Dublin before five o'clock and arrived in Smith's Engineering at seven o'clock on a dark morning An old factory, with a good site on the waterside. He walked around the outside perimeter.

A fire door opened; a head stuck out. 'And what might you be doing, nosing around my factory?' asked a small grey-haired fella with a heavy Wexford accent.

'I've an appointment with the general manager, Mister Bailey,' Liam replied.

'Oh, is it another one of them Dublin suits we have, visiting us? It's a wee bit early you are. Was your hotel bed lumpy or what?'

'No,' Liam replied. 'I drove down from Dublin this morning. Left early.'

That raised the man's eyebrows. 'It's an early bird we have? Didn't think we had any fellas like that in Dublin. Well, you better come in, so, and have a cup of tea.' He turned back into the factory. Liam followed the guy into a small caretaker's room where the teapot was just boiling on an old Primus stove. 'I've no sugar for you. Shure we're sweet enough, so we are, us Wexford men, and you can sit down on that,' he said, handing Liam the cup of tea and pointing to an old wooden crate, which Liam duly sat down on. 'My name is Danny,' he added, and he picked up his own cup and had his first close-up look at Liam. His hand stopped in midair. He put the cup down.

'Bejaysus,' he said, 'you're the new boss. Mister Cullen from Dublin. I saw your picture in the paper. I'm sorry I didn't recognise you. Shure it's in Mister Bailey's boardroom you should be. You'll get your trousers dirty on that ould crate.'

But Liam brushed off Danny's concerns. They got chatting, Liam talking about the famous Wexford hurling men he'd seen in Croke Park. The three Rackard brothers, Billy, Bobby and Nicky. What a game he'd seen in Croker for the 1955 All-Ireland hurling final, with Wexford beating the men from Galway by eight points.

'I was there meself, boy. Right behind the canal-end goal,' said Danny, and Liam responded, 'And you were looking straight over at meself on the railway-end wall.'

They had a great chat, with Liam able to join in the song of how the Wexford men fought and died for Ireland in the 1798 Rebellion — *the boys of Wexford/ who fought with heart and hand/ to burst in twain the galling chain/ and free our native land.* Harmony together.

Liam went into the offices when Mister Bailey arrived. He confirmed that the workers were anxious. Morale was low. There were rumours of the factory closing. What was Liam's intention?

'The only intention I have is to make this operation

profitable. But that's up to you, and all your people here. Renault in France have committed to a three-year component-supply contract for this plant. But you have to deliver the components on time, at the right price, to the right quality standards. And we have to make money on the contract. That's the bottom line.'

Bailey reached into his briefcase. 'Here's my business plan to cover those three years. We can meet Renault's criteria but I need a hundred-thousand-pound invest-ment in new machinery. Take this plan, and come back next week when your accounting team in head office have reviewed it. See if they'll agree,' said Bailey, handing him a two-inch-thick manuscript. Liam looked at it.

'I don't need a week, and we don't have an ac-counting team any more. Leave me here for one hour, till I digest this,' he said. It only took him half an hour to skim through the book. He wrote down the import-ant points. Called in Bailey.

'Okay, you need three new machines, costing one hundred thousand pounds. You want to go on three four-hour shifts a day to facilitate the workers, who are mainly women. Eliminate the quality-control division, make every worker responsible for their individual part of the process. Implement a performance-related bonus scheme: if we make profit, they get a share. That's what this is all about, right?' said Liam.

Bailey nodded. 'That's it in a nutshell, but we'll have to sell it to the workers. My team are edgy about it, and feel the plan might be rejected.'

Liam asked for all the workers to be assembled and gave them a review of the position. 'We don't want any redundancies. We want everyone to keep their jobs.

Only possible with new quality procedures, improved production and flexibility. Support and commitment from everyone. More money if it works. No jobs if it doesn't. We'll put in the new machinery, and it's in your own hands then. Mister Bailey becomes managing director as from today. You make the decisions down here, yourselves. A Wexford factory, run by Wexford people.'

It worked. Loud applause. Liam shook hands with Bailey. He got a full tour of the factory. Over lunch, Bailey was delighted with the new approach. No more long delays for decision-making. Controlling their own destiny. Liam threw in three conditions.

'First, we only have sixty grand for investment right now. You'll have to do with two machines and get the third one later out of profits.'

'Okay.'

'Secondly, Brendan Reville will be the Smith Group director responsible for your operation, and you'll report to him. He'll visit you weekly.'

'That's okay too; we know Brendan.'

'Thirdly, we are changing the name from Smith's Engineering to Wexford Electronix. Give your people some personal pride in their company.' That was more than okay. That was terrific.

'You know, the workers are over the moon,' Bailey said. I couldn't believe their positive reaction. It seems that Danny McCarthy was telling them he'd met you early this morning. That you weren't a Dublin suit. That you were a dacent man, who knew as much about the Wexford hurling team as he did. A man to believe in. That's what swung them behind you. Well done.'

Wexford Electronix became a great success story and

stormed into profitability. Eventually, Liam sold the factory to the local management team. It went on to double its staff. A great lesson for everyone. When the chips are down, it's up to yourself. Sink or swim. For Liam, another proof of Mother Darcy's wise saying: 'The early bird gets the worm.' Because Wexford Electronix was saved with the help of Danny the tea-maker.

*

The bank was worried. There was no sign of the over-draft reducing. The spring of 1987 was cold. The economy was on its knees. Unemployment was at its highest level ever. The dealer network was still negative. Liam got bad news from the finance director. 'The bank wants our cheque books. No more spending.' They couldn't do that. Might as well pull the plug on the whole operation. He phoned the bank manger who confirmed.

'It's head office. You were supposed to have reduced the overdraft by four million at this time. You've increased it by a million. They want me to call a halt,' he said.

Liam went into overdrive. Softly, softly. 'I have good news for you. Wexford Electronix is into profit this month. We're getting a deposit on Monday on the wallpaper premises on the Long Mile Road. And we have a draft contract for the sale of Murdoch's DIY in Dun Laoghaire. Plus, we've got an order for a hundred Renault vans for the post office. And we've a meeting with the Renault Dealer Council next week that we believe will bring them on stream,' he said. 'David, this is the turning point. Pull the plug now, and we'll all lose everything. Give me three more months and we'll be back on track. The overdraft will be down as planned. Just a bit behind time, that's all. And we'll monitor the results together, weekly, starting next Wednesday after our dealer meeting. We'll meet for lunch.'

Silence for a long moment. 'OK. We'll meet next week and I'll give you some more time. But the overdraft is now capped. No more ups. Only down, it has to go.' Relief all around.

But the economy was still flat through 1987 and into 1988. Dour days. The company had slimmed down. The bank overdraft was steadily reducing. But interest rates had pushed through the roof. They were paying twenty-five per cent on some loans. The rent on the recently built high-profile premises on the Naas Road was running at over four hundred thousand a year. Liam was searching for an alternative, cheaper location. And he found just what was needed. Fiat had moved into the city centre and their old headquarters in Ballyfermot were for sale. With property prices on the floor, he bought it for a song – a little over the cost of one year's rent where they were. And he now owned the premises that Fiat had not let him enter some years before. The Irish post office – SDS – took over the old premises.

The deal was done, and they moved from the big Naas Road property on Saint Patrick's Day of 1988. Springtime. Regeneration. For Renault, and indeed the whole country, that springtime brought the beginning of an economic resurgence. Interest rates began to fall back, house building started to increase, car sales began to pick up. It was clear that the country was coming out of recession, with Ray McSharry, the government minister of finance, plotting the way. Renault were slowly moving up the car-sales league table. The Smith Group name was changed to the Glencullen Group, to reflect the new owner and its Irish heritage. The bank overdraft was down to more manageable proportions. The company was profitable.

Liam had spent three years driving around the country with Fergus O'Rourke, who was the Renault sales director, a great affable character. He was a Leitrim man, now living in Meath, where one of his seven brothers was the captain of the great Meath football team that swept all before them at that time. Liam drove with Fergus through every county in Ireland, supporting and motivating the Renault dealer network, finding and establishing new dealers. Eventually, Fergus took over his own Renault dealership in Blanchardstown, where he became a star performer for Renault.

Liam worked his usual long hours to develop the base for the long-term growth of Renault in Ireland. Building and investing in new dealerships. He was determined to achieve his objective of making Renault a premier-league player in the Irish car market.

Through all the mental turmoil, Jackie was a tower of strength, help and support to Liam. Entertaining Renault visitors. Visiting car dealerships with him, all over the country. Making sure the home was an oasis of calm after a tough week's work. And kicking ass and motivating him when necessary!

36

END OF AN ERA

Dublin was experiencing the beginning of traffic con-
gestion. And of growing land prices. From his lovely
Stepaside Lodge in the mountains, Liam could see the
new housing estates developing rapidly out from the
city. It was now taking forty minutes to get to and from
the office. So Liam and Jackie decided to move south-
west of the city. They sold Stepaside Lodge and bought
a very old mansion on twenty acres, beside Sallins in
County Kildare. Osberstown House had been built in
1750. It was built to last, with walls three feet thick, by
one of the landed gentry. More Irish than the Irish
themselves. Sir John Esmonde had supported Lord
Edward Fitzgerald in the 1798 rebellion against the
English. He was captured, hanged, and his head was
stuck on a spike on O'Connell Bridge in Dublin.

Liam brought Mother Darcy down to see the house.
Her last motor-car journey. She was gobsmacked. She
sat in the magnificent drawing room, with the old pull
cords. In the past they had alerted the basement servants
that their services were required. Memories of her days
in Mountjoy Square as a servant girl.

'So this is what was upstairs. Lovely rooms, huge

hall. Giant bay windows.' She looked out of the window at the garden flowers, with a tear in her eye. Smiled at Liam. 'And my grandson upstairs. Like yar mammy said, it's a long, long way from penny apples.'

She was silent, with a dreamy smile on her face, all the way back to Dublin.

Molly was now in the convent of St Joseph's, right opposite her home, by special permission of the Archbishop. Spending her last days in the 'Home for Aged and Virtuous Females' – referred to locally as 'the Old Maids' Home' – a nursing home for the old nuns. Her devotion to that church had earned her the special concession, as she neared her hundredth birthday. In the winter, Liam would bring her a bottle of Lucozade, a yellow energy drink. He always added a little drop of Jameson whiskey.

'Great for heating up the old bones,' she'd say, 'but the stuff the others bring isn't as nice as yours, Liam. Tell them what shop ya buy it in, 'cause it's far nicer.' If she only knew, and her a teetotaller all her life.

It was on a Sunday morning that Liam and Vera were sitting talking to Mother Darcy. Half a dozen of Vera's kids were there. A great-great-granddaughter in Molly's lap. Chatting away about politics. Molly putting in her tuppenceworth. And her a hundred years old! Liam got up to leave.

'See you next week, Mother,' he said.

'Cheerio, son,' Molly replied, but as he moved off, she called him back. 'Here, you, give me a hug before ya go. Shure, I mightn't be here next week, an oul' one like me.' Liam smiled, and gave her a hug. Smelling the familiar scent of her snuff. Remembering the evenings beside the turf fire in her old tenement room.

'Yes, Mother,' he replied, 'we all know you want to go to heaven,' and Vera joined Liam in repeating her old phrase, 'but not yet.' Molly didn't join them as she usually did. When he got to the door, he felt her gaze on his back. Turning around, he saw she was smiling at him. A big smile. Just for him. With the baby on her knee, she lifted her right hand and blew him a kiss. He threw one back and she waved goodbye. As he walked into the hallway of his home, thirty minutes later, the phone was ringing.

'Liam, it's Vera. Mother Darcy went asleep, just after you left.' She had over a hundred direct descendants at her funeral in her beloved Saint Joseph's Church.

Bill and Bishop Eamonn Casey at the Clarinbridge Horse Show

*

The Da gave up his daily walking when the Ma died. Got dug into the telly. Loved the TV programmes. Loved being able to make his own choice with the remote control. The kids dropped in and out, so he had visitors every day. But he was living on his own.

Liam got a call from Vera. The Da had taken a fall, but she got him into the Mater Hospital. No bones broken, but he wasn't talking to anyone. Liam sat with him for two hours, but not a word. No speaky. Just gazing off into space.

On the second visit Liam found him strapped into a wheelchair. The nurse explained that he was having angry fits. Still no speaky. As Liam sat there, he could see the anger in the Da's face. Visualised the old days. The frustration, and banging the door off its hinges. He could see the veins swelling in his huge forearms. He was still strong as an ox, at eighty-four. But his jaw was clenched and his teeth were grinding.

The evening news came on the telly and the Da became instantly alert. He stiffened in the wheelchair as he stared at the box, listening to the news.

'Word has just come through that Bishop Casey has left Ireland. After the revelations regarding his love child with Annie Murphy, the disgraced Bishop of Galway has resigned and gone into hiding.'

Billy Cullen's face was scarlet with anger. By sheer physical strength, he was hopping the wheelchair off the ground. Snarling at the television pictures of the Bishop. And the words spat out.

'Fools we were. All our life wasted. Fooled by the priests. Mass every day. Prayers and Rosary every night.

Don't commit sin. And you fooling us all. The poor people of Ireland giving you their last penny. For what? For wine, women and song. Laughing at us. Do as I say, not as I do. Wasted, wasted, wasted. Thank God Mary isn't here to see this.' The words were like bullets. Venomous. His face was bulging as he pulled against the straps, hopping the wheelchair towards the television. Spitting at it.

Liam switched off the telly as the nurse quickly gave the Da a sedative. He slowly calmed. Tears were rolling down his cheeks. He was looking at Liam with red-rimmed eyes. A tortured, pleading look. He closed his eyes, shaking his head slowly from side to side. Slowly, slower, stopped. Chin on chest. Asleep. Liam took off the restraining straps and lifted his father into the bed. Shakespeare's seven stages.

Billy Cullen passed away quietly a few months later and was buried beside Mary. Together in peace at last. May the Virgin Mary beseech forgiveness for Bishop Casey. Lord, hear our prayers.

The end of an era. The ma, Mother Darcy, and now the Da, all gone. Liam becomes the patriarch figure. With Jackie now for twenty-two years. His daughter Anita with two lovely sons. Remembering Molly Darcy's words: 'You are the warrior. You have the strength.' William, the protector.

The Old Man

The tears have all been shed now
We've said our last goodbyes,
His soul's been blessed
He's laid to rest,

And it's now I feel alone.
He was more than just a father
A teacher, my best friend;
He can still be heard
In the tunes we shared
When I play them on my own.

I never will forget him
For he made me what I am;
Though he may be gone
Memories linger on —
And I miss him, the old man.

I thought he'd live forever
He seemed so big and strong
But the minutes fly,
And the years roll by
For a father and a son.
And suddenly when it happened —
There was so much left unsaid;
No second chance
To tell him 'Thanks'
For everything he'd done.

I never will forget him
For he made me what I am;
Though he may be gone
Memories linger on —
And I miss him, the old man.

Phil Coulter

Epilogue
Echoes of the Past

In writing *Penny Apples* I called on my family and friends for back-up information. The word got out around the inner city that 'Liamo is writin' the buke.' So a lot of new contacts were made. The next few pages give a sequel to some of the *Penny Apples* stories. They also help to authenticate some of my early memories.

Bill Cullen, October 2001

THE NORTH STRAND BOMBINGS: In 1998, a United Nations researcher was trawling through old World War II archives in a Munich air force base. He discovered a file code-named 'Operation Roman Helmet', containing instructions from Adolf Hitler to take retaliatory action against the Irish for helping the British after the Belfast bombing of 1941. 'Bomb their fire brigade stations in Dublin and frighten their president in his palace.' The North Strand bombing was deliberate. 'And that's a fact,' as Uncle Bob would say.

THE DA IN SUMMERHILL: I got a phone call from Yvonne Walsh, a pal of Rita's from the Summerhill tenements. She had emigrated to England, aged ten, when the tenements were demolished. Her abiding memory of Dublin was Mister Cullen, who marched down Summerhill like a soldier on parade.

THE DA HATED THE DRINK: Billy Cullen never went into a pub in his life. On the yearly Brooks Thomas bus excursions, he'd sit in the bus for hours while the lads were eating and drinking in the pub. It wasn't until after his funeral that I discovered that the Da's mother had been an alcoholic. Died young of the drink, she did. And the Da vowed never to touch the stuff himself. Bitter memories. He never realised that you have to let go. Forgive.

BETTY CULLEN RIP: One small page found in Billy Cullen's wallet after he died had a poem written on it that he had obviously carried around with him. It was well-worn and anonymous, about a little girl. It was only when Ulick O'Connor's diaries were published recently that I discovered the author. The poem was by Oliver St John Gogarty. It was called 'Golden Stockings':

> Golden stockings you had on
> In the meadow where you ran
> And your little knees together
> Bobbed like pippins in the weather
> When the breezes rush and fight
> For those pimples of delight
> And they dance from the pursuit
> And the leaf looks like the fruit.
>
> I have many a sight in mind
> That would last if I were blind
> Many verses I could write
> That would bring me many a sight
> Now I only see but one
> See you running in the sun
> And the gold dust coming up
> From the trampled buttercup.

It was Billy Cullen's way of remembering his young daughter, Betty, who died of pneumonia in the tenements.

THE SUMMERHILL POLICEMAN: I sat at a dinner table with Chief Commissioner Patrick Byrne of the Garda Siochána, the chief executive of the Irish police force. I told him the story of the Mountjoy jailbreakers. 'Isn't Ireland only a village, Bill,' he said to me. 'Sure, Garda Byrne, who was in Fitzgibbon Street station back in 1948, was my grandfather. A Portarlington man who served in the Dublin inner city all his life.'

THE CAMPILE BOMBING: I got a note from Bridie Sullivan. She was living in Campile in 1941 and saw the German airplane bombing Campile Co-op. She said that the plane went up and down the railway line looking for the Co-op. No accident, a deliberate retaliation.

CAPTAIN CARLSEN: After the trauma of the *Flying Enterprise*, Captain Kurt Carlsen retired to west Cork, around Baltimore, where he agreed that he should have brought his ship safely to shore.

MAGGIE TRIUMPHS: I got a phone call from Margaret Dempsey. She told me that she had been in the Magdalens' Laundry in Seán MacDermott Street, and that Mother Darcy got her a job in Neary's Hotel beside the Parnell Monument, with accommodation in a tenement room in Henrietta Street. She got married and has had a great life, raising her new family in Whitehall, a north Dublin suburb. She kept the name Margaret because she was conditioned to responding to Maggie. 'I don't ever want to remember my old name or my parents who banished me,' she said. 'But I was at Molly Darcy's funeral. God bless her for all she did for me, and she helped other girls like that too.'

UNCLE NED: Uncle Ned died of cancer in 1968. Cigarettes. He fought it for eighteen months. Weighed only six stone when he passed away.

UNCLE BOB: The cigarettes got Big Bob Darcy too. Just a while after Ned. But he went very quick. 'When you've gotta go, you've gotta go. And that's a fact.'

THE ROUNDY GLASS CASES: I got a call from Terry Brennan. Terry had two old glass cases, he said, that would suit the drawing room in Osberstown House. Bring them down. When I arrived home, the glass cases were in situ. I couldn't believe it. 'Terry, I bet you a thousand pounds I know where they came from,' I said, and walked over and looked under the lower shelf, 'with my initials scratched on the leg'.

'I got them out of Clery's, where we're doing a big renovating job,' said Terry. The same glass cases where Mary Darcy had parked her brood. Now at home with me. Things do go full circle. Lucky Cullen again.

THE AMBASSADOR CINEMA'S CHANDELIER: I spoke to Paul Anderson, who owned the Ambassador Cinema. It had the famous first-ever Waterford Crystal chandelier. He's now building a hotel on the site of the old Academy Cinema in Pearse Street. The chandelier will have pride of place in the foyer.

QUIT SLEEPING: I was at a motivational seminar in Orlando. The speaker was Mike Vance, author of *Think Outside the Box*. The first pearl of wisdom he gave us: 'The secret of success is two words – quit sleeping.' To reinforce his point, he said, 'For those who want to reduce sleeping hours, just put a coffin on your bed and climb in every night. See how much you sleep.' It cost two hundred dollars to get that advice. I got it from Mother Darcy for free, fifty years ago.

MISTER STACK, A REAL TEACHER: Sixteen years after leaving Saint Canice's School, I was standing in a queue in the Bank of Ireland at Cavendish Row. I got a tap on the shoulder, turned around and there was Mister Stack from Saint Canice's. 'Pinnacle,' he said to me.

I recognised the word from that month's *Reader's Digest*. 'Means highest point, of a mountain, of your career,' I replied.

Mister Stack smiled. 'Living up to your potential, you are, Liam. Well done.' And he walked away. Older, plumper, still motivating the young fellas. Well done, Mister Stack.

TONY MYLES: Walking up Grafton Street one Saturday morning in the 1970s, I saw Tony Myles coming down the street towards me. Older, greyer, but the same wide-shouldered, long-haired look. Aristocratic bordering on arrogant. A flicker of recognition but he passed me by. 'Hey, Mister Myles, don't you remember me?' I called after him. Myles stopped in his tracks. He turned around very slowly and looked Liam up and down with a sceptical smile on his face. 'And why, please tell me, should I remember you?' he said in Peter O'Toole fashion, pointing his chin upwards.

'I'm Liam Cullen from the Brú Mhuire, you were our physical training teacher. Taught me gymnastics.'

Myles nodded his head slowly. 'Oh, yes. Brú Mhuire. Cullen, is it?' He gave me the once-over again. 'Yes, yes, yes. I remember you. The best of a bad lot, you were. Just look at you now. And I thought I'd wasted those years. Guess I did have some success up there after all.' He smiled, gave a big wink and bounced off down the street with his get-out-of-my-way walk. Typical Myles. A showman, but he motivated a lot of Brú boys over the years.

ARTANE: I met Joseph McCarthy, who was in Artane from 1946 to 1954. He verified many of the horrific stories of that establishment.

I got a phone call in Renault from 'Blinky'. He's alive and well and living in Liverpool. He's a very happy grandfather and he's staying incognito. Emotional!

MICK O'CONNELL: Best Gaelic footballer ever, in most experts' opinion. Still one of the fittest men in Ireland at sixty-four years old. A great supporter of youth charities, he appears for the Ring of Kerry cycle every year. A hundred-mile charity event and Micko is always one of the first finishers.

THE TRAGEDY IN THE BREWERY: Paddy Walsh got my office messenger's job in Guinness in 1956. He tragically died in an industrial accident on the premises in 1984.

BRIAN THE ADVENTURER: After twenty years in the wilds of Saskatchewan, Brian fell from a high roof to an icy death. He was cremated. Jackie and I attended the services in Saskatoon, with Alice and Brian's three lovely daughters, Gaetane, Darcy and Lucretia. I brought his ashes on the long journey home and placed them at the foot of the grave with the Ma and Da. The wanderer returns. The small brass casket sits on my mantelpiece, with the inscription: 'And I never will play the Wild Rover no more.' May his restless spirit find peace at last. Lord, hear our prayers.

CAPE COD – RITA CULLEN VIDAL: Rita married Arthur Vidal in 1972, and her daughter, Mary Frances Vidal-Cullen, graduated *cum laude* in Berkeley College in Boston in 1996.

DUBLIN CHAMBER OF COMMERCE: I was invited to speak at the millennium luncheon of the Dublin Chamber of Commerce. I thanked them for the free lunch. Even if it was nearly forty years late.

KILLARNEY: Mesmerised by the beauty of Killarney's lakes and glens as a young fella, I opened Molly Darcy's pub-restaurant in the Muckross Park Hotel in 1991. It was a winner of an all-Ireland Pub of the Year Award.

JOHN F. KENNEDY: I stood in the drawing room of the US ambassador's residence in June 2001, saying goodbye to the outgoing ambassador, Mike Sullivan. A great friend of the Kennedy family – Dot Tubridy – came over as I admired a bronze bust of John F. Kennedy. 'You know, Bill,' she said, 'John F. Kennedy stood here with me on the last night of his visit in June 1963. Looking out at the sun going down, he said, "These have been the three most magnificent days of my life. Ireland

– it's just magic."' I hope he realised how much he inspired so many Irish people on his short visit.

EAMONN DORAN: Eamonn came home to Ireland in the 1990s and opened another pub in Temple Bar. Bill got his invitation for the opening night. All was forgiven.

STAINES AIR CRASH: Michael Smurfit told me that he was on the team scheduled for the London flight to the EEC headquarters in Brussels. But this achiever decided to go a few days earlier to look at takeover projects in Europe for his company. A lucky escape.

SENATOR JACK DALY: I became close friends with the Daly family in Killarney. They are Ford and BMW dealers, with a SuperValu empire on the Park Road roundabout.

HILARY CULLEN: My daughter Hilary registered for Trinity College to start her degree course. I had to tell the Da – he was not amused. 'What's the world coming to when a granddaughter of mine ends up in danger of being contaminated by them Protestants.' Hard to change the beliefs of a lifetime. In 1995, Hilary graduated from Trinity College. Part of the new Ireland.

BARCLAYS BANK: I was sitting in Stillorgan Park Hotel one evening, waiting for Jackie. 'Hi, Bill,' said an attractive young lady, 'you owe me a large brandy.' Didn't recognise her. The oul' brain is losing its power.

'And a large brandy it is,' I said, nodding to the barman, 'and how are you keeping since I saw you last.' Playing for time. And Jackie walks in the door. 'This is Jackie, and

I'm sorry, I just can't remember your name.'

'That's because you've never met me before,' was the reply, through a sip of brandy. 'You see, my husband handled the Renault account in Barclays Bank in your earlier days. Spent the first six months walking the floor every night, muttering about Bill Cullen and the Renault overdraft. So I feel I know you very well, and you do owe me this brandy. Cheers.'

DUBLIN LORD MAYOR'S AWARD: After the huge support that the Lord Mayor of Dublin, Alfie Byrne, had given to the Cullen family, 1998 saw the wheel turn full circle. I received the Lord Mayor's Award from John Stafford for my work with the Irish Youth Foundation in raising millions of pounds for disadvantaged young people. Alfie Byrne would be pleased.

EVENING HERALD: Now a tabloid. The wrong size for maximising toilet-paper sheets. Bit small for Kossick warmers. But, thank God, Ireland has moved on past all that.

HENRY FORD: I met Henry Ford II in Killarney in 1982. He got a commendation for his Fairlane Ford Dealership's record-breaking performance of 1981, with sixteen hundred new Ford vehicle sales.

WALDEN MOTOR COMPANY: Mister Wallace phoned Liam in Renault to ask him to join him for dinner. Old and frail now but a great walk down memory lane. Sitting in his living room on Howth Head ovelooking Dublin Bay. Magnificent! 'You know, Willum, I remember passing the garage at two o'clock in the morning going home from a late-night party. Saw the light in the office and went in. Found you at the desk finishing the enveloping of our month-end bills. Envelopes in two piles. 'This lot are for the post office and a tuppenny stamp on each, you said, 'but this lot are all within a mile of the garage. I'll deliver them on me bike on the way to work in the morning. Saves a few quid postage.' It was New Year's Eve. Told the wife that young Willum will be the man to run the garage before too long. And you did.'

A few months later I shed a tear with my old Walden pals at Mister Wallace's funeral in Glasnevin.

MITCHELL'S ROSARY BEADS: Gay Byrne confirmed that Alex Mitchell, the suave rosary bead maker, was a brother of the late Charles Mitchell who was famous as an RTÉ news broadcaster for so many years.

THE MA'S CONFIRMATION: Got a call from May Hughes who said she went to school with the Ma. "But we left school after the Holy Communion when we were seven. We were on the streets selling the fruit and fish with Molly Darcy when our class were making the Confirmation. We asked the teacher could we make our Confo. No she said, we were bold girls, mitching from school and didn't know our Catechism. So we missed the big day. But Molly Darcy kicked up murder with the head priest in the Pro-Cathedral and he said okay, eventually! So your Ma and meself borrowed a dress rig-out from our pals, and up we went in Uncle Bob's horse and cart to the Bishop's Palace in Drumcondra. Got our Confo from Archbishop Welch himself, in his palace, and we had tea and scones with him as well". What a story.

ROCK HUDSON 1952: Just to confirm the story of Rock Hudson being in Ireland. We had a call from our great friend Violetta Lawler, the previous owner of our home, Osberstown House. Vi confirmed that on his 1952 visit, Rock Hudson had a day out at the Curragh Races with his friend Barry Fitzgerald and they dined with her in Osberstown House. He played the piano in the drawing room as they all sang 'When Irish Eyes Are Smiling'. And me up in the tenements them days, but sure I was probably smiling too!

PADDY FITZPATRICK: Paddy Fitzpatrick is the founder of the Fitzpatrick Hotel Group with hotels in Ireland and America. The Lexington Avenue trio in New York is managed by young son John Fitzpatrick. At a Christmas lunch Paddy related the story of how three of Ireland's successful businessmen had all started their careers at Dublin's Gresham Hotel in 1952. Paddy himself was a trainee barman, Frank Conroy of Irish Racing Board fame was on wash-up duty in the kitchen and Bill Cullen was outside the front door selling newspapers. 'And haven't we all shown that success is ninety-nine per cent perspiration' said Paddy with his twinkling smile that epitomises his special brand of Irish hospitality.

Robert Emmet was hanged in Dublin in 1803 for plotting a rebellion against English rule. He made an eloquent speech before his execution, that contained an emotive and prophetic sentence: 'When my country takes her place among the nations of the earth, then, and not till then, let my epitaph be written.'

Two hundred years later, Emmet's dream has come true. Long may it last. May the Irish never forget their roots. Never forget how America welcomed our poor and needy emigrants. Never forget the debt we owe to our fellow-Europeans. Never forget the less well-off. We still have the problem of Northern Ireland. But hard work by men of peace brought about the Good Friday Agreement. A new sense of order. Of peace and reconciliation. A way forward together.

GLOSSARY OF DUBLIN SLANG
OF THE FORTIES

Bowsie	A bit of a thug, macho with malice
Chiseller	A youngster, a *garsún*
Culchie	A countryman, originally a man from Coillte Mách (Kiltimagh) in County Mayo
Gansey	Woollen sweater, pullover
Gaustering	Gossiping, loitering, hanging out
Gone for a burton	Dead (dressed in best suit from Burton tailors); also means fired from a job, expelled
Grush	Handful of coins thrown in the air, mainly at Dublin weddings
Gurrier	Street urchin, a young fella with cute tenacity
Hard shaw	Strong silent type, tough guy
Jackeen	A Dubliner, opposite to a culchie
Kossicks	Wellington boots, knee-high rubber boots
Lackery	As in 'giving out lackery': chastising
Latchico	Unreliable, bit of a coward, only one ball
Lee-a-roady	Balls, brave, courageous
Lose your rag	Get angry, lose your temper
Mooching	Checking things out, reconnoitring
Ossified	Stoned, intoxicated, legless, dead drunk
Rozzer	A policeman, a bobby, a peeler, a cop, a guard
Scrooching	Squeezing in, two onto one seat

Spunkers	Down-and-outs who drank methylated spirits
Under his oxter	Under his arm
Waster	Good for nothing, lazy, like a blister – only shows up when the work is done

INDEX

478

The pubishers would like to thank the following for granting permission to reproduce copyright material: an extract from 'Over the Rainbow', words by E. Y. Harburg, music by Harold Arden, © 1938 EMI Catalogue Partnership, EMI Feist Catalog Inc. and EMI United Partnership Ltd, USA, reproduced by permission of International Music Publications Ltd; an extract from 'Keep Your Sunny Side Up', by Buddy DeSylva, Lew Brown and Ray Henderson, © 1929 DeSylva, Brown and Henderson, Inc., lyric reproduction by kind permission of Redwood Music Ltd, London NW1 8BD; an extract from 'The Old Man', written by Phil Coulter, © Four Seasons Music Ltd; an extract from 'Whistle a Happy Tune', © Rodgers & Hammerstein; an extract from 'Golden Stockings' by Oliver St John Gogarty, © the estate of Oliver St John Gogarty; and the photograph on page 400, © the *Irish Times*.

Also available from Mercier Press

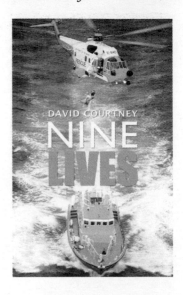

Nine Lives

David Courtney

978 1 85635 602 2

Nine Lives is an account of becoming a rescue pilot, from learning to fly, to the thrills and terrors of dangerous and complicated night rescues. As the story unfolds David Courtney introduces the reader to the people who work with rescue crews, and how the entire system works.

Courtney recounts his experiences, good and bad, in a way that is open and honest about fear, danger, disappointment, elation and happiness.

Contrasting the extraordinary with the everyday, Courtney delves into day-to-day family life, showing how it can empower each of us to confront the dramatic.

www.mercierpress.ie

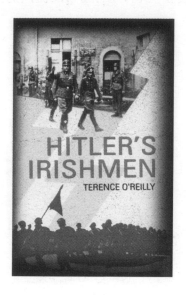

Hᴉᴛʟᴇʀ's Iʀɪsʜᴍᴇɴ

Terence O'Reilly

978 1 85635 589 6

James Brady and Frank Stringer originally joined an Irish regiment of the British army and but for a twist of fate would have ended up fighting against the Nazis. Instead, having been captured by the Germans in Guernsey, they switched sides. The pair were recruited to the German special forces, and even had the distinctive blood group tattoo of the SS.

Under the command of Otto Skorzeny, the man who had rescued Italian dictator Benito Mussolini from a mountain-top prison, they were involved in some of the most ferocious fighting of the war during the last days of the Third Reich.

This account draws heavily on the mens' own accounts and on state papers which have only been released in recent years.

www.mercierpress.ie

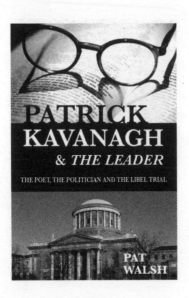

Patrick Kavanagh & *The Leader*
The Poet, the Politician and the Libel Trial

Pat Walsh

978 1 85635 664 0

One of the most traumatic episodes in the poet Patrick Kavanagh's life was played out in public over two weeks in February 1954. By suing *The Leader* magazine for defamation, Kavanagh initiated a sensational courtroom showdown with John A. Costello, noted barrister and twice Taoiseach of Ireland.

The country was electrified as Costello's masterful, relentless cross-examination dissected Kavanagh's public and private life, and revealed the tensions within Dublin's literary circle in the 1950s. When Kavanagh took the case against *The Leader* he could not have anticipated either the furore it would cause, or that the strain of the trial would shatter his considerable confidence and damage his health.

www.mercierpress.ie

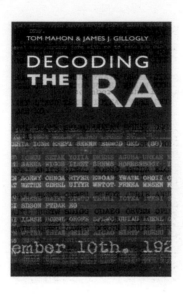

Decoding the IRA

Tom Mahon & James J. Gillogly

978 1 85635 604 6

Historian Tom Mahon and code breaker James J. Gillogly have spent the past few years breaking the IRA's communications code, used for the organisation's most secret messages. The newly decoded secret documents reveal the IRA's mindset in the years following the Civil War and the results are explosive as they expose IRA secrets that have been concealed for over 75 years.

Featuring facsimiles of the actual coded documents, the book delves into nearly every matter conceivable for a paramilitary organisation and provides an unnerving insight into how the IRA saw itself and conducted its dangerous business.

www.mercierpress.ie

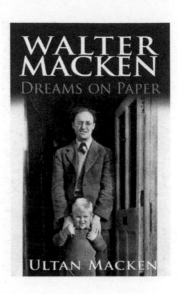

WALTER MACKEN
Dreams on Paper

Ultan Macken

978 1 85635 630 5

This new biography sheds light on the private life of one of Ireland's
most successful and popular writers, Walter Macken. Through his many
unpublished letters to his wife, sons, editors and friends, Walter's son,
Ultan charts his father's career and life, from his birth in Galway in 1915
to his untimely death in 1967.

Originally an actor, principally with An Taidhbhearc in Galway and
The Abbey Theatre in Dublin, Walter played lead roles on Broadway and
also acted in films, notably in Brendan Behan's *The Quare Fellow*. Acting
was to remain an important part of his life, but it was his stirring writing
that brought him true fame and acclamation.

www.mercierpress.ie

THE FIELD

John B. Keane

978 0 85342 976 0

The Field is John B. Keane's fierce and tender study of the love a man can have for the land and the ruthless lengths he will go to in order to obtain the object of his desire. It is dominated by Bull McCabe, one of the most famous characters in Irish writing today.

www.mercierpress.ie

Favourite Poems We Learned in School

Thomas F. Walsh

978 1 85635 051 8

Thomas F. Walsh has put together a collection of the most quoted and most memorable poems we learned in school. The poems in this anthology will remain with us until we reach the end of our journey in this life, mainly because we learned them when we were young, and consequently they have become part of us.

The poems are evocative and will stir a nostalgic chord in all our hearts.

www.mercierpress.ie

The Best of John B. Keane
Collected Humorous Writings

978 1 85635 265 9

John B. Keane is known nationally and internationally as a successful playwright, handling tragedy and comedy with equal art, and as a prose writer of great invention and skill. Yet an equal claim to fame is made by the hundreds of short pieces which have been published in more than a dozen highly popular collections, such as *Inlaws and Outlaws* and *Is the Holy Ghost Really a Kerryman?* Now harvested into a single volume, they represent the distillation of the experience of a funny, witty, wise and passionate observer of the bright tapestry of Irish life.

MERCIER PRESS

IRISH PUBLISHER - IRISH STORY

We hope you enjoyed this book.

Since 1944, Mercier Press has published books that have been critically important to Irish life and culture. Books that dealt with subjects that informed readers about Irish scholars, Irish writers, Irish history and Ireland's rich heritage.

We believe in the importance of providing accessible histories and cultural books for all readers and all who are interested in Irish cultural life.

Our website is the best place to find out more information about Mercier, our books, authors, news and the best deals on a wide variety of books. Mercier track the best prices for our books online and we seek to offer the best value to our customers, offering free delivery within Ireland.

Sign up on our website or complete and return the form below to receive updates and special offers.

www.mercierpress.ie
www.facebook.com/mercier.press
www.twitter.com/irishpublisher

Name:

Email:

Address:

Mercier Press, Unit 3b, Oak House, Bessboro Rd, Blackrock, Cork, Ireland